ESSENTIALS OF
BIOLOGICAL
CHEMISTRY

SECOND EDITION

Reinhold Chemistry Textbook Series

CONSULTING EDITORS

Harry S. Sisler

University of Florida
Gainesville, Florida

Calvin A. VanderWerf

Hope College
Holland, Michigan

Bonner and Castro—*Essentials of Modern Organic Chemistry*
Day and Selbin—*Theoretical Inorganic Chemistry*
Drago—*Physical Methods in Inorganic Chemistry*
Fairley and Kilgour—*Essentials of Biological Chemistry, Second Edition*
Fieser and Fieser—*Advanced Organic Chemistry*
Fieser and Fieser—*Topics in Organic Chemistry*
Heftmann—*Chromatography*
Heftmann and Mosettig—*Biochemistry of Steroids*
Klingenberg and Reed—*Introduction to Quantitative Chemistry*
Meyer—*Food Chemistry*
Reid—*Principles of Chemical Thermodynamics*
Sanderson—*Chemical Periodicity*
Smith and Cristol—*Organic Chemistry*

Selected Topics in Modern Chemistry

Harry H. Sisler and Calvin A. VanderWerf, Editors

Brey—*Physical Methods for Determining Molecular Geometry*
Cheldelin and Newburgh—*The Chemistry of Some Life Processes*
Eyring and Eyring—*Modern Chemical Kinetics*
Hildebrand—*An Introduction to Molecular Kinetic Theory*
Kieffer—*The Mole Concept in Chemistry*
Moeller—*The Chemistry of Lanthanides*
Morris—*Principles of Chemical Equilibrium*
Murmann—*Inorganic Complex Compounds*
O'Driscoll—*The Nature and Chemistry of High Polymers*
Overman—*Basic Concepts of Nuclear Chemistry*
Rochow—*Organometallic Chemistry*
Ryschkewitsch—*Chemical Bonding and the Geometry of Molecules*
Sisler—*Chemistry in Non-Aqueous Solvents*
Sisler—*Electronic Structure, Properties, and the Periodic Law*

✓Strong and Stratton—*Chemical Energy*
✓ VanderWerf—*Acids, Bases, and the Chemistry of the Covalent Bond*
✓ Vold and Vold—*Colloid Chemistry*

Selected Topics in Modern Biology

Peter Gray, Editor

Barish—*The Gene Concept*
Gottlieb—*Developmental Genetics*
✓ Keosian—*The Origin of Life*
Langley—*Homeostasis*
Morrison—*Functional Organelles*
Spratt—*Introduction to Cell Differentiation*

46734

Consulting Editor's Statement

The first edition of *Essentials of Biological Chemistry* marked a notable milestone in the history of biochemistry textbooks. The time had come for general introductory biochemistry to be presented as a *science* which related chemical structure to biological function. Fairley and Kilgour did just that. In *Essentials of Biological Chemistry, Second Edition*, they have broadened the scope of the first edition, and have brought its presentation up to date.

These two master teachers undertook the writing with one *objective*—to produce a text which would truly meet the needs of their own students, a typical group with widely varying backgrounds and diverse professional interests. Their *problem* was one that is shared by every teacher of general biochemistry: how to present the fundamentals of the science to students when the mass of biochemical information in any single area is becoming increasingly detailed and complex. Their *answer* was to develop that coherent picture of the metabolic and energetic activities of living cells which represents the heart and core of biochemistry. The *result* is *Essentials of Biological Chemistry, Second Edition*, an exciting contribution to the teaching in this field which, we are confident, will solve the problem for many another teacher of biochemistry.

Teacher and student alike will applaud the authors' decision to prune all that is nonessential or peripheral, in order to develop the basic story of the chemical constitution and major metabolic activities of living cells in sufficient depth to permit real understanding. Fairley and Kilgour have provided a truly sound and flexible ally to lead students of varied backgrounds and interests toward a mastery of the concepts that form the basis of our understanding of the phenomena of life in chemical terms.

June 1966   CALVIN A. VANDERWERF

ESSENTIALS OF

BIOLOGICAL CHEMISTRY

SECOND EDITION

JAMES L. FAIRLEY

Department of Biochemistry
Michigan State University
East Lansing, Michigan

GORDON L. KILGOUR

Department of Chemistry
San Fernando Valley State College
Northridge, California

REINHOLD PUBLISHING CORPORATION, NEW YORK

Preface to the Second Edition

Only a few years have elapsed since the first edition of this text was published. In that short time an ever-increasing tendency toward the teaching of certain biochemical principles in beginning biology courses has become apparent. Accordingly, many of our students can now handle material in these areas in greater depth than formerly was possible. The revision of the text reflects this trend. The major changes are the addition of material on protein and nucleic acid structure, and the expansion of the discussion of molecular genetics and protein synthesis into a new chapter. A quantitative treatment of Michaelis-Menten kinetics is provided for those who wish to include this subject. A variety of minor changes have been made throughout the text in response to the increases in knowledge which are the fruits of research. Several annoying errors, hopefully all of them, have been eliminated. Withal, the basic structure of the text remains the same. Unchanged too is the primary goal—the presentation of the fundamental concepts of biochemistry in a manner suited to the broad spectrum of students in our undergraduate classes.

JAMES L. FAIRLEY

GORDON L. KILGOUR

June, 1966

Preface to the First Edition

This book has been written specifically to serve as a text for the introductory course in biochemistry at the undergraduate level. With suitable supplementation it will also fill the needs of survey courses offered for graduate students whose areas of specialization require a basic familiarity with the principles of biochemistry, rather than a working knowledge of the field.

We were prompted to write this text by a definite need and our strong desire for a book which would present the fundamental concepts of biochemistry in a manner suited to the broad spectrum of students in the undergraduate classes at Michigan State University. These students come to us with widely varying preparations in chemistry and in biology and with major interests ranging from home economics through agriculture, veterinary medicine, microbiology, and other biological sciences to chemistry. The composition of these classes reflects in major degree the great impact that the unusually rapid growth of biochemical information has had upon all areas of biology. The resulting interest in biochemistry is gratifying to the biochemist, but it poses major problems for the instructors of introductory courses in the selection of material. On one hand, the students are being derived from an ever-widening pool of scientific interests, and on the other, the mass of biochemical information in any single area is rapidly becoming increasingly detailed and complex.

We feel that the logical solution of these problems requires major emphasis upon the basic concepts and fundamental information of general biochemistry rather than detailed information on a specific organism such as the human, or a superficial treatment which includes mention of every possible peripheral aspect of the field. Accordingly, our primary goal in this book is the presentation of a coherent picture of the major metabolic activities of living cells, a picture which places special attention on the relationship of chemical structure to biological function. This we firmly believe to be the core of the study of biochemistry. It is this material which a student must master as an approach to the understanding of the phenomena of life in chemical terms.

We have treated the material we feel to be basic in considerable depth, sufficiently, we believe, so as to permit real understanding. At the same time much material traditionally included in introductory courses has been omitted. This includes a certain amount of information on the purely chemical aspects of the compounds found in biological systems. We have discussed only those details most necessary for the comprehension of the processes of metabolism and of the research methods of the biochemist. Similarly, we have deleted many data related specifically to the understanding of human physiology and nutrition and to the clinical detection of disease or metabolic deficiencies. Much of this subject matter will currently be covered in courses in the student's own field and no longer need be considered as necessary in a general biochemistry course.

Suggestions for "Additional Reading" have been included at the end of each chapter in order to lead the way to the current literature for those who are so inclined. Where possible, we have chosen articles at several levels in order to provide a range between general background and precise detail.

The material on the chemical constitution of biological materials has been put into the first few chapters of the book in order to permit maximum flexibility in adapting the text to different classes having somewhat different backgrounds, particularly in organic chemistry. Students with a good chemistry background will be able to proceed with relative rapidity through the first few chapters and spend more time on the later material. Other classes may require more time for the first five chapters, and may cover the remaining material in less detail.

In Chapter 12, we have considered some of the current information regarding the chemical mechanisms by which metabolic activities are controlled within cells. This is an area of paramount importance for the maintenance of normal cellular structure and function. At the present time we have only a few glimpses of how the controls function, but they are so important that we felt justified in inserting some of this information even though it is only fragmentary.

In over-all approach, we have tried to proceed on what we feel to be a logical progression of complexity. Thus we begin with a consideration of the organic chemistry of cellular constituents, then go on to consider the most basic chemical feature of all life—the enzymatic catalysis of chemical reactions. The next step is to look at the chemical nature of an individual cell with emphasis on its energy-transfer mechanisms and the general means by which it maintains the living state. This leads readily into a rather extensive examination of many of the basic metabolic reaction sequences within cells, with consideration of their interactions and integration into a functional whole. The discussion of special problems peculiar to multi-cellular organisms or tissues has been left until the basic cellular groundwork has been laid.

We would like to express our thanks to the many colleagues and students who have read part or all of the manuscript during its preparation and have given us the benefit of their comments and suggestions. Our thanks also go to Mary Ann Kiesler, who prepared most of the figures for publication, and to the staff members of the Reinhold Publishing Corporation, who have been of so much assistance to us in proceeding from thoughts to print.

JAMES L. FAIRLEY
GORDON L. KILGOUR

Michigan State University
East Lansing, Michigan
April, 1963

Contents

Preface to the Second Edition   ix

Preface to the First Edition   xi

1. Some Pertinent Aspects of Organic Chemistry   1

    Functional Groups and Reactions, 1
    Isomerism, 11

2. Proteins, Amino Acids, and Peptides   14

    Proteins, 14
    Amino Acids, 15
    Peptides, 24
    Protein Structure, 26

3. Carbohydrates   43

    Monosaccharides, 43
    Glycosides, 56
    Disaccharides, 57
    Oligosaccharides, 59
    Polysaccharides, 59

4. Lipids 63

Fatty Acids, 64
Classification of Lipids, 65

5. Nucleic Acids and Nucleotides 79

Nitrogen Bases, 80
Nucleosides, 81
Nucleic Acid Structure, 82
Nucleotides of Metabolic Importance, 87

6. The Enzymes 92

Enzymes: General Comments, 93
Classification, 94
Chemical Nature of Enzymes, 94
Possible Mechanisms of Enzyme Catalysis, 98
Factors Affecting the Rates of Enzyme-Catalyzed Reactions, 104

7. Introduction to Metabolism 119

Structural Organization of the Cell, 120
Organization of Metabolic Activities, 122
Methods Used for the Study of Metabolism, 124
Interrelation of Metabolic Pathways, 131

8. Energy Transfer Process 133

Significance of Adenosine Triphosphate, 135
Biological Oxidations and ATP Production, 138
The Electron Transport System, 140
Photosynthesis, 148
Free Energy, 153

9. Metabolism of Carbohydrates 158

Digestion of Carbohydrates, 159
Metabolism of Sugars, 163

10. Metabolism of Lipids 196

Types of Lipids, 196
Hydrolysis of Lipids, 198
Metabolism of Fatty Acids, 201
Fatty Acid Biosynthesis, 204
Biosynthesis of Glycerol Lipids, 210
Biosynthesis of Cholesterol, 212
Metabolic Interconversion of Steroids, 214
Interaction of Carbohydrate and Lipid Metabolism, 216

11. Metabolism of Nitrogen Compounds   218

Sources of Amino Acids, 219
Specific Metabolic Roles of Individual Amino Acids, 228
Amino Acid Degradation, 242

12. Protein Synthesis and Gene Action   249

DNA and Genes, 251
DNA Duplication, 253
DNA and Protein Synthesis, 255
The Genetic Code, 260

13. The Control of Metabolic Activities   263

Substrate Concentration Effects, 264
Effects on Enzyme Activity, 265
Effects on Enzyme Synthesis, 267
Other Aspects of Metabolic Control, 271

14. Special Biochemistry of Higher Organisms   276

The Problem of Information Transfer, 276
The Problem of Control of Environment, 278
Hormones, 279
Biochemistry of Nerve Transmission, 292
Oxygen Transport, 294
Carbon Dioxide Transport and pH control, 297
Blood Coagulation, 299

Index   305

ESSENTIALS OF
BIOLOGICAL
CHEMISTRY

SECOND EDITION

Some Pertinent Aspects of Organic Chemistry

1

Certain aspects of organic chemistry are particularly important to a clear understanding of the structures, functions, and reactions of various compounds of biochemical importance. Some of these aspects have been selected for very brief review and re-emphasis at this point. More detailed information on any of the material presented in this chapter may be found in any standard text or reference book of organic chemistry.

FUNCTIONAL GROUPS AND THEIR REACTIONS

Alcohols R—OH

The alcohols can be classified into three groups on the basis of their structures:

Primary (those having at most one other carbon attached directly to the hydroxylated carbon), e.g.:

$$CH_3—OH, \quad and \quad CH_3—CH_2—OH$$

Secondary (those having two other carbons attached directly to the hydroxylated carbon), e.g.:

$$CH_3-\overset{\underset{\displaystyle CH_3}{|}}{CH}-OH \quad and \quad CH_3-CH_2-CH_2-\overset{\underset{\displaystyle CH_3}{|}}{CH}-OH$$

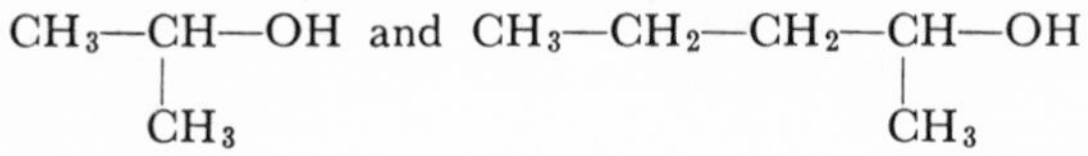

Tertiary (those having three other carbons attached directly to the hydroxylated carbon), e.g.:

$$CH_3-\overset{\overset{\displaystyle CH_3}{|}}{\underset{\underset{\displaystyle CH_3}{|}}{C}}-OH$$

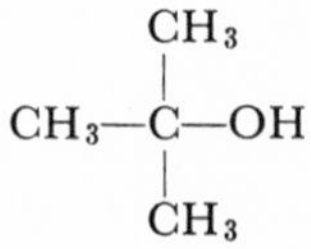

The differences in structure among the three groups are also reflected in differences in reactivities. Thus, for example, tertiary alcohols are most easily dehydrated, followed by the secondary and then by the primary alcohols. On the other hand, the reverse order of reactivity holds for ester formation.

REACTIONS

1. *Oxidation:* A *primary alcohol* is oxidized to the corresponding aldehyde, which in turn may be oxidized to a carboxylic acid:

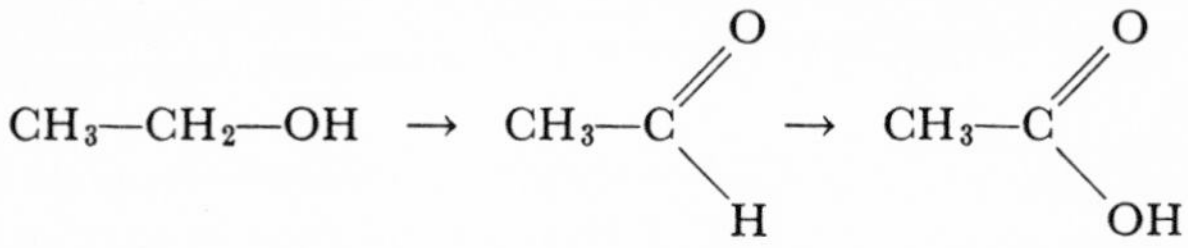

$$CH_3-CH_2-OH \;\rightarrow\; CH_3-C\overset{\displaystyle O}{\underset{\displaystyle H}{}} \;\rightarrow\; CH_3-C\overset{\displaystyle O}{\underset{\displaystyle OH}{}}$$

aldehyde   acid

Secondary alcohols are oxidized to ketones:

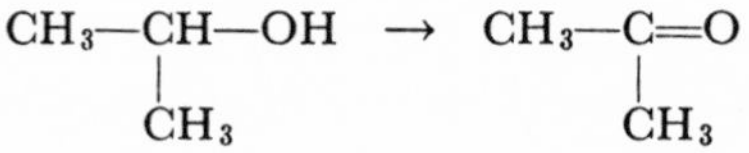

$$CH_3-\overset{\underset{\displaystyle CH_3}{|}}{CH}-OH \;\rightarrow\; CH_3-\overset{\underset{\displaystyle CH_3}{|}}{C}=O$$

ketone

Tertiary alcohols cannot be oxidized except under conditions which bring about rupture of the carbon chain.

The oxidation of an alcohol to an aldehyde or of an aldehyde to an acid actually involves the removal of two hydrogens with their electrons:

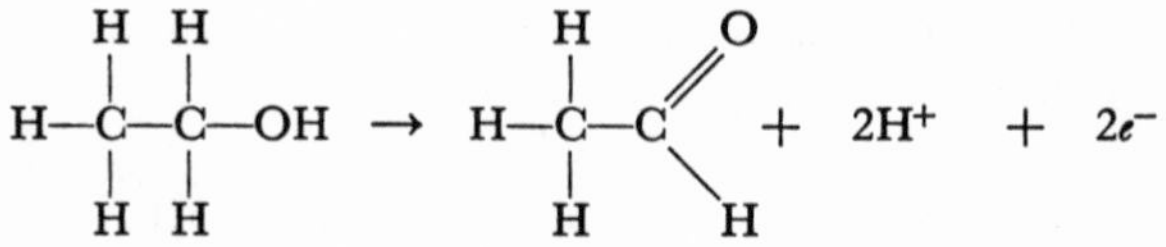

$$H-\overset{\overset{\displaystyle H}{|}}{\underset{\underset{\displaystyle H}{|}}{C}}-\overset{\overset{\displaystyle H}{|}}{\underset{\underset{\displaystyle H}{|}}{C}}-OH \;\rightarrow\; H-\overset{\overset{\displaystyle H}{|}}{\underset{\underset{\displaystyle H}{|}}{C}}-C\overset{\displaystyle O}{\underset{\displaystyle H}{}} \;+\; 2H^+ \;+\; 2e^-$$

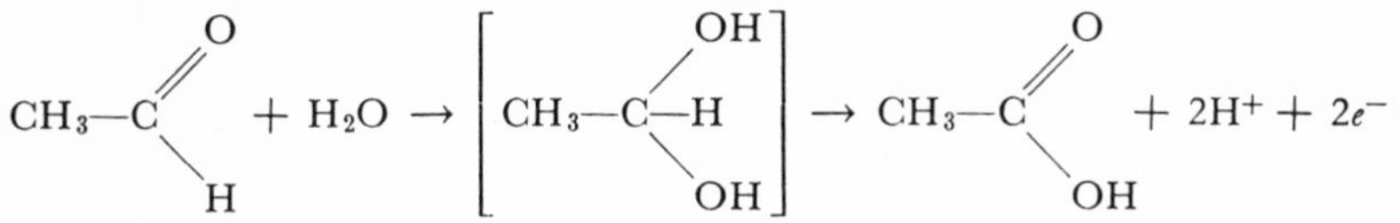

$$CH_3-C\underset{H}{\overset{O}{\big<}} + H_2O \rightarrow \left[CH_3-C\underset{OH}{\overset{OH}{\big<}}H\right] \rightarrow CH_3-C\underset{OH}{\overset{O}{\big<}} + 2H^+ + 2e^-$$

It is easier to see that the oxidation of the aldehyde to the acid does occur by removal of two hydrogens, when the aldehyde is written in the hydrated form. In fact, this form predominates in water solutions of simple aldehydes.

2. *Dehydration:* Under proper conditions, alcohols can be dehydrated to yield the corresponding unsaturated compound:

$$CH_3-CH_2-CH_2-OH \rightarrow CH_3-CH=CH_2 + H_2O$$

3. *Ester Formation:* When an alcohol and an acid are mixed together, they will react to produce some of the corresponding ester and an equivalent amount of water.

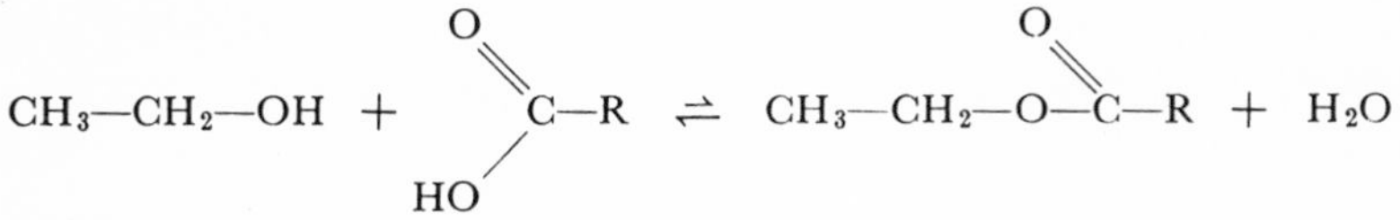

$$CH_3-CH_2-OH + \underset{HO}{\overset{O}{\big\backslash}}C-R \rightleftarrows CH_3-CH_2-O-\overset{O}{\overset{\big\backslash}{C}}-R + H_2O$$

Chemically, this equilibrium reaction is usually avoided by use of the anhydride of the acid and removal of the free acid that is formed during the reaction by the addition of excess base.

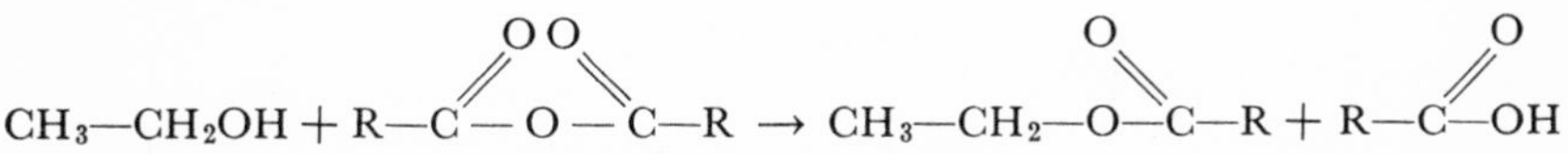

$$CH_3-CH_2OH + R-\overset{O\;O}{\overset{\big/\;\big\backslash}{C}}-O-C-R \rightarrow CH_3-CH_2-O-\overset{O}{\overset{\big\backslash}{C}}-R + R-\overset{O}{\overset{\big/}{C}}-OH$$

Note also that it is especially important for biochemical purposes to remember that the acid involved in ester formation need not be an organic acid, but can equally well be an inorganic acid such as phosphoric.

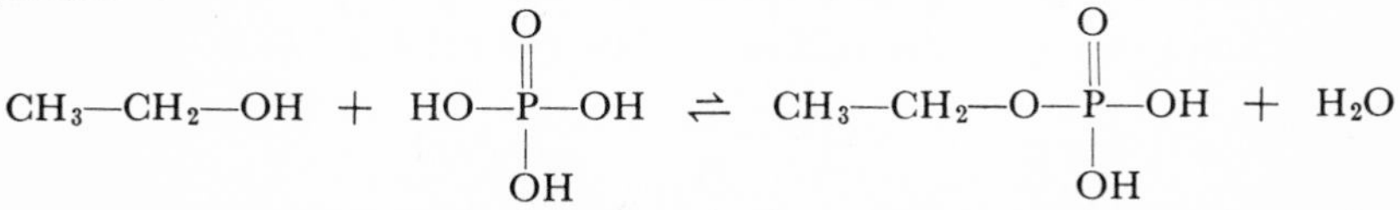

$$CH_3-CH_2-OH + HO-\underset{OH}{\overset{O}{\overset{\|}{P}}}-OH \rightleftarrows CH_3-CH_2-O-\underset{OH}{\overset{O}{\overset{\|}{P}}}-OH + H_2O$$

This product is called a *monoester* of phosphoric acid since only one of the three acidic groups is involved in the ester bond. A second group can be esterified to give a *phosphodiester;* this can react further to yield a *phosphotriester.* For example:

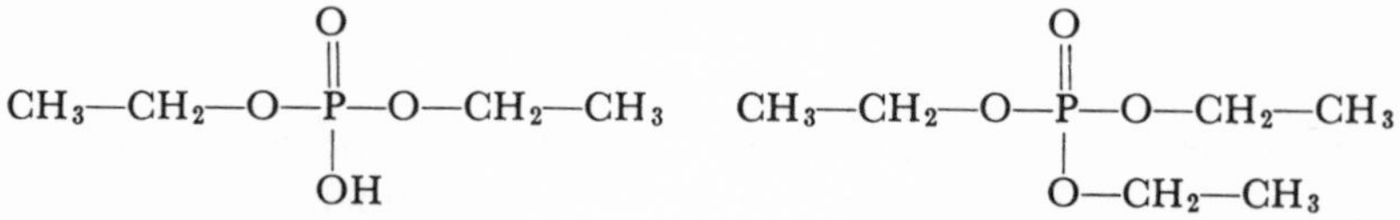

$$CH_3—CH_2—O—\overset{\overset{\textstyle O}{\|}}{\underset{\underset{\textstyle OH}{|}}{P}}—O—CH_2—CH_3 \qquad CH_3—CH_2—O—\overset{\overset{\textstyle O}{\|}}{\underset{\underset{\textstyle O—CH_2—CH_3}{|}}{P}}—O—CH_2—CH_3$$

a phosphodiester   a phosphotriester

Thioalcohols R—SH

The sulfur analogs of the alcohols in which a sulfur atom replaces an oxygen atom are called mercaptans or thioalcohols. The —SH group of a thioalcohol is referred to as a *thiol* or as a *sulfhydryl* group.

The thiols undergo many of the reactions of alcohols but have several outstanding differences:

REACTIONS

1. *Oxidation:* Thiols can be reversibly oxidized to form *disulfides:*

$$2\ CH_3—CH_2—SH \rightleftharpoons CH_3—CH_2—S—S—CH_2—CH_3 + 2H^+ + 2e^-$$

2. *Thioester Formation:* Reaction of a thiol with an acid (or acid anhydride) generally yields a *thioester:*

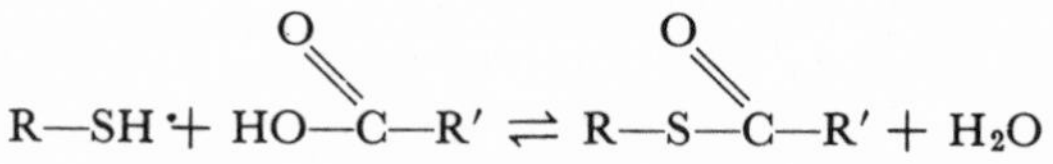

$$R—SH + HO—\overset{\textstyle O}{\overset{\diagdown}{C}}—R' \rightleftharpoons R—S—\overset{\textstyle O}{\overset{\diagdown}{C}}—R' + H_2O$$

Since thioalcohols are stronger acids than are alcohols, thioesters have a stronger tendency to act as anhydrides than do true esters. In particular, they may react to transfer the acid portion of the molecule to an alcohol; e.g.:

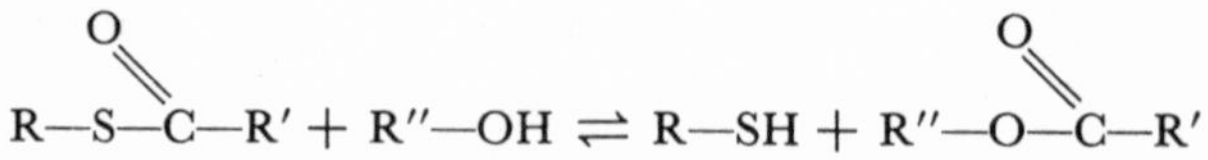

$$R—S—\overset{\textstyle O}{\overset{\diagdown}{C}}—R' + R''—OH \rightleftharpoons R—SH + R''—O—\overset{\textstyle O}{\overset{\diagdown}{C}}—R'$$

Aldehydes and Ketones $R—\overset{\overset{\textstyle O}{\|}}{C}—H$ and $R—\overset{\overset{\textstyle O}{\|}}{C}—R$

The aldehydes are generally named for the acid which is formed on their oxidation; e.g.:

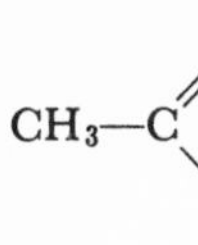

$$CH_3-\overset{\displaystyle O}{\underset{\displaystyle H}{\overset{\|}{C}}} \quad \text{acetaldehyde} \qquad CH_3-CH_2-\overset{\displaystyle O}{\underset{\displaystyle H}{\overset{\|}{C}}} \quad \text{propionaldehyde}$$

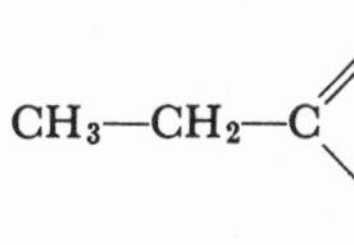

The ketones are named for the two groups which are attached to the carbon carrying the oxygen. (This C=O group as found in the aldehydes and ketones is referred to as a *carbonyl group*.) For example:

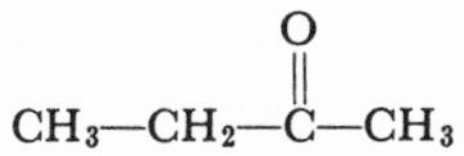

$$CH_3-CH_2-\overset{\displaystyle O}{\overset{\|}{C}}-CH_3 \quad \text{methyl ethyl ketone}$$

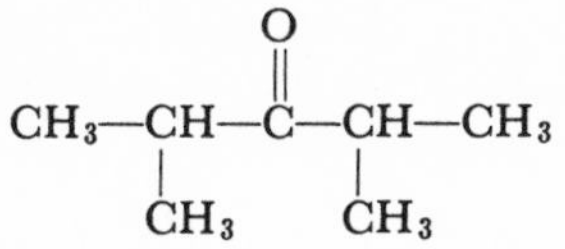

$$CH_3-\underset{\displaystyle CH_3}{\overset{\displaystyle}{CH}}-\overset{\displaystyle O}{\overset{\|}{C}}-\underset{\displaystyle CH_3}{\overset{\displaystyle}{CH}}-CH_3 \quad \text{diisopropyl ketone}$$

REACTIONS

1. *Reduction:*

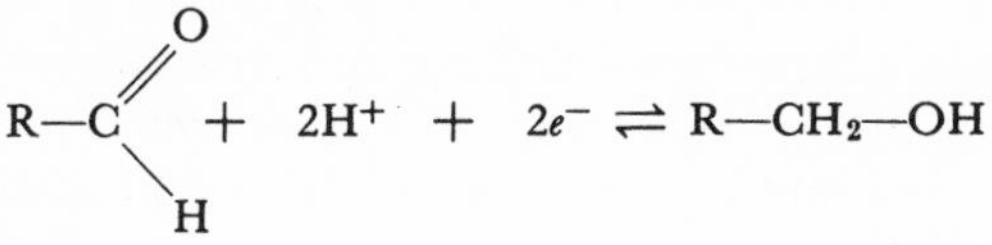

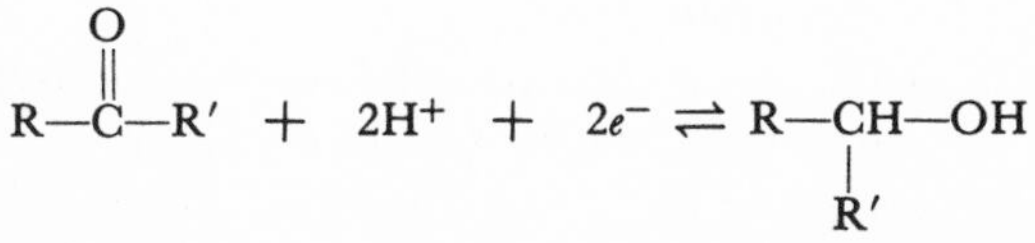

$$R-\overset{\displaystyle O}{\underset{\displaystyle H}{\overset{\|}{C}}} + 2H^+ + 2e^- \rightleftharpoons R-CH_2-OH$$

$$R-\overset{\displaystyle O}{\overset{\|}{C}}-R' + 2H^+ + 2e^- \rightleftharpoons R-\underset{\displaystyle R'}{\overset{\displaystyle}{CH}}-OH$$

2. *Addition to Carbon-Oxygen Double Bonds:* In each of the following cases, the hydrogen from the compound being added across the double bond goes to the oxygen; the remainder of the compound becomes attached to the carbon. One important example is the addition of an alcohol to an aldehyde to yield a *hemi-acetal*.

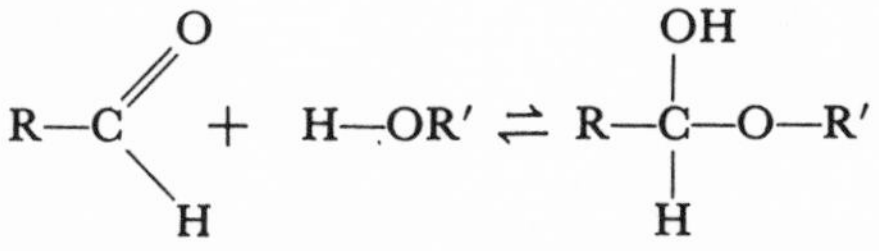

$$R-\overset{\displaystyle O}{\underset{\displaystyle H}{\overset{\|}{C}}} + H-OR' \rightleftharpoons R-\underset{\displaystyle H}{\overset{\displaystyle OH}{\overset{\displaystyle|}{\underset{\displaystyle|}{C}}}}-O-R'$$

hemi-acetal

The formation of a hemi-acetal (or hemi-ketal if formed from a ketone) is a true addition reaction. That is, two molecules are joined together to form a new molecule without loss or gain of atoms. Hemi-acetals are constantly in equilibrium with the free aldehyde and alcohol. This equilibrium usually lies far to the left. Exceptions to this are certain ring structures, common among the sugars, in which the equilibrium is very much in favor of the hemi-acetal.

Hemi-acetals react with alcohols to yield *acetals*. This reaction is a dehydration involving the hemi-acetal and alcohol hydroxyl groups and is *not* an addition reaction. The corresponding derivative of a ketone is usually called a *ketal*.

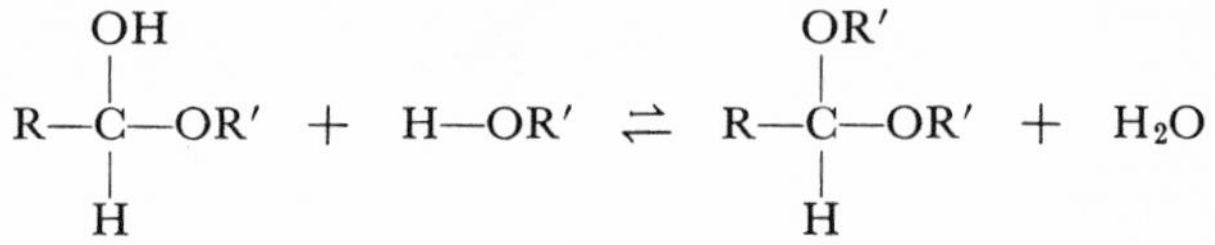

$$
\begin{array}{c}
\text{OH} \\
| \\
\text{R—C—OR}' \\
| \\
\text{H}
\end{array}
+ \ \text{H—OR}' \ \rightleftarrows \
\begin{array}{c}
\text{OR}' \\
| \\
\text{R—C—OR}' \\
| \\
\text{H}
\end{array}
+ \ \text{H}_2\text{O}
$$

A second type of addition reaction, involving *active methylene groups*, is also common in biological systems. When a compound has one or more electron-withdrawing groups adjacent to a methylene (or some-times a methyl) group, the methylene group is more acidic than usual. Accordingly this type of methylene group is more reactive in car-bonyl-group addition reactions. We often refer to such methylene groups as "active methylene groups." Electron-withdrawing groups include phenyl groups, esters, acids, carbonyl groups, and, under some circumstances, double bonds.

A compound with an exceptionally active methylene group is malonic acid (or its esters). Here the two carboxyl or ester groups are so effective in decreasing the electron density at the central carbon that the ester becomes sufficiently acidic to form salts in such solvents as ethyl alcohol:

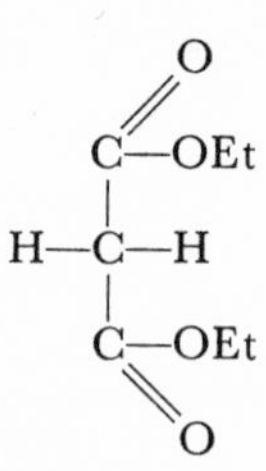

$$
\begin{array}{c}
\quad \text{O} \\
\quad \diagup\!\diagup \\
\text{C—OEt} \\
| \\
\text{H—C—H} \\
| \\
\text{C—OEt} \\
\diagdown\!\diagdown \\
\quad \text{O}
\end{array}
\qquad\qquad
\begin{array}{c}
\quad \text{O} \\
\quad \diagup\!\diagup \\
\text{C—OEt} \\
| \\
\text{H—C}^- \ \text{Na}^+ \\
| \\
\text{C—OEt} \\
\diagdown\!\diagdown \\
\quad \text{O}
\end{array}
$$

diethyl malonate 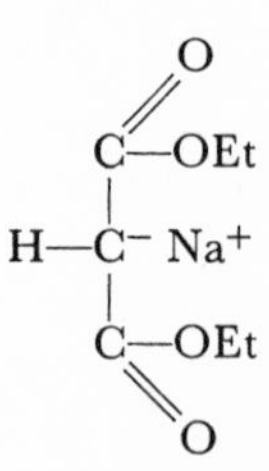   sodium diethyl malonate

Examples of typical additions of active methylene groups to carbonyl double bonds are:

(a)

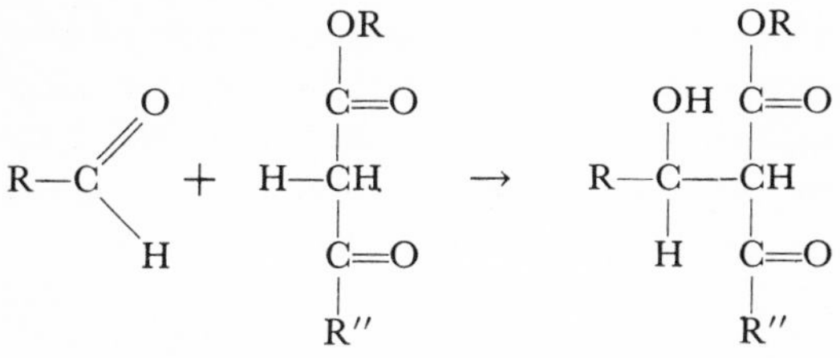

$$R-C\overset{O}{\underset{H}{\diagdown}} \quad + \quad H-\underset{\underset{R''}{|}}{\overset{\overset{OR}{|}}{\underset{C=O}{CH}}} \quad \rightarrow \quad R-\underset{\underset{H}{|}}{\overset{\overset{OH}{|}}{C}}---\underset{\underset{R''}{|}}{\overset{\overset{OR}{|}}{CH}}$$

(b)

$$\underset{\underset{COOH}{|}}{\overset{\overset{COOH}{|}}{\underset{CH_2}{C=O}}} \quad + \quad \underset{|}{\overset{\overset{S-R}{|}}{\underset{H-CH_2}{C=O}}} \quad \rightarrow \quad HO-\underset{\underset{COOH}{|}}{\overset{\overset{COOH}{|}}{\underset{CH_2}{C}}}-CH_2-\overset{O}{\overset{||}{C}}-S-R$$

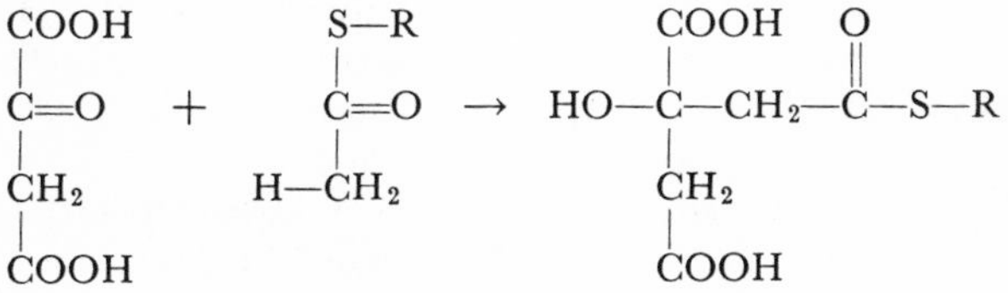

A third type of addition to carbonyl double bonds involves compounds of the general type H_2N-X, where the X represents a variety of groups ranging from a hydroxyl group to substituted ring systems. A water molecule is usually lost after the initial addition reaction. A typical example is the reaction of an aldehyde with an amine:

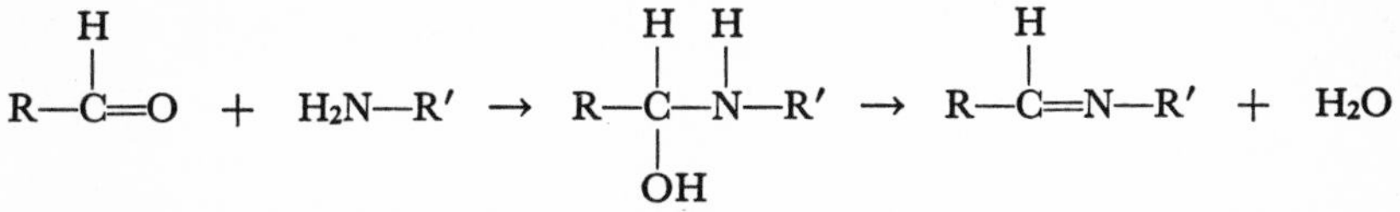

$$R-\overset{\overset{H}{|}}{C}=O \; + \; H_2N-R' \; \rightarrow \; R-\underset{\underset{OH}{|}}{\overset{\overset{H}{|}}{C}}-\overset{\overset{H}{|}}{N}-R' \; \rightarrow \; R-\overset{\overset{H}{|}}{C}=N-R' \; + \; H_2O$$

The product in this case is called a "Schiff base" and is very unstable in water solution. However, stable products are formed in reactions of aldehydes with compounds such as hydroxylamine or phenylhydrazine. The products, oximes and phenylhydrazones, respectively, are readily crystallized and are often prepared to assist in the identification of unknown aldehydes or ketones.

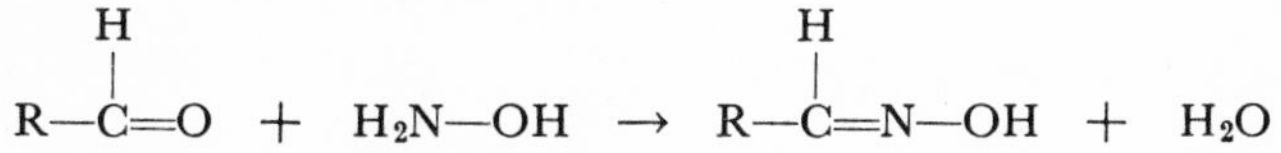

$$R-\overset{\overset{H}{|}}{C}=O \; + \; H_2N-OH \; \rightarrow \; R-\overset{\overset{H}{|}}{C}=N-OH \; + \; H_2O$$
$$\text{hydroxylamine} \qquad\qquad \text{an oxime}$$

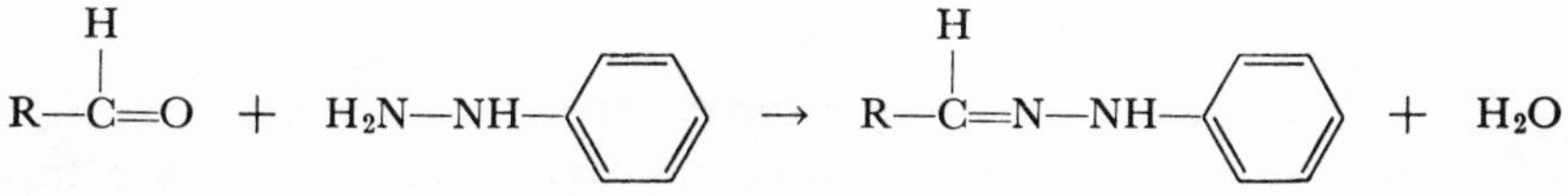

$$R-\overset{\overset{H}{|}}{C}=O \; + \; H_2N-NH-\bigcirc \; \rightarrow \; R-\overset{\overset{H}{|}}{C}=N-NH-\bigcirc \; + \; H_2O$$
$$\text{phenylhydrazine} \qquad\qquad \text{a phenylhydrazone}$$

Acids R—COOH

The following is a list of common unbranched-chain monocarboxylic acids. The common name is shown first, followed by the more systematic IUPAC nomenclature in parentheses:

H—COOH	formic (methanoic) acid
CH_3—COOH	acetic (ethanoic) acid
CH_3CH_2—COOH	propionic (propanoic) acid
$CH_3CH_2CH_2$—COOH	butyric (butanoic) acid
$CH_3CH_2CH_2CH_2$—COOH	valeric (pentanoic) acid
$CH_3CH_2CH_2CH_2CH_2$—COOH	caproic (hexanoic) acid
CH_3—$(CH_2)_{10}$—COOH	lauric (dodecanoic) acid
CH_3—$(CH_2)_{12}$—COOH	myristic (tetradecanoic) acid
CH_3—$(CH_2)_{14}$—COOH	palmitic (hexadecanoic) acid
CH_3—$(CH_2)_{16}$—COOH	stearic (octadecanoic) acid

It should be noted that for those acids having four or more carbon atoms, a variety of isomers is possible, depending upon the arrangement of the carbons in the side chain; for example, *n*-butyric (butanoic) and *iso*-butyric (2-methylpropanoic) acids. The positions of substituents on the carbon chain of the acids may be indicated either by numbering of the carbons, or by the use of Greek letters as shown below:

$$\overset{6}{R}-\overset{5}{C}H_2-\overset{4}{C}H_2-\overset{3}{C}H_2-\overset{2}{C}H_2-\overset{1}{C}H_2-COOH$$
$$\quad\;\epsilon\qquad\delta\qquad\gamma\qquad\beta\qquad\alpha$$

Generally, the numbers are used with the IUPAC system of nomenclature and the Greek letters when the common names are employed. For example:

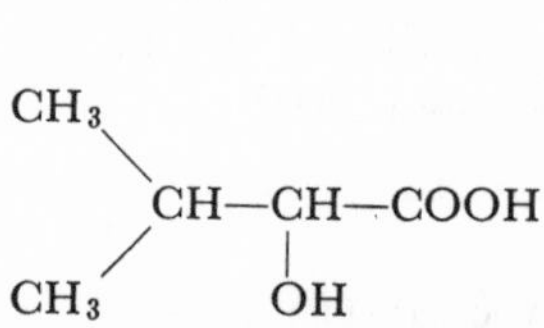

$$\begin{array}{c} CH_3 \\ \diagdown \\ CH-CH-COOH \\ \diagup \quad\;\; | \\ CH_3 \quad\;\; OH \end{array}$$

α-hydroxy-*iso*-valeric acid
or
2-hydroxy-3-methylbutanoic acid

Another important group of acids contains two carboxylic groups per molecule and is referred to as *dicarboxylic acids*. The more important ones for our purposes are:

$$
\begin{array}{c}
\text{COOH} \\
| \\
\text{COOH}
\end{array}
$$

oxalic acid

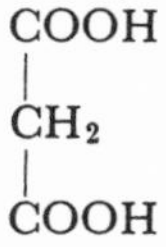

$$
\begin{array}{c}
\text{COOH} \\
| \\
\text{CH}_2 \\
| \\
\text{COOH}
\end{array}
$$

malonic acid

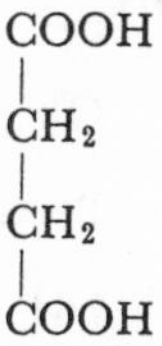

$$
\begin{array}{c}
\text{COOH} \\
| \\
\text{CH}_2 \\
| \\
\text{CH}_2 \\
| \\
\text{COOH}
\end{array}
$$

succinic acid

$$
\begin{array}{c}
\text{COOH} \\
| \\
(\text{CH}_2)_3 \\
| \\
\text{COOH}
\end{array}
$$

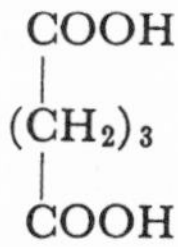

glutaric acid

REACTIONS

1. *Decarboxylation:* The loss of carbon dioxide from a carboxyl group is termed decarboxylation. The general reaction is

$$ R\text{—COOH} \rightarrow R\text{—H} + CO_2 $$

Two special cases of biological importance are the decarboxylation of α- and β-keto acids. Some specific examples are:

(a) 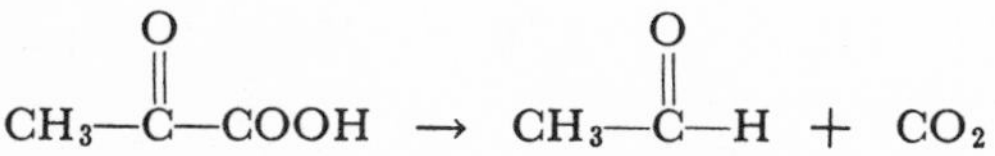
$$
CH_3\text{—}\overset{\overset{\displaystyle O}{\|}}{C}\text{—COOH} \rightarrow CH_3\text{—}\overset{\overset{\displaystyle O}{\|}}{C}\text{—H} + CO_2
$$

pyruvic acid acetaldehyde

(b) 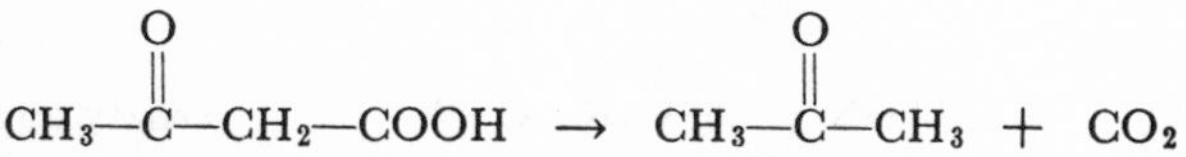
$$
CH_3\text{—}\overset{\overset{\displaystyle O}{\|}}{C}\text{—CH}_2\text{—COOH} \rightarrow CH_3\text{—}\overset{\overset{\displaystyle O}{\|}}{C}\text{—CH}_3 + CO_2
$$

acetoacetic acid acetone

Note that an α-keto acid gives an aldehyde on decarboxylation; a β-keto acid a ketone.

2. *Anhydride Formation:* An *acid anhydride* is the product of a reaction involving the removal of a water molecule from two acidic groups. Upon hydrolysis of the anhydride, the two acids will be formed. A variety of different types of acid anhydrides is possible; some of the different possibilities are:

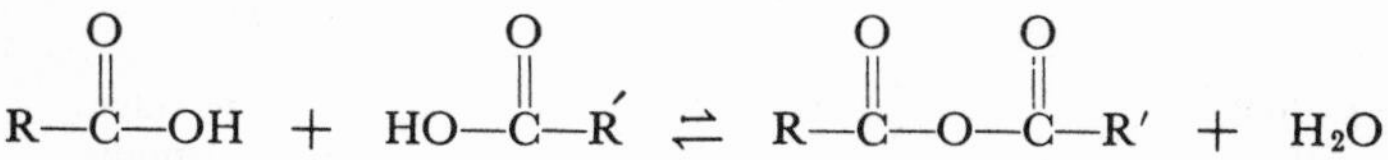

$$
R\text{—}\overset{\overset{\displaystyle O}{\|}}{C}\text{—OH} + HO\text{—}\overset{\overset{\displaystyle O}{\|}}{C}\text{—R}' \rightleftarrows R\text{—}\overset{\overset{\displaystyle O}{\|}}{C}\text{—O—}\overset{\overset{\displaystyle O}{\|}}{C}\text{—R}' + H_2O
$$

$$R-\overset{\overset{\displaystyle O}{\|}}{C}-OH \; + \; HCl \; \rightleftharpoons \; R-\overset{\overset{\displaystyle O}{\|}}{C}-Cl \; + \; H_2O$$

$$R-\overset{\overset{\displaystyle O}{\|}}{C}-OH \; + \; HO-\underset{\underset{\displaystyle OH}{|}}{\overset{\overset{\displaystyle O}{\|}}{P}}-OH \; \rightleftharpoons \; R-\overset{\overset{\displaystyle O}{\|}}{C}-O-\underset{\underset{\displaystyle OH}{|}}{\overset{\overset{\displaystyle O}{\|}}{P}}-OH \; + \; H_2O$$

$$R-O-\underset{\underset{\displaystyle OH}{|}}{\overset{\overset{\displaystyle O}{\|}}{P}}-OH \; + \; HO-\underset{\underset{\displaystyle OH}{|}}{\overset{\overset{\displaystyle O}{\|}}{P}}-OH \; \rightleftharpoons \; R-O-\underset{\underset{\displaystyle OH}{|}}{\overset{\overset{\displaystyle O}{\|}}{P}}-O-\underset{\underset{\displaystyle OH}{|}}{\overset{\overset{\displaystyle O}{\|}}{P}}-OH \; + \; H_2O$$

We must emphasize the fact that significant amounts of anhydrides are formed by these reactions only under conditions which overcome the very unfavorable equilibrium. Chemically, this is usually accomplished by removal of the water as it is formed.

3. *Amide Formation:* The simple mixture of organic acids with ammonia or amines does not readily lead to amide formation. The amides can be formed easily if an anhydride of the acid is employed. The type of amide formed will depend upon the type of amine (or ammonia) used.

$$R-C\!\!\begin{array}{c}\nearrow O \\ \\ \searrow X\end{array} \; + \; \left\{\begin{array}{lll}
H_3N & \rightarrow \; R-\overset{\overset{\displaystyle O}{\|}}{C}-NH_2 & \text{primary amide} \\
\\
H_2N-R' & \rightarrow \; R-\overset{\overset{\displaystyle O}{\|}}{C}-NH-R' & \text{secondary amide} \\
\\
H-N\!\!\begin{array}{c}\nearrow R' \\ \\ \searrow R''\end{array} & \rightarrow \; R-\overset{\overset{\displaystyle O}{\|}}{C}-N\!\!\begin{array}{c}\nearrow R' \\ \\ \searrow R''\end{array} & \text{tertiary amide}
\end{array}\right.$$

an acid anhydride

Amines

Like the alcohols, the amines may also be classified into three groups depending upon their structures, i.e.,

$$R-NH_2 \qquad\qquad \begin{array}{c}R \\ \searrow \\ \quad N-H \\ \nearrow \\ R'\end{array} \qquad\qquad \begin{array}{c}R \\ \searrow \\ \quad N-R'' \\ \nearrow \\ R'\end{array}$$

primary amine   secondary amine   tertiary amine

In this case, however, it is the number of carbons attached to the nitrogen which determines whether it is a *primary*, *secondary*, or *tertiary* amine, and the actual structure of the groups which are attached to the nitrogen has no bearing upon the matter.

ISOMERISM

In order that two compounds may be called "isomers," it is first necessary that they contain the same number of atoms of each type, i.e., that they have the same empirical formula. Beyond this, however, it is possible to have a variety of types of isomerism depending upon the manner and degree in which the two compounds differ from each other. Examples of differing types of isomerism are given below:

STRUCTURAL ISOMERS

Those isomers which have wide variations in the arrangements of the atoms, especially of the carbon chain.

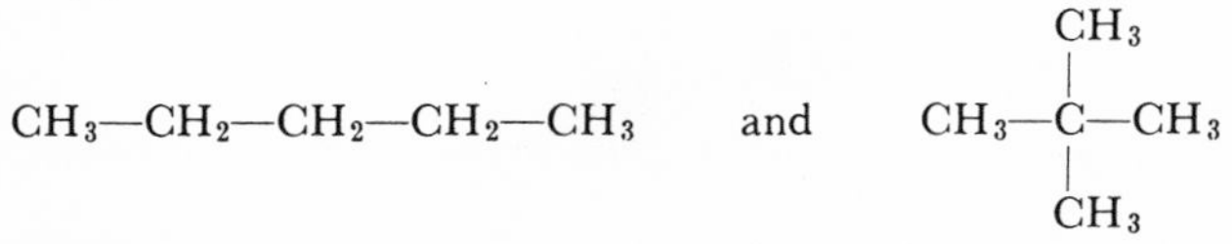

$$CH_3-CH_2-CH_2-CH_2-CH_3 \quad \text{and} \quad CH_3-\overset{\displaystyle CH_3}{\underset{\displaystyle CH_3}{C}}-CH_3$$

POSITIONAL ISOMERS

Those isomers which have the same basic carbon chain but having the functional group or groups in different positions.

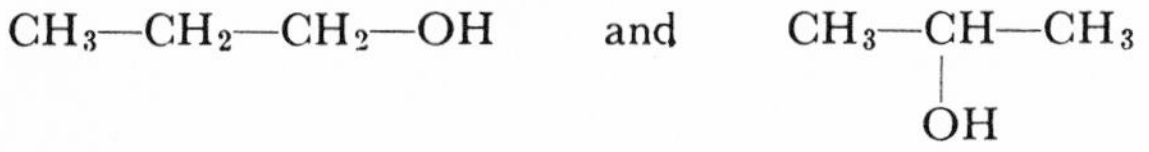

$$CH_3-CH_2-CH_2-OH \quad \text{and} \quad CH_3-\underset{\displaystyle OH}{CH}-CH_3$$

GEOMETRICAL ISOMERS

Those isomers which arise from the peculiar geometry of compounds having a double bond within the carbon chain.

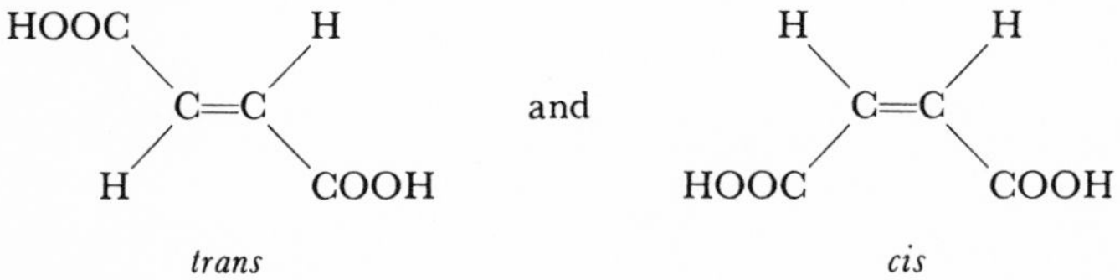

trans   and   *cis*

OPTICAL ISOMERS

Optical isomerism results basically from a lack of symmetry. It is only when there is no point, line, or plane of symmetry possible in a molecule that it displays optical isomerism. For organic compounds, this occurs most commonly when four different groups are attached to one carbon atom. Under these conditions, the carbon involved is usually referred to as an "asymmetric carbon atom." It must be remembered, however, that a molecule may include several "asymmetric carbons" but not show optical isomerism because of the existence of symmetry in the molecule as a whole. This emphasizes that it is not truly the carbon atom that is asymmetric but rather the arrangement of groups around the carbon atom.

The simplest case of optical isomerism involves a single asymmetric carbon atom. A generalized representation of the two possible isomers is shown below:

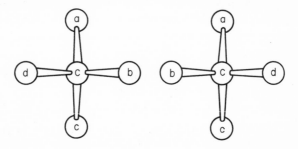

It is important to note that these two isomers have certain properties:

(1) All atoms are connected to the same atoms in each case *and* each atom has the same group of "nearest neighbors." Only the 3-dimensional arrangement of the atoms in space differs.

(2) The two isomers are mirror images of each other.

(3) The molecules are nonsuperimposable, i.e., no matter how one of the isomers is twisted or turned around, it can not be superimposed on the other in such a way that all of the atoms will coincide with like atoms.

(4) Either one of these isomers, as a crystal or in solution, will cause the plane of polarized light to be rotated. One will rotate the plane a certain amount to the right ($+$), the other an equal amount to the left ($-$).

Isomers having these properties are called *enantiomorphs*. Examples of several simple optical isomers are:

$$
\begin{array}{ccc}
\text{COOH} & & \text{COOH} \\
| & & | \\
\text{H--C*--NH}_2 & \text{and} & \text{H}_2\text{N--C*--H} \\
| & & | \\
\text{CH}_3 & & \text{CH}_3
\end{array}
$$

alanine (an amino acid)

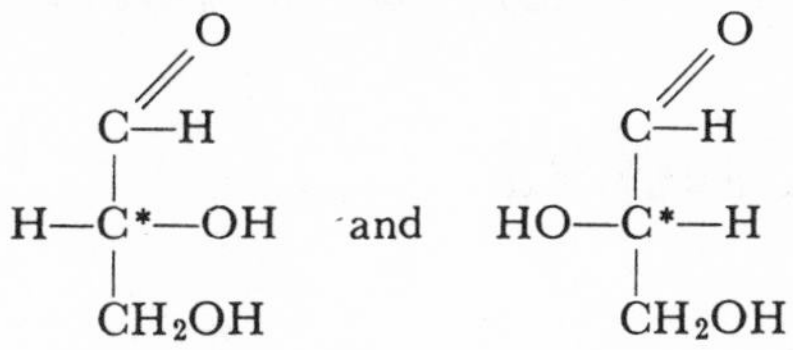

$$
\begin{array}{cc}
\overset{\displaystyle O}{\overset{\displaystyle \diagup\!\!\!\diagdown}{C-H}} & \overset{\displaystyle O}{\overset{\displaystyle \diagup\!\!\!\diagdown}{C-H}} \\
\mid & \mid \\
H-C^*-OH \quad \text{and} \quad & HO-C^*-H \\
\mid & \mid \\
CH_2OH & CH_2OH
\end{array}
$$

glyceraldehyde (a simple sugar)

The asterisks mark the asymmetric carbon in each case.

An example of a compound having "asymmetric carbons" but no other enantiomorphic form, is *meso*-tartaric acid.

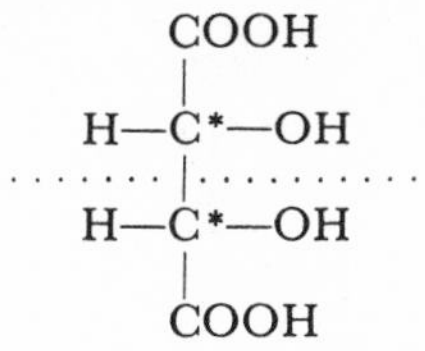

$$
\begin{array}{c}
COOH \\
\mid \\
H-C^*-OH \\
\cdots\cdots\cdots\mid\cdots\cdots\cdots \\
H-C^*-OH \\
\mid \\
COOH
\end{array}
$$

meso-tartaric acid

Here there is a plane of symmetry passing through the molecule as indicated by the dotted line.

Both geometrical isomers and optical isomers are subdivisions of the more general class of *steroisomers*, those differing only in the arrangement of their atoms in space.

SUGGESTED ADDITIONAL READING

White, E.H., "Chemical Background for the Biological Sciences," Prentice-Hall, Inc., Englewood Cliffs, N. J., 1964.

Fieser, L.F., and Feiser, M., "Introduction to Organic Chemistry," D.C. Heath & Co., Boston, 1957.

Hart, H., and Schuetz, R.D., "A Short Course in Organic Chemistry," 3rd ed., Houghton Mifflin Co., Boston 1966.

Morrison, R.T., and Boyd, R.N., "Organic Chemistry," Allyn & Bacon, Inc., Boston, 1959.

Proteins, Amino Acids, and Peptides

2

PROTEINS

The group of compounds called "proteins" account, on the average, for about one half of the total dry weight of living materials. While some proteins do serve as structural materials or as important components of extracellular fluids, the most striking characteristic of these compounds is their ability to function within living cells as biological catalysts. As will be explained in more detail in a later chapter, almost all reactions occurring within living cells require the presence of specific catalysts. These catalysts, which are called *enzymes*, vary greatly in biological activity and properties but have in common the fact that they are all proteins of one kind or another. It has been estimated that as much as 90 per cent of the total protein within a cell is in fact enzyme protein.

The proteins are often referred to as macromolecules because of the high molecular weight of the individual molecules. The proteins are further characterized by the fact that they are all polymers, that is, they are chain-like molecules produced by the linking together of a number of similar small units. The small units of the proteins are chiefly *α-amino acids* of the following general structure:

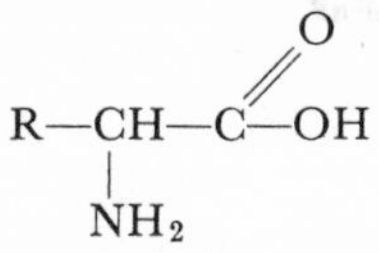

$$R—CH—\overset{\displaystyle O}{\overset{\|}{C}}—OH$$
$$\underset{NH_2}{|}$$

These units are joined through the carboxyl and amino groups to give the primary structure of the protein chain shown below:

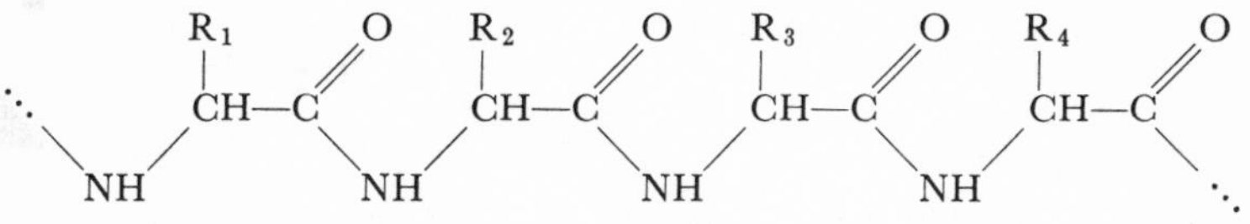

$$\cdots \underset{NH}{\overset{R_1}{CH}}—C \overset{O}{\diagup} \underset{NH}{\overset{R_2}{CH}}—C \overset{O}{\diagup} \underset{NH}{\overset{R_3}{CH}}—C \overset{O}{\diagup} \underset{NH}{\overset{R_4}{CH}}—C \overset{O}{\diagup} \cdots$$

The bond between each pair of amino acids is a special kind of amide bond and is commonly called a *peptide* bond.

The chain lengths of known proteins vary from about fifty to several thousand amino acid units. In addition, proteins differ in relative content of the twenty or so amino acids which are common constituents, and in the order in which the amino acids are linked together in the chain. It should be clear that with twenty different units to fill as many as several thousand places, the total number of possible proteins approaches infinity.

AMINO ACIDS

Most of the amino acids which occur as components of proteins are *α*-amino acids and fit the general structural formula given above.

When we consider any of the *α*-amino acids other than glycine ($H_2N—CH_2—COOH$), we see that there are at least two possible optical isomers. The two forms of a typical amino acid can be represented as:

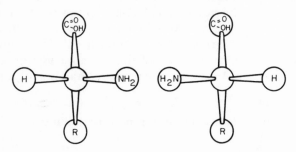

Because of the difficulty of representing three-dimensional molecules in the two dimensions available on a sheet of paper, the structures are usually presented in a conventional "projection" form. To make such a projection, the first step is to arrange the structures as shown above, with the carboxyl group at the top and the hydrogen and amino groups above the plane of the paper. A projection of this structure onto the plane of the paper then appears as shown below, where the amino group in one case falls to the *right* of the carbon chain and in the other case to the *left*.

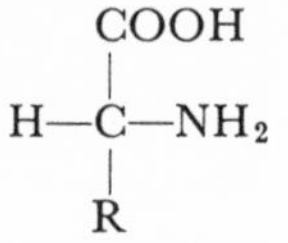

$$
\begin{array}{cc}
\text{COOH} & \text{COOH} \\
| & | \\
\text{H—C—NH}_2 & \text{H}_2\text{N—C—H} \\
| & | \\
\text{R} & \text{R} \\
\text{a D-amino acid} & \text{an L-amino acid}
\end{array}
$$

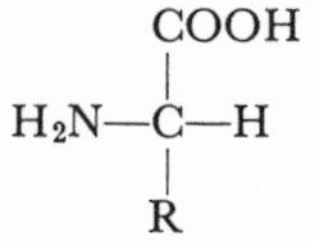

By convention, those compounds which under these circumstances have their amino group to the *right* are called D- compounds, and those having the amino group to the *left* are called L- compounds. It should be noted that this D- or L- has nothing to do with the direction in which a solution of the compound will rotate the plane of polarized light. This direction can be specified by a ($+$) or ($-$) designation.

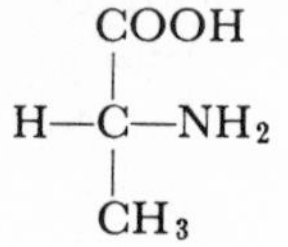

$$
\begin{array}{cc}
\text{COOH} & \text{COOH} \\
| & | \\
\text{H—C—NH}_2 & \text{H}_2\text{N—C—H} \\
| & | \\
\text{CH}_3 & \text{CH}_3 \\
\text{D-(+)-alanine} & \text{L-(−)-alanine}
\end{array}
$$

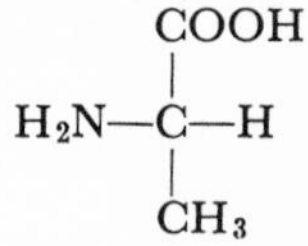

While some D-amino acids do occur in living cells, only the L-amino acids are used for protein synthesis. Similar specificities for one optical isomer are common in a wide variety of biochemical reactions.

Structures and Classification of Amino Acids Common to Most Proteins

The chemical classification of the amino acids is based chiefly upon the composition of the side-chain or R-group in that this is the feature which varies from one amino acid to another while the α-carbon, carboxyl, and amino groups are common to all. No single means of classification can be used for all of the amino acids; hence we shall find that a compound may appear in more than one of the classes.

SIMPLE AMINO ACIDS

Those amino acids which contain no functional groups in the side-chain:

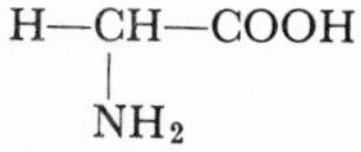

$$H—CH—COOH$$
$$\qquad | $$
$$\qquad NH_2$$

glycine

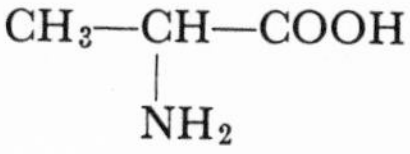

$$CH_3—CH—COOH$$
$$\qquad\quad | $$
$$\qquad\quad NH_2$$

alanine

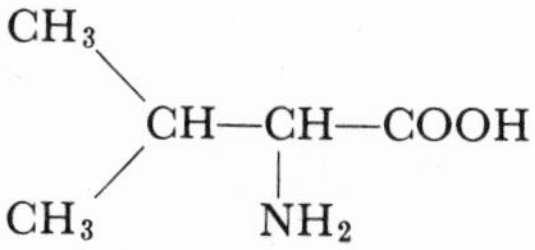

$$CH_3$$
$$\quad\diagdown$$
$$\qquad CH—CH—COOH$$
$$\quad\diagup\qquad | $$
$$CH_3\qquad NH_2$$

valine

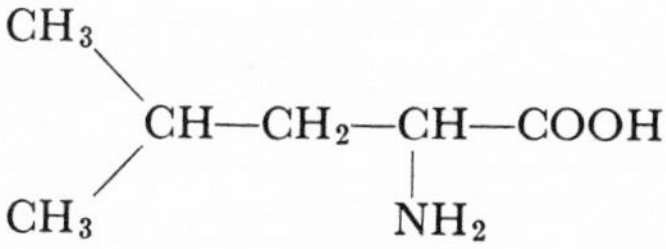

$$CH_3$$
$$\quad\diagdown$$
$$\qquad CH—CH_2—CH—COOH$$
$$\quad\diagup\qquad\qquad | $$
$$CH_3\qquad\qquad NH_2$$

leucine

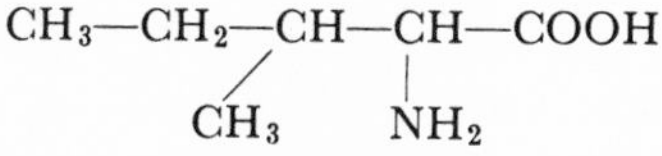

$$CH_3—CH_2—CH—CH—COOH$$
$$\qquad\qquad\diagup\quad | $$
$$\qquad\quad CH_3\quad NH_2$$

isoleucine

HYDROXY AMINO ACIDS

Those which contain an alcohol group in the side-chain:

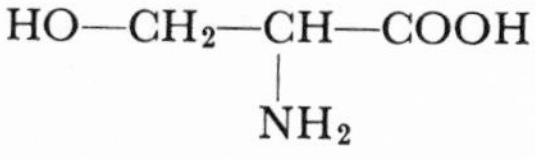

$$HO—CH_2—CH—COOH$$
$$\qquad\qquad | $$
$$\qquad\qquad NH_2$$

serine

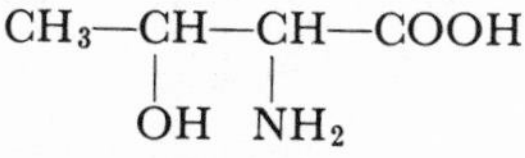

$$CH_3—CH—CH—COOH$$
$$\qquad\ | \quad | $$
$$\qquad OH\ \ NH_2$$

threonine

SULFUR-CONTAINING AMINO ACIDS

Those having a sulfur atom in the side-chain:

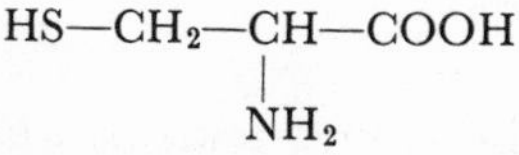

$$HS—CH_2—CH—COOH$$
$$\qquad\qquad | $$
$$\qquad\qquad NH_2$$

cysteine

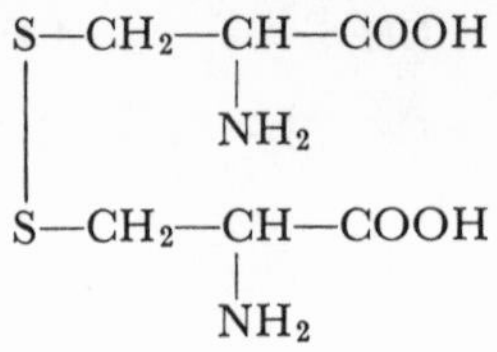

$$S—CH_2—CH—COOH$$
$$\vert$$
$$NH_2$$

$$S—CH_2—CH—COOH$$
$$\vert$$
$$NH_2$$

cystine

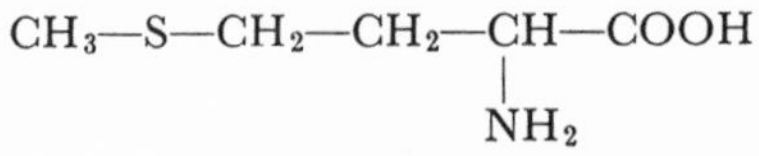

$$CH_3—S—CH_2—CH_2—CH—COOH$$
$$\vert$$
$$NH_2$$

methionine

BASIC AMINO ACIDS

Those having a basic group in the side-chain:

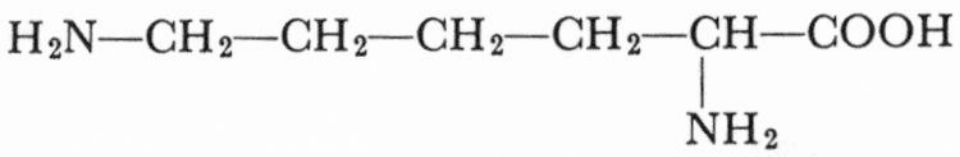

$$H_2N—CH_2—CH_2—CH_2—CH_2—CH—COOH$$
$$\vert$$
$$NH_2$$

lysine

$$NH$$
$$\vert\vert$$
$$H_2N—C—NH—CH_2—CH_2—CH_2—CH—COOH$$
$$\vert$$
$$NH_2$$

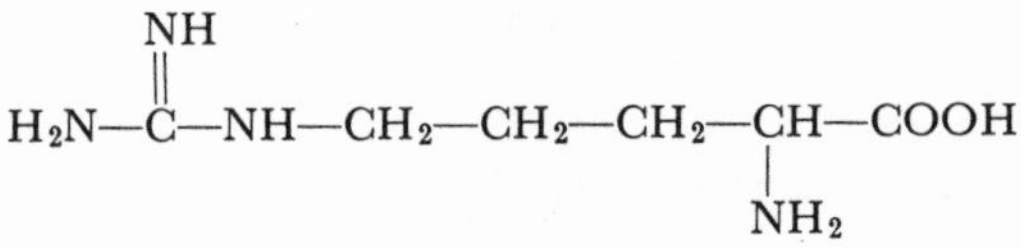

arginine

ACIDIC AMINO ACIDS

Those having a carboxyl group in the side-chain:

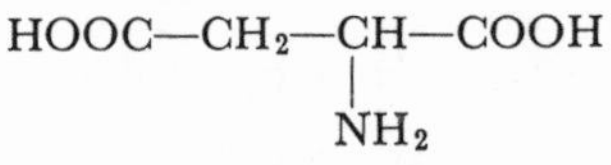

$$HOOC—CH_2—CH—COOH$$
$$\vert$$
$$NH_2$$

aspartic acid

$$HOOC—CH_2—CH_2—CH—COOH$$
$$\vert$$
$$NH_2$$

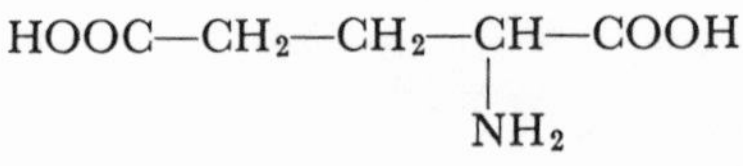

glutamic acid

Amino Acid Amides

Derivatives of the acidic amino acids in which one of the carboxyl groups has been converted to an amide:

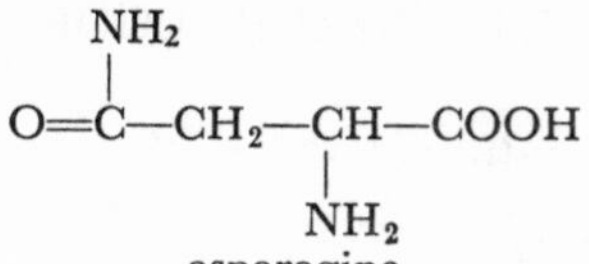

$$\underset{\underset{NH_2}{|}}{O=C}-CH_2-\underset{\underset{NH_2}{|}}{CH}-COOH$$

asparagine

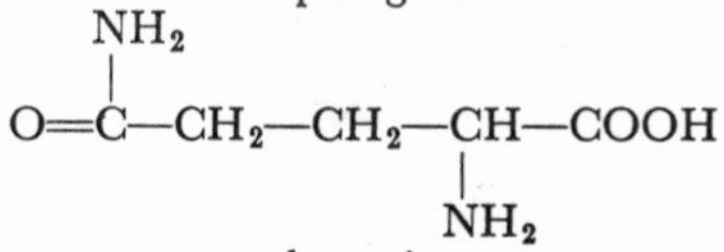

$$\underset{\underset{NH_2}{|}}{O=C}-CH_2-CH_2-\underset{\underset{NH_2}{|}}{CH}-COOH$$

glutamine

HETEROCYCLIC AMINO ACIDS

Those in which the side-chain includes a ring involving at least one atom other than carbon:

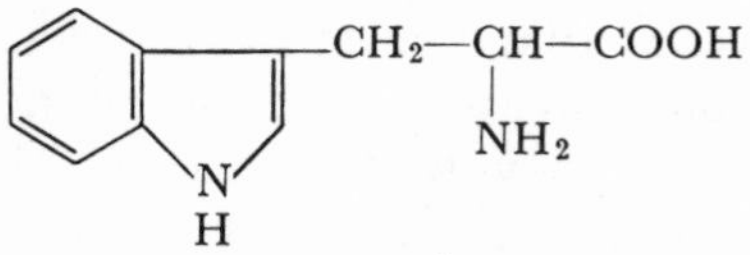

tryptophan

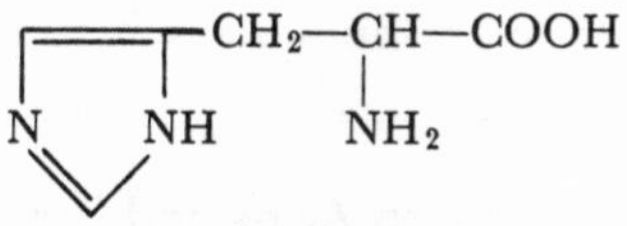

histidine

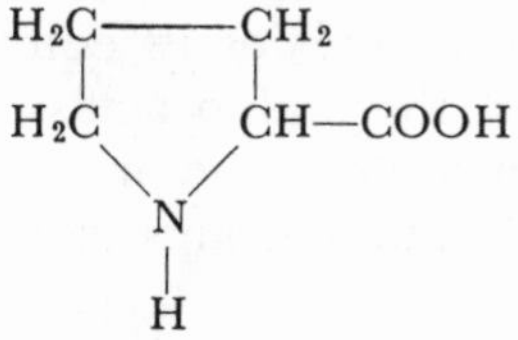

proline

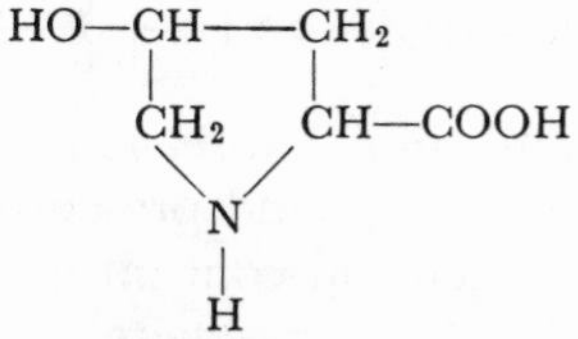

hydroxyproline

Those having an aromatic (benzene-like) group in the side-chain:

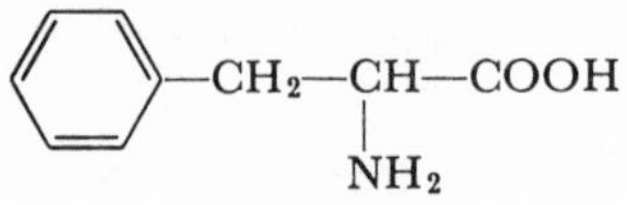

$$\text{C}_6\text{H}_5-\text{CH}_2-\underset{\underset{\text{NH}_2}{|}}{\text{CH}}-\text{COOH}$$

phenylalanine

$$\text{HO}-\text{C}_6\text{H}_4-\text{CH}_2-\underset{\underset{\text{NH}_2}{|}}{\text{CH}}-\text{COOH}$$

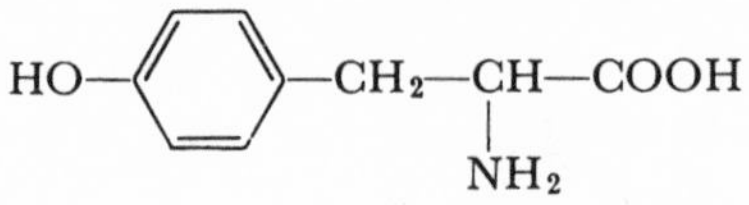

tyrosine

. . .　　. . .　　. . .

It must be emphasized that a number of the amino acids may be placed in more than one category. The classification given is perhaps the most useful; however, tryptophan and histidine are commonly included with the aromatic amino acids, histidine with the basic amino acids and hydroxyproline with the hydroxy amino acids. Also, a separate class is sometimes used for proline and hydroxyproline in that these two are the only amino acids which do not have a primary amino group.

Acidic and Basic Nature of Amino Acids and Proteins

All free amino acids contain at least one acidic group (—COOH) and one basic group (—NH₂ or its equivalent). In order to understand the behavior of the amino acids, and eventually of proteins, we must first consider some of the properties of these groups.

Both carboxyl and amino groups take part in ionization reactions as follows:

$$\text{R}-\underset{\underset{\text{OH}}{}}{\overset{\overset{\text{O}}{\|}}{\text{C}}} \rightleftharpoons \text{H}^+ + \text{R}-\underset{\underset{\text{O}^-}{}}{\overset{\overset{\text{O}}{\|}}{\text{C}}} \tag{1}$$

$$\text{R}-\text{NH}_3^+ \rightleftharpoons \text{H}^+ + \text{R}-\text{NH}_2 \tag{2}$$

Since these are equilibrium expressions, the relative amounts of ionized and un-ionized compound present at any given time will be governed by the hydrogen ion concentration in the solution, in accord with the Mass Law for any chemical reaction. In quantitative terms, this can be expressed for the reactions just shown as

$$\frac{[H^+] \times [R\text{—}COO^-]}{[R\text{—}COOH]} = K$$

and

$$\frac{[H^+] \times [R\text{—}NH_2]}{[R\text{—}NH_3^+]} = K$$

where the square brackets are used to indicate the molar concentrations of each of the species indicated, and the K's are the individual equilibrium constants (in this case ionization or dissociation constants). The exact value of K will depend on the particular compound involved. Typical values might be 1×10^{-5} for the dissociation of R—COOH and 1×10^{-8} for R—NH$_3^+$.

If we substitute these general values for the ionization constants into the equations above, along with any given value of the hydrogen ion concentration, we can obtain a value for the ratio of ionized to un-ionized molecules in the solution. For example, at pH 7 ([H$^+$] = 1×10^{-7}M.) we obtain

$$1 \times 10^{-5} = \frac{(1 \times 10^{-7}) \times [R\text{—}COO^-]}{[R\text{—}COOH]}$$

$$\text{i.e.,} \quad 10^2 = \frac{[R\text{—}COO^-]}{[R\text{—}COOH]}$$

That is, for every molecule of un-ionized R—COOH, there will be 100 molecules of R—COO$^-$. Another way to state this is to say that the acid is about 99 percent ionized at this pH.

Similarly, for the amine,

$$1 \times 10^{-8} = \frac{(1 \times 10^{-7}) \times [R\text{—}NH_2]}{[R\text{—}NH_3^+]}$$

$$\text{or} \quad 10^{-1} = \frac{[R\text{—}NH_2]}{[R\text{—}NH_3^+]}$$

In this case, there are ten ionized molecules for each un-ionized one, or the amine is about 91 percent ionized. The manner in which percent ionization will vary with pH for each of these groups is shown in the form of a graph in Figure 2–1.

When the hydrogen ion concentration is equal to K, the equations reduce to the simple ratios

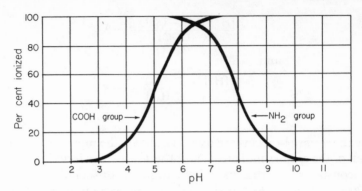

Figure 2-1.   Graph of Ionization Versus pH for Typical Carboxyl and Amino Groups.

$$\frac{[\text{R}-\text{COO}^-]}{[\text{R}-\text{COOH}]} = 1 \quad \text{at} \quad [\text{H}^+] = 10^{-5}, \text{ i.e., pH} = 5,$$

and

$$\frac{[\text{R}-\text{NH}_2]}{[\text{R}-\text{NH}_3^+]} = 1 \quad \text{at} \quad [\text{H}^+] = 10^{-8}, \text{ i.e., pH} = 8.$$

The pH at which this occurs is known as the pK for the particular ionizing group involved. Under these circumstances, the groups are half in the ionized and half in the un-ionized form. The pK is thus an expression of the hydrogen ion concentration present at half-ionization; in this way it serves as an indication of the relative ease with which the ionization takes place. That is, it indicates the strength of an acid or base.

If we consider a typical amino acid having one of each type of group, we get

$$
\begin{array}{ccc}
 & \overset{\displaystyle O}{\underset{\displaystyle R}{\overset{\displaystyle \parallel}{\underset{\displaystyle |}{C-OH}}}} & \overset{\displaystyle O}{\underset{\displaystyle R}{\overset{\displaystyle \parallel}{\underset{\displaystyle |}{C-O^-}}}} \\
\text{at low pH:} \quad H-C-NH_3^+, & \text{and at high pH:} \quad H-C-NH_2.
\end{array}
$$

At some intermediate pH the number of molecules having the carboxyl group ionized and the number of molecules having the amino group ionized will be equal; at this point almost all of the molecules will be in the doubly ionized or *dipolar ion* form:

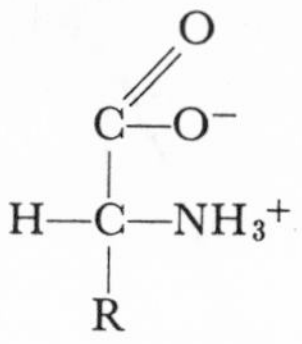

$$
\begin{array}{c}
O \\
\diagup\!\!\!\diagup \\
C\!-\!O^- \\
| \\
H\!-\!C\!-\!NH_3{}^+ \\
| \\
R
\end{array}
$$

The pH at which this occurs is known as the *isoelectric point* of the particular compound. It is the pH at which there is no *net* positive or negative charge *on the molecule* itself.

In proteins of course, the alpha-amino and carboxyl groups of the amino acids are joined together in peptide linkages (except at the ends of chains) and thus are unable to ionize. However, if we look at the side-chains on a number of the amino acids, it is obvious that a variety of ionizing groups would be present as part of any protein. If we consider all of these ionizing groups as either carboxyl or amino groups, we can readily extend the above discussion to the protein molecule.

In this case we will wish to look, not at large numbers of molecules, but at a single molecule with relatively large numbers of both kinds of ionizing groups. At extremes of pH, we would then get for a protein molecule:

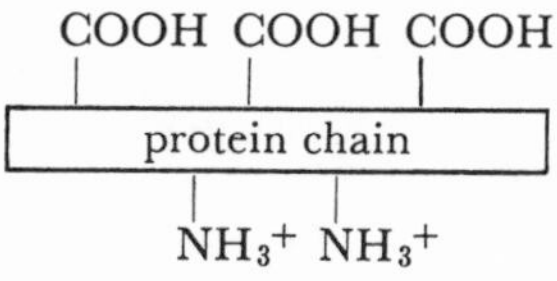

$$
\begin{array}{c}
COOH\ \ COOH\ \ COOH \\
|\qquad\ |\qquad\quad | \\
\boxed{\ \ \text{protein chain}\ \ } \\
|\qquad\ | \\
NH_3{}^+\ \ NH_3{}^+
\end{array}
\qquad \text{and} \qquad
\begin{array}{c}
COO^-\ \ COO^-\ \ COO^- \\
|\qquad\ |\qquad\quad | \\
\boxed{\ \ \text{protein chain}\ \ } \\
|\qquad\ | \\
NH_2\ \ NH_2
\end{array}
$$

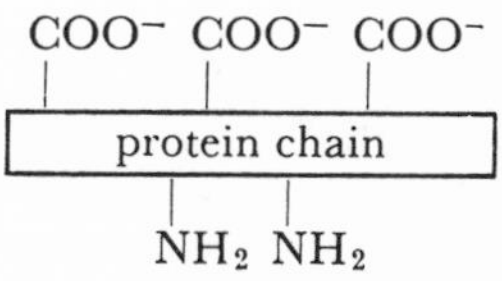

Somewhere in between these extremes, however, we would get a form such as is shown below, i.e., with no net effective charge on the protein molecule:

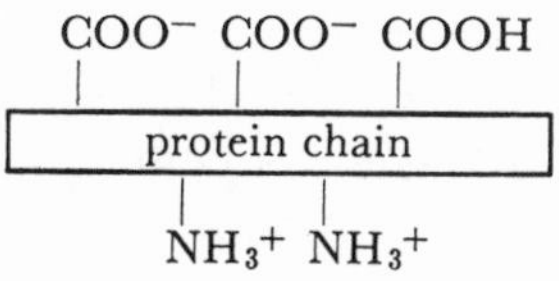

$$
\begin{array}{c}
COO^-\ \ COO^-\ \ COOH \\
|\qquad\ |\qquad\quad | \\
\boxed{\ \ \text{protein chain}\ \ } \\
|\qquad\ | \\
NH_3{}^+\ \ NH_3{}^+
\end{array}
$$

The pH at which this occurs is again referred to as the isoelectric point for that particular protein. It should also be clear that those proteins having an excess of carboxyl groups or their equivalent will tend to have a lower isoelectric point, while those having an excess of amino groups or their equivalent will tend to have a higher isoelectric point. For proteins especially, the isoelectric point is usually determined by finding the pH at which the molecules will not move toward either the anode or the cathode when subjected (in solution) to an electrical field.

PEPTIDES

When two or more amino acids are joined together by amide bonds, the resulting compound is termed a *peptide*. A small peptide may be classified according to the number of amino acid units as a dipeptide (2 amino acids), tripeptide, etc. Larger units composed of many amino acids are called *polypeptides*. Strictly speaking, proteins are polypeptides; however, most proteins have structural complexities not displayed to the same degree by a chain of amino acids linked by peptide bonds. Therefore, many biochemists draw a line of indefinite placement between the proteins and the less complex polypeptide chains.

Certain aspects of the structure and nomenclature of peptides may best be presented in conjunction with a specific example. Consider, then, a peptide composed of glycine, alanine, and serine with the structure shown below:

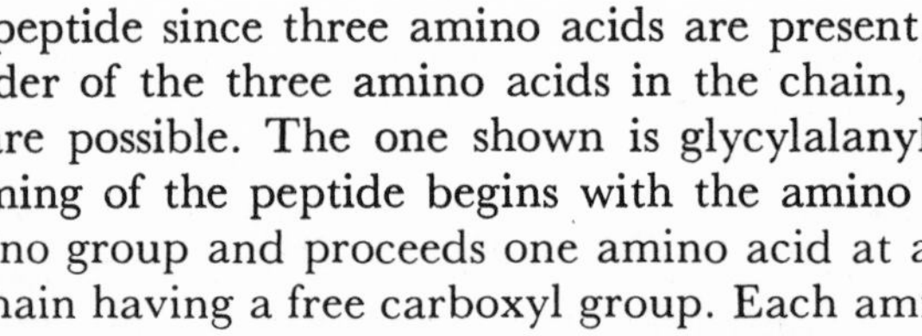

$$H_2N \diagup CH_2 \diagdown C(=O) \diagup N(H) \diagdown CH(CH_3) \diagup C(=O) \diagdown N(H) \diagup CH(CH_2OH) \diagdown C-OH(=O)$$

This is a tripeptide since three amino acids are present. Depending upon the order of the three amino acids in the chain, six different tripeptides are possible. The one shown is glycylalanylserine. Note that the naming of the peptide begins with the amino acid having a free α-amino group and proceeds one amino acid at a time to the end of the chain having a free carboxyl group. Each amino acid unit except the last one is named as an acyl group. This involves the use of the root of the name for the amino acid and the suffix *-yl*.

In discussing naturally occurring peptides or those obtained by the cleavage of the natural compounds into smaller molecules, it is not normally necessary to indicate that the amino acids are of the L-series. This is simply understood to be the case. Should the specification of the optical isomerism be desirable, the compound shown above might be named as glycyl-L-alanyl-L-serine.

Note that the formation of two secondary amide or peptide bonds leaves only one free amino and one free carboxyl group per molecule, occurring at opposite ends of the peptide chain. The ends of the chain are referred to as the amino and carboxy terminals or commonly as the N- and C- terminals. These two terminal groups, one basic and one acidic, will be the only ionizable groups of any peptide chain unless amino acid units are present which have acidic or basic groups in their side-chains.

Small peptides are comparatively rare in biological material. However, a number of these are of sufficient importance to be mentioned here. *Glutathione* is a widely distributed tripeptide of glutamic acid, cysteine, and glycine. The compound appears to function in certain oxidation-reduction reactions, although a variety of other specific roles have also been suggested. *Oxytocin* and *vasopressin* are examples of a rather unusual group of cyclic peptides. These compounds are hormones; that is, each is a substance produced in small amounts in one part of a complex organism which significantly affects a biochemical process at some other site in the organism. Oxytocin stimulates the contraction of smooth muscle and is particularly important during childbirth. Vasopressin acts to increase the blood pressure, but is perhaps most important by virtue of its participation in the control of the excretion of water by the kidneys. The structure of oxytocin may be diagrammatically represented as:

$$\begin{array}{ccc}
\text{isoleucine} & \text{---------glutamic acid amide} \\
| & | \\
\text{tyrosine} & \text{aspartic acid amide} \\
| & | \\
\text{(H}_2\text{N)---cysteine---(S---S)---cysteine---proline---leucine---glycine amide}
\end{array}$$

Vasopressin differs only in that leucine is replaced by a basic amino acid such as lysine, and isoleucine is replaced by phenylalanine.

There are several points of particular interest in this structure. One of these is the cyclical nature of the compound resulting from the presence of a disulfide linkage between two cysteine units separated from each other in the peptide chain by four other amino acid units. Disulfide bonds of this general type are also of considerable importance in the architecture of protein molecules. A second point of importance is the presence of three molecules of ammonia bound in amide linkage to the three carboxyl groups of the C-terminal glycine and the two acidic amino acids, glutamic acid and aspartic acid. This, too, is of common occurrence in proteins.

A further point is derived from the comparison of oxytocin and vasopressin. The structures are quite similar, differing only with respect to two amino acids. Nevertheless, the two compounds have different physiological activities, demonstrating that relatively minor differences in peptide structure can have far-reaching effects upon biological properties. This emphasizes the specificity of peptide structure with respect to amino acid composition and sequence. A given peptide, including the proteins as major examples, must have certain amino acids arranged in a certain order before its biological role can be fulfilled.

Amino Acid Sequence

The order in which amino acids are joined together in a peptide chain is called the *amino acid sequence* of that chain. Since proteins are often composed of hundreds of amino acid units, with the same ones occurring in many places in a chain, the job of determining such a sequence is a staggering one. However, it is possible to determine rather rapidly the sequence of amino acids in a smaller unit, such as a di- or tripeptide. To do this, the peptide is treated with one of a number of reagents which will react only with the free amino or carboxyl group, or alternatively, only with the peptide bonds. As an example, let us consider the use of dinitrofluorobenzene and of hydrazine for determining the amino acid sequence of a tripeptide (p.27).

In each case the unusual products must be separated from the others and identified by various means, often involving chromatographic separations.

From the reactions shown, it is clear that in our example glycine was on the end of the peptide having the free amino group (i.e., the N-terminal end) and valine was on the end with the free carboxyl (i.e., the C-terminal end). The peptide must then be glycylalanylvaline.

Following this idea, Sanger and his associates hydrolyzed insulin, a very small protein, into a large number of peptides. Each peptide was isolated and its amino acid sequence determined by procedures such as we have described above. From the known sequences of all these peptides, Sanger was able to reconstruct (on paper) the entire sequence of each of the peptide chains of the original insulin molecule. Similar methods have since been used to determine the sequences of several other proteins of somewhat larger size.

PROTEIN STRUCTURE

The proteins may be viewed as very large peptides. However, a number of the properties of the proteins are considerably different

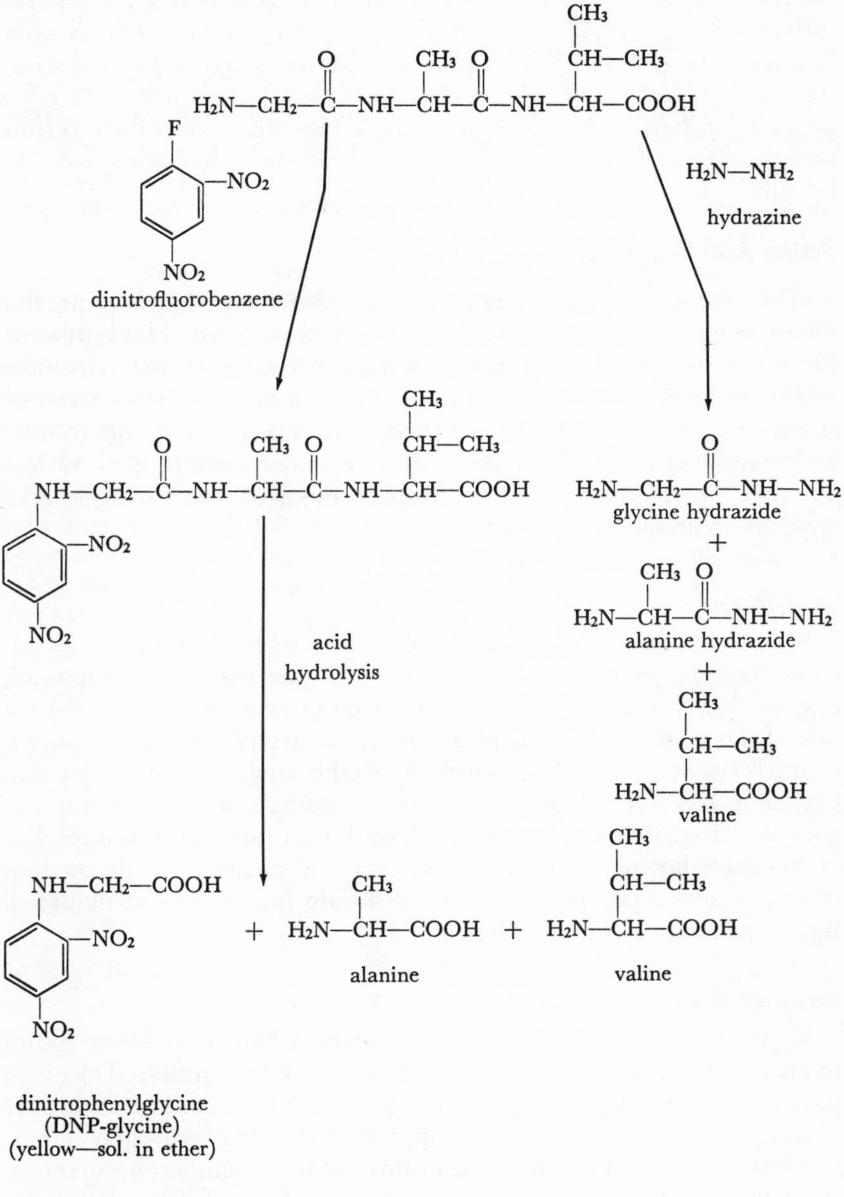

$$
\begin{array}{c}
& & & & & & CH_3 \\
& & O & & CH_3 & O & CH-CH_3 \\
& H_2N-CH_2-C-NH-CH-C-NH-CH-COOH
\end{array}
$$

dinitrofluorobenzene

H_2N-NH_2

hydrazine

$$
\begin{array}{c}
& & & & CH_3 \\
& O & CH_3 & O & CH-CH_3 \\
NH-CH_2-C-NH-CH-C-NH-CH-COOH
\end{array}
$$

acid
hydrolysis

$$
\begin{array}{c}
& O \\
H_2N-CH_2-C-NH-NH_2
\end{array}
$$
glycine hydrazide

+

$$
\begin{array}{c}
CH_3 & O \\
H_2N-CH-C-NH-NH_2
\end{array}
$$
alanine hydrazide

+

$$
\begin{array}{c}
CH_3 \\
CH-CH_3 \\
H_2N-CH-COOH
\end{array}
$$
valine

$$
\begin{array}{c}
NH-CH_2-COOH
\end{array}
$$

+

$$
\begin{array}{c}
CH_3 \\
H_2N-CH-COOH
\end{array}
$$
alanine

+

$$
\begin{array}{c}
CH_3 \\
CH-CH_3 \\
H_2N-CH-COOH
\end{array}
$$
valine

dinitrophenylglycine
(DNP-glycine)
(yellow—sol. in ether)

from those to be expected for a long chain of amino acids connected by peptide bonds. Such a chain should resemble a long, thin worm, continually twisting and turning in solution to assume different conformations, different shapes at different times. There is no doubt that peptide chains are a primary aspect of protein structure; yet each protein occurs in nature in a particular, relatively fixed, three-dimensional configuration. Some are essentially linear, others resemble coiled springs, still others may have both linear areas and coiled areas and in addition be complexly folded to give very compact, globular molecules.

The apparent discrepancy between the expected properties of a peptide chain and the actual properties of the protein is due to the presence in proteins of a variety of bonds other than peptide bonds. These "secondary" bonds hold the peptide chain in the naturally occurring or "native" configuration. A number of different types of bonds may be involved in creating and maintaining the overall structure of any particular protein. The major ones of general importance are hydrogen bonds, disulfide linkages, salt linkages, and "hydrophobic bonds."

DISULFIDE BONDS

We have already seen that the thiol groups of two cysteine molecules may be reversibly oxidized to give the disulfide compound, cystine. When this reaction involves two cysteine units in a polypeptide chain or in different peptide chains, a strong covalent linkage is formed between the two portions of the molecule or molecules. Oxytocin has already been given as an example of the formation of a cyclic structure from a peptide chain by an internal disulfide. The polypeptide hormone, insulin, is an excellent example of the binding together of two peptide chains by disulfide bonds. The structure of this compound is given in Figure 2-2.

HYDROGEN BONDS

Hydrogen bonds form readily whenever a hydrogen atom bound to an oxygen or nitrogen atom is approached by an unshared electron pair of another oxygen or nitrogen. In that proteins contain a number of oxygen and nitrogen atoms capable of forming hydrogen bonds, it is not surprising that this type of linkage is of common occurrence. Particularly important in many proteins are hydrogen bonds involving the $>$NH and $>$C$=$O groups of the peptide bonds. In some cases bonds of this type link a number of peptide chains together. In other

Figure 2-2. The Structure of Beef Insulin.
Each amino acid is represented by the first few
letters of its name. The —NH₂ groups shown
indicate the presence of glutamine and asparagine
rather than glutamic and aspartic acids. Glycine
and phenylalanine are the N-terminal amino
acids; asparagine and alanine the C-terminals.

cases a single peptide chain is held in a coiled or helical form by hydrogen bonds. Specific examples will be presented below.

SALT LINKAGES

Some amino acid side-chains may contain positively charged
groups, others negatively charged groups. If properly positioned,
these groups may give rise to bonding between different portions of a
given molecule or between two or more protein chains.

It should be noted that this type of bonding is in large measure
responsible for the very tight binding between the negatively charged
nucleic acids and the positively charged proteins involved in the formation of nucleoprotein complexes.

A number of the amino acids have side-chains which are of hydro-carbon nature. These are hydrophobic groups in that they do not form hydrogen bonds with water molecules. On the other hand, water molecules have a strong tendency to form hydrogen bonds among themselves. As the result of the hydrogen bonding among water molecules, hydrocarbons are forced out of any water phase in which they may be placed. Similarly the hydrocarbon side-chains of the various amino acids tend to be forced together as a result of the hydrogen bonding among water molecules. The association of hydrocarbon side-chains can in this fashion lead to relatively strong bonding between different portions of a peptide chain.

Protein Conformations

It has previously been mentioned that each protein exists in its natural state in a specific three-dimensional conformation. This particular structure is maintained by secondary bonding of the types mentioned above. The secondary bonding which is possible, and hence the configuration assumed by a particular peptide chain, is in large measure determined by the kinds of amino acids present and by their location in the molecule. It should be clear, for example, that the formation of a disulfide bond requires that two cysteine units be present in positions allowing their interaction. Similar considerations apply to the other kinds of secondary bonding.

Proteins may exist in a number of possible conformations. However, we will limit our discussion to the three major types.

THE EXTENDED CHAIN

A number of the structural proteins, particularly those which form fibers, are essentially linear peptide chains. The conformation is maintained by multiple hydrogen bonding among a number of peptide chains lying side-by-side. One example is that of fibroin, the major component of silk fibers. A diagrammatic representation of portions of two chains of fibroin linked by hydrogen bonds is given in Figure 2-3. Note that the two chains run in opposite directions. It should be apparent that each of the chains could also form hydrogen bonds with still another protein, and so on. Very large protein aggregates can thus be formed. Structures of this type can be formed readily only if the R groups are relatively small. Otherwise the chains are held too far apart for hydrogen bonding to occur. Silk fibroin, for example, is composed mainly of glycine, alanine and serine units.

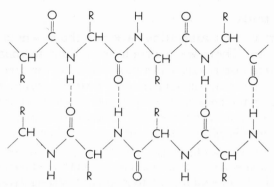

Figure 2-3. Diagram of a Portion of the Structure of Silk Fibroin.

The dashed lines indicate hydrogen bonds linking the peptide chains.

THE ALPHA-HELIX

A number of other structural proteins, although essentially linear in gross form, are found to be of coiled or helical nature. The coiling is maintained chiefly by hydrogen bonding of the $>$NH group of each amino acid with the $>$C$=$O group of the amino acid three units away down the chain. The result is a relatively rigid, tube-like structure called an α-helix. Figure 2-4 is a representation of a portion of an α-helix. The heavy lines indicate portions of the coil closer to the viewer. The side-chains on the α-carbons have been omitted in an attempt for clarity. These side-chains project outwardly, away from the center of the helix.

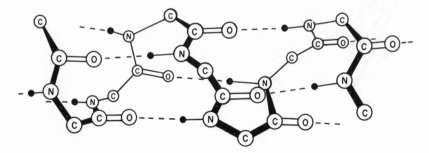

Figure 2-4. Diagram of a Portion of an α-Helix.

The dashed lines indicate hydrogen bonding between successive turns of the helix. The hydrogen atoms involved in hydrogen bonding are shown as small solid circles.

A common example of a protein having the α-helix conformation is the keratin of wool. An additional structural feature in this case is the fact that a number of α-helix chains are bound together to yield very large fibrous aggregates. The individual helices are bound to one another by extensive disulfide bonding and by hydrogen bonding involving the side-chains.

FOLDED CONFORMATIONS

The protein conformations which have just been described are those of structural proteins. You should recall that they are basically of linear nature. On the other hand most biologically active proteins, such as the various enzymes, are probably rather compact structures, roughly globular or ovoid in general shape. Some of these may have more than one chain, but many consist of a single peptide chain folded many times and held in place by any or all of the types of bonding that have been described. Although the conformations of these proteins are generally quite irregular and therefore difficult to determine, it has recently been possible to obtain a good picture of the structure of myoglobin, an iron-porphyrin protein of muscle tissue. This protein appears to consist of α-helical portions connected by portions of random nature. These last portions easily bend or twist to produce the folding. A diagram of the structure of myoglobin appears as Figure 2-5.

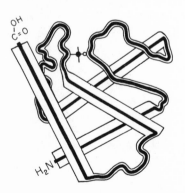

Figure 2-5.   The Three-dimensional Structure of Myoglobin.

Probably most of the globular proteins possess these general structural aspects. Naturally the content of α-helix or other conformations and the extent of folding will vary greatly depending upon the amino acid composition. In this regard it may be mentioned that areas of a peptide chain containing adjacent valine units cannot easily exist as an α-helix. There simply is not sufficient room for the bulky side-chains close to the backbone of the peptide. Also, proline units lack a hydrogen atom on the α-nitrogen and therefore cannot hydrogen-bond in the α-helix. These may also be weak points in the helix which can give rise to a change in direction of folding.

In discussing the structures of the globular proteins, it is often desirable to indicate aspects of varying degrees of complexity. For this purpose the term *primary structure* is used to designate the amino acid sequence of the peptide chain. Here the concern is with the bonding of each amino acid by peptide bonds to its immediate neighbors. Structural aspects arising from the linkage of amino acid units which are not immediate neighbors but are relatively close to each other, as in the α-helix, are referred to as *secondary structure*. Interactions among amino acids relatively widely separated in primary position yield *tertiary structure*.

A fourth degree of complexity, that of *quaternary structure*, has recently been recognized to be of great importance in a number of proteins. This term refers to aspects of molecular structure arising from the interaction of individual peptide chains to form a specific aggregate. We have already described a number of such interactions in the fibrous proteins and have underscored their importance in determining the structures of the various fibrous and membranous components of the cell. It is now clear that numerous globular proteins also have quaternary structure; that is, they are composed of a number of sub-unit peptide chains linked together by any or all of the forces that can act between amino acid side-chains. As before, the nature of the interactions is determined by the types of amino acid residues involved and the distribution of them in the peptide chains.

In some cases, globular proteins having quaternary structure are composed of two or more identical sub-units. In other cases, several kinds of peptide chains are bound together to form the protein.

Hemoglobin, the oxygen-transporting protein of blood, provides an excellent example of quaternary structure. This protein consists of four peptide chains of two types. Each of these sub-units is itself complexly folded, resembling myoglobin to a considerable degree. The two pairs of folded peptides interact with each other to give a quite stable, compact bundle, which is the active protein.

Numerous enzymes have also been shown to possess quaternary structure, that is, to be composed of sub-units. In some cases the component peptide chains may dissociate and recombine readily. In other examples the complete structure, like that of hemoglobin, retains its identity unless exposed to severely disruptive conditions.

Denaturation of Proteins

The conformation of a protein as it is assumed to occur in cells and tissues is termed the *native state*. This is the conformation that is most stable from an energetic standpoint under the particular chemical and physical conditions existing in the cells or tissues of the living organism. If a protein is exposed to a different set of environmental conditions, its conformation may change, with attendant alterations in its physical properties and, most significantly, in the ability of the protein to perform its biological role. Such a change in a protein is termed *denaturation*.

Denatured protein molecules often tend to form large aggregates and to precipitate from solution—a process decribed as *coagulation*.

We cannot describe precisely for any protein the changes that occur as it becomes denatured. Presumably a number of relatively weak secondary bonds are broken and new bonds form in a different pattern. These processes require but little energy; hence proteins may be denatured by rather mild conditions, such as physical agitation, pH changes, or elevated temperatures. A common example of a protein easily denatured by agitation or by heat is the albumin of egg white.

Classification of Proteins

In that they are all polymers made up of the same 20 or so amino acids, the proteins are remarkably similar in general composition and chemical reactions. Until very recently, little was known about the exact chemical nature of any protein. Consequently, it was not really possible to classify them on the basis of precise structure. Still, some classification was desired to reduce confusion, and so a number of essentially operational classification systems were developed in the early stages of protein chemistry.

Several systems which distinguish among protein classes on different bases are as follows:

(A) Classification on the basis of their composition:

    (1) *Simple Proteins:* these contain only amino acids as structural components.

    (2) *Conjugated Proteins:* these contain one or more compounds in addition to amino acids; these would include:

        (a) *Chromoproteins:* amino acids plus a colored pigment (e.g., hemoglobin);

        (b) *Glycoproteins and Mucoproteins:* amino acids plus carbohydrate (e.g., mucin of saliva);

      (c) *Phosphoproteins:* amino acids plus phosphoric acid (e.g., casein of milk);

      (d) *Lipoproteins:* amino acids plus lipids (e.g., lipovitellin of egg yolk);

      (e) *Nucleoproteins:* amino acids plus nucleic acids (viruses may be regarded as huge molecules of nucleoprotein).

(B) Classification on the basis of the shape of the molecule:

      (1) *Globular Proteins:* those which have a relatively spherical or ovoid shape; these, as a rule, are relatively soluble.

      (2) *Fibrous Proteins:* those which resemble long ribbons or fibers in nature; these tend to be insoluble, and are usually found as components of the tougher types of tissues. Examples are the keratins of skin, hair, and feathers; the collagens of cartilage and tendons; the elastins of ligaments; and silk fibroin, the principal constituent of the fibers of silk.

(C) Classification on the basis of solubility:

      (1) *Albumins:* soluble in distilled water, dilute salt solutions, dilute acids and bases. They are precipitated (usually without denaturation) by saturating the solution with ammonium sulfate. Common examples are the albumins of egg white and of blood serum.

      (2) *Globulins:* insoluble in distilled water but soluble in dilute salt solutions (for example, 5 percent sodium chloride). These are precipitated by half-saturating the solution with ammonium sulphate. Common examples are the globulins of egg white; of blood serum; and of a variety of seeds, including squash, soybean, hemp, and others.

      (3) *Protamines and Histones:* very soluble, small, and stable proteins. Unlike almost all other proteins, they are not coagulated by heat. They contain a very high proportion of basic amino acids and will form salts with mineral acids, acidic proteins, and nucleic acids. Since the nucleic acid salts are generally insoluble, this reaction is sometimes used to remove unwanted nucleic acids during protein purifications. Another useful salt is protamine-zinc insulin; in this form the insulin is rendered somewhat more stable toward heat and is made less soluble, so that it is more slowly absorbed and is thus effective over a longer period of time. The major differ-

ence between the two proteins is that the histones are somewhat weaker bases and are thus insoluble in ammonium hydroxide solutions, whereas protamines are soluble.

(4) *Glutelins:* insoluble in distilled water and alcohol but soluble in dilute acid or base solutions. They are commonly found in various plant seeds. Glutelins in flour are in large measure responsible for the stickiness of dough mixtures.

(5) *Prolamines:* insoluble in distilled water, but soluble in dilute acid or base and in 70 to 80 percent alcohol solutions. They may be isolated from various plant seeds; for example, zein from corn.

(6) *Scleroproteins:* insoluble in water and other common solvents. These are chiefly the "Fibrous Proteins" described above.

Purification of Proteins

The separation of proteins from one another and from other substances presents some unique problems. The proteins are all very similar in their chemical properties, can only rarely be crystallized from an impure solution, and at all costs must be protected from denaturation during isolation. Thus, separation methods usually must take advantage of the differences in molecular charge and/or molecular size and density. They must at the same time avoid heat, strong acid or base, or other denaturing agents. Some of the specific procedures commonly used are as follows:

(1) *Salt Precipitation:* Different proteins have differing solubilities in various salt solutions. By stepwise increases in the concentration of a salt, it is possible to precipitate a whole series of protein fractions. Ammonium sulfate is the salt most commonly employed, mainly because of its high solubility at low temperatures.

(2) *Solvent Precipitation:* This procedure is analogous to salt precipitation in that protein fractions are precipitated by the stepwise addition of a solvent such as ethanol or acetone. The danger of denaturation of the proteins is much greater in this case than with salt precipitation; near-freezing temperatures must be maintained throughout the procedures.

(3) *Gel Adsorption:* Various proteins, because of their net charge, molecular size and shape, etc., are specifically bound to certain gels (for example, calcium phosphate or alumina) under proper conditions

of pH, salt concentration, etc. Proteins which are not adsorbed may then be washed off the gel. The bound protein may then be removed by changing the pH or salt concentration of the solution used to wash the gel.

(4) *Zone Electrophoresis:* Any substance in solution which carries a net charge will tend to migrate when subjected to a direct-current electrical field. Positively charged materials will move toward the negative electrode, and negative charges toward the positive electrode. For protein molecules, the rate of motion will be a function chiefly of the strength of the electrical field, the magnitude of the net charge on the molecule, and the size of the molecule.

In order to minimize the extent of diffusion and be able to recover the separated materials, a support which permits migration but holds the molecules in a relatively restricted location or *zone*, is usually employed. Typical materials used for this purpose are starch pastes or gels, fine cellulose sponges, synthetic chemical gels, and thick filter papers saturated with suitable buffer solutions. After separation, the different protein zones may be located by staining with dyes or (in the case of enzymes) by locating areas having specific catalytic activity. A schematic diagram of the apparatus used for this type of separation and of the separation obtained with a typical protein mixture is shown in Figure 2-6.

(5) *Ion-Exchange Separations:* A complete discussion of ion-exchange materials and their uses is beyond the scope of this book. We will mention only that they are generally insoluble materials which carry as part of their structures ionizing groups of one type or another; and discuss briefly the essential separation process. These ionized groups can form salts with ions of opposite charge, and they will "exchange" these ions for others when the relative salt concentrations in the solution are varied.

Ion-exchange materials are often produced in the form of very small plastic beads carrying the desired ionizable groups. For protein separations, however, various "modified cellulose" ion-exchange materials are usually employed. These are cellulose powders that are chemically treated in order to attach various ionizing groups; they are usually named on the basis of the attached group. Examples are diethylaminoethyl cellulose, cellulose phosphate, carboxymethyl cellulose, etc.

In practice, a mixture of proteins is passed through a column of the modified cellulose (held in a glass tube) and permitted to become attached to the column material. Increasing concentrations of salt and/or buffers of varying pH's are then passed through the column.

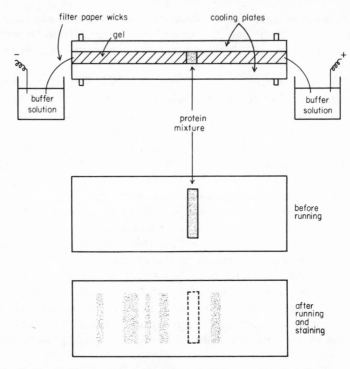

Figure 2-6. Separation of Protein Mixtures by Gel Electrophoresis.

The top figure represents a side view of a typical apparatus used
for gel electrophoresis. The other two figures show top view of a
gel slab at the beginning of an experiment and at the end of the
electrophoretic separation. The protein bands are assumed to have
been rendered visible by the use of appropriate stains.

Proteins will be washed off the column at different times depending
on their side-groups, net charges, and molecular structures. The essential process is represented diagrammatically in Figure 2-7. A typical
separation of proteins obtained on such a column is shown in Figure
2-8.

(6) *Molecular Sieve Separations:* All of the preceding procedures are
concerned to some extent with the electrical properties and/or shape
of the protein molecules. In contrast, separation by means of "molecular sieves" depends almost entirely on the effective sizes of the molecules.

The materials used are generally gels composed of particles having
defined pore sizes, each particle resembling a very small sponge.

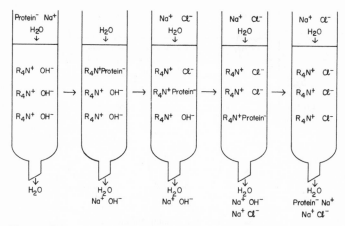

Figure 2-7. Illustration of the Processes Occurring as a Protein Is Absorbed by, and Eluted from, an Ion-exchange Column.

In this example the material of which the column is made is assumed to be an insoluble polymer having free substituted amine groups.

Large molecules cannot pass through the pores to the interior of the particles, and thus pass rapidly between the particles through a column of the gel. Smaller molecules can enter the particles, so their flow through the column is hindered and they emerge at a later time if a buffer solution (or water) is passed continuously through the column.

The effect is that of an "inverse sieve," which allows large molecules to go through and holds up small ones. Proteins up to a molecular weight of about 200,000 have been separated by this technique.

Determination of Protein Purity

If methods of protein purification are to be applied intelligently, it is obviously necessary to be able to determine when an increase in purity has been achieved. For a protein that is an enzyme, the relative purity can be obtained by following the amount of catalytic activity per unit of protein weight.

There are, however, several physical methods of determining purity which are more generally useful:

(1) *Analytical Electrophoresis:* This method differs from the zone electrophoresis above in that the separations are carried out in solutions in the absence of supporting gels or filter paper. This requires rather

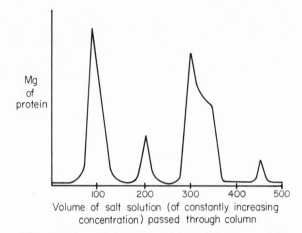

Volume of salt solution (of constantly increasing concentration) passed through column

Figure 2-8. Diagrammatic Representation of the Separation of Proteins on a Diethylaminoethyl Cellulose Column.

The original protein mixture has been separated into four fractions. The third fraction is not a single compound but contains at least two substances incompletely separated from each other. The symmetrical nature of the other three protein peaks indicates that each of these fractions may be a solution of a single pure protein.

elaborate instrumentation and careful techniques, but provides excellent information as to whether a given protein sample contains a single protein species or is a mixture. The procedure may also be used for the quantitative estimation of the concentration of each of the proteins present in a mixture, and has been used to a considerable extent in determining the concentrations of the various proteins of blood as an aid to the diagnosis of certain disease states.

(2) *Analytical Ultracentrifugation:* Protein molecules have been described as *macro*molecules to emphasize their relatively large size. Under conditions of sufficiently high centrifugal acceleration, these molecules can be made to sediment toward one end of a special centrifuge tube. By optical means it is possible to follow the rate of sedimentation. The rate for any given protein in a given solution under a certain centrifugal force will depend on the density, size, and shape of the molecule. By this technique it is possible to get not only an estimate of the purity of a protein, but (somewhat indirectly), information as to its molecular weight and approximate dimensions.

Specific Chemical Reactions of Amino Acids and Proteins

There are several reactions which are common to all amino acids and/or peptides and/or proteins, which are useful for detection and sometimes for quantitative estimation of these materials.

The true *ninhydrin reaction* is given by all α-amino acids. This reaction is shown below:

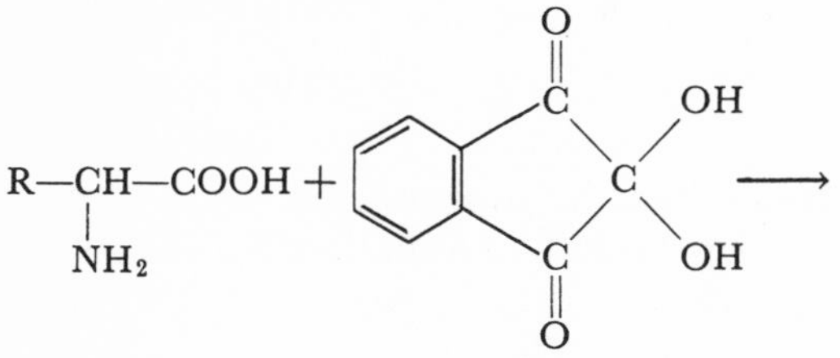

amino acid   ninhydrin

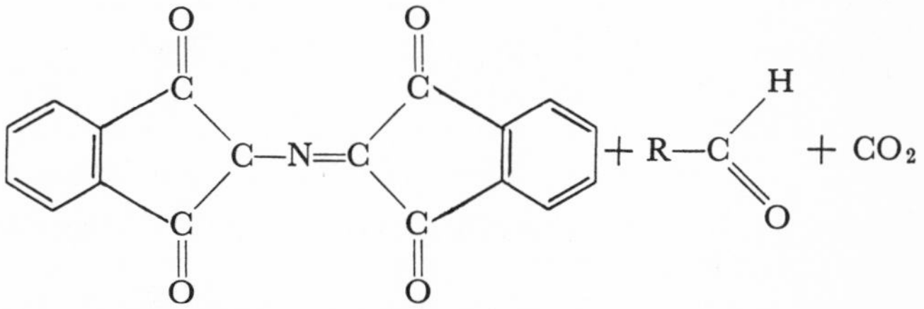

(purple color)

The reaction can be followed by measuring the color of the complex product or by measuring the CO_2 evolved, or both. Ammonia, many amines, peptides, and any protein will give a blue to purple color with ninhydrin. Unless they have a carboxyl group next to the amino group, however, they will not yield CO_2.

This reaction is often used for the quantitative estimation of amino acids (especially those formed by the hydrolysis of a purified protein) after they have been separated by ion-exchange chromatography or similar methods. It is extremely sensitive and gives reliable results with very small amounts of material.

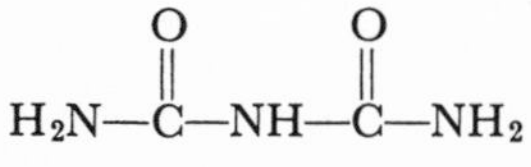

The *biuret reaction* is named for one of the simplest compounds capable of exhibiting the typical reaction. If biuret or any similar structure having two amide bonds linked by not more than one other atom, is mixed with cupric ion in very basic solution, a violet color is produced. Any peptide having more than three amino acid units clearly meets the requirement.

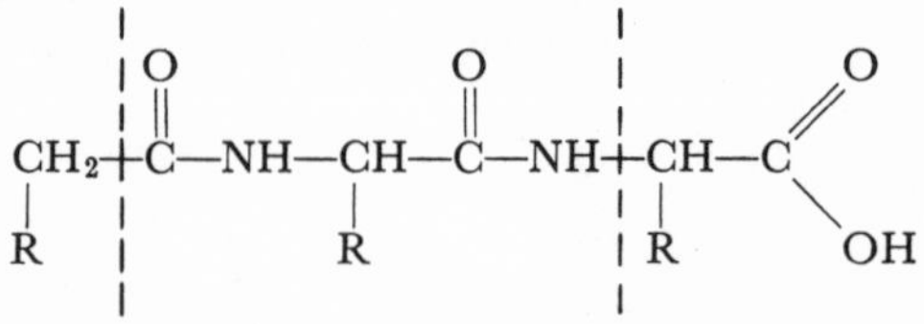

$$CH_2\text{---}\underset{\underset{R}{|}}{\overset{\overset{O}{\|}}{C}}\text{---}NH\text{---}\underset{\underset{R}{|}}{CH}\text{---}\overset{\overset{O}{\|}}{C}\text{---}NH\text{---}\underset{\underset{R}{|}}{CH}\text{---}\overset{O}{\underset{OH}{C}}$$

The required unit is shown between the broken lines.

The biuret reaction is used widely both as a qualitative test for proteins and as a quantitative measure of protein concentrations.

Several other color tests that are specific for only one or a small group of amino acids are also in common use as either qualitative or quantitative reagents. The more common are those which give reactions with tyrosine (Folin-Ciocalteau Reagent), tyrosine and tryptophan (Millon's Reagents) or specifically with tryptophan (Hopkins-Cole Reagent).

SUGGESTED ADDITIONAL READING

Perutz, M. F., "The Hemoglobin Molecule," *Scientific American*, **211**, No. 5, 64 (November, 1964).

Kendrew, J. C., "Three-Dimensional Structure of a Protein," *Scientific American*, **205**, No. 6, 96 (December, 1961).

Stein, W. H., and Moore, S., "The Chemical Structure of Proteins," *Scientific American*, **204**, No. 2, 81 (February, 1961).

Steiner, R. F., "The Chemical Foundations of Molecular Biology," D. Van Nostrand Company, Inc., Princeton, N. J., 1965.

Scheraga, H. A., "Protein Structure," Academic Press, New York and London, 1961.

Brookhaven Symposia in Biology, No. 13, "Protein Structure and Function," Office of Technical Services, Department of Commerce, Washington, 1960.

Carbohydrates

3

The term "carbohydrate" was originally derived from the fact that the large bulk of the compounds being described fit the empirical formula $C_n(H_2O)_n$. This is now considered to be excessively restrictive, and a more useful definition might be "polyhydroxy aldehydes and ketones and their derivatives." This would include deoxy sugars, amino sugars, and even sugar alcohols and acids.

Carbohydrates occur in a variety of forms, including simple sugars (incapable of being hydrolyzed to simpler compounds) and a variety of derivatives and polymers, such as starch and glycogen.

MONOSACCHARIDES

Compounds possessing a free (or "potentially free") aldehyde or ketone group and two or more hydroxyl groups are called *monosaccharides* or *simple sugars*.

The simplest compounds which meet these requirements are glyceraldehyde and dihydroxyacetone. Having three carbon atoms, these are known as *trioses*. Sugars having four carbon atoms are then *tetroses;* five carbons, *pentoses;* six carbons, *hexoses*, etc. They may be further differentiated on the basis of the functional group involved into *aldo-* or *keto-* sugars. Thus, for example, glyceraldehyde is an *aldotriose* and dihydroxyacetone is a *ketotriose*.

$$
\begin{array}{cc}
\overset{\displaystyle O}{\diagdown} & \\
\text{C—H} & \text{CH}_2\text{OH} \\
| & | \\
\text{H—C—OH} & \text{C=O} \\
| & | \\
\text{CH}_2\text{OH} & \text{CH}_2\text{OH} \\
\text{glyceraldehyde} & \text{dihydroxyacetone}
\end{array}
$$

When the three-dimensional structure of the glyceraldehyde molecule is arranged and projected according to the Fischer system (aldehyde on top and primary alcohol at bottom; hydrogens and hydroxyl groups on other carbons projecting up out of the plane of the paper), we find that two different enantiomorphic structures are possible:

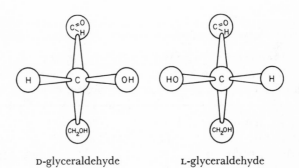

D-glyceraldehyde   L-glyceraldehyde

The form in which the hydroxyl group next to the primary hydroxyl is projected to the right of the carbon chain is designated as the D-form and the form in which it is projected to the left, the L-form. These D- and L-designations have nothing to do with the direction in which the compound rotates the plane of polarized light. If it is desired to indicate the direction of rotation, the name may be written D-(+)-glyceraldehyde.

Whatever else may be inserted between the aldehyde and the alcohol next to the primary alcohol, the assignment to the D- or L-series of compounds still depends on whether the hydroxyl of the asymmetric carbon atom farthest from the aldehyde (i.e., next to the primary hydroxyl) is projected to the right or the left. For example:

$$
\begin{array}{ccc}
\underset{\text{D-glucose}}{
\begin{array}{c}
\text{O} \\
\diagdown\!\diagup \\
\text{C}-\text{H} \\
| \\
\text{H}-\text{C}-\text{OH} \\
| \\
\text{HO}-\text{C}-\text{H} \\
| \\
\text{H}-\text{C}-\text{OH} \\
| \\
\text{H}-\text{C}-\text{OH} \\
| \\
\text{CH}_2\text{OH}
\end{array}}
&
\underset{\text{L-glucose}}{
\begin{array}{c}
\text{O} \\
\diagdown\!\diagup \\
\text{C}-\text{H} \\
| \\
\text{HO}-\text{C}-\text{H} \\
| \\
\text{H}-\text{C}-\text{OH} \\
| \\
\text{HO}-\text{C}-\text{H} \\
| \\
\text{HO}-\text{C}-\text{H} \\
| \\
\text{CH}_2\text{OH}
\end{array}}
&
\underset{\text{L-galactose}}{
\begin{array}{c}
\text{O} \\
\diagdown\!\diagup \\
\text{C}-\text{H} \\
| \\
\text{HO}-\text{C}-\text{H} \\
| \\
\text{H}-\text{C}-\text{OH} \\
| \\
\text{H}-\text{C}-\text{OH} \\
| \\
\text{HO}-\text{C}-\text{H} \\
| \\
\text{CH}_2\text{OH}
\end{array}}
\end{array}
$$

When we go from glyceraldehyde to a four-carbon aldose, we get the possibility of four stereoisomers because, as shown by the asterisks, there are two asymmetric carbon atoms.

$$
\begin{array}{cccc}
\underset{\substack{\text{D-erythrose} \\ 1}}{
\begin{array}{c}
\text{O} \\
\diagdown\!\diagup \\
\text{C}-\text{H} \\
| \\
\text{H}-\text{C}^*-\text{OH} \\
| \\
\text{H}-\text{C}^*-\text{OH} \\
| \\
\text{CH}_2\text{OH}
\end{array}}
&
\underset{\substack{\text{L-erythrose} \\ 2}}{
\begin{array}{c}
\text{O} \\
\diagdown\!\diagup \\
\text{C}-\text{H} \\
| \\
\text{HO}-\text{C}-\text{H} \\
| \\
\text{HO}-\text{C}-\text{H} \\
| \\
\text{CH}_2\text{OH}
\end{array}}
&
\underset{\substack{\text{D-threose} \\ 3}}{
\begin{array}{c}
\text{O} \\
\diagdown\!\diagup \\
\text{C}-\text{H} \\
| \\
\text{HO}-\text{C}-\text{H} \\
| \\
\text{H}-\text{C}-\text{OH} \\
| \\
\text{CH}_2\text{OH}
\end{array}}
&
\underset{\substack{\text{L-threose} \\ 4}}{
\begin{array}{c}
\text{O} \\
\diagdown\!\diagup \\
\text{C}-\text{H} \\
| \\
\text{H}-\text{C}-\text{OH} \\
| \\
\text{HO}-\text{C}-\text{H} \\
| \\
\text{CH}_2\text{OH}
\end{array}}
\end{array}
$$

Of these, 1 and 2 constitute a pair of enantiomorphs (i.e., a DL-pair), as do 3 and 4. However, 1 *or* 2 together with either 3 *or* 4 does not form a pair of mirror images. These are compounds with different chemical and physical properties. Optical isomers of this type are called *diastereoisomers*.

For aldopentoses, there are eight isomers; the D- forms are shown below (for each of these there is a mirror image L- form):

$$
\begin{array}{cccc}
\underset{\text{D-ribose}}{
\begin{array}{c}
\text{O} \\
\diagdown\!\diagup \\
\text{C}-\text{H} \\
| \\
\text{H}-\text{C}^*-\text{OH} \\
| \\
\text{H}-\text{C}^*-\text{OH} \\
| \\
\text{H}-\text{C}^*-\text{OH} \\
| \\
\text{CH}_2\text{OH}
\end{array}}
&
\underset{\text{D-arabinose}}{
\begin{array}{c}
\text{O} \\
\diagdown\!\diagup \\
\text{C}-\text{H} \\
| \\
\text{HO}-\text{C}-\text{H} \\
| \\
\text{H}-\text{C}-\text{OH} \\
| \\
\text{H}-\text{C}-\text{OH} \\
| \\
\text{CH}_2\text{OH}
\end{array}}
&
\underset{\text{D-xylose}}{
\begin{array}{c}
\text{O} \\
\diagdown\!\diagup \\
\text{C}-\text{H} \\
| \\
\text{H}-\text{C}-\text{OH} \\
| \\
\text{HO}-\text{C}-\text{H} \\
| \\
\text{H}-\text{C}-\text{OH} \\
| \\
\text{CH}_2\text{OH}
\end{array}}
&
\underset{\text{D-lyxose}}{
\begin{array}{c}
\text{O} \\
\diagdown\!\diagup \\
\text{C}-\text{H} \\
| \\
\text{HO}-\text{C}-\text{H} \\
| \\
\text{HO}-\text{C}-\text{H} \\
| \\
\text{H}-\text{C}-\text{OH} \\
| \\
\text{CH}_2\text{OH}
\end{array}}
\end{array}
$$

Both D-ribose and D-xylose occur widely in nature, while lyxose is most uncommon. Arabinose is a special case, since L-arabinose is the common form rather than the D-isomer. This is the only L-series sugar known to occur in any appreciable quantity in nature.

For the aldohexoses, there are 16 possible stereoisomeric forms; Fischer projection formulas for the eight D-isomers are shown below:

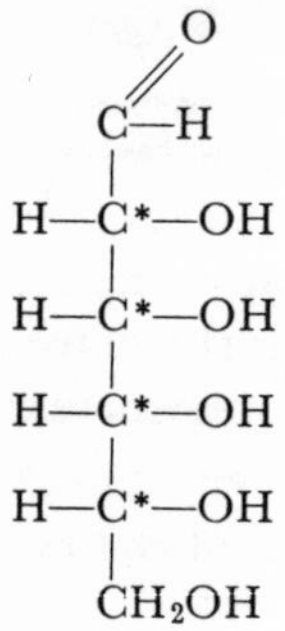

$$
\begin{array}{cccc}
\text{O} & \text{O} & \text{O} & \text{O} \\
\diagdown\diagup & \diagdown\diagup & \diagdown\diagup & \diagdown\diagup \\
\text{C--H} & \text{C--H} & \text{C--H} & \text{C--H} \\
\text{H--C*--OH} & \text{HO--C--H} & \text{H--C--OH} & \text{HO--C--H} \\
\text{H--C*--OH} & \text{H--C--OH} & \text{H--C--OH} & \text{H--C--OH} \\
\text{H--C*--OH} & \text{H--C--OH} & \text{HO--C--H} & \text{HO--C--H} \\
\text{H--C*--OH} & \text{H--C--OH} & \text{H--C--OH} & \text{H--C--OH} \\
\text{CH}_2\text{OH} & \text{CH}_2\text{OH} & \text{CH}_2\text{OH} & \text{CH}_2\text{OH} \\
\text{D-allose} & \text{D-altrose} & \text{D-gulose} & \text{D-idose}
\end{array}
$$

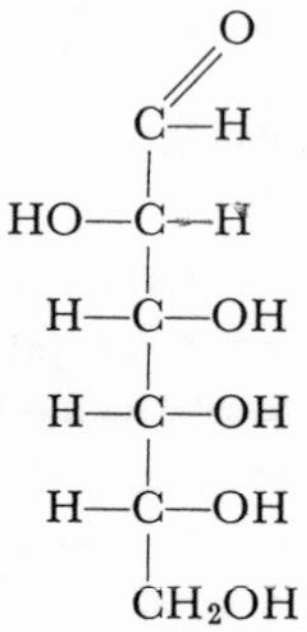

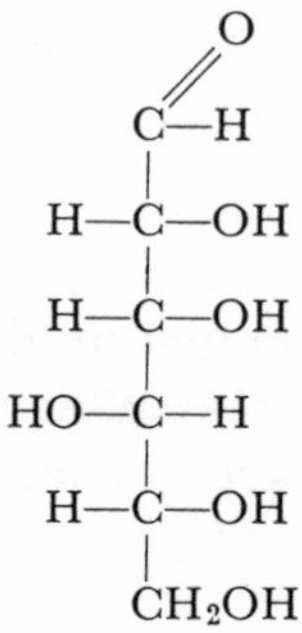

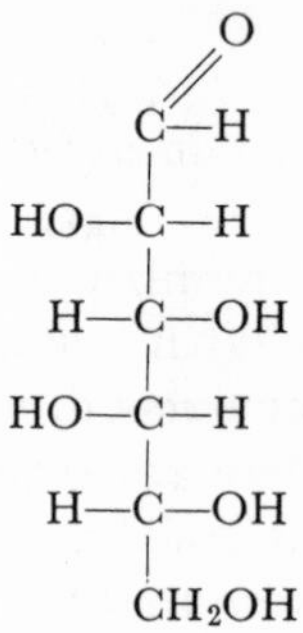

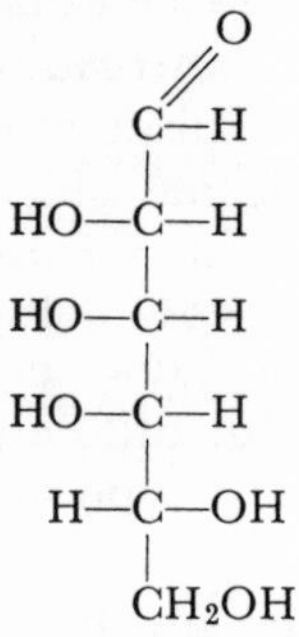

$$
\begin{array}{cccc}
\text{O} & \text{O} & \text{O} & \text{O} \\
\diagdown\diagup & \diagdown\diagup & \diagdown\diagup & \diagdown\diagup \\
\text{C--H} & \text{C--H} & \text{C--H} & \text{C--H} \\
\text{HO--C--H} & \text{H--C--OH} & \text{HO--C--H} & \text{H--C--OH} \\
\text{HO--C--H} & \text{HO--C--H} & \text{HO--C--H} & \text{HO--C--H} \\
\text{HO--C--H} & \text{H--C--OH} & \text{H--C--OH} & \text{HO--C--H} \\
\text{H--C--OH} & \text{H--C--OH} & \text{H--C--OH} & \text{H--C--OH} \\
\text{CH}_2\text{OH} & \text{CH}_2\text{OH} & \text{CH}_2\text{OH} & \text{CH}_2\text{OH} \\
\text{D-talose} & \text{D-glucose} & \text{D-mannose} & \text{D-galactose}
\end{array}
$$

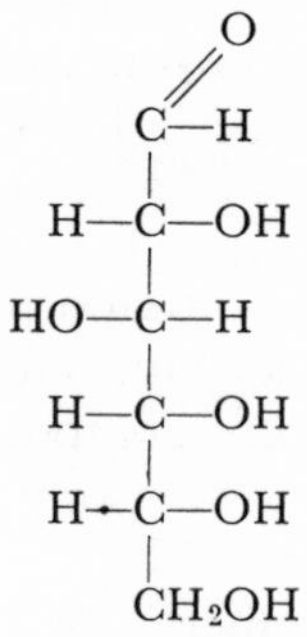

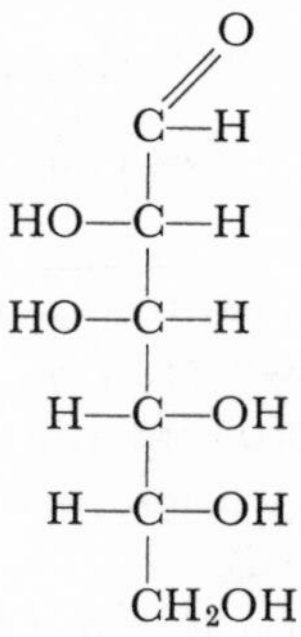

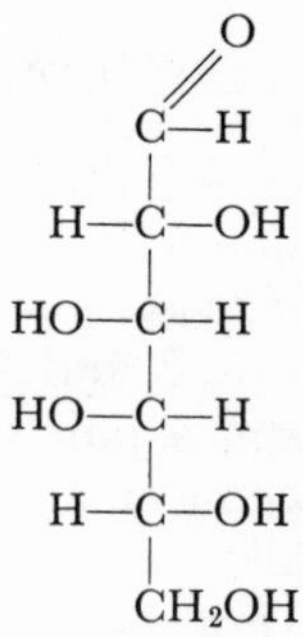

Of these 16 isomers, only D-glucose, D-mannose, and D-galactose are commonly found in nature.

At this point we can see that every time we add another asymmetric carbon atom, we double the number of stereoisomers that are possible. That is, the maximum possible number of stereoisomers = 2^n, where n = the number of asymmetric carbon atoms.

For the ketoses, a series of sugars can similarly be formed, all of which will be related to dihydroxyacetone.

$$CH_2OH \qquad\qquad CH_2OH \qquad\qquad CH_2OH$$
$$|\qquad\qquad\qquad |\qquad\qquad\qquad |$$
$$C{=}O \qquad\qquad\quad C{=}O \qquad\qquad\quad C{=}O$$
$$|\qquad\qquad\qquad |\qquad\qquad\qquad |$$
$$H{-}C{-}OH \qquad\quad H{-}C{-}OH \qquad HO{-}C{-}H$$
$$|\qquad\qquad\qquad |\qquad\qquad\qquad |$$
$$CH_2OH \qquad\quad H{-}C{-}OH \qquad\quad H{-}C{-}OH$$
$$|\qquad\qquad\qquad |$$
$$CH_2OH \qquad\quad H{-}C{-}OH$$
$$|$$
$$CH_2OH$$

a D-ketotetrose	a D-ketopentose	a D-ketohexose
(D-erythrulose)	(D-ribulose)	(D-fructose)

A number of the keto sugars, and their derivatives, play important roles in cellular metabolism. D-Fructose is of particularly common occurrence; the other ketohexoses are found only to a limited extent. Derivatives of the ketopentoses ribulose and xylulose are important intermediates in carbohydrate metabolism related to photosynthesis. Note that the ending *-ulose* designates a keto sugar.

Cyclic Forms of Sugars

The Fischer projection formulas for the sugars obscure the fact that the aldehyde group and the alcohol group of carbon 5 can readily approach each other. For example, Figure 3-1 is a more realistic representation of one possible configuration of a glucose molecule which takes into account the normal bond angles. It is also possible for the molecule to twist in such a way that the alcohol group of carbon 4 is brought close to the aldehyde group. Similarly, the keto group of a keto sugar can approach the alcohol group of either carbon 6 or carbon 5.

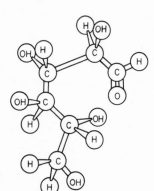

Figure 3-1. A Three-dimensional Representation of One Possible Configuration of a Glucose Molecule.

The close proximity of an aldehyde (or ketone) group and an alcohol group in the sugars facilitates their reaction to give cyclic hemiacetals (or hemiketals). Of course this can occur with the alcohol group of either carbon 4 or of carbon 5.

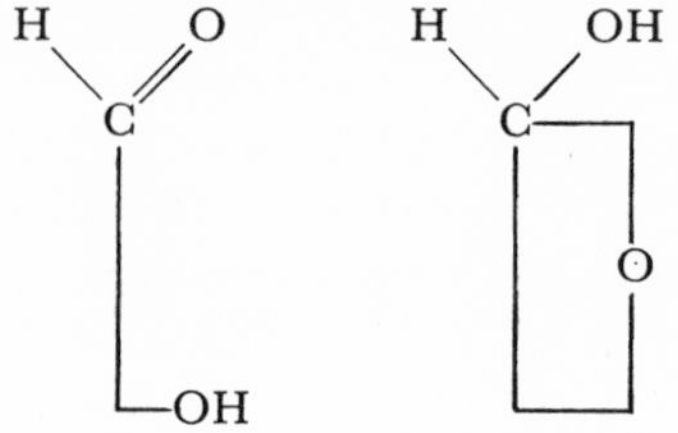

aldehyde   cyclic hemiacetal

This reaction does not involve the loss or gain of any atoms by the sugar molecule; hence the aldehyde and cyclic forms are isomers. The sugar is said to exist in either the aldehyde or hemiacetal form. The cyclic forms are actually the most important forms of the sugar molecules. Glucose, for example, exists in the crystalline state or in water solution almost entirely as one or another hemiacetal, not as the free aldehyde. The sugars display many reactions typical of aldehydes only because hemiacetal formation is an equilibrium process, so that small amounts of free aldehyde are always present in solution. Incidentally, the use of the term "potentially free aldehyde" in the definition of the monosaccharides is necessary because of the existence of hemiacetals.

The formation of the cyclic forms introduces two new structural problems into the chemistry of the sugars. There is first the question of the size of the ring. As we indicated above, a cyclic hemiacetal can be formed which involves either carbon 4 or carbon 5. In the first case

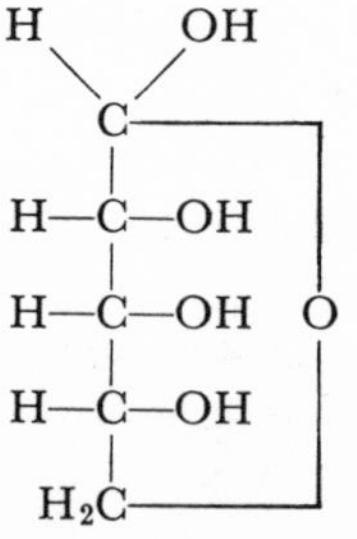

a pyranose form
of D-ribose
(α-D-ribopyranose)

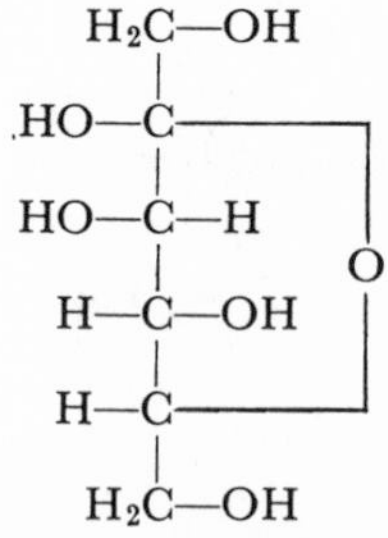

a furanose form
of D-fructose
(β-D-fructofuranose)

a ring consisting of four carbon atoms and one oxygen atom is created; this is called a *furanose* ring. In the second case the ring contains five carbon atoms in addition to the oxygen; this is a *pyranose* ring.

The second structural problem originating with the cyclic forms of the sugars is the question of the stereochemistry of the hemiacetal or hemiketal carbon. Examination of the structures given above should reveal that a new asymmetric center exists at the position of the original carbonyl: C_1 for ribose and C_2 for fructose. We find, therefore, that each ring form of a sugar can exist as either of two isomeric structures. These are termed the α- and β-isomers.

In depicting the structure of an α-isomer, we place the hydroxyl group of the hemiacetal or hemiketal carbon on the same side of the carbon chain as the hydroxyl group which determines whether the sugar is D or L. In practical terms, if the sugar structure is given in the Fischer method, the hydroxyl will be written to the right for a D-series sugar. Similarly, a β-isomer of a D-series sugar would be shown with the hydroxyl group of the critical carbon projecting to the left. The ribose molecule shown above is therefore an α-isomer; the fructose compound, a β- form.

Another complication introduced with the ring forms of the sugars arises from the reversible nature of hemiacetal formation and from the possibility that either furanose or pyranose and α or β isomers can be formed. A solution of a sugar actually contains all the possible forms in a freely reversible equilibrium. Regardless of which crystalline form of a sugar is dissolved in water, an equilibrium mixture will result.

Thus D-glucose in aqueous solution exists as an equilibrium mixture of five compounds, as shown on the facing page.

Haworth Projections

The Fischer projection, while very useful to indicate differences in configuration at various asymmetric centers, does not represent very accurately the ring forms of the sugars. For this purpose we have a second conventional picture of the molecule which is known as the Haworth projection. In this system, the basic structures of the two ring forms are:

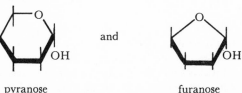

pyranose   furanose

When the rings are viewed in this manner, the attached groups will be found to lie either above or below the plane of the ring. Instead of trying to twist the Fischer structure around mentally, or actually constructing a molecular model, we may follow certain "rules" which permit us to obtain the correct Haworth form.

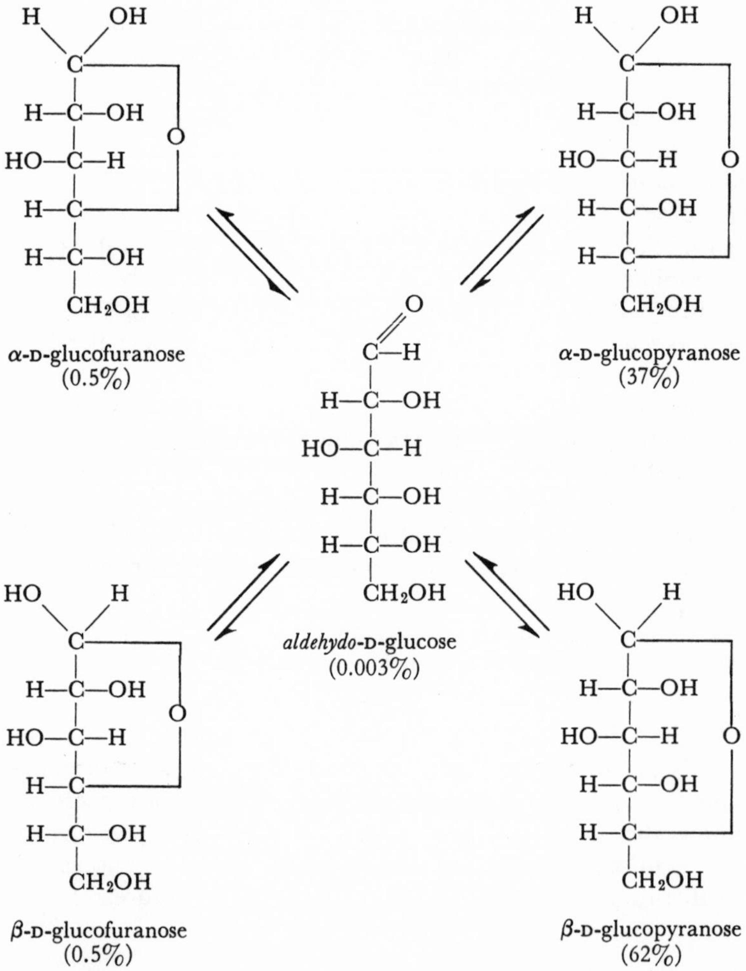

α-D-glucofuranose
(0.5%)

aldehydo-D-glucose
(0.003%)

α-D-glucopyranose
(37%)

β-D-glucofuranose
(0.5%)

β-D-glucopyranose
(62%)

The figures in parentheses indicate the mole percentage present in an equilibrium mixture at neutral hydrogen ion concentration (pH). It should be noted that *aldehydo-* or *keto-* and/or furanose forms are present in much higher concentrations for some sugars, e.g., ribose and lactose.

The first rule for translation of Fischer projections to Haworth forms is that any group to the *right* of the carbon chain is written *down;* those to the left are written up (i.e., above the plane of the ring). Thus, for example:

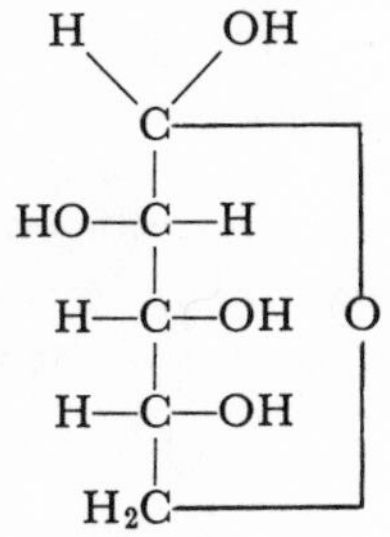

becomes

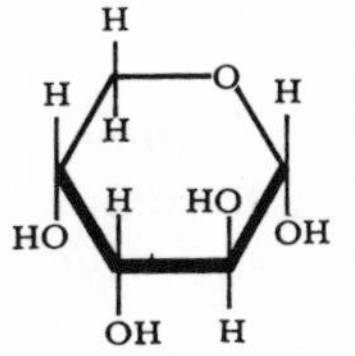

When there are more carbon atoms in the sugar than are involved in ring formation, it becomes necessary to determine whether they should be written above or below the plane of the ring. Here, the rule is that if the ring is to the *right*, the extra carbon or carbons will be *up* (i.e., above the plane). For example:

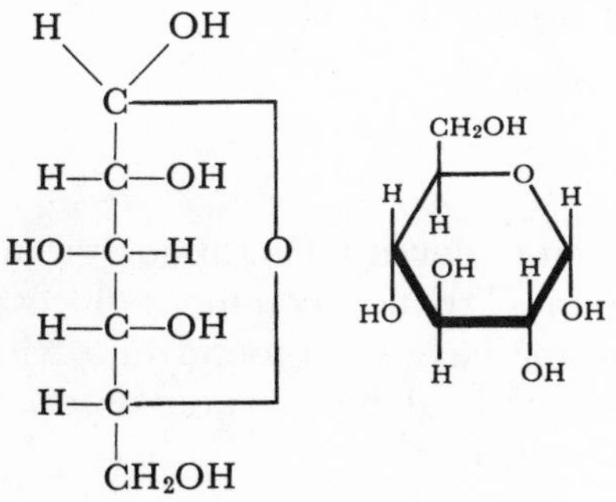

α-D-glucopyranose 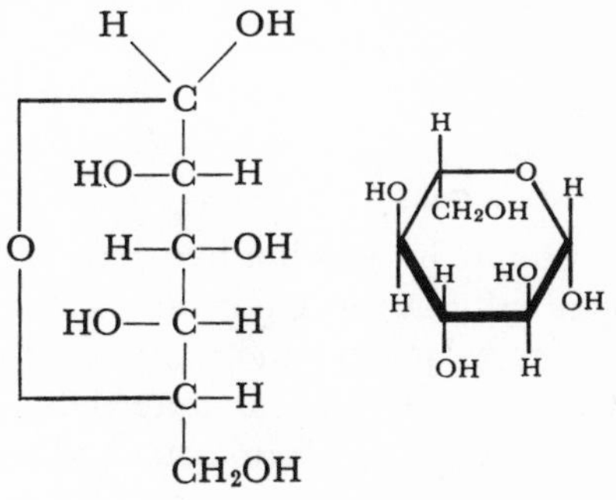   β-L-glucopyranose

In the case of a ketohexose in the furanose form, the position of the 6-carbon will be determined as above; the 1-carbon will be up or down depending on whether the sugar is in the α- or β-form:

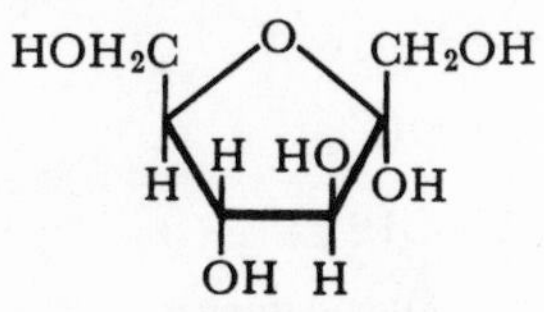

α-D-fructofuranose 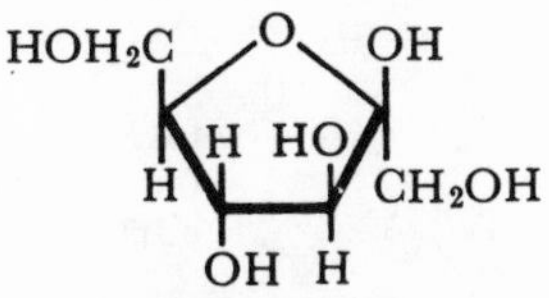   β-D-fructofuranose

Sugar Derivatives

In defining the carbohydrates as a class, we agreed to include a number of sugar derivatives. The more common of these are the following:

DEOXY SUGARS

Sugars in which one of the hydroxyl groups is replaced by a hydrogen. The most common example is 2-deoxy-D-ribose (or D-2-deoxyribose). This sugar is one of the major components of the nucleic acids of cell nuclei.

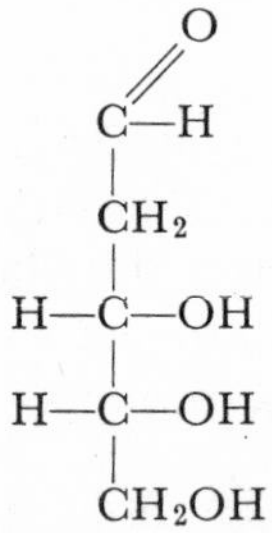

$$
\begin{array}{c}
\quad\quad O \\
\quad\quad \| \\
C\!-\!H \\
| \\
CH_2 \\
| \\
H\!-\!C\!-\!OH \\
| \\
H\!-\!C\!-\!OH \\
| \\
CH_2OH
\end{array}
$$

D-2-deoxyribose

AMINO SUGARS

Sugars in which a hydroxyl has been replaced by an amino group, generally at the 2-position. Hexosamines are most common; glucosamine, galactosamine, and mannosamine have been found in a wide variety of biological materials. Frequently these compounds occur with an acetyl group attached to the nitrogen.

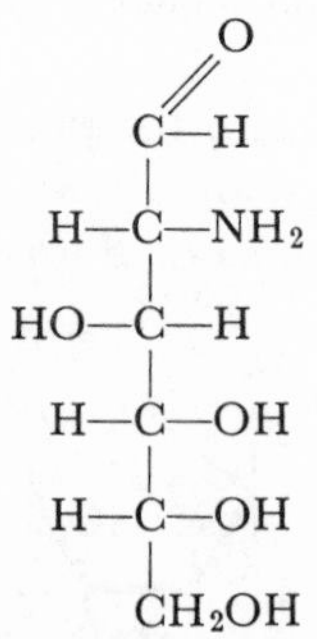

$$
\begin{array}{c}
\quad\quad O \\
\quad\quad \| \\
C\!-\!H \\
| \\
H\!-\!C\!-\!NH_2 \\
| \\
HO\!-\!C\!-\!H \\
| \\
H\!-\!C\!-\!OH \\
| \\
H\!-\!C\!-\!OH \\
| \\
CH_2OH
\end{array}
\qquad\qquad
\begin{array}{c}
\quad\quad O \\
\quad\quad \| \\
C\!-\!H \quad\quad O \\
| \qquad\qquad \| \\
H\!-\!C\!-\!NH\!-\!C\!-\!CH_3 \\
| \\
HO\!-\!C\!-\!H \\
| \\
H\!-\!C\!-\!OH \\
| \\
H\!-\!C\!-\!OH \\
| \\
CH_2OH
\end{array}
$$

D-glucosamine or   *N*-acetylglucosamine
D-2-deoxy-2-aminoglucose

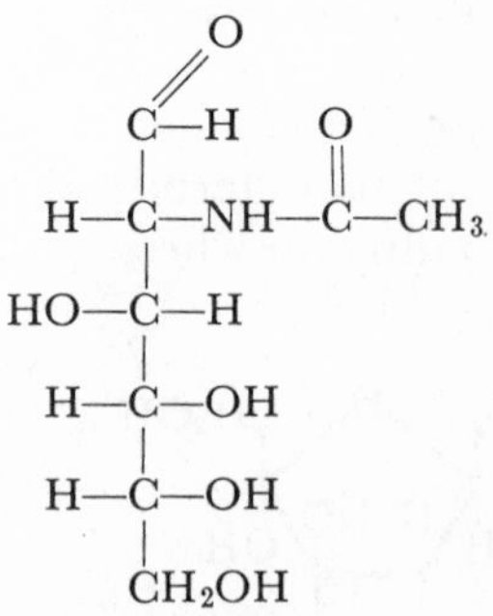

SUGAR ACIDS

These fall into several categories. The *uronic acids* are most closely related to the sugars since they still contain an aldehyde group. They are formed by oxidation of the primary alcohol to a carboxyl group.

The *glyconic acids* are formed by oxidation of the aldehyde group of the sugar.

The *glycaric acids* are formed by oxidation at both ends of the sugar. These are sometimes called "saccharic acids."

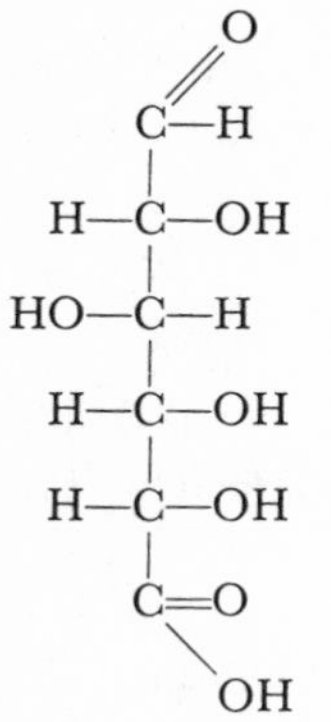

D-glucuronic acid (a uronic acid)	D-gluconic acid (a glyconic acid)	D-glucaric acid (a glycaric acid)
$\begin{array}{c} \text{O} \\ \parallel \\ \text{C—H} \\ \mid \\ \text{H—C—OH} \\ \mid \\ \text{HO—C—H} \\ \mid \\ \text{H—C—OH} \\ \mid \\ \text{H—C—OH} \\ \mid \\ \text{C=O} \\ \backslash \\ \text{OH} \end{array}$	$\begin{array}{c} \text{O} \\ \parallel \\ \text{C—OH} \\ \mid \\ \text{H—C—OH} \\ \mid \\ \text{HO—C—H} \\ \mid \\ \text{H—C—OH} \\ \mid \\ \text{H—C—OH} \\ \mid \\ \text{CH}_2\text{OH} \end{array}$	$\begin{array}{c} \text{O} \\ \parallel \\ \text{C—OH} \\ \mid \\ \text{H—C—OH} \\ \mid \\ \text{HO—C—H} \\ \mid \\ \text{H—C—OH} \\ \mid \\ \text{H—C—OH} \\ \mid \\ \text{C=O} \\ \backslash \\ \text{OH} \end{array}$

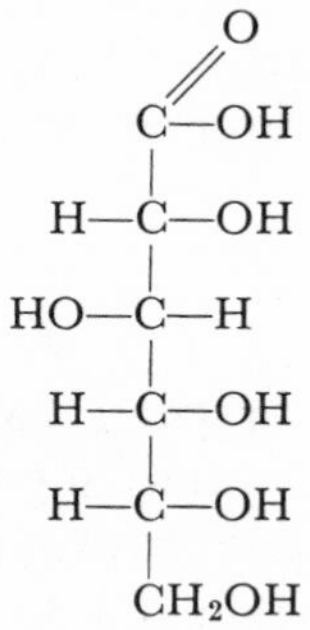

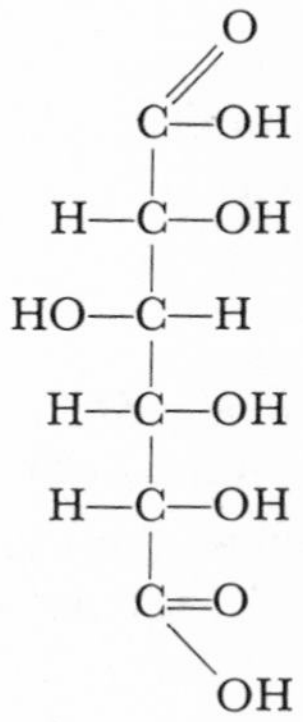

SUGAR ALCOHOLS

These are obtained on reduction of the aldehyde or ketone group of a sugar. Typical examples of sugar alcohols are shown below. Common names are in wide use for the sugar alcohols of glucose and galactose. These are shown in parentheses.

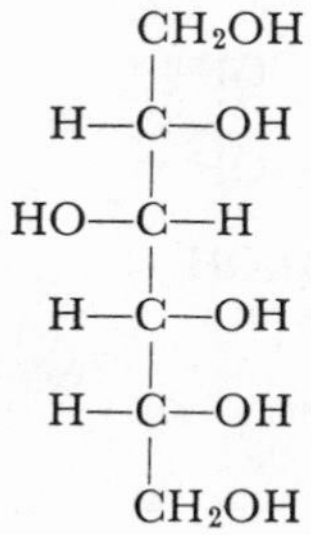

D-glucitol (sorbitol)	galactitol (dulcitol)	ribitol
$\begin{array}{c} \text{CH}_2\text{OH} \\ \mid \\ \text{H—C—OH} \\ \mid \\ \text{HO—C—H} \\ \mid \\ \text{H—C—OH} \\ \mid \\ \text{H—C—OH} \\ \mid \\ \text{CH}_2\text{OH} \end{array}$	$\begin{array}{c} \text{CH}_2\text{OH} \\ \mid \\ \text{H—C—OH} \\ \mid \\ \text{HO—C—H} \\ \mid \\ \text{HO—C—H} \\ \mid \\ \text{H—C—OH} \\ \mid \\ \text{CH}_2\text{OH} \end{array}$	$\begin{array}{c} \text{CH}_2\text{OH} \\ \mid \\ \text{H—C—OH} \\ \mid \\ \text{H—C—OH} \\ \mid \\ \text{H—C—OH} \\ \mid \\ \text{CH}_2\text{OH} \end{array}$

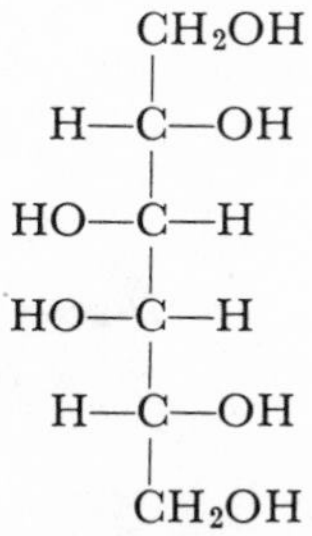

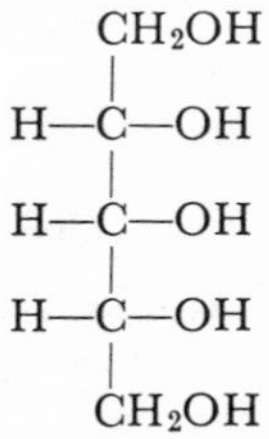

A related group of compounds of biochemical interest are the cyclitols, best illustrated by the most common example, *myo*-inositol.

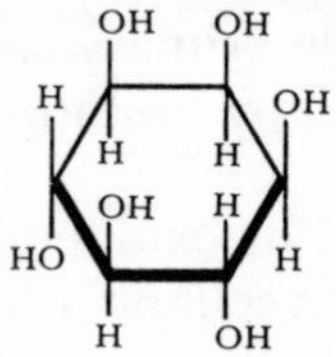

This compound is widely distributed in nature in the free form, as a component of phospholipids, and as phytic acid (the hexaphosphoric acid ester).

OTHERS

Ascorbic Acid (Vitamin C) is a special case of a sugar acid. It is shown below in its normal form as the internal ester, called a *lactone*. The acid hydrogens are those of the enolic hydroxyl groups.

Sialic Acids are a group of acylated aminosugar acids of wide occurrence in nature. The sialic acid of human blood plasma, N-acetylneuraminic acid, is also shown below.

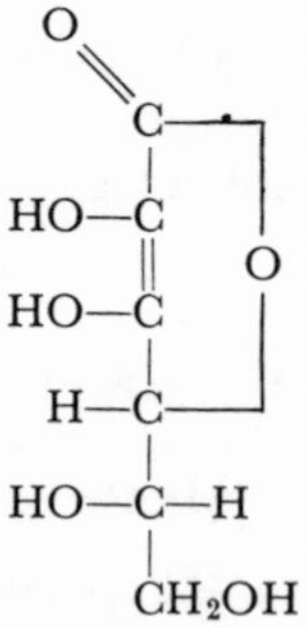

ascorbic acid 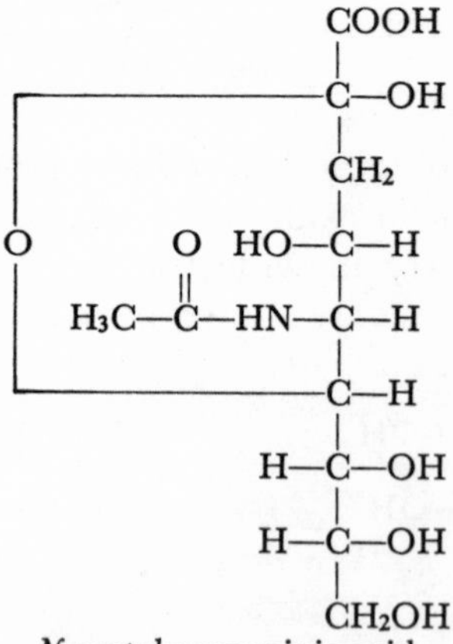   *N*-acetylneuraminic acid

Special Reactions of Sugars

The sugars, being polyhydroxy aldehydes and ketones, generally are capable of undergoing all of the normal reactions of alcohols and

of carbonyl groups, e.g. oxidation, reduction, dehydration, esterification, ether formation, addition to the carbonyl double-bond, etc.
Several of these reactions having unusual applications to carbohydrate chemistry are mentioned below:

"REDUCING" AND "NONREDUCING" SUGARS

Any free aldehyde or α-hydroxy ketone is capable of being oxidized,
thus causing the reduction of some other substance. Any of the sugars
in the free aldehyde or ketone form, or in any form in equilibrium
with the free aldehyde or ketone, will fit this category. This will
include all of the hemiacetal forms.

A variety of agents may be used to carry out the oxidation (and be
themselves reduced). The most common is cupric ion, which is the
active ingredient in Fehling's, Benedict's, and Barfoed's reagents for
the detection of reducing sugars. The reaction is:

$$\text{reducing sugar} \;+\; 2\,Cu^{++} \;\rightarrow\; \text{oxidized sugar} \;+\; 2\,Cu^{+}$$
$$\text{blue}$$

$$2\,Cu^{+} \;+\; 2\,OH^{-} \;\rightarrow\; \underline{2\,CuOH} \;\rightarrow\; \underline{Cu_2O} \;+\; H_2O$$
$$\text{yellow} \qquad \text{red}$$

Any carbohydrate capable of giving this reaction without having to
be hydrolyzed first, is designated as a "reducing" carbohydrate: others
are then "nonreducing." Obviously, all free monosaccharides must
be "reducing" carbohydrates.

FURFURAL FORMATION

A number of tests which are used to detect carbohydrates in general, whether reducing or nonreducing, depend on the ability of the
compounds to be dehydrated to furfural or a derivative of this compound. The reaction is illustrated for glucose, a typical hexose.

Trioses and tetroses are incapable of undergoing this reaction, since
they do not possess the necessary minimum of five carbon atoms.

The furfural derivative may then be reacted with any one of a
variety of phenols or aromatic amines to yield a colored material.
The Molisch test, given by all carbohydrates larger than tetroses, and
Bial's orcinol test, given by pentoses and uronic acids, are among the
procedures based on this type of reaction.

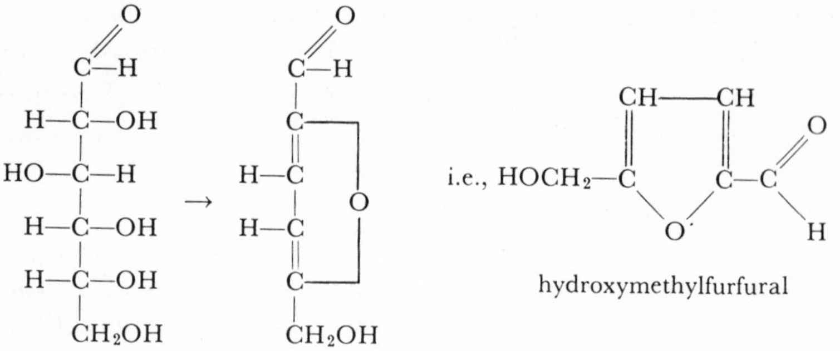

glucose   i.e., $HOCH_2$— ... hydroxymethylfurfural

GLYCOSIDES

Since all of the sugars in the ring forms are hemiacetals, it is possible for them to react with another alcohol to form acetals. These are given the general class name of *glycosides;* when a particular sugar is involved, a more specific name is applied, e.g., glucoside, galactoside, fructoside, etc. Further, it is of course possible to have α- and β-forms and pyranose or furanose ring structures. When all of these are specified, we get, for example:

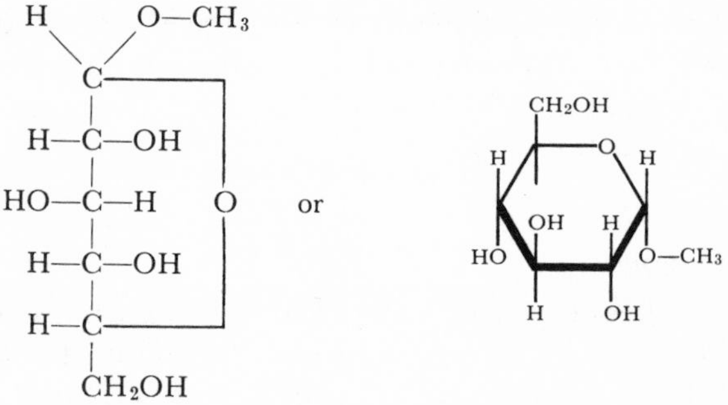

methyl-α-D-glucopyranoside

In contrast with hemiacetals, in which the α- and β-forms are always in equilibrium with each other through the free aldehyde or ketone, α- and β-glycosides are individually stable with respect to such transformations.

DISACCHARIDES

When the alcohol used in formation of a glycoside is part of another sugar molecule, we obtain a disaccharide as a product. Some common examples are:

Maltose (two glucoses; α-1,4-glucoside linkage):

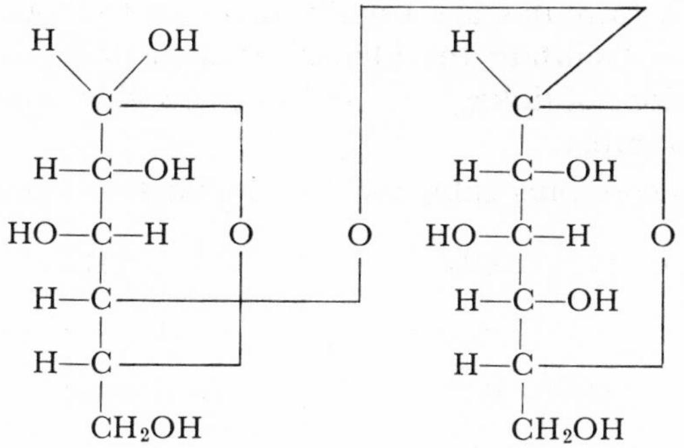

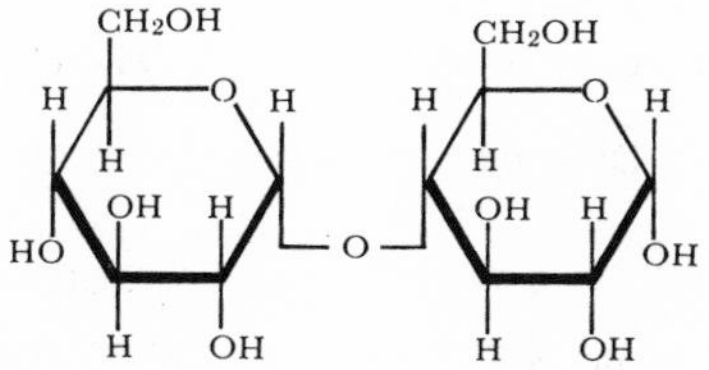

Maltose is obtained as an intermediate during the digestion of starch to glucose.

Note that because of the free hemiacetal form of one of the sugar units, maltose in solution will consist of an equilibrium of three forms the α-, β-, and *aldehydo*-forms:

α-maltose *aldehydo*-maltose β-maltose

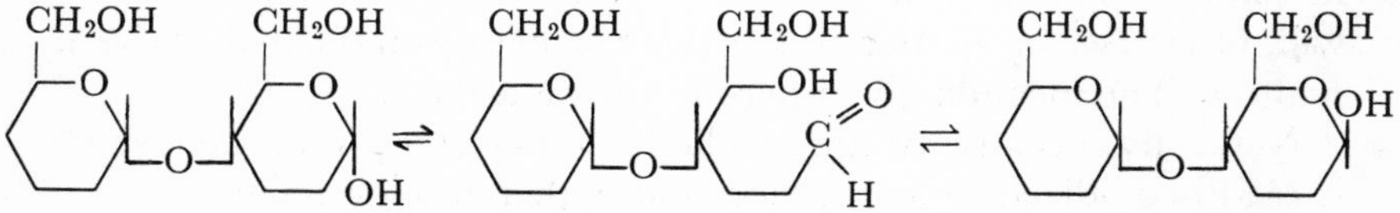

For simplicity, the H's and OH's of most of the carbons have been omitted.

It may be emphasized that the designation of α- or β- maltose refers only to the hemiacetal configuration; the linkage between the two glucose units in maltose is *always* an α-1,4-glucoside.

Because of the free aldehyde form, maltose will reduce Fehling's and Benedict's solution, etc., and is thus a "reducing disaccharide."

You will note that the Fischer projection formulas become very ungainly when depicting di- and polysaccharides. This is one reason that Haworth formulas are usually used for this purpose. Both are shown here to facilitate the identification of the component sugars and the positions of linkage, as well as to provide practice in converting one to the other.

Lactose (glucose plus galactose; β-1,4-galactoside linkage):

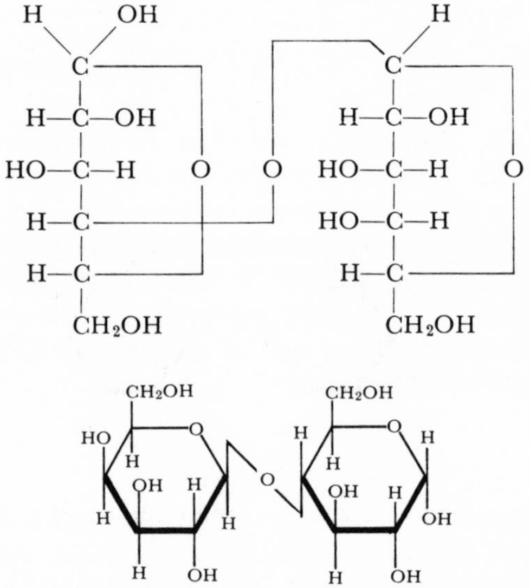

This molecule, like maltose, has one free hemiacetal group (carbon 1 of the glucose portion of the molecule). Consequently, it too, exists in solution as a mixture of α-, β-, and *aldehydo*-compounds. These will, of course, be similar to the three structures indicated above for maltose. The formula given here is for the α-form.

Naturally, because of the available hemiacetal group, lactose also is readily oxidized by cupric ion and is therefore designated as a reducing disaccharide.

The occurrence of lactose in nature, in contrast to most carbohydrates, is restricted to the animal kingdom. Here it is found as the major carbohydrate component of mammalian milks.

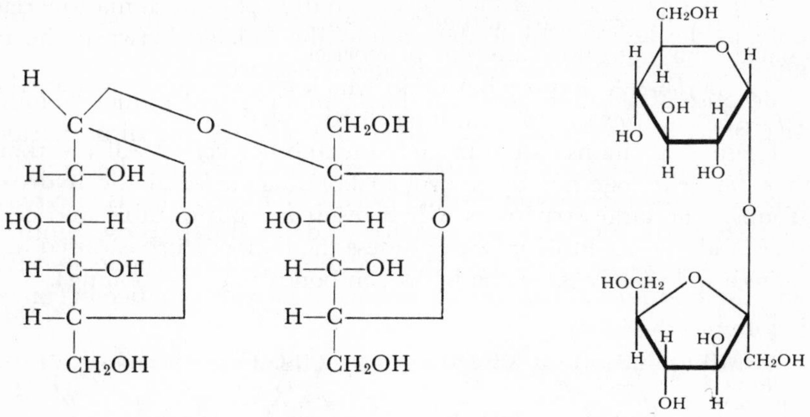

Sucrose (glucose plus fructose; α-D-glucopyranosyl-β-D-fructo-furanoside):

Sucrose is very widely distributed in plants. In the case of sugar cane, sugar beets, and sugar maple, the concentration is sufficiently high to make its isolation commercially feasible.

Since both of the carbonyl groups are involved in formation of the glycoside bond, neither will be in equilibrium with its free form. Thus, there exists only one form of sucrose, and that form is incapable of reacting with Benedict's or similar reagents. Consequently, sucrose is a nonreducing disaccharide.

OLIGOSACCHARIDES

These are compounds containing "a few" sugar units. Aside from a few naturally occurring trisaccharides, these are usually hydrolysis products of larger structures.

POLYSACCHARIDES

These are polymeric structures containing many units. Those in which the units are all the same sugar are called homopolysaccharides and those composed of two or more different sugars are called hetero-polysaccharides.

STARCH

This is the name given to the material comprising the major storage form of carbohydrate in plants. Starch usually occurs in the form of compact insoluble grains inside the plant cells.

The starch grains are actually composed of two different polysaccharides having quite different properties:

(1) *Amylose:* A polysaccharide in which glucose units are joined in *α-1,4-glucoside linkages* to form long slender chains.

These long chains can approach one another very readily and can then be held together by hydrogen bonding between the hydroxyl groups. The large structures which result are quite stable and compact, and are insoluble in water unless the temperature is raised high enough to break most of the hydrogen bonds (e.g., by boiling).

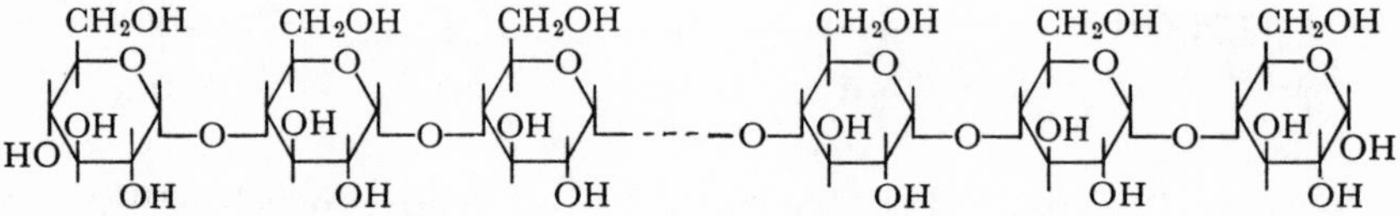

(2) *Amylopectin:* This polysaccharide possesses the same basic chain of *α-1,4-glucoside* linkages as does amylose, but has in addition a number of side chains attached by *α-1,6-glucoside* linkages, as shown:

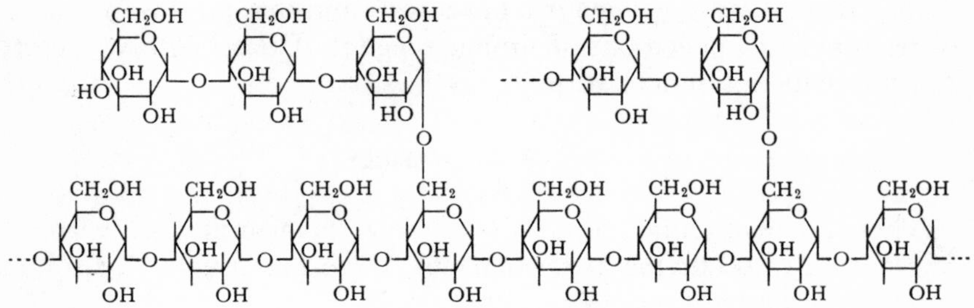

This branching decreases the ability of the chains to get together with one another and increases the binding of water molecules to the chains. Thus the amylopectins are reasonably soluble in warm water.

GLYCOGEN

This is the major carbohydrate reserve in animals. In most mammals, deposits of glycogen are maintained especially in the liver and in the skeletal muscles.

The structure of glycogen is essentially the same as that of the amylopectins, except that there is much more extensive branching.

This confers an increased solubility, to the degree that glycogen is quite readily put into suspension even in cold water.

CELLULOSE

This is one of the major structural components of plants. It is similar in structure to amylose, except that all of the glucose units are held together by *β-1,4-glucoside* linkages.

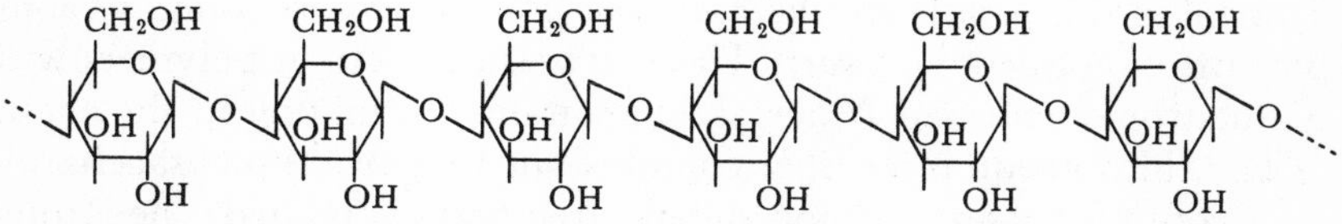

For the reasons mentioned in connection with the amyloses, this yields an insoluble macromolecule. The cellulose chains are rather longer and more efficiently held together, and the aggregated molecules are thus very large and extremely insoluble. However, these are just the properties that make them so useful as fibres for paper, cloth, etc.

Animals that do their own digesting are unable to make any use of cellulose as a food, since none of them possesses an enzyme capable of catalyzing the cleavage of β-glucoside bonds. Ruminants and a variety of wood-eating insects are able to use cellulose only because the microorganisms of their digestive tracts do possess such enzymes and use them to the mutual benefit of microorganism and animal.

CHITIN

This is apparently a linear (straight-chain) polymer of *N*-acetyl-glucosamine units. It forms a major component of the shells of crustaceans and some insects, and is very resistant to hydrolysis.

PECTINS

The pectins of fruits and berries are polymers of D-galacturonic acid. Only the aldehyde and hydroxyl groups are involved in formation of the polymer, leaving the carboxyl groups free. A varying percentage of these carboxyl groups is always found to be in the form of the methyl ester.

Polymers of similar structure but composed of D-mannuronic acid have been obtained from seaweed.

MUCOPOLYSACCHARIDES

This term is used to denote those heteropolysaccharides which contain aminosugars or their derivatives.

The members of this class may be separated into several subgroups. First, the *neutral* mucopolysaccharides, such as the immunologically important blood-group substances, which contain only an *N*-acetylhexosamine and a hexose.

A second group is distinguished by the presence of a hexuronic acid (such as D-glucuronic acid), along with an *N*-acetylhexosamine. Typical of this group are the *hyaluronic acids* which are found as components of connective tissue. These are straight-chain polymers with D-glucuronic acid and *N*-acetylglucosamine alternating in the chain.

The third group is a rather complex one in which a polysaccharide may contain hexoses, amino sugars (free and acetylated), hexuronic acids, and sugar sulfates. Examples are *chondroitin sulfate* of cartilage (*N*-acetylgalactosamine, glucuronic acid, and sulfate esters of these sugars), and *heparin*, the natural anticoagulant of blood (glucosamine *N*-sulfate, glucuronic acid, and their sulfate esters).

Glycosidic linkages involving uronic acids or aminosugars are unusually resistant to chemical hydrolysis. Consequently, the polysaccharides containing these units tend to be extremely stable and are often found where strength and chemical resistance are most important, e.g., in skin, connective tissues, insect exoskeletons, umbilical cord, etc.

OTHERS

Various vegetable gums and mucilages (e.g., *gum arabic, plum gum,* etc.) contain a variety of pentoses, hexoses, and uronic acids. Hemicelluloses of plants have similar structures.

Agar, from seaweed, is composed of a mixture of D- and L-galactoses. Mannose polymers (called *mannans*) are common in plants. A polymer of D-fructose (*Inulin*) is obtained from the tubers of the Jerusalem artichoke.

All of the polysaccharides mentioned above are merely selected examples of different types of structures. Many other similar compounds are to be found in nature.

SUGGESTED ADDITIONAL READING

Pigman, W., Ed., "The Carbohydrates," Academic Press, New York, 1957.

Lipids

4

$\mathbf{A}$ttempts at a rigorous definition of the class of compounds to be called *lipids* usually become either hopelessly complicated or completely misleading. Generally, however, the lipids include those compounds which can be extracted from biological materials by organic solvents such as ether-alcohol mixtures, acetone, or various chlorinated hydrocarbons.

The terms "fats" and "oils" are commonly used to denote crude lipid mixtures which are obtained from natural sources in specific ways (such as lard and cottonseed oil). The distinction between the two terms is solely on the basis of the physical state at room temperature; fats are solids, oils are liquids. On the other hand, most chemists use these same terms to identify esters of glycerol with fatty acids. The obvious likelihood of confusion makes it preferable to avoid these designations when possible.

Fortunately, the *fatty acids* are much more readily defined. They are simply those monocarboxylic acids which are more soluble in organic solvents than they are in water, i.e., essentially those with four or more carbon atoms.

The fatty acids occur in nature largely as components of more complex lipid materials. Before proceeding to a classification system for the lipids as a whole, we will therefore consider the various types of fatty acids which are of common occurrence.

FATTY ACIDS

The naturally occurring fatty acids include almost all of the saturated acids having an even number of carbon atoms in the range from 4 to 30 carbons. Other prominent fatty acid species are the 18- and 20-carbon unsaturated fatty acids, various hydroxy acids, and a few cyclic fatty acids.

SATURATED FATTY ACIDS

The general formula for these acids is CH_3—$(CH_2)_n$—$COOH$. Among those occurring most commonly are the following (the subscript numbers refer to the total number of carbon atoms):

Butyric acid	C_4			Palmitic acid	C_{16}
Lauric acid	C_{12}	Myristic acid	C_{14}	Stearic acid	C_{18}

UNSATURATED FATTY ACIDS

The following are the most important of the unsaturated fatty acids:

Oleic acid (C_{18}, one double bond) $CH_3(CH_2)_7CH{=}CH(CH_2)_7COOH$

Linoleic acid (C_{18}, two double bonds)
$$CH_3(CH_2)_4CH{=}CH{-}CH_2{-}CH{=}CH(CH_2)_7COOH$$

Linolenic acid (C_{18}, three double bonds)
$$CH_3CH_2{-}CH{=}CH{-}CH_2{-}CH{=}CH{-}CH_2{-}CH{=}CH(CH_2)_7COOH$$

Arachidonic acid (C_{20}, four double bonds)
$$CH_3(CH_2)_4CH{=}CH{-}CH_2{-}CH{=}CH{-}CH_2{-}CH{=}CH{-}CH_2{-}CH{=}$$
$$CH(CH_2)_3COOH$$

Humans, along with many other animal species, are capable of inserting the one double bond to convert stearic acid to oleic acid, but are unable to convert oleic acid into either linoleic, linolenic, or arachidonic acid. The maintenance of normal structure and function, particularly of skin tissue, requires that cells have available some one of these acids. Since they cannot be synthesized by the cells, they must be obtained from the dietary materials. However, most animal systems can interconvert linoleic, linolenic, and arachidonic acids. Therefore, the diet need contain only one of these. The actual functioning acid is unknown; there is some evidence that it is arachidonic acid.

HYDROXY ACIDS

An example is ricinoleic acid derived from castor oil:

$$CH_3-(CH_2)_5-\overset{\overset{\displaystyle OH}{|}}{CH}-CH_2-CH=CH-(CH_2)_7-COOH$$

CYCLIC FATTY ACIDS

These are rather rare, the best examples being chaulmoogric and hydnocarpic acids, which occur in chaulmoogra oil (used in the treatment of leprosy):

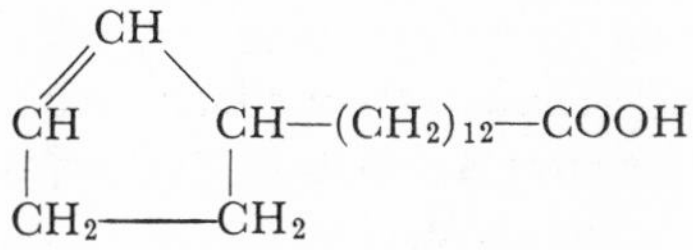

$$\begin{array}{c} CH \\ \diagup \quad \diagdown \\ CH \qquad CH-(CH_2)_{12}-COOH \\ | \qquad\qquad | \\ CH_2\text{------}CH_2 \end{array}$$

chaulmoogric acid

CLASSIFICATION OF LIPIDS

It is possible to classify the lipids in a variety of ways. One method that has been extensively used in the past is based on the nature of the products obtained on hydrolysis. "Simple lipids," on this basis, are defined as those which yield only one or more fatty acids and an alcohol on hydrolysis. "Complex lipids" yield, in addition to fatty acids and an alcohol, compounds such as phosphoric acid, sugars, etc. "Derived lipids" are those which contain no ester linkages but which may be considered to have been derived from naturally occurring esterified materials. Most of these are alcohols of complex nature.

Since the structures of many of the lipids are becoming better known, it has become more common to classify the lipids with regard to the structure of the molecules. Since most of the lipids are esters, it is most convenient to do this on the basis of the alcohol portion of the molecule. The following classification is constructed in this manner:

Glycerol Lipids

SIMPLE GLYCERIDES

These are the simple neutral esters of glycerol and fatty acids, and include the mono-, di-, and triglycerides. It is obvious that a large number of these compounds are possible, varying in the nature of the fatty acids involved and in the positions and order of their attachment to the glycerol molecule.

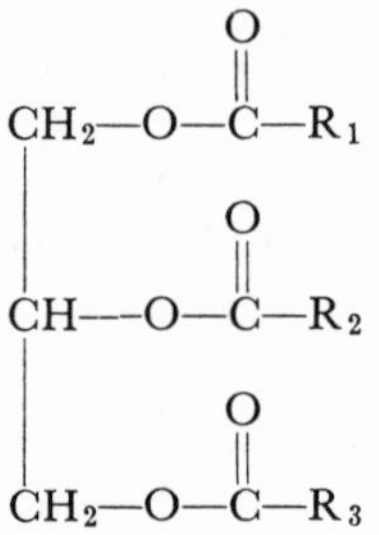

$$
\begin{array}{c}
\quad\quad\quad\quad O \\
\quad\quad\quad\quad \| \\
CH_2{-}O{-}C{-}R_1 \\
\\
\quad\quad\quad\quad O \\
\quad\quad\quad\quad \| \\
CH{-}{-}O{-}C{-}R_2 \\
\\
\quad\quad\quad\quad O \\
\quad\quad\quad\quad \| \\
CH_2{-}O{-}C{-}R_3
\end{array}
$$

a triglyceride

Obviously when the groups attached to carbons 1 and 3 differ, a center of asymmetry occurs at carbon-2. The two isomers may be represented diagrammatically as:

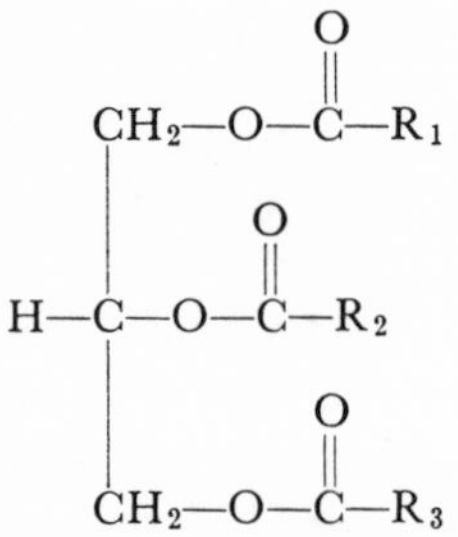

$$
\begin{array}{c}
\quad\quad\quad\quad O \\
\quad\quad\quad\quad \| \\
CH_2{-}O{-}C{-}R_1 \\
\quad\quad\quad\quad O \\
\quad\quad\quad\quad \| \\
H{-}C{-}O{-}C{-}R_2 \\
\quad\quad\quad\quad O \\
\quad\quad\quad\quad \| \\
CH_2{-}O{-}C{-}R_3 \\
I
\end{array}
\quad\quad\quad
\begin{array}{c}
\quad\quad\quad\quad O \\
\quad\quad\quad\quad \| \\
CH_2{-}O{-}C{-}R_1 \\
\quad O \\
\quad \| \\
R_2{-}C{-}O{-}C{-}H \\
\quad\quad\quad\quad O \\
\quad\quad\quad\quad \| \\
CH_2{-}O{-}C{-}R_3 \\
II
\end{array}
$$

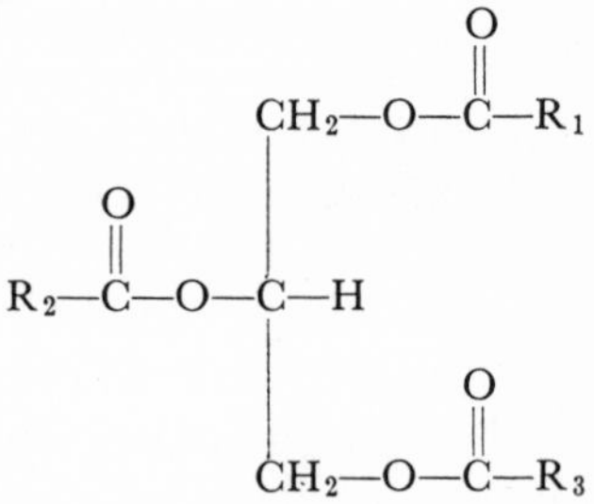

While the naturally occurring glycerol lipids are normally based on the II structure, we will for convenience not specify the isomeric forms in the formulas given in this chapter.

In order to name a specific glyceride, we must be able to specify clearly the positions of attachment of the fatty acids. Two alternate systems are in common use for achieving this purpose; in the one case, the carbons of the glycerol portion are designated as α, β, and α' carbons, and in the other case they are simply numbered 1, 2, 3 in either direction.

Compound A (shown below) is then described as α-butyro-β-stearo-α'-olein or 1-butyro-2-stearo-3-olein, or with equal correctness it may be described as α-oleo-β-stearo-α'-butyrin or 1-oleo-2-stearo-3-butyr-in. Any one of these names will specify clearly and unambiguously the structure of the triglyceride.

$$
\begin{array}{ll}
\text{CH}_2\text{—O—}\overset{\displaystyle O}{\overset{\|}{\text{C}}}\text{—(CH}_2)_2\text{—CH}_3 & \text{CH}_2\text{—O—}\overset{\displaystyle O}{\overset{\|}{\text{C}}}\text{—(CH}_2)_{10}\text{—CH}_3 \\
\\
\text{CH—--O—}\overset{\displaystyle O}{\overset{\|}{\text{C}}}\text{—(CH}_2)_{16}\text{—CH}_3 & \text{CH—O—}\overset{\displaystyle O}{\overset{\|}{\text{C}}}\text{—(CH}_2)_{14}\text{—CH}_3 \\
\\
\text{CH}_2\text{—O—}\overset{\displaystyle O}{\overset{\|}{\text{C}}}\text{—C}_{17}\text{H}_{33} & \text{CH}_2\text{—OH} \\
\qquad\qquad (A) & \qquad\qquad (B)
\end{array}
$$

For the diglyceride B, acceptable names would be α-lauro-β-pal-mitin and 1-lauro-2-palmitin.

In most animals, the reserve energy supply is stored predominantly in the form of triglycerides. This is relatively efficient, since lipids of this type yield, on oxidation, a great deal more energy for a given weight of stored material than either carbohydrates or proteins.

GLYCEROL PHOSPHOLIPIDS

Any lipid containing phosphorus is included in the general class of *phospholipids*. Of these the glycerol phospholipids (sometimes referred to as phosphatides) are by far the most common. The different types of phospholipids appear to have certain biological functions in common. These can be related to the fact that the phospholipids are all good emulsifying agents. Large concentrations are usually found in cell membranes and in subcellular structures where lipids and water-soluble materials must be capable of intimate interaction. The phospholipids may therefore promote the transportation, absorption, and metabolic interactions of the other lipid substances. There is some evidence that each specific class of phospholipid has its own specific functions, but in most cases these are not yet clearly known to us.

The different types of glycerol phospholipids are outlined below. You will find that a number of them have the same essential structure, varying only in the nature of one of the groups linked to the phosphate portion of the molecule. Note also that most of the compounds are of phosphodiester nature and provide our first biological example of this type of bonding.

Phosphatidic Acids: These compounds are not found in tissue ex-tracts in any significant concentration. However, they have been found to play important roles as intermediates in the biosynthesis of the other glycerol lipids.

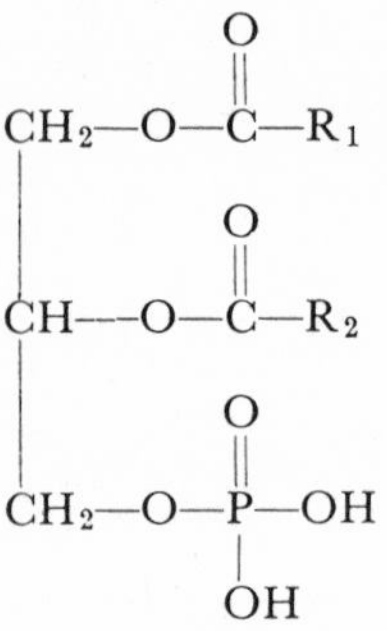

$$
\begin{array}{c}
\quad\quad\quad\quad O \\
\quad\quad\quad\quad \| \\
CH_2\!-\!O\!-\!C\!-\!R_1 \\
\\
\quad\quad\quad\quad O \\
\quad\quad\quad\quad \| \\
CH\!-\!-\!O\!-\!C\!-\!R_2 \\
\\
\quad\quad\quad\quad O \\
\quad\quad\quad\quad \| \\
CH_2\!-\!O\!-\!P\!-\!OH \\
\quad\quad\quad\quad | \\
\quad\quad\quad\quad OH
\end{array}
$$

Phosphatidyl Cholines (Lecithins): This is probably the most common form of phospholipid, at least in animals. The lecithins are required for normal transport and utilization of other lipids, especially in the liver. Anything which interferes with the synthesis of choline will also block the synthesis of lecithins, and thus interrupt the normal transportation of lipids to and from the liver. This usually results in the accumulation of lipid material in the liver, giving rise to the condition called "fatty liver."

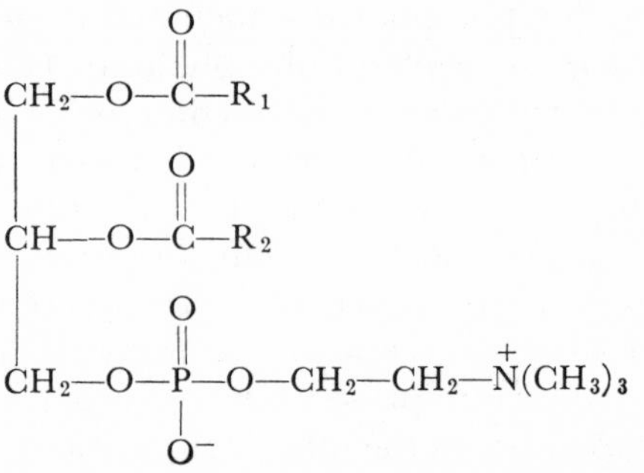

$$
\begin{array}{c}
\quad\quad\quad\quad O \\
\quad\quad\quad\quad \| \\
CH_2\!-\!O\!-\!C\!-\!R_1 \\
\\
\quad\quad\quad\quad O \\
\quad\quad\quad\quad \| \\
CH\!-\!-\!O\!-\!C\!-\!R_2 \\
\\
\quad\quad\quad\quad O \\
\quad\quad\quad\quad \| \\
CH_2\!-\!O\!-\!P\!-\!O\!-\!CH_2\!-\!CH_2\!-\!\overset{+}{N}(CH_3)_3 \\
\quad\quad\quad\quad | \\
\quad\quad\quad\quad O^-
\end{array}
$$

Free choline is a compound with an alcohol group. Its linkage to the phosphate portion of a lecithin, like that of the glycerol to the phosphate, is that of a phosphate ester.

$$HO\!-\!CH_2\!-\!CH_2\!-\!\overset{+}{N}(CH_3)_3$$

choline

Phosphatidyl Ethanolamines, Phosphatidyl Serines, and Phosphatidyl Inositols: These phospholipids are similar in structure to the lecithins (above) but have the choline portion replaced by one of the compounds indicated.

$$HO—CH_2—CH_2—NH_2$$

ethanolamine

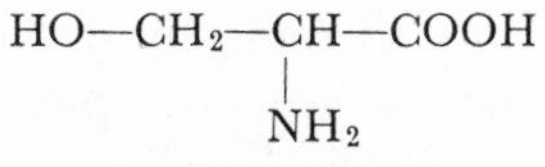

$$HO—CH_2—CH—COOH$$
$$NH_2$$

serine

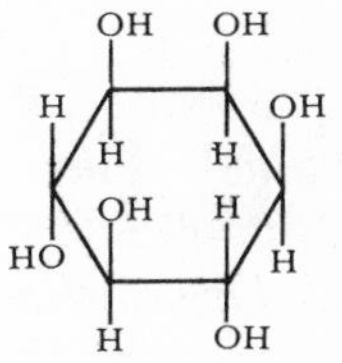

OH   OH

H   OH
  H   H
  OH   H
HO   H

H   OH

myo-inositol

The ethanolamine and serine compounds are often referred to as the cephalins. They were originally distinguished from the lecithins on the basis of different solubility characteristics in mixed solvents.

In animals, the ethanolamine, serine and inositol phospholipids are found in highest concentration in nerve tissues. Their exact functions there are not known.

Plasmalogens: These phospholipids are characterized by the fact that on treatment with acid they give rise to a long-chain fatty aldehyde. This aldehydogenic group replaces one of the fatty acids in a typical phospholipid structure.

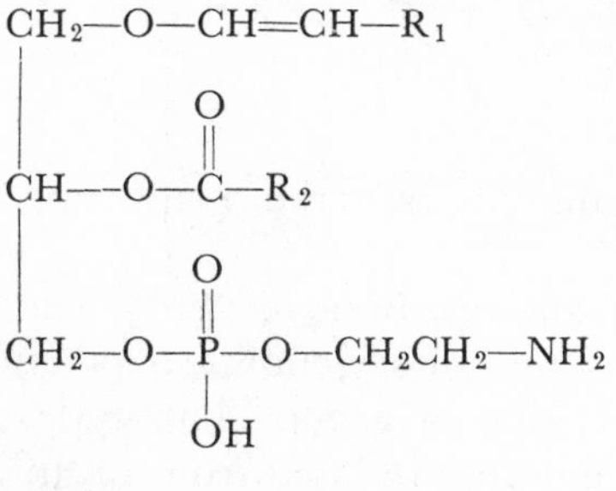

$$CH_2—O—CH{=}CH—R_1$$

$$CH—O—\overset{O}{\overset{\|}{C}}—R_2$$

$$CH_2—O—\overset{O}{\overset{\|}{P}}—O—CH_2CH_2—NH_2$$
$$OH$$

The structure shown is that of one of the common plasmalogens; the ethanolamine is often replaced by choline, and the aldehydogenic group may be attached to the β-position rather than the α-position as shown.

SPHINGOSINE LIPIDS

These contain as the alcohol portion either the long-chain amino alcohol *sphingosine,* or the related saturated form *dihydrosphingosine.*

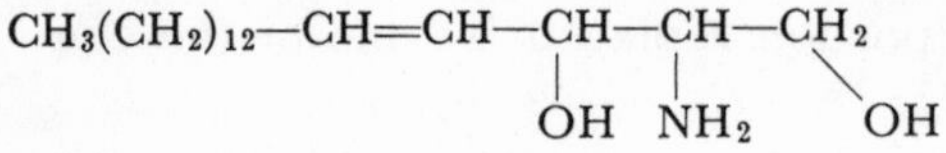

$$CH_3(CH_2)_{12}-CH=CH-CH-CH-CH_2$$
$$\underset{OH}{|}\quad\underset{NH_2}{|}\quad\underset{OH}{\diagdown}$$

sphingosine

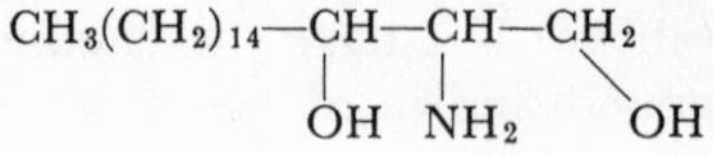

$$CH_3(CH_2)_{14}-CH-CH-CH_2$$
$$\underset{OH}{|}\quad\underset{NH_2}{|}\quad\underset{OH}{\diagdown}$$

dihydrosphingosine

The structures of many of these lipids have not as yet been well defined. Those listed below are examples of some of the types of sphingolipids that have been isolated and characterized.

Sphingomyelins: These lipids contain sphingosine plus a fatty acid attached in the form of an amide linkage and phosphorylcholine attached to the primary alcohol group.

$$CH_3$$
$$|$$
$$(CH_2)_{12}$$
$$|$$
$$CH$$
$$\|$$
$$CH$$
$$|$$
$$CH-OH$$
$$|$$
$$\overset{\displaystyle O}{\underset{\displaystyle \|}{}}$$
$$CH-NH-C-R$$
$$|$$
$$\overset{\displaystyle O}{\underset{\displaystyle \|}{}}$$
$$CH_2-O-P-O-CH_2CH_2-\overset{+}{N}(CH_3)_3$$
$$|$$
$$O^-$$

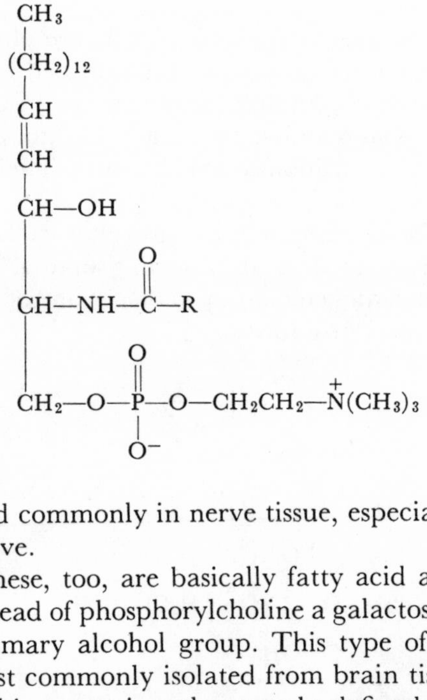

They are found commonly in nerve tissue, especially in the myelin sheath of the nerve.

Cerebrosides: These, too, are basically fatty acid amides of sphingosine, having instead of phosphorylcholine a galactose oligosaccharide joined to the primary alcohol group. This type of structure occurs widely but is most commonly isolated from brain tissue.

Gangliosides: This group is rather poorly defined. Attached to the fatty amide structure it is possible to find one or more molecules of glucose, galactose, *N*-acetylglucosamine, *N*-acetylneuraminic acid, and perhaps other sugar derivatives. The exact composition and structure of the molecules varies considerably with the source. The gangliosides are most commonly isolated from nerve or spleen tissues.

Phytoglycolipids: A wide variety of these are present in various plant sources. Generally, they appear to be based on the fatty acid amide of sphingosine or dihydrosphingosine, and contain in addition an assortment of sugars and often *myo*-inositol. Relatively few members of this group have been well characterized.

Waxes

An ester of a high-molecular-weight alcohol and a high-molecular-weight fatty acid is called a *wax*. The acids and alcohols most commonly involved are those having carbon chains of the order of 16 to 40 carbon atoms.

Most of the natural waxes are mixtures of esters. Beeswax contains waxes derived from alcohols having 24 to 30 carbons. A typical example would be n-hexacosanyl palmitate

$$[CH_3—(CH_2)_{14}—\overset{\displaystyle O}{\overset{\|}{C}}—O—(CH_2)_{25}—CH_3]$$

Spermaceti, from the head of the sperm whale, is rich in cetyl palmitate

$$[CH_3—(CH_2)_{14}—\overset{\displaystyle O}{\overset{\|}{C}}—O—(CH_2)_{15}—CH_3]$$

Steroids and Sterols

All steroid compounds have in common the basic ring structure which is known as a cyclopentanoperhydrophenanthrene nucleus.

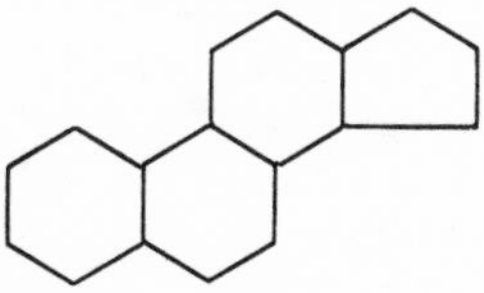

As the name implies, this is a fully saturated ring system. Various natural steroids, however, may have one or more double bonds as added embellishments. These compounds comprise one of the most ubiquitous and versatile families of compounds in nature. Small variations in structure or in the nature of attached groups are found to result in profound changes in biological activity. The structures of a number of different types of steroids having greatly varying biological activities are shown below:

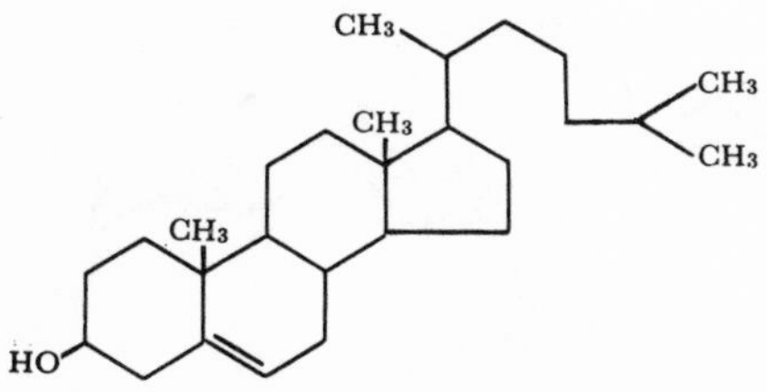

cholesterol

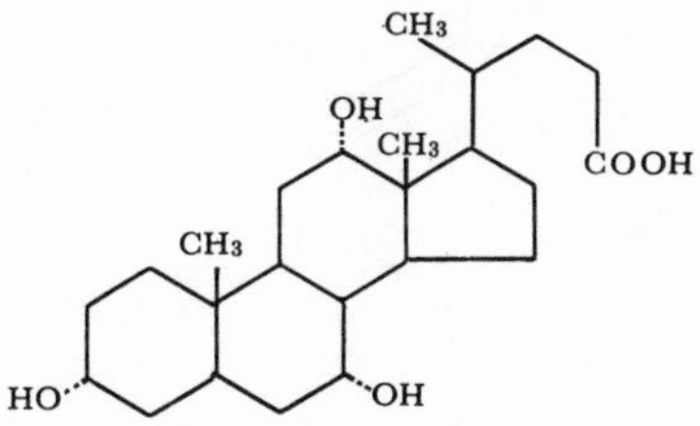

cholic acid

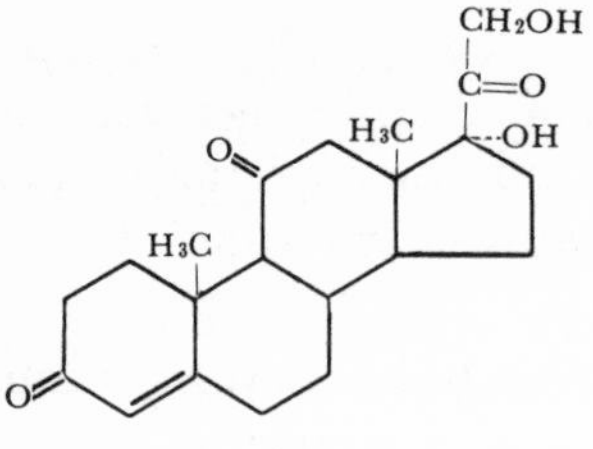

CH₂OH
C=O
H₃C   ..OH

cortisone

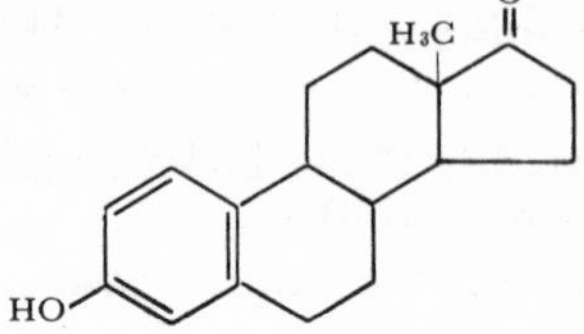

estrone

While the total chemical synthesis of certain steroids has been accomplished, it is an extremely difficult process involving many reactions. One of the problems involved is the necessity to obtain the correct optical isomer at each of at least five asymmetric centers in the molecule. Consequently, synthesis of new pharmacologically active steroids is normally accomplished by either chemical or microbiological modification of some suitable naturally occurring steroidal compound.

Without even considering substituent groups, we find six possible asymmetric centers involved in the ring system itself.

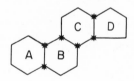

Fortunately for the synthetic chemist, the naturally occurring steroids differ only in the configuration of the carbons joining rings A and B. They thus fall into two groups in which the A to B junction is either "cis" or "trans." Structures for these two are shown below in accurate conformational form just to indicate a closer approximation to the actual shapes of the molecules.

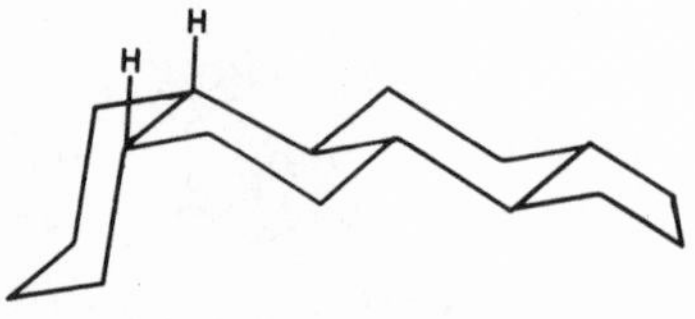

cis 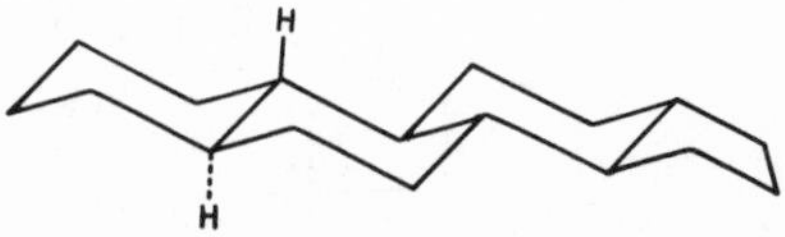   trans

The bonds available for various substituents can be viewed as extending either above or below the overall plane of the molecule. In order to indicate this in the common formulas and names, those below the plane are denoted by a broken line and are called "α"-substituents. Solid lines are then used to denote bonds above the plane attaching "β"-substituents. These conventions have been used in the specific steroid formulas shown above.

Certain steroids, containing a hydroxyl group as their only functional one, are often referred to as *sterols*. The common examples of these are cholesterol, ergosterol, and stigmasterol; the last two occur in plants and the first in animals.

Hydrocarbons

Hydrocarbons occur in major concentration in biological materials only in a relatively small number of special cases. Where they do occur, such as in rubber-producing plants or in certain species of sharks, they are usually highly unsaturated and have a high degree of carbon-chain branching. Many of them appear to be formed by the condensation of isoprene-type units. Examples are the terpenes, such as limonene, and miscellaneous compounds such as squalene (which

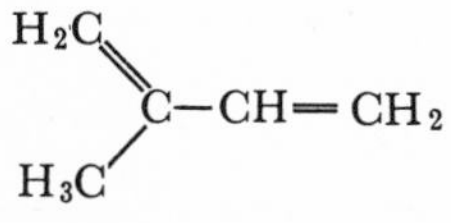

isoprene

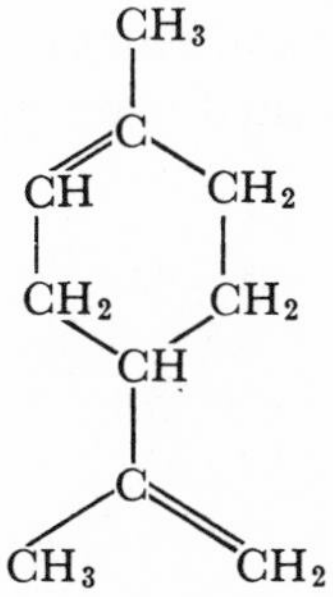

limonene

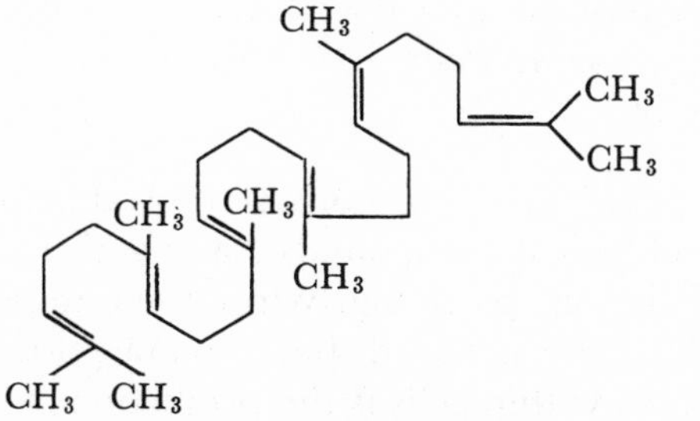

squalene

is an important intermediate on the route of biological synthesis of steroids). In addition, the major components of rubber latex are essentially long, linear polymers of isoprene units.

Fat-Soluble Vitamins

Certain lipid compounds are vitamins, that is, they are required in small amounts in the diet for proper nutrition of some organisms (usually animals). Vitamins A, D, and K are required for humans and a variety of other animals. A definite need for Vitamin E has been shown for many animals, but not for humans.

In referring to Vitamins A, D, K, or E, we are not really referring to a single chemical compound but to a type of compound which will have a specified physiological effect. Thus in each case there exist small families of closely related compounds, each of which will have, for example, "Vitamin A activity." In the brief discussion of the fat-soluble vitamins that follows, we will show structures only for the most common or most representative example in each case.

Vitamin A is involved in the processes of vision, maintenance of epithelial tissues, and growth in general. The chemical compounds having this activity are all closely related to the carotenoid plant pigments (which will be mentioned shortly) and, in fact, normally occur in the diet chiefly in the form of the various carotenes. Vitamin A is then formed from this material in the animal body.

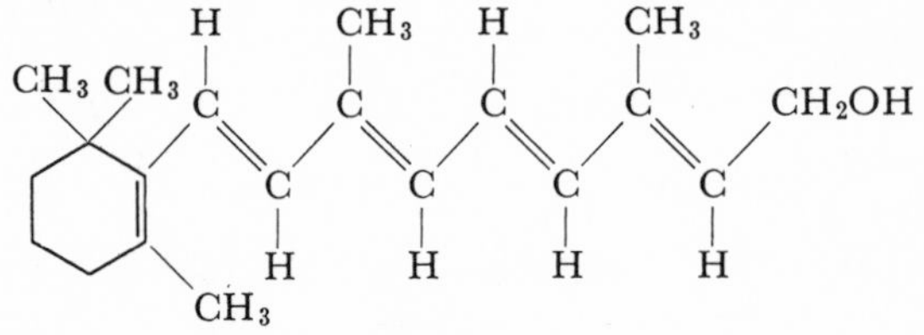

Vitamin A₁

Vitamin D is important for the control of absorption and the utilization of calcium. As a result, it is necessary for proper formation of bones and teeth.

Vitamin E is required for normal reproduction in many animal species. The chemical compounds having this activity are all very efficient antioxidants, particularly in preventing oxidation of unsaturated fatty acids. It is believed that a major portion of the function of these compounds within cells is the protection of cellular constituents from fortuitous oxidation.

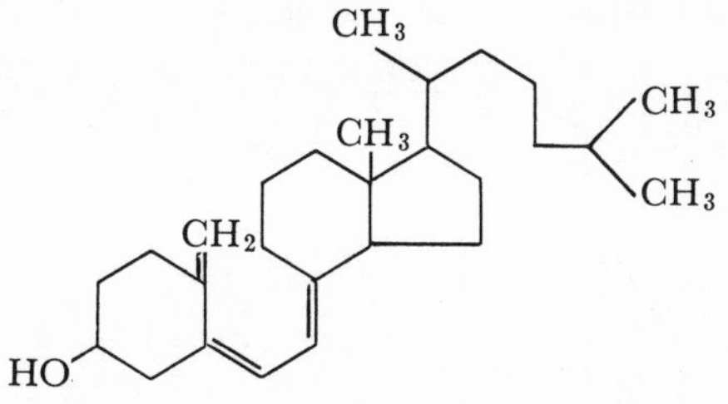

Vitamin D$_3$

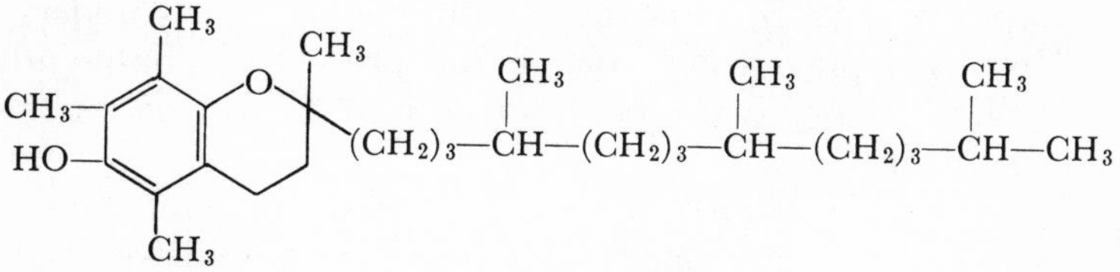

Vitamin E
(alpha-tocopherol)

Vitamin K is most notable in that it is required for synthesis of some of the compounds required for normal blood clotting. In addition, it is now believed that the Vitamin K compounds or similar structures may have other more general roles in the oxidative processes of cells.

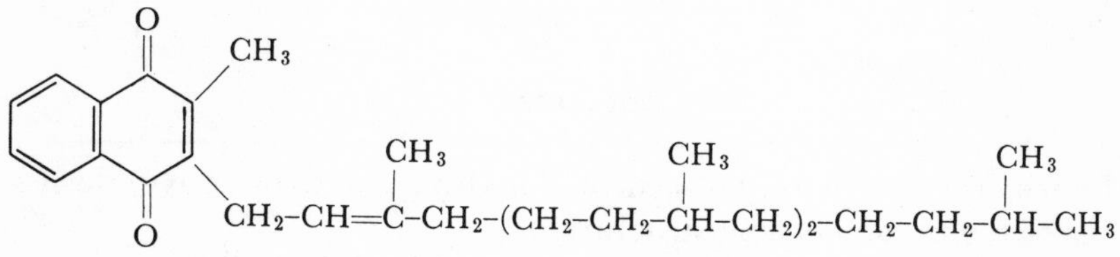

Vitamin K$_1$

It is interesting that a simple synthetic naphthoquinone derivative called menadione is several times more active than the naturally occurring compounds, and is commonly used in commercial vitamin preparations.

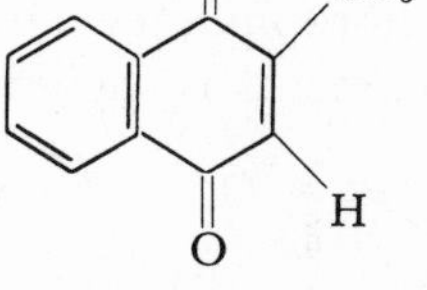

menadione

Plant Pigments

This grouping includes a number of compounds that are alike only in that they are colored, occur in plants, and are extractable with organic solvents.

By far the most ubiquitous of the plant pigments are the *chlorophylls*. These contain a complex nitrogen-containing ring system called a *porphyrin*. The nitrogen atoms of the porphyrin are bonded to a magnesium ion. In addition, this whole complex is linked to a specific protein molecule. The similarity between the chlorophyll structure and the heme portion of the hemoglobins is striking and is illustrated on the opposite page. By some mechanism not yet clearly understood, the chlorophylls play a key role in the process of photosynthesis, where radiant energy is trapped and utilized to provide energy for key synthetic reactions.

The *carotenes* form another important group of pigments. Like some of the hydrocarbons mentioned above, these are essentially polymers of isoprene-type units; owing to the extended conjugated double-bond system, they are generally yellow in color. While their functions in plants are not clear, in animals the carotenes can be converted in whole or in part to Vitamin A structures.

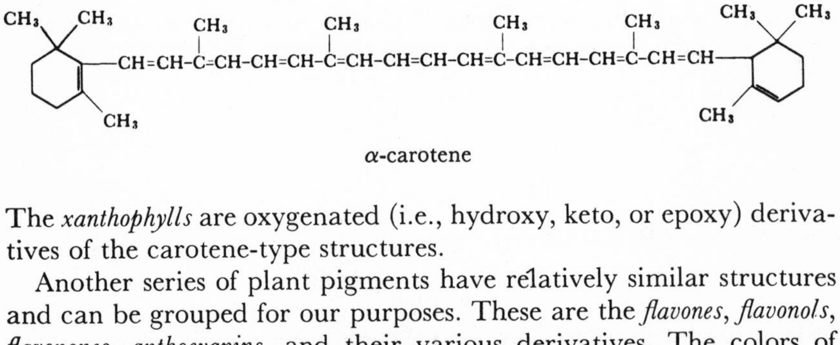

α-carotene

The *xanthophylls* are oxygenated (i.e., hydroxy, keto, or epoxy) derivatives of the carotene-type structures.

Another series of plant pigments have relatively similar structures and can be grouped for our purposes. These are the *flavones, flavonols, flavonones, anthocyanins,* and their various derivatives. The colors of these range from the yellows of the flavones and flavonols to the reds and blues of some of the anthocyanins. The compounds are present in plants in rather high concentrations, but the colors are often masked by the preponderance of chlorophylls. The brilliant autumn colors become apparent as the chlorophyll level in the leaves decreases. The basic structure of these pigments is shown below.

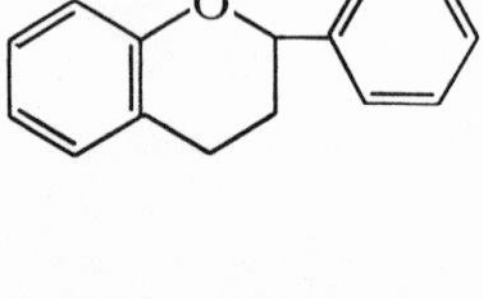

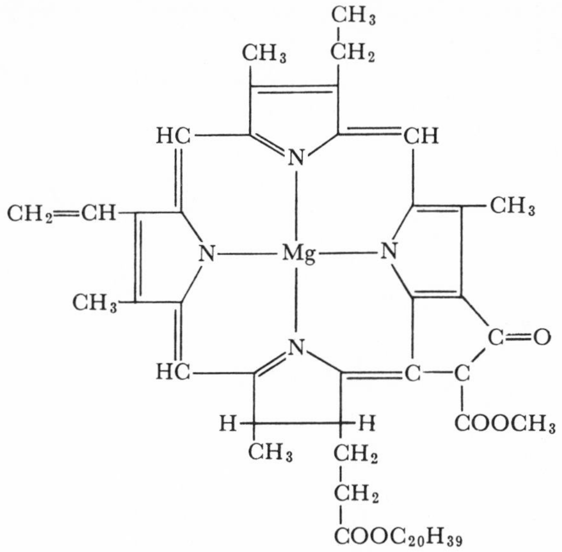

$$CH_3$$
$$CH_3 \quad CH_2$$

$$HC \quad N \quad CH$$

$$CH_2{=}CH \quad N \quad Mg \quad N \quad CH_3$$

$$CH_3$$

$$C{=}O$$

$$HC \quad N \quad C{-}C$$

$$COOCH_3$$

$$H \quad H$$

$$CH_3 \quad CH_2$$

$$CH_2$$

$$COOC_{20}H_{39}$$

chlorophyll a

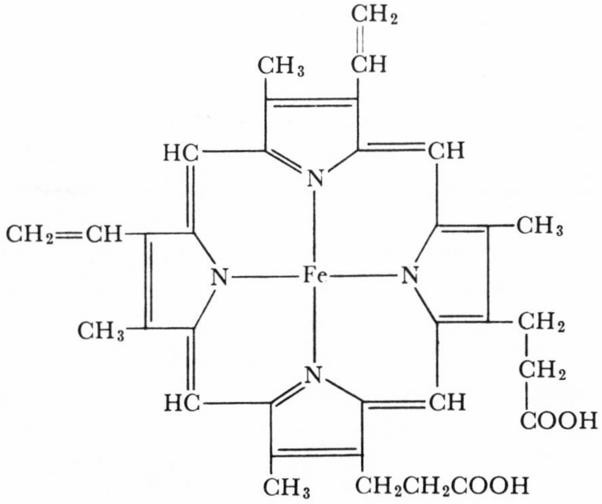

$$CH_2$$
$$CH_3 \quad CH$$

$$HC \quad N \quad CH$$

$$CH_2{=}CH \quad N \quad Fe \quad N \quad CH_3$$

$$CH_2$$

$$CH_3 \quad CH_2$$

$$COOH$$

$$HC \quad N \quad CH$$

$$CH_3 \quad CH_2CH_2COOH$$

heme portion of hemoglobin

The naturally occurring compounds have at least one, and commonly several, hydroxyl groups substituted on one or more of the rings. In addition, these are often bound to sugars, so that the pigments commonly occur as glycosides. Examples of two types of these pigments appear below.

An Anthocyanidin: The complete anthocyanin is made up of an anthocyanidin ring structure joined to a carbohydrate portion through a phenolic glycoside linkage.

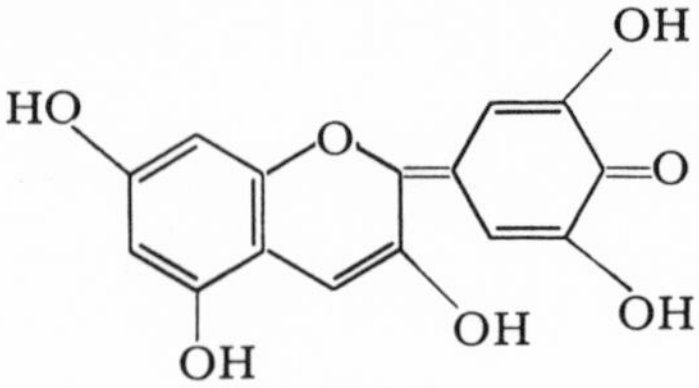

delphinidin

A Flavonol:

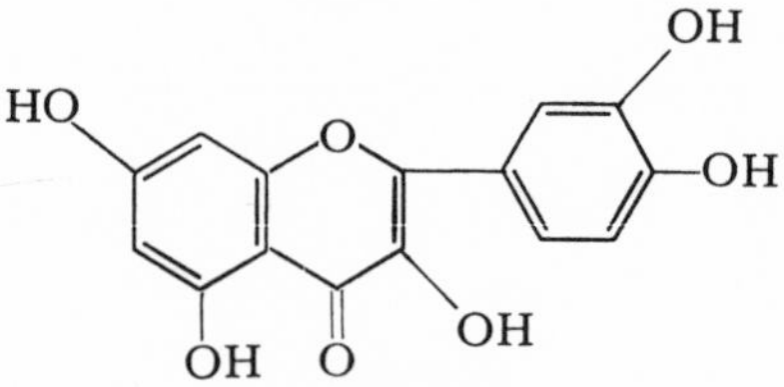

quercitin

SUGGESTED ADDITIONAL READING

Hanahan, D. J., "Lipide Chemistry," John Wiley & Sons, Inc., New York and London, 1960.

Fieser, L. F., and Fieser, M., "Steroids," Reinhold Publishing Corp., New York, 1959.

Burton, B. T., Ed., "Heinz Handbook of Nutrition," McGraw-Hill Book Co., New York, 1959.

Clevenger, S., "Flower Pigments," *Scientific American*, **210**, No. 6, 84 (June, 1964).

Nucleic Acids
and Nucleotides

5

The nucleic acids, like the proteins and polysaccharides, are another class of biological polymer or macromolecule that occurs in all living cells. In addition, a nucleic acid is an essential component of all viruses. The main function of the nucleic acids is the storage, transmission and use of the genetic information upon which the continuation of cell structure depends.

The monomeric unit of the nucleic acids is termed a *nucleotide*. This monomer, in contrast to the amino acids and the monosaccharides, is susceptible to further hydrolysis. Each nucleotide yields in this way three subunits: a nitrogen-containing ring compound (a nitrogen base), a pentose, and a molecule of phosphoric acid. Two general classes of nucleic acids may be distinguished on the basis of their hydrolysis products. One of these yields D-ribose as the only sugar component, and is thus called *ribonucleic acid* (*RNA*). The other yields D-2-deoxyribose and accordingly is designated as *deoxyribonucleic acid* (*DNA*).

DNA is found in cells almost exclusively as a major component of the *chromosomes* of the nucleus. Small amounts of DNA have quite recently been shown to reside in the chloroplasts of green plants and in the mitochondrial particles of cell cytoplasm. Certain viruses, including many of the bacterial viruses or bacteriophages, are DNA-protein particles.

The RNA of cells is quantitatively of two major types. One of these, *ribosomal-RNA*, occurs in combination with proteins in the small sub-cellular particles called *ribosomes*. These particles are distributed throughout the cell, chiefly in the cytoplasm. The second type, *soluble-RNA*, is found in free form in the cytoplasm. A third type of RNA, *messenger-RNA*, occurs in small quantities, commonly associated with ribosomes. RNA molecules, again in conjunction with proteins, are major components of many viruses.

NITROGEN BASES

The two types of nucleic acids differ also in the nitrogen-containing ring structures found in their nucleotide units. Both types contain adenine, guanine, and cytosine, but RNA contains in addition uracil while DNA contains thymine.

On the basis of the ring structures, adenine and guanine may be classified as examples of a group of organic compounds called *purines;* similarly, cytosine, uracil and thymine are representatives of *pyrimidines*. The structures of these compounds appear below.

Nucleic acid purines:

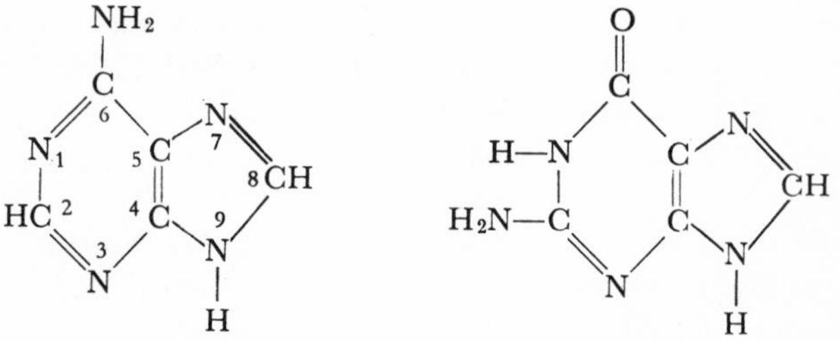

adenine   guanine

Nucleic acid pyrimidines:

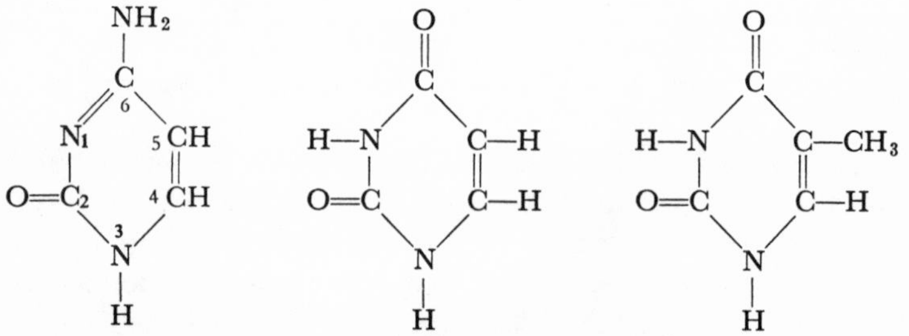

cytosine   uracil   thymine

Systems in common use for the numbering of the atoms of the rings are also given.

NUCLEOSIDES

When a heterocyclic nitrogenous base such as one of those mentioned above is connected through one of its nitrogen atoms to the glycosidic carbon of a sugar, the resulting compound is called a *nucleoside*. If the sugar is ribose, the compound is a ribonucleoside or simply a riboside. Similarly, deoxyribose gives a deoxyriboside. The riboside of uracil is depicted below as an example of the structure of a pyrimidine riboside. Note that the glycosidic linkage is of the β-type and that the ring form is furanose. These structural points are common to all the nucleosides of the nucleic acids. In the pyrimidine nucleosides the glycosidic linkage is with the 3-nitrogen; in the purine ribosides with the 9-nitrogen atom.

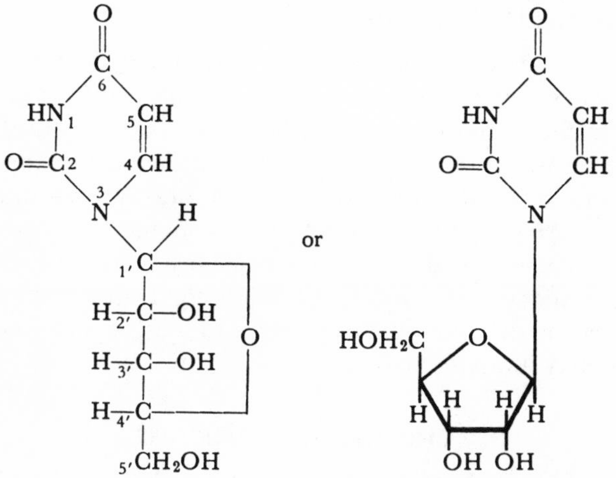

uracil riboside

NUCLEOTIDES

A *nucleotide* is a phosphate ester of a nucleoside. The designations "ribotide" and "deoxyribotide" are used to specify the nucleotides of the pertinent sugar. From the structures of the ribosides it should be apparent that three alcohol groups are available for esterification, those on the 2'-, 3'-, and 5'-carbon atoms of the sugar. For deoxyribose derivatives, only two positions are possible, the 3'- and 5'-, since the

2'-hydroxyl has been replaced by a hydrogen atom. All these possible isomeric nucleotides are known; most of them occur in biological material. The structure of the 5'-deoxyribotide of adenine is shown below as a typical example of a purine nucleotide.

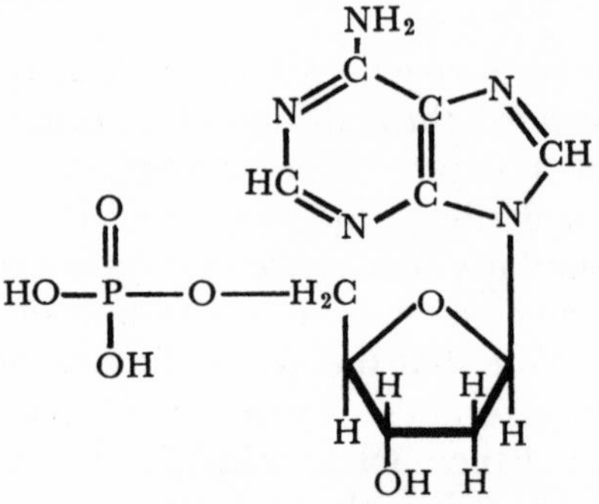

adenine-5'-deoxyribotide
(deoxyadenosine-5'-phosphate)

Nucleoside and Nucleotide Terminology

Most of these compounds were named before their structures were known, hence trivial names have been the rule. Unfortunately, several sets of additional names were applied after the structures were elucidated. All of these are still current and are used interchangeably. The most common designations for the ribosides and 5'-ribotides of the RNA bases are presented in Table 5-1. It should be apparent that the 2'- and 3'-isomers of the ribotides can be named in similar fashion. Also, the names of the deoxy compounds can be formed by adding the prefix *deoxy-*, to give, for example, deoxyadenosine, cytosine deoxyriboside, 2'-deoxyguanylic acid, etc.

NUCLEIC ACID STRUCTURE

The nucleic acids are high-molecular-weight polymers of mononucleotide units, into which they may be converted by hydrolysis under selected conditions. Nucleic acids are often called *polynucleotides*. Titration of a nucleic acid demonstrates that only one of the two acidic groups of the phosphate portion of each mononucleotide is present in free form in the polynucleotide. The second acidic group must then be involved in the internucleotide linkage. Further, certain enzymes catalyze the hydrolysis of nucleic acids quantitatively to the 3'-nucleotides; other similar enzymes yield only the 5'-nucleotides.

Table 5-1. Naming of the Ribosides and 5'-Ribotides of the RNA Bases.

Base	Riboside	5'-Ribotide
Adenine	adenosine adenine riboside	adenosine-5'-phosphate 5'-adenylic acid 5'-adenosine monophosphate (AMP)
Guanine	guanosine guanine riboside	guanosine-5'-phosphate 5'-guanylic acid 5'-guanosine monophosphate (GMP)
Cytosine	cytidine cytosine riboside	cytidine-5'-phosphate 5'-cytidylic acid 5'-cytidine monophosphate (CMP)
Uracil	uridine uracil riboside	uridine-5'-phosphate 5'-uridylic acid 5'-uridine monophosphate (UMP)

Clearly, the nucleotides must be joined one to the other by 3'-5' phosphodiester linkages.

The backbone of the polynucleotide chain thus is formed by alternating pentose and phosphate groups. The various bases are free to project from the chain much as do the side-chains of the amino acid units of a polypeptide. A representation of a portion of a poly-deoxyribotide chain illustrating these features appears as Figure 5-1. A polyribotide has the same basic structure.

We must emphasize that RNA and DNA represent classes of nucleic acids. Within each class are many individual kinds of nucleic acid molecules, differing basically in the proportions of the four nucleotide monomers and in the sequences in which the nucleotides are linked together. Just as the amino acid sequence of a protein is its prime characteristic, so too, as we shall see later, is the nucleotide sequence of a nucleic acid. The variable feature in both cases is the sequential arrangement of the projecting side-groups. We shall describe in a later chapter how this sequential arrangement of bases in the nucleic acid molecules of the cell in effect encodes the genetic information.

The DNA Double Helix

The properties of DNA cannot be completely explained on the basis of a simple polynucleotide chain. For example, the molecules

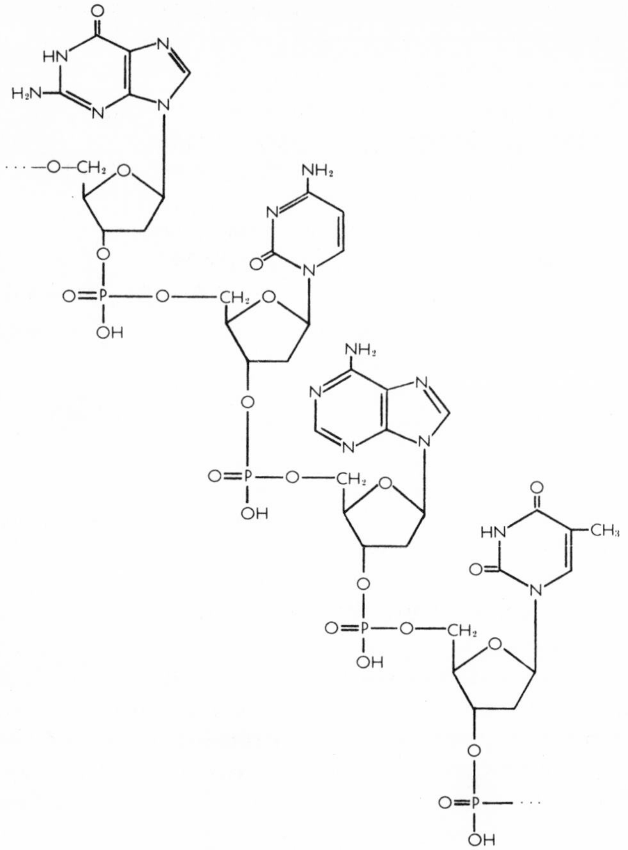

Figure 5-1. A Portion of a DNA Chain.

behave in solution as if they were very long, very rigid rods rather than as the flexible chains we might expect. Also, heating a DNA solution or changing the pH markedly results in great changes in the properties of the molecules. The "denatured" DNA behaves as if it now is a simple, flexible chain. Obviously the native molecule must possess structural features beyond those of the primary structure.

The first model of DNA secondary structure which adequately explained the properties of the molecules was proposed by Crick and Watson in 1953. Certain minor modifications have since been made, but this model has met every test yet applied and is now generally accepted as a valid representation of the actual structure of DNA.

The major features of the Crick-Watson structure for DNA are depicted in Figure 5-2. Briefly, two polydeoxyribotide chains are coiled together in helical array around the same axis. The nitrogen bases of both chains project toward the center of the axis. These bases are all flat or planar molecules. In the DNA double helix the bases are arranged so that the planes in which their atoms lie are all parallel to each other and perpendicular to the central axis (that is, perpendicular to the page in the case of the figure shown). This arrangement, along with the diameter of the helix, is such that the bases of opposite chains can interact to form hydrogen bonds with each other. This bonding provides part of the force required to maintain the two chains in the helical configuration. It is now clear that other forces are involved as well, among them electronic interactions among the stacked bases in a direction parallel to the axis of the helix.

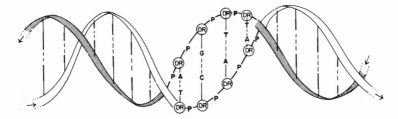

Figure 5-2. A Representation of the Double Helix Structure of a DNA Molecule.

A, T, G, and C represent adenine, thymine, guanine, and cytosine, respectively.

Perhaps the most important aspect of the Crick-Watson proposal is the limitation placed on the base pairs which may form hydrogen bonds. Any of the free mononucleotides can form at least one hydrogen bond with any of the other nucleotides. But the dimensions of the DNA helix and the three-dimensional arrangement of the bases are such that multiple hydrogen bonding can occur only between adenine and thymine or between guanine and cytosine. For the first pair, two hydrogen bonds can form, while three bonds are possible for the guanine-cytosine pair. These interactions are shown in Figure 5-3.

The base-pairing limitation in secondary structure imposes a major restriction on the primary structure of each of the two polydeoxyribotide chains. Each nucleotide unit in one chain must be matched by its base-pair counterpart in the other chain. Every thymine must be matched by an adenine, every adenine by a thymine, every guanine by a cytosine and every cytosine by a guanine. Given the nucleotide sequence of one chain, one could therefore write the sequence of nucleotides in the second chain. The two chains are said to be *complementary* with respect to nucleotide sequence. We will return to consider some of the implications of this point when we discuss the biological role of DNA.

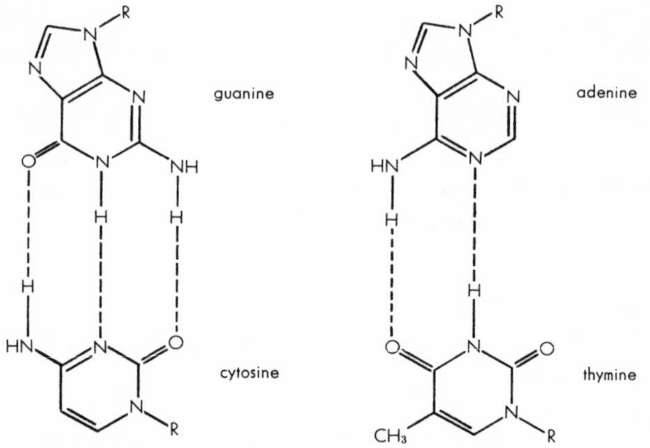

Figure 5-3.   A More Detailed Picture of the Hydrogen Bonding Between the Nitrogen Bases of DNA.

Secondary Structure of RNA

Free RNA generally occurs as single polyribotide chains, probably lacking fixed secondary structure. However, each chain is free to fold back upon itself many times in numerous ways. Some of these folded forms can lead to fortuitous base-pairing between different sections of the chain. This will produce short stretches of a helical nature, similar to DNA, interspersed with areas of random configuration. RNA as it occurs bound to other substances, primarily proteins, in ribosomes and viruses probably has a definite structural alignment.

Soluble-RNA molecules, on the other hand, appear to have precise secondary structures in which many of the bases are hydrogen bonded, although the exact structures are unknown. The simplest picture, probably oversimplified, which is consistent with the available data is one in which the single chain is folded back on itself in one or more hairpin-like bends. The bases at the loops remain free while the remainder form typical base-pairs. Much of the molecule is therefore of helical nature resembling DNA.

Size of Nucleic Acids

The nucleic acids are truly *macro*molecules. The smallest, the soluble-RNA molecules, have molecular weights of about 30,000. This is much like a typical polypeptide chain, but most nucleic acids are much larger. The single RNA chain of a Tobacco Mosaic Virus particle has a molecular weight of somewhat over 2 million, corresponding to about 6,500 nucleotide units. Ribosomal-RNA is of similar size.

The molecular weight of the DNA duplex of T_2-bacteriophage is 130 million, each chain consisting of about 200,000 nucleotide units. The DNA molecules of true cells may have much higher molecular weights. The evidence suggests that all the DNA of the chromosome of the bacterium, *Escherichia coli*, is one unit with a molecular weight of about 10^9. The molecular weights of the purified DNA preparations usually obtained from cells range up to 10 million or so. However, these may be only fragments produced from larger units by the isolation procedures.

NUCLEOTIDES OF METABOLIC IMPORTANCE

In the preceding discussions we have emphasized the nucleotides which are structural components of the nucleic acids. Living cells also contain a variety of low-molecular-weight nucleotides which have important roles as reaction intermediates in the complex, integrated chemical reactions of the cell which we call metabolism. Some of these nucleotides are close chemical relatives of the nucleic acid nucleotides. In others the purine or pyrimidine ring is replaced by some other nitrogen compound.

Nucleoside Triphosphates

Many metabolic reactions involve the transfer of energy from one molecule to another. Commonly this occurs with the transfer of a phosphate group from a nucleoside triphosphate, which then becomes a nucleoside diphosphate.

The most important nucleoside triphosphate is *adenosine triphosphate*, commonly abbreviated at ATP. This compound, shown below, is involved in numerous metabolic reactions. Considerable space will be devoted in a later chapter to the processes by which this compound is formed and utilized in biological systems. The triphosphates of uridine, cytidine, and guanosine (UTP, CTP, and GTP) and of certain deoxyribosides are also of importance in specific reactions occurring in the metabolism of sugars, phospholipids, and related compounds.

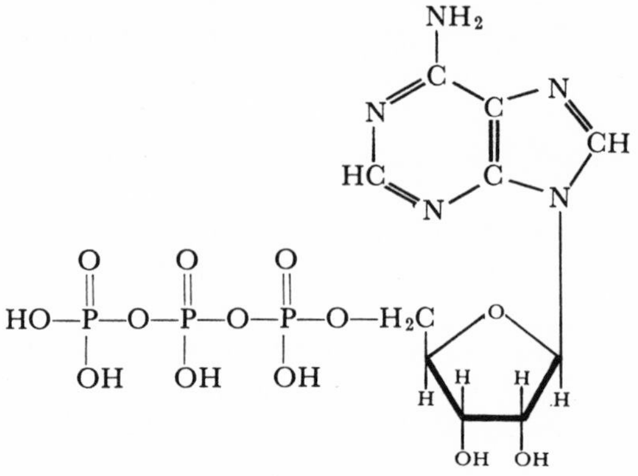

adenosine triphosphate

Note that the phosphate group is connected to the sugar by a typical ester linkage, while the phosphate groups are linked to one another by anhydride bonds.

Oxidation-Reduction Nucleotides

This is a very important group of nucleotides, which are capable of being reversibly oxidized and reduced. They are thus all capable of serving as oxidizing and/or reducing agents, and are found to be intimately involved with essentially all of the oxidation and reduction reactions occurring within living cells. One important example, depicted on the following page, is diphosphopyridine nucleotide (DPN) or nicotinamide adenine dinucleotide (NAD).

First, note that this structure may be regarded as being put together from two nucleotide units: adenosine monophosphate (AMP) and nicotinamide mononucleotide (NMN). This type of structure is generally referred to as a *dinucleotide*.

Secondly, we find here our first example of the active biological form in which a vitamin exerts its specific function, the nicotinamide nucleotide (NMN) portion of DPN being derived from the dietary supply of nicotinamide (niacin amide).

Diphosphopyridine Nucleotide (DPN) or
  Nicotinamide Adenine Dinucleotide (NAD):

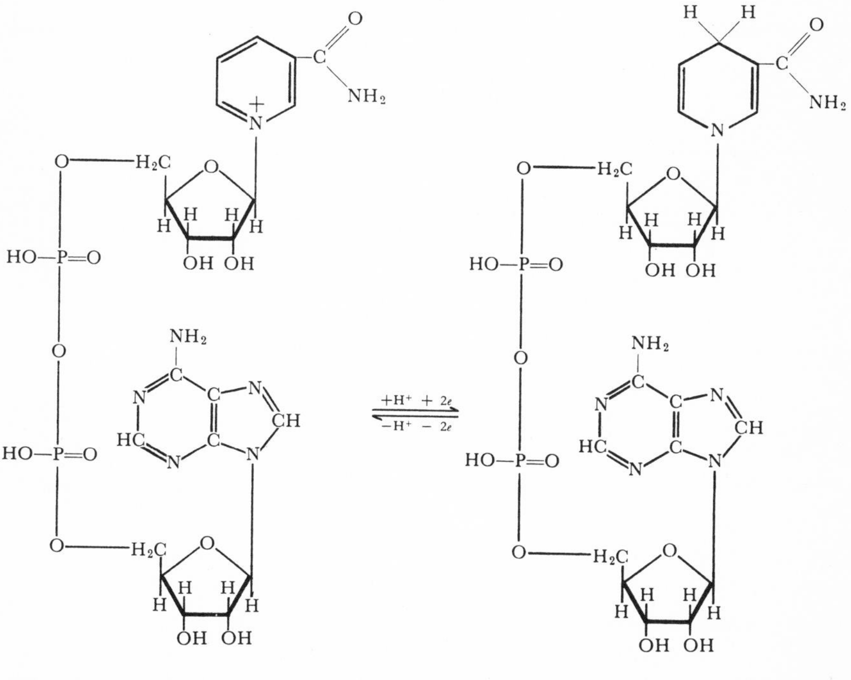

$$+H^+ + 2e \atop -H^+ - 2e$$

DPN$^+$	DPNH
(NAD$^+$)	(NADH)
(oxidized form)	(reduced form)

Triphosphopyridine Nucleotide (TPN) or
  Nicotinamide Adenine Dinucleotide Phosphate (NADP)

The structure of this compound is essentially identical with that of DPN, except that it has in addition a phosphate ester group attached to the 2′-hydroxyl group of the ribose portion of the adenosine unit.

Flavin Adenine Dinucleotide (FAD):

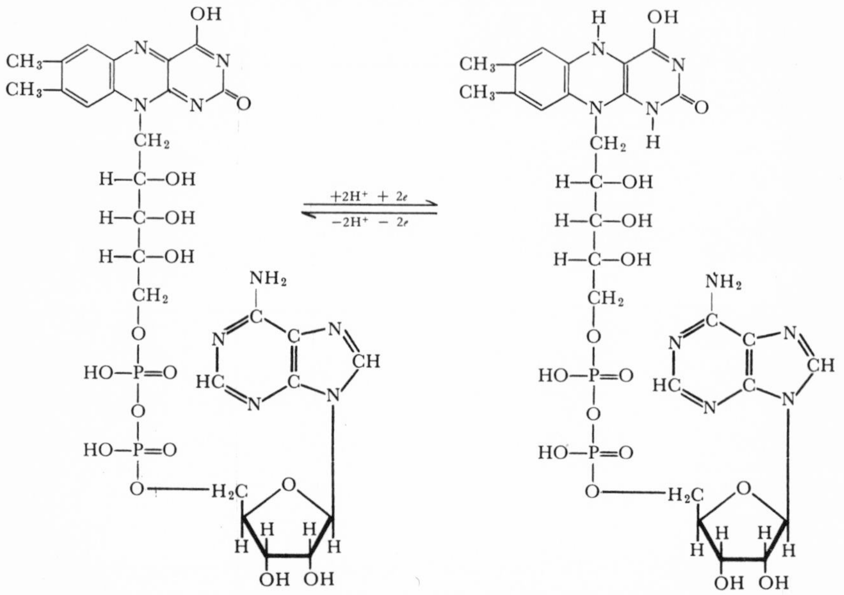

FAD
(oxidized form)

FADH$_2$
(reduced form)

This is another dinucleotide, one half of which is a molecule of AMP. The other nucleotide here is riboflavin-5′-phosphate or flavin mononucleotide (FMN). Actually, riboflavin phosphate is regarded as a nucleotide only as a sort of courtesy; unlike all the other nucleotides, the sugar portion in this case is not a true sugar but rather a sugar alcohol (ribitol).

Flavin Mononucleotide (FMN, Riboflavin-5′-phosphate): This is simply half of the above structure. It is specifically required for certain reactions.

Both FMN and FAD represent metabolically active forms of the vitamin riboflavin (Vitamin B$_2$).

Other Important Nucleotides

Coenzyme A: This is yet another compound, having as part of its structure a molecule of AMP. Coenzyme A is required for a number of the metabolic reactions in which organic acids are involved.

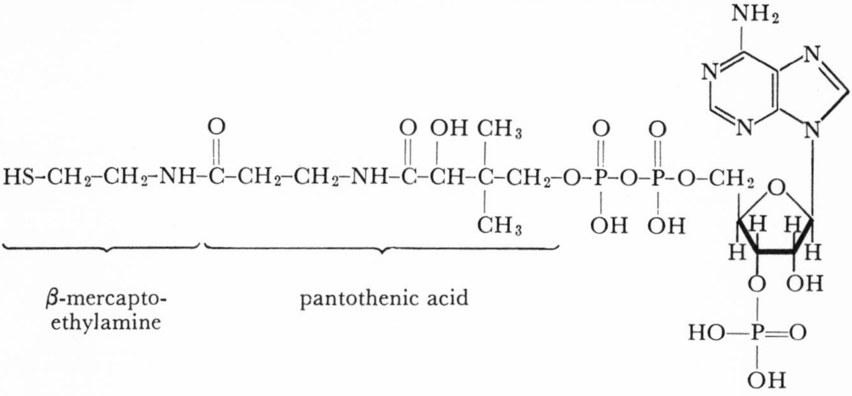

$$\text{HS-CH}_2\text{-CH}_2\text{-NH-}\overset{\overset{\displaystyle O}{\|}}{C}\text{-CH}_2\text{-CH}_2\text{-NH-}\overset{\overset{\displaystyle O}{\|}}{C}\text{-}\overset{\overset{\displaystyle OH}{|}}{CH}\text{-}\overset{\overset{\displaystyle CH_3}{|}}{\underset{\underset{\displaystyle CH_3}{|}}{C}}\text{-CH}_2\text{-O-}\overset{\overset{\displaystyle O}{\|}}{\underset{\underset{\displaystyle OH}{|}}{P}}\text{-O-}\overset{\overset{\displaystyle O}{\|}}{\underset{\underset{\displaystyle OH}{|}}{P}}\text{-O-CH}_2$$

β-mercapto-
ethylamine   pantothenic acid

$$\text{HO—}\overset{}{\underset{\underset{\displaystyle OH}{|}}{P}}\text{=O}$$

   This is also an example of a compound that represents the functional form of a vitamin. In this case the vitamin involved is *pantothenic acid.*

   Vitamin B$_{12}$: One portion of the complex Vitamin B$_{12}$ molecule is a nucleotide having the structure shown below.

   This is the only nucleotide known to occur in nature in which the nitrogen-glycoside bond is an α-linkage. In all other cases, the sugars are present as β-glycosides. The remainder of the Vitamin B$_{12}$ structure is composed chiefly of a cobalt porphyrin complex (cf. chlorophyll, hemoglobin).

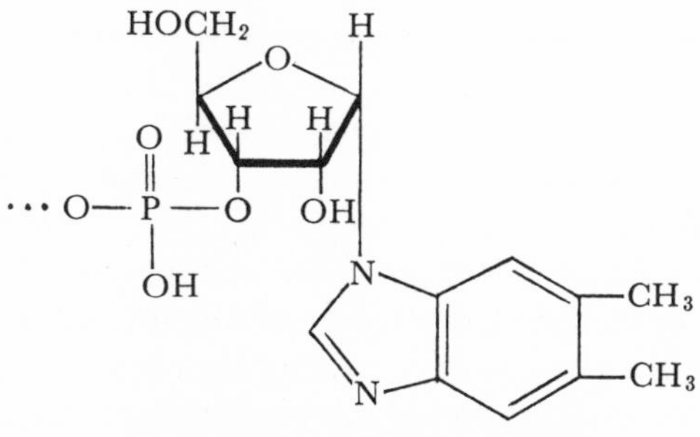

SUGGESTED ADDITIONAL READING

Crick, F. H. C., "Nucleic Acids," *Scientific American*, **197**, No. 3, 188 (September 1957).

Jordan, D. O., "The Chemistry of Nucleic Acids," Butterworths, Washington, 1960.

Potter, V. R., "Nucleic Acid Outlines, Vol. 1, Structure and Metabolism," Burgess Publishing Co., Minneapolis, 1960.

Fraenkel-Conrat, H., "Design and Function at the Threshold of Life: The Viruses," Academic Press, New York and London, 1962.

The Enzymes

6

Most chemical reactions of organic compounds occur very slowly at the low temperatures and the atmospheric pressure under which living cells carry on their life processes. Yet in living cells these reactions proceed at extremely high rates, often very much higher than those the organic chemist could obtain in the laboratory with very high temperatures and pressures. It should be apparent that the reactions in cells must be catalyzed, that is, their rates must be increased by the presence of catalysts. The biological catalysts are called *enzymes*. With no known exceptions, the enzymes are proteins. Furthermore, the enzymes are *specific* catalysts; each enzyme is a certain kind of protein molecule which catalyzes only one particular reaction or at most a group of very closely related reactions.

Enzymes do not require the specific environment obtaining within a living cell for the expression of their catalytic properties, but may be removed from the cell, separated by use of the standard techniques of protein purification, even crystallized, without effect on their catalytic abilities. These abilities must therefore reside solely in the particular structure of the individual protein molecule constituting each enzyme, and the action of enzymes must in turn eventually be capable of complete explanation in chemical terms.

ENZYMES : GENERAL COMMENTS

Every cell must synthesize its own enzymes; being proteins, these molecules can pass through cell membranes only under unusual circumstances. Most of the enzymes produced by a cell operate within that cell and hence are called *endoenzymes*. The sum of all chemical processes occurring within a cell is termed *metabolism*, and the endoenzymes are therefore metabolic enzymes. Certain enzymes are liberated by living cells and catalyze useful reactions in the cell's environment. These are called *exoenzymes;* they act chiefly as digestive enzymes, catalyzing the hydrolysis of complex substances to simpler compounds which can readily be absorbed by the cell.

Life as we know it would be impossible in the absence of biological catalysts such as the enzymes. An understanding of the action of these substances is essential to the understanding of biochemical processes. Before we turn to the examination of these processes, it seems desirable, therefore, to examine the enzymes as a class of compounds, to describe their properties, and to attempt to explain their catalytic abilities.

NAMING OF ENZYMES

While a systematic procedure has been devised for the naming of enzymes, to the point that a given enzyme can be described by a sequence of numbers, the names most commonly used will continue to be what we must now call "trivial" names. For many years it has been common practice in naming a new enzyme to try to indicate the nature of the reaction catalyzed and the specific reacting molecule or group of molecules. The suffix *"ase"* is then added to identify the substance as an enzyme. Thus *L-glutamic dehydrogenase* indicates an enzyme catalyzing a dehydrogenation (H removal; oxidation) reaction involving L-glutamic acid. However, certain enzymes were named before these general rules came into common use, examples being digestive enzymes such as pepsin and trypsin.

In the systematic nomenclature for enzymes developed by the International Union of Biochemistry, all enzymes are divided into six major classes:

1. Oxidoreductases   4. Lyases
2. Transferases   5. Isomerases
3. Hydrolases   6. Ligases (synthetases)

The "lyases" are enzymes which catalyze the removal of structural portions of their substrates (other than by hydrolysis), in the process producing double bonds. Of course, the same enzymes will also catalyze the reverse processes. "Ligases" (also called synthetases) catalyze the joining together of two molecules, usually by a process which involves breakdown of a nucleoside triphosphate or similar compound.

Sub-classes are then developed on the basis of (a) the nature of the substrate and/or the type of reaction involved, and (b) more detailed considerations of coenzymes and acceptors, groups removed or changed, or the nature of the products. The assignment of any given enzyme to major and minor classes and sub-classes can be specified by a series of numbers, the last one simply being its serial number within the sub-sub-class.

This systematic nomenclature is important for the purpose of unequivocally identifying an enzyme, and has the added advantage of permitting numerical identification of each enzyme, a useful feature in this age of computer data handling. However, for general use the common names will continue to predominate.

CLASSIFICATION

Enzymes are commonly classified on the basis of the kinds of reactions which they catalyze, although this leads to some problems because a single reaction may technically fall into more than one class. The list given below indicates the major groups of enzymes which we shall encounter in the study of metabolism.

Oxidation-Reduction Enzymes

These enzymes obviously catalyze reactions in which one compound is oxidized, another reduced. More precisely, they catalyze electron-transfer reactions. *Oxidases* are members of this class in which molecular oxygen is one of the reactants. *Dehydrogenases* are enzymes catalyzing reactions in which the electron transfer is accompanied by the transfer of hydrogen atoms.

Hydrolases

The hydrolases catalyze the hydrolysis of a compound. The subgroup, *esterases*, hydrolyze esters to alcohols and acids. *Lipases* are esterases acting upon triglycerides and related compounds; *phosphatases* catalyze hydrolysis of phosphate esters.

Another subgroup is the *carbohydrases*. These enzymes catalyze the hydrolysis of the acetal linkages in compounds such as di- and polysaccharides and glycosides.

Proteases, or proteolytic enzymes, catalyze the hydrolysis of peptide bonds in proteins and related compounds.

Group-Transfer Enzymes

Enzymes which catalyze the migration of a group from one compound to another are often called *transferases.* Subclasses are named according to the group transferred, e.g., *transaminases, transmethylases, transaldolases,* etc.

Others

The groups given above contain the most members. Many other groups with relatively few examples could be given. The group names are so infrequently used that they will be of little service to us; however, the existence of many other kinds of enzymes should not be overlooked.

CHEMICAL NATURE OF ENZYMES

As we have already stated, enzymes are protein molecules. Some enzymes are simple proteins; others are conjugated proteins. The non-protein (or non-amino acid) part of a conjugated protein is usually called a *prosthetic group.* This term may be used in discussing conjugated protein enzymes, but the term *coenzyme* is more generally employed. This latter term was coined in early work with biological catalysts when it was found that dialysis of some enzymes led to loss of catalytic activity—activity which was regained on mixing the material remaining within the dialysis membrane (a large protein) with the material outside the membrane (a small compound capable of passing through the pores of the membrane). This suggested that the actual catalyst was a conjugated protein which was in ready equilibrium with its two constituents. The intact structure was termed a *holoenzyme,* the protein portion an *apoenzyme,* and the dialyzable component a *coenzyme.*

$$\text{Holoenzyme} \rightleftharpoons \text{apoenzyme} + \text{coenzyme}$$

or:

$$\text{Conjugated protein enzyme} \rightleftharpoons \text{protein} + \text{prosthetic group}$$

Coenzymes and Vitamins

The term *coenzyme* originally meant a substance which had to be present for the activity of the enzyme, without specifying the part played by the substance. Today, many biochemists employ the term *cofactor* in this general way, and reserve coenzyme for those cofactors which have been demonstrated to participate in the catalytic process. Some cofactors may be necessary only indirectly, as in serving to maintain an —SH group of an enzyme in the reduced state. Others may help establish a certain three-dimensional structure necessary for catalytic activity of the protein. These are not coenzymes in the modern sense. Also, coenzyme often is used to designate only organic prosthetic groups, leaving the metal ions of metallo-protein enzymes to be covered by the general description, *cofactor*.

The organic coenzymes are often, but by no means always, of nucleotide structure. Furthermore, many of these compounds, again not all, are composed in part of a vitamin. A *vitamin* may be defined as an organic compound which must be available to an organism in very small amounts from its nutrient materials if normal physiological conditions are to be maintained. This implies that the organism requires the compound for specific metabolic purposes yet cannot synthesize the compound from other available substances. It is becoming increasingly clear that the need for the majority of the vitamins is directly associated with their roles as building-blocks of coenzymes, explaining the marked biological effects of very small quantities of the compounds.

All living cells make use of the same molecules as coenzymes; however, some cells do not have the ability to synthesize completely one or more of these substances. The portions they cannot make are vitamins for these organisms. A given compound can be a vitamin for one organism and not for the next. Therefore it is preferable to use chemical names such as thiamine, even though they be trivial names, rather than designations such as Vitamin B_1. The compound thiamine is needed by all living things as part of a coenzyme; it is a vitamin only for a relatively few organisms. Similarly, ascorbic acid, Vitamin C, is a vitamin only for primates and the guinea pig, although it is necessary in a metabolic sense for a wide variety of organisms. It is important here, as in the cases of essential amino acids and essential fatty acids to be encountered later, to distinguish carefully between the metabolic necessity of a compound and the necessity that it be obtained preformed from the diet or the culture medium.

In this connection, it should be realized that the need for the presence in the diet of a compound such as a vitamin implies that the organism concerned has lost the ability to produce one or more enzymes required for the synthesis of the compound from other simple dietary constituents. The fact that genetic deficiencies of this type are widespread among living organisms implies that they do not present much of a hazard to survival, and that through the history of evolution the necessary compounds were readily obtained from the diet in adequate amounts. However, it should be noted that a diet restricted in amount or in variety of foods may well supply inadequate amounts of a variety of substances, including vitamins.

The vitamins which have been clearly shown to be built into coenzymes are chiefly those which have been grouped as the "B complex." These compounds are related only by virtue of their tendency to occur in high concentrations in the same kind of biological material, and in being soluble in water. The "B complex" and ascorbic acid (Vitamin C) constitute the *water-soluble* vitamins in contrast to those soluble in organic solvents—the *fat-soluble* group which we have discussed previously. This is not the place to detail the physical

Table 6-1.   Relationships Among Water-soluble Vitamins, Their Coenzyme Forms, and Metabolic Reactions in Which They Participate.

Vitamin	Coenzyme	Types of Reactions
Thiamine (B_1)	thiamine pyrophosphate	decarboxylation of α-keto acids; certain reactions of keto sugars.
Riboflavin (B_2)	flavin mononucleotide flavin-adenine-dinucleotide	several kinds of oxidation-reduction reactions.
Pyridoxine (B_6)	pyridoxal phosphate	several kinds of reactions involving amino acids, e.g., decarboxylation, transamination.
Niacin	diphosphopyridine nucleotide triphosphopyridine nucleotide	numerous oxidation-reduction reactions.
Pantothenic acid	Coenzyme A	many reactions of fatty acids, particularly those involving the transfer of acetyl groups.
Biotin	enzyme-bound biotin	certain carbon dioxide fixation reactions.
Folic acid	tetrahydrofolic acid	various reactions involving single carbon compounds.
Cyanocobalamin (B_{12})	several "cobamide" coenzymes	carbon chain isomerizations. certain methyl group transfers

abnormalities which are attendant upon the lack of a particular vitamin. But we *would* like to emphasize that these abnormalities are the result of the inability of the organism to catalyze one or more chemical reactions. A list of the B-complex vitamins, with the names of the coenzymes and some major reactions with which they are associated, is given in Table 6-1.

Inorganic Cofactors

Many of the inorganic substances required by cells, particularly the metal ions, also are needed primarily because of their function as cofactors or coenzymes. This is again consistent with their being needed only in trace amounts, for these are the "trace elements" of animal nutrition, of bacterial culture media, and of fertilizers. Obviously, no organism can synthesize a metal ion; hence these substances, in contrast to vitamins, must be obtained from the environment by all living things.

Typical examples of enzymes requiring metal ions for catalytic activity are: carbonic anhydrase (catalyzing the reaction of CO_2 with H_2O to give H_2CO_3), which requires Zn^{++}; arginase (catalyzing the hydrolysis of arginine to give ornithine and urea), requiring Mn^{++}; and tyrosinase (catalyzing the oxidation of tyrosine) requiring Cu^{++}. Magnesium ion functions as a cofactor for numerous enzymes, particularly those which catalyze reactions of phosphorylated compounds.

POSSIBLE MECHANISMS OF ENZYME CATALYSIS

Any catalyst is a substance which alters the rate at which a chemical reaction approaches equilibrium without itself being consumed in the process. The final equilibrium concentrations are not changed, demonstrating that the catalyst must affect both the forward and reverse reactions to the same degree. Most metabolic reactions are reversible; therefore a single enzyme may catalyze both the net synthesis and the net degradation of a compound at different times, depending upon the relative concentrations of the components of the reaction mixture. This does not imply that all biological compounds are formed and degraded by the same reactions. In fact, we commonly find that the synthesis and degradation processes follow entirely different routes.

An enzyme may generally be studied only in terms of its effect on the rate of the reaction it catalyzes. Usually we do not determine the time required to reach equilibrium, but rather the initial rate, the rate at which the reaction proceeds in the first few minutes before the accumulation of products makes the reverse reaction significant.

A molecule undergoing, or capable of undergoing, a particular enzyme-catalyzed reaction is termed a *substrate* of that enzyme. If we carry out a series of experiments, identical in all ways except that the initial substrate concentration is varied, we obtain results typified by Figure 6-1. Here the reaction rate must be determined by analysis either for the amount of product formed or for the amount of substrate which reacted in a given time period.

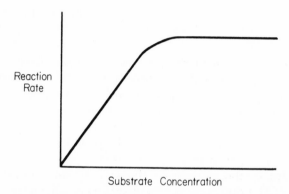

Reaction Rate

Substrate Concentration

Figure 6-1. The Effect of Substrate Concentration on the Rate of an Enzyme-catalyzed Reaction.

At high substrate concentrations, the rate remains constant in spite of further increases in concentration. To the early biochemists, this was an anomalous finding. In general in chemical reactions, as the concentrations of the reactants are increased a corresponding increase in reaction rate is observed. In the case of enzymic reactions, we see this only for relatively low substrate concentrations. This apparent anomaly could be explained only by assuming that the enzyme was an active participant in the reaction process, rather than a passive component of the reaction mixture. Furthermore, it was then necessary to assume that the over-all reaction occurred, not as a single step, but as a multistep process. For example, a hydrolysis reaction might be written simply as:

$$S + H_2O \overset{E}{\rightleftharpoons} P_1 + P_2$$

This tends to convey the erroneous impression that the effect of the enzyme, E, on the rate of hydrolysis of the substrate, S, to the products, P_1 and P_2, is simply a reflection of its physical presence. The assumptions given above led to the suggestion that the actual process was of the following nature.

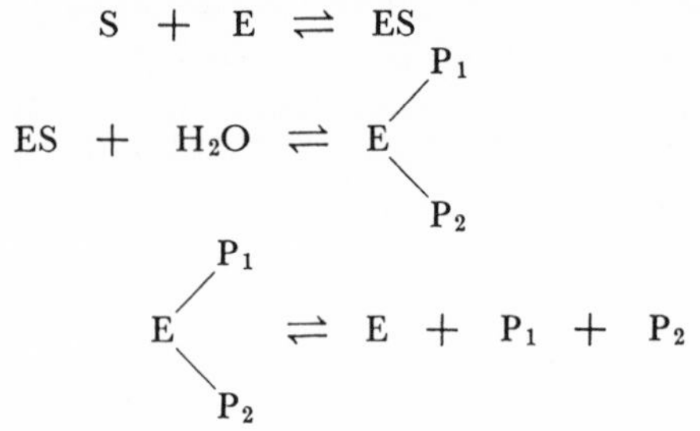

$$S \;+\; E \;\rightleftharpoons\; ES$$

$$ES \;+\; H_2O \;\rightleftharpoons\; E \Big\langle {}^{P_1}_{P_2}$$

$$E \Big\langle {}^{P_1}_{P_2} \;\rightleftharpoons\; E \;+\; P_1 \;+\; P_2$$

In this representation of the process, it is clear that the enzyme molecule must combine with the substrate as a prelude to the actual hydrolysis, giving a new compound which is termed the enzyme-substrate intermediate. This enzyme-substrate compound then undergoes hydrolysis of a susceptible bond, yielding yet another substance, the enzyme-product complex. Finally, the products are released from the enzyme, leaving it in its original state.

This picture of the enzyme-catalyzed reaction provides a ready explanation of the observed effects of substrate concentration on the reaction rate. To show this, let us first simplify the equations shown above to a more general form.

$$E \;+\; S \;\rightleftharpoons\; ES \;\rightarrow\; E \;+\; \text{Products}$$

Here consideration is being restricted to the initial stage of the reaction, when the concentration of products is so low that the interaction of the products with the enzyme can be ignored as an effect on the rate. Thus, $ES \longrightarrow P$ is not depicted as a reversible process in the reactions shown above.

Clearly the rate of appearance of products at any instant should be directly proportional to the concentration of the enzyme-substrate compound. The problem reduces then to that of understanding how the concentration of this intermediate changes as the substrate concentration is changed. If we examine the first step alone, the equilibrium reaction of E and S to give ES, we should expect that an increase in S, at low concentrations, would be accompanied by a shift in the equilibrium to give a higher concentration of ES and thus a higher rate of reaction. But as S continues to be increased, a maximum concentration of ES should eventually be reached since this value can never exceed the total concentration of the enzyme. The amount of enzyme present therefore determines the maximum concentration of ES. A further increase in S beyond the point at which essentially all of the enzyme is in the form of the ES compound cannot appreciably increase the reaction rate, and a plateau in the graph of rate versus substrate concentration should result.

Our qualitative observations agree closely with the experimental observations depicted in Figure 6-1. A quantitative treatment is furnished at the end of this chapter for those wishing more information.

This picture of enzyme-catalyzed reactions, indeed of all catalyzed reactions, as involving an intermediate combination of the catalyst with at least one of the reactants, has received ample confirmation and is now widely accepted. Furthermore, it has been demonstrated that the usual interaction of an enzyme and its substrate occurs at a specific location on the protein molecule. This portion of the enzyme with which the substrate or substrates combine and at which the transformation of substrate to product occurs, is called the *active site* of the enzyme.

It also seems clear that in most cases the interaction of the enzyme and substrate involves multiple bonding. This leads to a ready explanation of enzyme specificity, for it implies that in order for the enzyme to accept a given molecule as a substrate, the molecule must have a number of functional groups so arranged in space that each can simultaneously interact with correspondingly specific functional groups of the enzyme. These reactive groups of the enzyme have a relatively fixed arrangement in space—fixed by virtue of the specific folding of the protein chain. The absolute specificity of some enzymes toward one of a pair of DL isomers seemingly can be explained only by assuming that at least three groups of the substrate must interact with three groups of the enzyme.

Many kinds of enzyme-substrate interaction are possible: covalent bonds, hydrogen bonds, charge dipoles, etc.—the same forces that are involved in determining protein structure. Figure 6-2 presents an entirely imaginary, but entirely possible example of an enzyme-substrate intermediate in which a thiohemiacetal bond, a charge dipole, and a hydrogen bond are involved.

This idea of the specific, multiple interaction of enzyme and substrate as a necessary preliminary also provides a clear explanation of the observed sensitivity of enyzmes to any condition which would denature the protein, i.e., alter its specific three-dimensional structure. Upon denaturation, the necessary functional groups would no longer have the requisite arrangement in space for correct combination with the substrate.

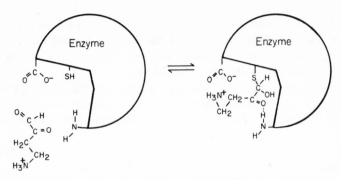

Figure 6-2. Formation of a Hypothetical Enzyme-Substrate Intermediate.

A great number of enzyme-catalyzed reactions are bimolecular in nature, i.e., they involve a reaction between two different substrate molecules. In many of these cases, the two reacting molecules must both be bound to the enzyme, bound in such a way that the reacting portions of the molecules are very close together. The active site of such an enzyme would include the binding sites of both substrates.

The picture of the interaction of enzyme and substrate which has been presented should, if the picture is an accurate one, be capable of leading us toward an explanation of the basic question of catalysis— what is the cause of the increased reaction rate? Although a specific, mechanistic explanation cannot yet be provided for any enzyme, a number of possibilities, based on the fundamental assumption of the specific combination of the enzyme with its substrate, have become evident.

Perhaps the most important of these possible explanations of the enzymatic process is derived from the realization that a substrate bound to an enzyme can differ greatly from a substrate molecule in the free state. The reactivity of any molecule is determined by a number of factors, among them the distribution of electrons in space around the various atoms. You will recall that bonds among atoms are basically electronic in nature. It should be apparent, then, that multiple bonding of enzyme and substrate, also involving interactions of electrons with atoms, will produce a change in the distribution of electrons among the atoms of the original substrate. The specific interaction of enzyme and substrate can lead in this way to a specific electron redistribution, increasing the reactivity of a discrete portion of the substrate molecule.

A second factor to consider is the necessity that two molecules must collide in order for a reaction between them to occur. Furthermore, among organic molecules simple molecular collision is not enough; rather, the collisions which can lead to reactions are only those in which the reacting groups of the molecules are brought close together for a time period sufficiently long for interaction to occur. The enzyme, therefore, can expedite a reaction simply by binding one substrate, holding it in place until the second substrate comes by, and then binding this second substrate in a manner which insures that the reacting groups are brought together. In effect, the probability of the two substrates colliding in the correct way is increased, and this correct relationship is maintained until the reaction takes place.

A number of other factors tending to explain the catalytic action of an enzyme could be given. However, these become increasingly specific, and thus more restricted to a particular enzyme. The two factors described above are probably of most general importance, each to varying degrees, in many enzyme-catalyzed reactions.

At this stage we should point out that a coenzyme is actually one of the reactants in a bimolecular reaction. The coenzyme may be viewed simply as one of two substrate molecules which interact while bound to the enzyme. It differs in the usual case from the substances most commonly called substrates in being bound more firmly to the apoenzyme both before and after the reaction, and in being restored to its initial state by a second process. A single coenzyme molecule is used over and over again, reacting with a substrate molecule, being regenerated, reacting with a second molecule of the substrate, being regenerated, and so on. This cyclical role of a coenzyme is presented diagrammatically for an oxidation-reduction reaction in Figure 6-3.

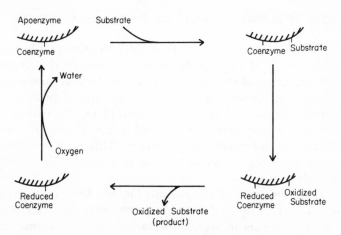

Figure 6-3.   The Cyclic Nature of Coenzyme Action in an Oxidation-Reduction System.

In this example, the coenzyme is seen to undergo reduction and then oxidation while bound to the apoenzyme. In other cases, the reduced coenzyme is released, reoxidized, and then recombined with the protein portion of the enzyme.

Metal-ion cofactors may act in similar fashion; for example, a cupric ion bound to an enzyme may be reduced to a cuprous ion by a reaction with an organic substrate, and then reoxidized by a second reaction with oxygen. Such cases merit the term "coenzyme." In other cases, a metal ion cofactor may serve simply as one of the binding points for a substrate or coenzyme. Magnesium ion, for example, is a cofactor for almost every enzyme having as its substrate a phosphate compound. Presumably the metal ion acts as a bridge to bind the phosphate group of the compound to the enzyme, as in the diagrammatic representation shown in Figure 6-4.

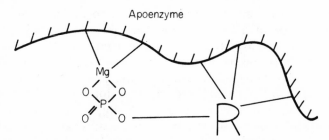

Figure 6-4.   An Illustration of One Possible Role of Metal Ions in Enzymatic Reactions.

FACTORS AFFECTING THE RATES OF ENYZME-CATALYZED REACTIONS

Enzyme-catalyzed processes are subject to appreciable changes in rate as the result of apparently minor changes in the physical and chemical attributes of the solution in which the reactions occur. To a major degree this reflects the unusual sensitivity of protein structure to external influences. The most important factors which alter the rates of enzymic reactions are described below. Recall that one major factor is that of substrate concentration. This was described in another context in an earlier section of this chapter and will not be repeated here.

In considering each of the various factors, keep in mind that the nature of its effect upon the reaction rate must be determined by a series of experiments in which the factor under examination is the only variable. All other experimental conditions should be identical.

Only thus can a specific result be ascribed to a specific cause. In particular, the substrate concentration should be sufficiently high so that it does not change appreciably during the course of the experiment.

Enzyme Concentration

Preceding discussions have emphasized that an enzyme must react chemically with the substrate as the first of a sequence of reactions which ultimately regenerates the enzyme and yields the reaction products. The enzyme is accordingly a reacting molecule, and its concentration should be expected to influence the reaction rate in the same manner as that of the other reactant, the substrate (see p. 99). Therefore we might anticipate that as the enzyme concentration is increased, the rate would also increase to a certain point and then become constant. This should happen theoretically; actually it does not—for practical reasons. Here we must recall that the molecular weight of an enzyme is high, often about 100,000. The preparation of a one-molar solution of an enzyme would therefore require the solution of 100,000 grams of enzyme in water to give a final volume of 1 liter—an obvious impossibility. Under normal conditions the enzyme concentration rarely exceeds 0.001 molar.

Practically, then, we are restricted to working with low concentrations of enzyme. Under these conditions the reaction rate is directly proportional to the concentration of the enzyme, as shown in Figure 6-5.

One further point should be made in connection with this figure. Note that at zero enzyme concentration the rate of reaction is indi-

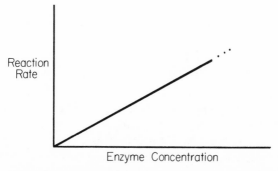

Figure 6-5. The Effect of Enzyme Concentration on the Rate of an Enzyme-catalyzed Reaction.

cated to be zero. It is, of course, not true that reactions do not occur unless enzymes are present. They may be slow, but many occur at a measurable rate. For this reason, in working with enzyme-catalyzed reactions, one always must run a "blank" or "control" experiment in which the enzyme is absent. Any reaction which occurs is then subtracted from that obtained in the presence of the enzyme. The difference between the two values is the effect caused by the enzyme.

The linear relation between enzyme concentration and reaction rate has much practical importance because it allows one to measure the relative concentration of one enzyme in impure protein preparations, or even directly in the great mixtures of proteins in biological materials. We can express this relation as:

$$\text{Rate} = K \times E$$

where E = enzyme concentration and K = a constant of proportionality.

The reaction rate is the amount of reaction which occurs in a unit of time. It is usually measured and expressed as the amount of product formed in a particular time-period.

$$\text{Rate} = \frac{\text{amount of product}}{\text{time of reaction}} = K \times E$$

or

$$E = \frac{\text{amount of product}}{\text{time of reaction} \times K}$$

If we always use the same time-period in studying a particular enzymic reaction, then this too is constant. The product of two constants is, of course, another constant. Let us designate this as C, giving:

$$E = \frac{\text{amount of product}}{C}$$

The enzyme concentration is therefore directly proportional to the amount of product formed when all other factors are identical (including the time allowed for the reaction).

Naturally if in one experiment 0.2 mg of product is formed and in another experiment 0.6 mg, the second case involved three times as much enzyme as the first. Note that we obtain only a relative measure of the enzyme content, not an absolute value. We can convert the relative values to absolute values only if pure enzyme is available as a standard.

Measurements of relative enzyme concentrations are of great importance as aids in the purification of an enzyme for further study. In addition, such measurements are frequently performed in clinical laboratories. Deviations from the normal concentrations of a variety of enzymes in blood reflect the presence of certain disease states. Enzyme measurements are therefore a useful diagnostic tool.

Temperature

Experiments designed to determine the effect of temperature on the rate of an enzyme-catalyzed reaction often give data of the type presented in graphical form in Figure 6-6. Note that at $0°C$ the rate is close to zero. As the temperature is raised the reaction rate increases until a maximum is reached. At still higher temperatures the rate decreases very rapidly back toward zero. The temperature at which the maximum rate is observed is termed the *optimum* temperature.

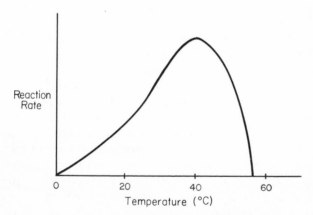

Figure 6-6. Typical Effect of Temperature on the Rate of an Enzyme-catalyzed Reaction.

The form of the graph shown in Figure 6-6 suggests at once that two factors are operating—one, predominant at low temperatures, acting to increase the rate, and one predominant at high temperatures, tending to decrease it. The first factor is the typical increase in reaction rate with increased temperature found for most chemical reactions. This is due to the greater energy of the molecules at higher temperatures, enhancing both the inherent reactivity of the molecules and the frequency of their collisions. The temperature coefficient (the Q_{10}) for such a reaction is often of the order of 2; that is, the reaction rate is doubled for each $10°C$ increase. In the figure shown, this general phenomenon is followed closely until a temperature near 30°C is reached.

The second factor is that of enzyme denaturation. Enzymes are of course proteins, molecules of almost unique complexity whose structures are maintained in major part by relatively weak forces. As the result of this structural complexity the temperature coefficient for the rate of denaturation of an enzyme for a 10°C change in temperature may be of the order of 10 rather than the usual 2. As a few of the secondary bonds responsible for maintaining the native configuration are broken by the increased thermal activity, it becomes increasingly easy for more bonds to rupture, until finally a point is reached at which the entire structure collapses to a random chain.

Because of the high Q_{10} for denaturation, an enzyme may be stable for weeks at 0°, days at 10°, hours at 30°, but only a few seconds at 70°C. You should be able to calculate that the rate of denaturation at 70°C would be one million times that at 10°, assuming a Q_{10} equal to 10.

The rapidly increasing rate of enzyme denaturation and the accompanying loss of catalytic activity is responsible for the rapid decrease in reaction rate shown in Figure 6-6 for temperatures above 40°C.

The optimum temperature is simply the temperature at which the two opposing factors reach a balance. It has been traditional to assume that enzymes have optimum temperatures near 38°C, the body temperature of humans. However, the apparent optimum temperature is greatly influenced by experimental conditions. It varies with pH, with the concentration of other compounds of the solution, and particularly with the time allowed for the reaction to proceed before the amount of product is measured. The shorter the time, the higher the optimum temperature. The peak reaction rate may occur at 60° or 70° if a reaction time of a minute or two is used. At these temperatures the enzyme is a very active catalyst as long as it lasts; it just doesn't last long. If we waited ten minutes before measuring the amount of product, no active enzyme may have been present for the last nine, all the product being formed in the first minute. The average rate for the 10-minute period is obviously only one tenth of the actual rate for the first minute.

Also, different enzymes are affected to different degrees by temperature. Small, simple proteins are much less subject to denaturation than large, complex ones. Also, the greater the content of disulfide linkages the more stable an enzyme will be. These bonds are not subject to thermal disruption at the temperatures used in this type of experiment. Consequently they tend to maintain the basic structure of the molecule. Even if secondary bonds are broken, there is a much greater chance for them to reform in the original pattern.

It may be of interest to note that a number of enzymes of microorganisms living in hot springs have been shown to resist denaturation to a greater degree than the usual animal enzymes, thus having higher optimum temperatures under the same conditions. However, for most higher organisms, it does appear that temperatures near 40°C are the most efficient. This is not simply because 40°C is the optimum temperature for the enzymes, but a major factor does seem to be that near this temperature the best balance between reaction rates and denaturation rates is obtained. The denaturation rates, of course, must be held to a level at which they do not seriously strain the capacity of the organism to synthesize new enzyme molecules.

We would like to draw your attention to one further aspect of Figure 6-6—the fact that the reaction rate approaches zero at 0°C. It must be realized that as 0°C is neared, water molecules form crystalline aggregates which interfere with the ability of the substrate and enzyme to interact. Of course as soon as the solution is frozen solid, collisions between enzyme and substrate molecules become exceedingly few.

The effect of temperature on enzymatic reactions imposes certain restrictions on the capabilities of living organisms. Remember that the activities of organisms, including all physical activities, are based on enzyme-catalyzed reactions. Therefore a change in the temperature of their environment will have marked effects upon the metabolic and physical activities of "cold-blooded" organisms—those unable to control their internal temperatures to an appreciable extent. These creatures expire rather quickly on being exposed to high temperatures because their enzymes and other proteins are rapidly denatured. Pasteurization is a common example of the useful application of this fact, useful to us but not to the bacteria! Similarly a rattlesnake will soon die if it is kept in the direct rays of a Death Valley summer sun.

On the other hand, "cold-blooded" organisms become sluggish and even completely dormant as the environmental temperature is lowered toward the freezing point because the rates of all their metabolic processes are greatly reduced. This does permit survival through a frigid winter, the food requirement needed to maintain the lowered activity being met by reserve materials stored in the tissues.

The "warm-blooded" animals have mechanisms which normally stabilize their internal temperatures within quite narrow ranges. Within limits, these organisms are capable of essentially constant metabolic activity regardless of wide variations in environmental temperature, permitting them to be physically active in all seasons and in all climates. Counteracting these advantages to some extent is the inability of most warm-blooded animals to survive very long under conditions wherein their body temperatures do change significantly. However, true hibernation, such as by the chipmunk, is accompanied by significant lowering of body temperature.

Hydrogen Ion Concentration

The hydrogen ion concentration of an enzyme solution also has a marked effect on the enzyme activity. Low catalytic activities are usually found in quite acidic or basic solutions. These effects are due in major degree to the gross denaturation of the enzyme protein. However, denaturation is not the whole explanation for the striking changes of activity shown by many enzymes with only minor changes in pH, a phenomenon illustrated in Figure 6-7. Rather, this involves a change in the degree of ionization of functional groups of the enzyme. If we assume, for example, that a positively charged group and a negatively charged group are necessary at the active site of a particular enzyme in order for the enzyme-substrate intermediate to form, then any enzyme molecule in which one or the other of these groups is uncharged would be catalytically inactive. Of course, changes in ionization of other groups of the protein may lead to minor alterations in structure with attendant alterations in catalytic activity.

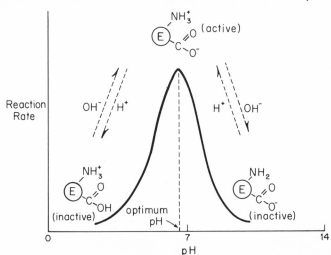

Figure 6-7.   Typical Effect of pH on the Rate of an Enzyme-catalyzed Reaction.

Another common effect of pH variation is upon the substrate molecule. Many of these compounds are also of ionic nature, just like the enzyme. The concentration of any particular one of the various possible ionic forms, as well as the uncharged form, will vary as the pH is altered. Only one of these various forms may be able to combine with the active site of the enzyme. Accordingly, the *effective* substrate concentration is a function of the pH even though the total amount of substrate is constant.

Other conditions being equal, the maximum rate of the reaction will be obtained at a pH which provides for the best balance among these different effects. This is termed the *optimum pH*. This optimum varies widely from one enzyme to another, depending upon the precise structure of the enzyme and the nature of the ionizable groups of both enzyme and substrate. Most enzymes have optima in the pH range of 5 to 8; however, some few are most active in very acidic media, others in quite alkaline solutions. In the living organism, then, the pH will not necessarily be at the optimum for each enzyme. Any change in pH will obviously alter the balance of enzyme activities. If cells are to maintain metabolic control, this necessitates control of pH within rather narrow limits, usually near neutrality, by the selective excretion of acids or bases. In higher organisms, the pH of the extracellular fluids must also be under control. Buffer systems are here the first line of defense against pH change, but ultimately the organism must be able to excrete preferentially the excess of acid or base.

Inhibitors

Since enzymes are proteins, they possess a variety of functional groups which are capable of interacting with many different substances. Any such reaction which results in appreciable alteration of the structure of an enzyme is likely to affect its catalytic activity, even though the reaction may not directly involve a group of the active site. In most cases the effect of the reaction is the production of a protein which is a poorer catalyst than the original enzyme. Compounds which adversely affect the rate of enzymic reactions are called *inhibitors* and the process is that of *enzyme inhibition*. Most of the substances commonly referred to as poisons are harmful in that they inhibit one or more essential enzymes.

The inhibitors may be classed in two broad groups. First, compounds or ions which are specific in their effect, inhibiting only one enzyme or several closely related enzymes. And second, substances which are nonspecific, inhibiting many enzymes.

In most cases of specific inhibition, the inhibitor molecule is a structural analog of the normal substrate of the enzyme; that is, it is chemically similar to the substrate. The inhibitor is capable of combining with the active site much as does the substrate, by virtue of its similar structure; yet it is sufficiently different so that it cannot undergo the reaction that would follow the combination of the substrate with the active site. As long as the active site is bound to the inhibitor, the enzyme is not a catalyst. However, most such combinations are equilibrium situations. In a solution containing enzyme (E), inhibitor (I), and substrate (S) molecules, the following equilibria would occur:

$$\begin{array}{c} \text{E} \;+\; \text{S} \;\rightleftharpoons\; \text{ES} \;\rightarrow\; \text{E} \;+\; \text{products} \\ + \\ \text{I} \\ \updownarrow \\ \text{EI} \end{array}$$

A major factor determining whether an enzyme molecule combines with I or with S will be the relative concentrations of these two substances. Inasmuch as both are in a sense competing for combination with the same active site, the term *competitive inhibition* is often used. Most cases of specific inhibition are competitive in nature.

The phenomenon of specific inhibition of enzymes is one of great practical importance. It is employed whenever one wishes to prevent the growth of one organism in the presence of another—bacteria in an animal, crabgrass in a lawn, the lamprey eel in a trout stream, or the insects on a fruit tree. The basis of these effects is usually the presence in one organism of an enzyme which catalyzes a necessary metabolic process and which can be inhibited by a suitable compound. The second organism either does not require the particular process or is able to accomplish it by a different mechanism, using different enzymes. This second organism will not be affected by the inhibitor; the growth of the first will be slowed, even halted.

The classical example of such inhibition is provided by the class of compounds called the sulfa drugs. These are structural analogs of para-aminobenzoic acid, a compound required by many bacteria for certain metabolic processes but which is not used by higher organisms such as man. The sulfa drugs inhibit growth of the bacteria in man by competing with the para-aminobenzoic acid for the active site of some bacterial enzyme.

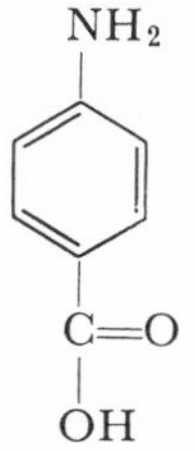

NH$_2$

C=O

OH

para-aminobenzoic
acid

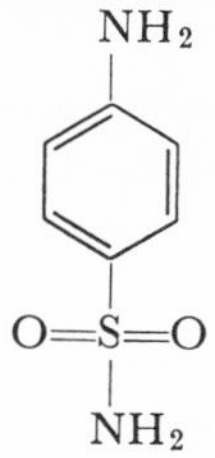

NH$_2$

O=S=O

NH$_2$

sulfanilamide

Absolutely specific inhibitors are rare because most organisms use the same kinds of enzymes for the same purposes. However, small differences in a single kind of enzyme do occur from organism to organism, leading to differing degrees of inhibition by a competitive inhibitor. Rather than an all-or-none situation, we usually find that a compound may inhibit one organism strongly, another only slightly.

NONSPECIFIC INHIBITION

Every protein molecule has a number of reactive groups present as side chains of the constituent amino acids, groups such as —CO$_2$H, —SH, —NH$_2$, etc. Any substance capable of combining with a common group of this type is a potential inhibitor of all, or at least of a great number, of enzymes. In other words, such substances are likely to be nonspecific inhibitors. Heavy-metal ions are a common example of this type of inhibitor. These can bind rather strongly to a number of protein groups, in particular —SH and —CO$_2$H. Should such binding alter the three-dimensional arrangement of the protein or involve groups at the active site, impairment of the catalytic ability of the enzyme would obviously result. In sufficient concentration, heavy-metal ions will inhibit most enzymes and are therefore poisonous to all living things. We should note again that some of these same heavy-metal ions, Cu^{++}, Zn^{++}, Co^{++} for example, are absolute requirements in low concentrations for cells as cofactors for a variety of enzymes. Obviously, the classification of a substance as a poison is dependent on its concentration.

Most, but certainly not all, nonspecific inhibition is *noncompetitive* in nature; that is, the inhibitor cannot be displaced from the enzyme by the substrate, often because the inhibitor has reacted at a site other than the active site. Even though the active site may still be available for combination with substrate, no reaction of the substrate will occur, because the nature of the active site has been altered by the interaction of the protein and the inhibitor.

Activators

In some cases the addition of a substance to a solution containing an active enzyme gives enhanced catalytic activity. This process is called *enzyme activation* and the substances which produce such effects are called *activators*.

Some examples of the activation of enzymes represent cases in which the combination of an enzyme with another compound yields an altered protein which is a better catalyst than the original one. For example, chloride ion is highly stimulatory to the activity of α-amylase, an enzyme catalyzing the hydrolysis of glucose polymers, and phosphate ion produces a further enhancement of activity.

Some examples which are commonly described as activation probably represent the restoration of a cofactor which has been lost by some of the enzyme molecules in the course of their isolation. Metal-ion cofactors are sometimes called activators, for example.

In still other cases the activator reacts with an inactive, altered protein to restore the original state. For example, H_2S is an activator for several enzymes, as they are usually isolated. The H_2S may act in two ways; by reacting with and removing metal-ion inhibitors or by reducing disulfide bonds to the sulfhydryl stage.

A final phenomenon also described as activation is a normal biological process. A variety of enzymes, particularly those involved in digestive reactions and in the coagulation of blood, are synthesized in inactive forms. A specific chemical reaction, often catalyzed by another enzyme, is necessary to convert the inactive species to active enzyme. The inactive forms are called *zymogens* or *proenzymes*. This type of enzyme activation generally appears to involve the cleavage of a particular peptide bond. The rearrangement of the structure of the remaining molecule yields the catalytically active protein.

Allosteric Effects

We have mentioned several times that an activator or inhibitor can alter the catalytic efficiency of an enzyme by combining with it in a way that results in a change in the conformation of the protein. Such effects are called *allosteric* effects. They appear to be particularly important for enzymes comprised of more than one peptide chain sub-unit. The combination of a compound with one of the sub-units alters the interaction of the various units of the complete protein so that the nature of the active site or access to the active site is changed. The inhibitor or activator may combine with the protein at a site far from that which binds the substrate, often on a different peptide chain of multi-unit enzymes.

A major reason for recent interest in allosteric effects has been the discovery that they are of considerable importance in the metabolic control processes of living organisms. Many normal cell metabolites are now known to act as allosteric activators or inhibitors of various enzymes. Thus the enzymatic activities of living cells change in response to changes in the concentration of cell metabolites. We shall defer further discussion of these aspects to Chapter 13.

The Michaelis Equation

Early in this chapter we discussed in qualitative terms the variation in the rate of an enzyme-catalyzed reaction with variation in substrate concentration. The first satisfactory quantitative treatment of this subject was provided by Michaelis and Menten in 1913 with the development of an equation which is commonly called the Michaelis Equation.

This equation can be derived rather simply with the aid of certain assumptions. The first of these is that the enzymatic process occurs as a stepwise set of reactions, which can be depicted in the early stages as

$$E \;+\; S \;\rightleftharpoons\; ES \;\rightarrow\; E \;+\; P$$

The second assumption made by Michaelis, now known to be essentially correct for most, but not all, enzymes, is that the process of reaching equilibrium between E, S, and ES is quite rapid compared to the rate of reaction of ES to give free enzyme and products.

One might expect no problems in describing the kinetics of these reactions in mathematical terms; indeed there is no theoretical problem, only a practical one. The difficulty arises from our own inability in most cases to determine the concentration of the enzyme-substrate complex, or even the concentration of the enzyme. This was particularly true in Michaelis' day. The success of his derivation lay in replacing these immeasurable quantities with ones that could be measured experimentally.

We noted earlier that the rate of appearance of products, v (for *velocity*), should be proportional to the concentration of the enzyme-substrate complex, ES.

(1) $$v = k \text{ x ES}$$

For simplicity we shall omit the brackets generally used to indicate that it is the molar concentration of the substance that is intended. Remember that in these equations the symbols ES, S, and E refer to the *molar concentrations* of the enzyme-substrate complex, the substrate, and the enzyme respectively.

The maximum reaction rate possible, V_{max}, will occur at a substrate concentration sufficiently high so that essentially all of the enzyme is bound to substrate. The maximum concentration of ES which is possible is thus equal to the total enzyme concentration, and accordingly,

(2) $$V_{max} = k \text{ x } E_{Total}$$

Dividing equation 1 by equation 2 gives

(3)
$$\frac{v}{V_{max}} = \frac{ES}{E_{Total}}$$

Here we have an equation which allows us to express the immeasurable quantities ES and E_{Total} in terms of reaction rates that can be experimentally measured.

Turning now to the first step in the enzymatic process, we can write the equilibrium constant for the dissociation of the ES complex as

(4)
$$K_m = \frac{E \times S}{ES}$$

This gives us a second equation containing the quantity ES, but with E rather than E_{Total}. Here E must be the concentration of *free* enzyme. But E_{Total}, ES, and E are related in the following way:

(5)
$$E = E_{Total} - ES$$

Substituting this value for E in 4 gives

(6)
$$K_m = \frac{(E_{Total} - ES) \times S}{ES}$$

Algebraic rearrangement of equation 6 yields

(7)
$$\frac{ES}{E_{Total}} = \frac{S}{K_m + S}$$

Now equation 3 can be used to eliminate the enzyme concentrations, giving

(8)
$$\frac{v}{V_{max}} = \frac{S}{K_m + S}$$

Equation 8, the Michaelis Equation, adequately describes the kinetics of most enzyme-catalyzed reactions. One can use this equation and experimentally determined reaction rates at various substrate concentrations to calculate K_m. This equilibrium constant, usually called the Michaelis constant, is a measure (in the ideal case) of the affinity of an enzyme for its substrate. The more strongly an enzyme interacts with its substrate, the greater will be the proportion of the enzyme which is combined with substrate as ES, the lower the concentration of free enzyme, E, and the lower the value for K_m. This can readily be understood by the examination of equation 4. Note that the lower the K_m, the greater the affinity of enzyme and substrate. Typical values for the Michaelis constants of various enzyme-substrate pairs range from 10^{-2} to 10^{-6} molar.

Lineweaver-Burk Plots

The major application of the Michaelis equation has been in the study of enzyme inhibition, particularly as an aid in distinguishing between competitive and non-competitive inhibition. An approach widely used is a *Lineweaver-Burk* or *double-re-*

ciprocal graph obtained from reaction rates at various substrate concentrations in the absence and in the presence of the inhibitor.

The Michaelis equation can be rewritten as

$$v = \frac{V_{max} \times S}{K_m + S} \qquad \text{i.e.,} \qquad \frac{1}{v} = \frac{K_m + S}{V_{max} \times S}$$

or

$$\frac{1}{v} = \frac{K_m}{V_{max}} \times \frac{1}{S} + \frac{1}{V_{max}}$$

The final equation is of the form $y = mx + b$ if one considers the variables to be $1/v$ and $1/S$. When one plots the reciprocals of the experimental velocities against the reciprocals of the corresponding substrate concentrations, i.e., $1/v$ *versus* $1/S$, a straight line should result. The slope of the line should be K_m/V_{max} and the $1/v$-intercept should be $1/V_{max}$. While it is not as obvious from the equation in this form, the $1/S$-intercept should be $-1/K_m$. A typical graph of this type is illustrated in Figure 6-8. This procedure provides a graphical means for determining the value of the Michaelis constant; it also permits determination of the maximum rate of the reaction for the amount of enzyme used.

If the experiments are repeated with the same concentration of an inhibitor present in all of the reaction mixtures, new, slower rates will be obtained. The reciprocals of these velocities are again plotted against the reciprocals of the substrate concentrations. The resulting line will commonly be one of the two major possibilities indicated in Figure 6-8. One of these has the same $1/V$-intercept, that is, the same V_{max}, as in the absence of inhibitor but an apparent increase in the Michaelis constant (a

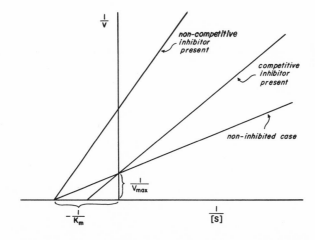

Figure 6-8.   Double Reciprocal Plots Illustrating Competitive and Non-competitive Inhibition.

smaller value for its reciprocal). This we should expect for a case of *competitive inhibition*. The binding of E and S is affected by the inhibitor, but the same maximum rate should be obtained when the concentration of S is very high with respect to the concentration of inhibitor.

The second possibility is a line with the same 1/S-intercept but a different 1/v-intercept; that is, the same Michaelis constant but a different, lower, maximum velocity. This is *non-competitive* inhibition. The observed effect is the same as we would obtain using a lower enzyme concentration without inhibitor. In non-competitive inhibition the *effective* enzyme concentration is lowered because some of the enzyme is present in an inactive form combined with the inhibitor. In this case the percentage of inhibited enzyme molecules is determined only by the ratio of inhibitor to enzyme and is unaffected by variations in the substrate concentration.

SUGGESTED ADDITIONAL READING

Neilands, J. B., and Stumpf, P. K., "Outlines of Enzyme Chemistry," 2nd ed., John Wiley & Sons, New York, 1958.

Gaebler, O. H., Ed., "Enzymes: Units of Biological Structure and Function," Academic Press, New York, 1956.

Ingraham, L. L., "Biochemical Mechanisms," John Wiley & Sons, New York, 1962.

Introduction to
Metabolism

7

Up to this point, our chief concern has been with the chemical nature of the molecular constituents of living cells; the concept that living things are composed solely of chemical compounds and ions has been implicit in the discussion. The remainder of this book will emphasize the chemical activities of living organisms. Here, too, it is important to realize that all of the activities of organisms—their growth, their responses to external stimuli, their movement, their production of new cells and new organisms—are either chemical processes or physical processes based directly on chemical reactions.

In the past there was much resistance to acceptance of the idea that the activities of living organisms could be explained in chemical terms, chiefly because man understood so little of the great complexities of even the simplest living cell. Of course it was apparent that biological material contained chemical compounds and carried out chemical reactions, but the obvious organization of the chemical compounds into cellular structures and the organization of the chemical reactions along precisely controlled lines seemed to be beyond understanding and to require metaphysical interpretation.

The attribute of organization is a central one to the phenomenon of life. Disruption of the organization leads to rapid death. So perhaps it was natural for men to believe that anything so intimately related to life itself could never be described in mundane terms. Yet at the present time, even though our knowledge is barely rudimentary, it has become clear that there are firm chemical bases upon which explanations of the organization of cellular components and of cellular activities can rest. An introduction to these bases follows. Later chapters of this book will consider certain aspects of the question of organization in greater detail.

STRUCTURAL ORGANIZATION OF THE CELL

The living cell is not simply a bag containing a homogenous solution of chemical compounds. Rather, the inspection of a cell by means of light and electron microscopy reveals the presence of many particles or structures. The structures most important to our discussions (by no means all the structures present in cells) are diagrammed in Figure 7-1. Chief among these are the various *membranes* such

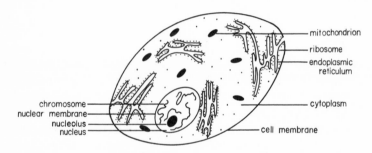

Figure 7-1. A Highly Generalized and Simplified Diagram of an Animal Cell.

as those delimiting the cell and the nucleus, the *mitochondria* and the *ribosomes* of the cytoplasm, and the *chromosomes* of the nucleus. The cells of a green plant would also contain *chloroplasts*, egg-shaped particles somewhat larger than mitochondria.

Even the smallest of these particles is composed of thousands of molecules which interact to form the specific multimolecular aggregates or complexes. The larger particles, such as chloroplasts and mitochondria, can be viewed as specific aggregates of smaller particles. They have surrounding membranes and complex internal structures. A mitochondrion, for example, appears to be divided into a series of compartments by a system of internal, folded membranes called *cristae*. Apparently attached to the cristae are numbers of small dense particles called *electron transport particles*.

A similar situation applies to the cell cytoplasm, which contains a three-dimensional network of membranous material to which the ribosomes appear to be attached. This network is called the *endoplasmic reticulum*.

The details of the physical aspects of the cell structures are beyond the scope of this book. Much further data is available in any text of cytology. Here we wish mainly to emphasize that a variety of different subcellular particles exist, and that these particles are composed of many molecules which interact in a specific fashion to give a particular particle. As generalizations, it is noteworthy that membranes of various sorts are chiefly lipid-protein aggregates, that ribosomes are RNA-protein complexes, and that chromosomes are mainly aggregates of DNA and certain proteins. The other structures are composed essentially of a variety of different proteins.

The factors governing the assemblage of certain numbers of certain kinds of molecules to give a particular subcellular particle are imperfectly understood. However, it seems logical to assume that such aggregation is in major degree a normal chemical result of the structural features of the molecules involved, just as the specific folding of a protein is based on its specific chemical composition. Indeed, the chemical interactions which link molecules together in a particle are in all probability those which we discussed in connection with protein structure—hydrogen bonds, hydrophobic bonds, salt linkages, and the like.

This implies that if we were to disrupt a subcellular particle, the molecules would tend to reassemble in the original pattern, each molecule finding its place like a piece of a jigsaw puzzle. This has not yet been accomplished with the usual cell particles. A major difficulty lies in the separation of the molecules without chemical or physical alteration of their structures. However, the Tobacco Mosaic Virus particle, which is an aggregate of about 2000 apparently identical protein molecules and one giant RNA molecule, can be disrupted into components which will spontaneously recombine to an appreciable extent in the original manner (as shown in Figure 7-2). The heating of a DNA double helix in water results in the cleavage of the hydrogen bonds, yielding the two polynucleotide chains. On cooling the solution, some of the chains reunite to restore the original structure. The hypothesis that the organization of molecules into cellular structures is inherent in the specific chemical nature of the molecules therefore seems to be a valid one.

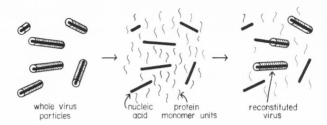

whole virus particles   nucleic acid   protein monomer units   reconstituted virus

Figure 7-2. Disruption and Recombination of Tobacco Mosaic Virus.

ORGANIZATION OF METABOLIC ACTIVITIES

The explanations of the organization of the metabolic activities of living cells rest on rather firm ground, even though we must again emphasize that many of the details are not yet known. Certainly the very efficient protein catalysts, the enzymes, are responsible for much of the organization. With few exceptions, each chemical reaction which occurs in a living cell is catalyzed by a particular kind of enzyme. We have already seen that the presence of these catalysts accounts for the striking rapidity of biochemical reactions (the existence of very high reaction-rates associated with living organisms was another problem which could not be explained until quite recent times). Perhaps it is more difficult to visualize how the enzymes contribute to the *organization* of these processes. Most uncatalyzed reactions are far too slow to be of significance in the chemical economy of the cell. Thus it may be seen that the chemical activities of any cell are limited chiefly to those reactions for which enzymes are available. Cells do not produce enzymes for all possible reactions, only for a relatively limited number. Therefore many processes which are theoretically possible are automatically excluded.

If we examine the chemical reactions which cells perform, we find that very commonly a compound is carried with high efficiency through a long series of consecutive reactions to a definite end-product. Very little of the compound is lost in *random* side-reactions. This is the first step toward organization along specific chemical lines. It should not be difficult to decide that the sequential nature of these reactions and their high efficiency is a result of the presence of certain enzymes. Consider a series of reactions in which A can be converted to B, to C, and finally to D. Ordinarily we might expect, as indicated below, that the various compounds might also undergo a variety of *other* reactions.

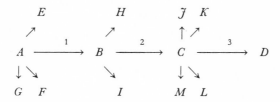

In the absence of catalysts, each possible reaction would proceed at its own inherent rate, and very few molecules of A would be converted to D. But if to this system were added three catalysts, one for each of the reactions designated as 1, 2, and 3, then these would become much more rapid than the others, and A could be converted to D with little loss to side-reactions. This is the situation in living systems. Enzymes are present for each step of long sequences, leading to an organized flow of molecules through these reactions rather than their diversion to random interactions.

Another factor which is sometimes of major importance in the channeling of reactions in certain directions is the physical separation of the enzymes catalyzing one sequence from those catalyzing another. For example, the mitochondria of higher organisms contain within their membranes the enzymes necessary to catalyze certain important oxidative processes. Furthermore, a number of these enzymes occur bound together in the small *electron transport particles*. Accordingly a compound can be carried through a complete sequence without being lost to other areas of the cell at an intermediate stage.

The fundamental question which remains unanswered here is that of how a cell manufactures only certain specific proteins—some which will interact to form specific structures, others which catalyze specific reactions. This we will examine in a later chapter in connection with the general problem of protein synthesis. For the present, it is perhaps sufficient to state that the synthesis of each protein molecule in a cell is under genetic control; and, furthermore, that most genes of a cell are probably involved in the control of its synthesis of protein compounds.

METHODS USED FOR THE STUDY OF METABOLISM

A compound in a cell is generally metabolized very rapidly, through a series of stepwise alterations of its structure, to a substance which may be viewed as an end-product. The end-products of different reaction sequences may be either waste materials to be excreted or necessary functioning components of the cell such as enzyme proteins or nucleic acids. A sequence of reactions of this type is often termed a *metabolic pathway*. The various compounds which are formed in transitory fashion as the original compound is converted to the end-product are called *intermediates* of the pathway.

The study of metabolic pathways must overcome several major obstacles. One of these is the fact that the concentration of each of the intermediate compounds is usually very low, often being only about 10^{-5} molar. The detection, separation, and identification of the compounds are accordingly almost impossible by traditional methods of organic chemistry unless one is prepared to begin with a truckload of material. In addition, many of the intermediates of the various metabolic sequences are rather unstable, easily altered or destroyed by the usual chemical procedures for the separation of organic compounds.

The early biochemists generally could not overcome these obstacles. They were often forced to be content with feeding organisms large quantities of a compound, collecting the excreta, and analyzing these for the presence of compounds which might have been formed from the substance fed.

Cell-Free Systems and Enzyme Inhibitors

A major advance in the study of metabolism was made by Buchner in 1897 with the finding that a complete metabolic pathway could operate in the absence of living cells. Buchner discovered that an extract of yeast rapidly converted glucose to carbon dioxide and ethanol, a process now known to involve 12 consecutive reactions. Prior to this finding, many scientists believed that such processes could not occur in the absence of an organizing "vital force" supplied by the living cell.

With systems such as Buchner's, many experiments which could not be carried out with living organisms became possible. The system could be dialyzed, for example, with the loss of ability to convert (i.e., to *ferment*) the glucose to ethanol and CO_2. Various substances could then be added to the nondialyzable material in attempts to restore its activity. In this way the great importance of phosphate ions in the metabolism of glucose was discovered.

It also became apparent that the use of enzyme inhibitors with such systems could yield valuable information. These experiments were based on the fact that if a reaction sequence is blocked at one of the intermediate steps, the reactions preceding this step will continue to occur. The compound whose further metabolism is blocked becomes the end-product of a shortened sequence of reactions and will tend to accumulate in relatively large quantities, sometimes to the point where it can be isolated and identified.

Again using the fermentation of glucose by an extract of yeast as an example, it was found that if iodoacetic acid were added, the production of ethanol and CO_2 was halted even though the glucose still disappeared. The reaction medium was then found to contain relatively large amounts of the phosphate esters of three-carbon sugars. It was logical to guess that one reaction in the fermentation of glucose was the cleavage of the hexose to two triose derivatives, and that some necessary reaction of these compounds was inhibited by iodoacetate ion. The necessity of phosphate ion for the fermentation process could also be related to the formation of sugar phosphates in some other step.

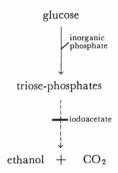

In still other experiments with the same system, the use of fluoride ion as an enzyme inhibitor led to the discovery of glyceric acid-2-phosphate as an intermediate, and the use of bisulfite led to the discovery of acetaldehyde. Furthermore, if acetaldehyde was added to the yeast extract, ethanol was formed but no CO_2. The phosphoglyceric acid and the triose-phosphates, on the other hand, gave rise to both ethanol and CO_2. In this way a general picture of the kinds of reactions occurring was obtained. Guesses could then be made as to other likely intermediates, and the compounds tested to see whether they could indeed be fermented to ethanol and CO_2.

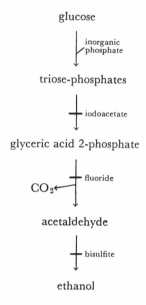

glucose

inorganic phosphate

triose-phosphates

iodoacetate

glyceric acid 2-phosphate

CO_2 fluoride

acetaldehyde

bisulfite

ethanol

The use of cell extracts to unravel the sequence of reactions occurring with the fermentation of glucose has been cited here primarily because of its historical importance. Basically the same methods have been and are still being used in the study of many other systems.

Biochemical Mutants

The use of biochemical mutants is another approach which has been of much value in the study of metabolism. Certain natural mutations (inherited genetic changes) have provided useful data, but the mutations induced in organisms such as bacteria or molds by high-energy radiation have been of greatest service.

A biochemical mutation is generally the loss by the organism of the ability to synthesize a particular enzyme. The reaction normally catalyzed by the enzyme can no longer occur at any appreciable rate, effectively blocking the metabolic pathway at this point. Consider, for example, a sequence:

$$A \; \rightarrow \; B \; \overset{x}{\rightarrow} \; C \; \rightarrow \; D \; \rightarrow \; E$$

Assume that the enzyme catalyzing the production of C from B has been lost by mutation. Compound B would then be expected to accumulate and the production of E would cease. Furthermore, if E is an end-product which is important for other processes in the cell, say an amino acid or a nucleotide, then the microorganism could no longer grow in a simple medium, but could develop normally only if compound E were present in the growth medium.

Given such a biochemical mutant, one has the opportunity to determine which other compounds can be converted to compound E, that is, which compounds are metabolic *precursors* of E. In the example given, the organism could grow if it were provided with either C or D as well as with E, suggesting that they were intermediates of the synthetic pathway.

A different mutant of the same organism might be able to grow in the presence of D, but not in that of C. The conclusion would then be that C is normally converted to D and that in this second case it is the enzyme for this reaction which is lacking.

It is still true that the first clue to the nature of a metabolic pathway is often derived from nutritional studies of this type with mutant organisms.

Radioisotope Tracers

Much of the great progress toward elucidation of metabolic pathways that has been made in the last twenty years has been due to two developments, the use of isotopic compounds and of chromatographic means for separating the components of the cell. Most commonly and most successfully these two techniques have been employed together.

Although a number of isotopes are being used in biochemical research, those of oxygen, sulfur, nitrogen, and hydrogen for example, the isotope of carbon, called *carbon-14* and designated as C^{14}, has been most common and will form the basis of this discussion.

Carbon-14 differs from the normal C^{12} isotope of carbon in that the nucleus of the atom contains two additional neutrons. This is an unstable nucleus and sooner or later will disintegrate with the release of β-rays. Any reasonable quantity of carbon-14 contains so many atoms (recall that 14 grams will be composed of 6.02×10^{23} atoms) that at any given instant it is likely that some few of them will decompose. In effect, a C^{14} sample will emit a continual stream of radiation which can be detected in a variety of ways, most commonly by use of one of several modifications of the Geiger radiation counter.

In most respects carbon-14 resembles the normal carbon-12 quite closely. It can be incorporated into organic compounds, which are then essentially identical with the usual C^{12} compounds except that they are radioactive. A compound containing an isotopic atom is said to be a *labeled* compound.

A labeled compound fed to an organism or placed in a cell extract will be metabolized by the same reactions as the nonlabeled substance. However, the compounds formed from the C^{14}-labeled compound will also contain C^{14} and hence will be radioactive. If we separate the various compounds of the organism and determine which are radioactive, we know that they have been formed from the labeled compound which was originally supplied.

Isotopic compounds can therefore be employed to trace the course of metabolic pathways. This has led to the use of the term *tracer technique* for an experiment of this type. The tracer technique is equally suited for experiments with living organisms and with cell extracts or homogenates.

Chromatographic Separations

Much of the usefulness of the tracer techniques, and of other procedures as well, would be lost in the absence of methods for the separation from each other of the hundreds of compounds found in biological materials. It is not surprising that the development of such methods has proceeded hand in hand with the development of radioactive tracer techniques.

Of the various separation procedures that have been devised, that of *paper chromatography* has been outstanding in simplicity and in general usefulness. The method known as two-dimensional paper chromatography has been particularly valuable for the separation of mixtures containing a large number of compounds.

The first step in this technique is to place a small volume (usually about 0.05 ml) of the solution containing the compounds to be separated on a small area near one corner of a large sheet of filter paper. The paper sheet is then dried and placed so that one edge dips into a trough of solvent, usually a mixture of water and one or more organic solvents. This stage is illustrated in the first part of Figure 7-3.

The solvent will flow slowly, by capillary action, through the paper. When the solvent reaches the spot containing the compounds of the original sample solution, these compounds will usually be subjected to two opposing forces. On the one hand, they will tend to be held at the original spot by one or more types of interaction (such as hydrogen bonding) with hydroxyl groups of the cellulose, or more

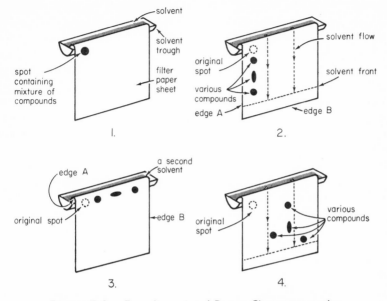

Figure 7-3. Two-dimensional Paper Chromatography.
It must be emphasized that the various compounds will not normally be visible on the paper. They are usually located by spraying the paper with a reagent which will react with the compounds to give colored areas.

commonly perhaps with water molecules which are in turn bound to the cellulose. On the other hand, the various compounds will also tend to be carried away from the original spot by the moving solvent, because there will usually be forces of interaction such as hydrogen bonding, hydrophobic bonding, and the like between the compounds and the molecules of solvent. In a simplified sense, the situation may be viewed as a competition for solution of the compounds between the moving organic compounds and the fixed cellulose-water phase.

The balance of these opposing forces would naturally be expected to be different for different compounds. For example, a compound which is very soluble in the moving solvent and which does not interact with the paper will move with the leading edge of the solvent. A water-soluble (hydrophilic) compound with a low solubility in the organic solvent will move down the paper only at a very slow rate. Compounds having properties between these extremes will move at various intermediate rates. For a mixture of compounds, the result will usually be similar to that shown in part 2 of Figure 7-3; that is, the compounds will be distributed in different areas along the length of the paper.

Sometimes this single development stage is sufficient to bring about separation of the specific compound or compounds in which we are interested, from other materials. With complex mixtures, however, two or more compounds will often be incompletely separated from one another. In this case, the paper sheet is removed from the trough, dried, turned through 90 degrees, and then inserted into a trough containing a second solvent, differing in composition from the one used previously. Part 3 of the figure illustrates this step.

In the new solvent system, a new balance of forces will exist for each of the compounds. Compounds which move at the same rate in the first solvent may be found to differ greatly in their rates in the second solvent. The result, if the solvents have been chosen correctly, will be similar to that shown in part 4 of the figure. Two compounds which occur at one area after the first solvent development have now been separated from one another, completing the separation of the four substances present in the original solution.

The next requirement is that of detecting and locating the compounds. In most cases the completed *chromatogram* is colorless, with no indication of the presence of any compounds. Also the amount of each of the compounds present is commonly of the order of several thousandths of a milligram. Often sensitive color reactions, such as the ninhydrin reaction for amino acids, are used to locate the substances. The reagent is sprayed on the paper, the reaction occurs, and colored spots develop at the site of the compounds.

However, if the solution chromatographed is one derived from a tracer experiment, the compounds of particular interest will be radioactive and can be located either by using a Geiger counter or by placing the paper against a sheet of X-ray film (all in the dark!). The β-rays from the radioactive compounds will expose the film, and on development, the negative will show dark spots at the site of each radioactive compound. Such a developed negative is called a *radioautograph.*

The remaining problem is that of identifying a colored spot or a radioactive area as being due to a particular compound. Of use here is the R_f, the ratio of the distance a compound travels on the paper to the distance traveled by the solvent front. The R_f's of many compounds in various solvents are available in the literature. A new, previously unknown compound requires the most ingenious and delicate chemical sleuthing. Each is a new problem.

Enzyme Studies

Once clues to the nature of the reactions of a metabolic pathway are available, the way is clear for the detailed examination of each step. This normally involves, as a major goal, the isolation of each enzyme in relatively pure form. Naturally, procedures must first be developed for assaying the activity of each enzyme preparation at different stages of purification. Once purified enzymes are available, the precise nature of the reacting molecules and the possible requirements for coenzymes or other cofactors can be determined. The purification of any enzyme is a major task; the detailed description of any metabolic pathway is rarely accomplished by one worker, but is the result of contributions from many laboratories.

INTERRELATION OF METABOLIC PATHWAYS

In a previous section of this chapter we emphasized that most metabolic processes are carried out via highly ordered sequences of reactions. This may suggest that the metabolism of a hexose, an amino acid, and a fatty acid are entirely independent processes. Nothing could be further from the truth. This is easiest to see for a green plant, because the carbon atoms of every compound made by the organism must be derived by sequences of chemical reactions from the same original organic compound, a carbohydrate. But even in animals, the metabolic pathways of all the major compounds are interconnected by a variety of chemical reactions. The carbon atoms of a fatty acid molecule entering a cell may eventually appear as part of an amino acid in a protein, a purine component of DNA, or a sugar unit of a polysaccharide. Similarly, the atoms of a glucose molecule may be incorporated into any of these compounds or into the fatty acid portion of a triglyceride. Any alteration, qualitative or quantitative, in the metabolism of one kind of compound will therefore have far-reaching effects on the metabolism of numerous compounds which may seem to be unrelated.

It is patently impossible to discuss all the concurrent metabolic activities simultaneously. In the following chapters we shall look at the metabolism of carbohydrates, lipids, and nitrogen compounds as units dissected from the complete body of metabolism. Keep in mind as we proceed that these units cannot operate by themselves, but are highly interrelated and interdependent. It is only the limited ability of humans to communicate which makes the piecemeal discussion necessary.

SUGGESTED ADDITIONAL READING

Brachet, J., "The Living Cell," *Scientific American*, **205,** No. 3, 50 (September 1961).

Swanson, C. P., "The Cell," 2nd ed., Prentice-Hall Inc., Englewood Cliffs, N. J., 1964.

Langley, L. L., "Cell Function," Reinhold Publishing Corp., New York, 1961.

Baldwin, E., "Dynamic Aspects of Biochemistry," 3rd ed., The Macmillan Co., New York, 1957.

Heftmann, E., Ed., "Chromatography," Reinhold Publishing Corp., New York, 1961.

Energy Transfer Processes

8

Energy may be defined as the capacity to perform work. Within a system, whether this be the universe, a living cell, or a molecule, energy cannot be created or destroyed. Energy can be transferred, however, from one system to another in a variety of ways, such as by thermal, mechanical, electrical, or chemical means. It is only in conjunction with the transfer of energy by one of these means that work can be performed.

It is obvious that living cells perform work of a mechanical nature. The physical movement of an animal from place to place and the growth of a plant against gravity are common examples of energy-transfer processes which overcome resisting forces. Perhaps it is not so obvious that living cells must do a great amount of work of a chemical nature, work which involves the transfer of energy from one molecule to another. In this respect it is important to realize that the structural components of the cell, as well as many of the other compounds which a cell synthesizes, cannot be formed to any appreciable degree by equilibrium processes. For example, in a cell there is much protein, few free amino acids; yet the equilibrium

$$\text{protein} + H_2O \rightleftharpoons \text{amino acids}$$

lies far toward the amino acid side. This is one illustration of the generality that life is a nonequilibrium phenomenon in the chemical sense. Any such departure from equilibrium conditions can be brought about and maintained only by doing work.

The cell-system will of itself tend to proceed toward equilibrium, as will any isolated system. Therefore the energy required to maintain the nonequilibrium situation must be derived from some other system in the environment of the cell. In the absence of energy-transfer into the cell from some external source, the cellular processes will all proceed toward equilibrium and the cell will die.

Green plants and certain microorganisms obtain the necessary energy as the visible radiant energy which we call light. The source of the light is normally the thermonuclear fusion reactions taking place in the sun. As we shall see later, this radiant energy is used by the plant cells for the synthesis of various organic molecules. In effect, nuclear energy is transformed in the sun into radiant energy and the radiant energy is transformed in the green plant into the energy of molecular structure which we can call chemical energy.

All other living cells fill their need for energy through the assimilation from the environment of chemical compounds with their associated chemical energy. For most cells these compounds are organic substances such as glucose, fatty acids, and amino acids, with glucose playing a major role. The ultimate origin of these materials is obviously the green plant. A few microorganisms are exceptional in that they utilize the chemical energy of inorganic substances such as ammonia, sulfur, or ferrous iron.

Subsequent to the absorption of energy, either as light or as energy of chemical compounds, many consecutive energy-transfer steps take place in order to make possible the synthesis of complex cellular components. It is important to realize that these processes cannot be accomplished by thermal means. A gasoline engine performs work by transfer of energy from the molecules of the fuel to a moving piston. In this case the energy-transfer involves a chemical reaction of oxidative nature. The chemical energy of the reacting molecules is transformed in part into the kinetic energy of the gaseous molecules which are the products of the reaction. This kinetic energy is often referred to as heat. The increase in kinetic energy results in the expansion of the gases, pushing a piston and doing mechanical work. Such changes would be of little help in doing the work necessary in the synthesis of a protein. Furthermore, temperature changes of any appreciable magnitude would lead to the imbalance of enzymic activities and denaturation of the enzymes.

The energy-transfer processes of living cells commonly involve oxidation reactions. However, these must be accomplished at rather constant temperature and under rather constant pressure-volume relationships. These requirements are met by reactions which involve the transfer of energy directly from one molecule to another in the form of chemical rather than kinetic energy. Any energy released as heat is lost to the cell for most chemical purposes, although this heat is important in maintaining the body temperature of a warm-blooded animal.

SIGNIFICANCE OF ADENOSINE TRIPHOSPHATE

In order for a living cell to maintain its normal state, a great number of different kinds of chemical reactions leading to the synthesis of a wide variety of cellular constituents must continually be taking place. These reactions are chiefly energy-requiring processes. They can occur only if energy is made available by energy-yielding reactions. We shall see in later chapters that there are a number of types of reactions which yield chemical energy in a form suitable for use in the synthetic processes of the cell.

As we emphasized in the previous section, the energy-transfers which occur in living cells do not result in the liberation of raw energy but involve reactions which transfer chemical energy from one molecule to another. If the energy available from an energy-yielding process is to be utilized to drive an energy-requiring process, it is necessary that a single chemical compound be a product of the energy-yielding process and a reactant in the energy-requiring process.

It would be theoretically possible to have a metabolic system in which each one of the various energy-yielding reactions is coupled with a specific energy-requiring process. However, obvious advantages would be gained by having a single, common intermediate, one compound which could be formed by all energy-yielding processes and in turn used in all energy-requiring processes. This ideal state is approached in living systems with the use of adenosine triphosphate. All living cells employ this compound, commonly abbreviated as ATP, as the major intermediate in energy-transfer processes. The energy-yielding reactions, such as occur with the absorption of light by chlorophyll or with the oxidation of molecules such as glucose, are linked to the production of ATP from adenosine diphosphate (ADP) and inorganic phosphate ion (P_i). The energy-requiring reactions, such as the contraction of a muscle fiber or the absorption of glucose through a cell membrane are in turn linked to the cleavage of ATP to give ADP and ultimately phosphate ion. In essence, energy is transferred to ADP and P_i to produce ATP, and then the energy is

$$NH_2$$

adenosine triphosphate (ATP)

transferred from ATP to another process, regenerating ADP and P_i. It is worth emphasizing that the reactions which involve ATP are reactions in which an acid anhydride linkage is formed, as ADP is converted to ATP, or in which an acid anhydride linkage is cleaved, as ATP is transformed back to ADP.

The cyclical formation and cleavage of ATP in various energy-transfer processes is illustrated diagrammatically in Figure 8-1. Several typical energy sources are shown; a number of others would serve equally well for the formation of ATP.

Note that in addition to the synthesis of complex compounds, which we have previously mentioned as needing ATP, many of the physical

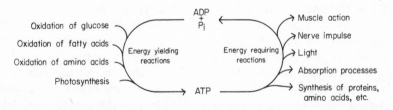

Figure 8-1. The Formation and Cleavage of ATP in Energy-transfer Processes.

activities of organisms similarly require this compound as a direct source of energy. The processes shown are common to all animals. Plants, of course, do not have typical muscle or nervous systems. On the other hand, some specialized organisms utilize the energy of ATP in processes which are not shown. Prominent examples are the production of light by the firefly and the shocking behavior of the electric eel.

Compounds such as ATP are often described as "high-energy" or "energy-rich" compounds. However, it should be recognized that on an equivalent basis glucose has a much greater energy content than is involved in the ATP-ADP interconversion. The importance of ATP lies not so much in its energy content, though this is important, as in the ability of this molecule, in contrast to glucose, to participate directly in the variety of energy-transfer reactions required by the cell. This is one major basis for the selection of ATP by living systems as their "energy-intermediate."

Also it may be well to mention that ATP is often said to have a "high-energy phosphate bond." The term is a very poor one but is in wide use to indicate that the pyrophosphate (phosphate anhydride) linkage is a very reactive portion of the molecule. A better expression is the statement that ATP has "high phosphate-group transfer potential," to indicate that the phosphate group readily can be transferred by chemical reactions to other compounds.

Before we proceed to discuss some of the problems of ATP formation, it may be of interest to mention that the role of ATP in biological systems was discovered in 1929 by Lohmann. We have previously mentioned the use of iodoacetic acid as an inhibitor in yeast of one of the reactions of glucose oxidation. This same compound also was found to cause the rapid loss of ability of an isolated muscle fiber of an animal to undergo contraction. Lohmann found that the addition of ATP to the medium containing the muscle fiber restored temporarily the contractile ability. The way was then clear to suggest that ATP was formed by the oxidation of glucose and utilized in muscle contraction. This led to much experimentation concerning the role of ATP in other systems and the detailed mechanisms for the production and use of the compound.

Formation of ATP

Most of the ATP synthesized from ADP and P_i by living organisms is derived from two major processes. One of these is based on the oxidation of organic substances in the mitochondria of cells; the other on the utilization by chloroplasts of radiant energy in photochemical reactions. We shall see that these two processes are actually closely related, the significant reactions in both cases being the phosphorylation of ADP in the course of electron transfer from one compound to another.

BIOLOGICAL OXIDATIONS AND ATP PRODUCTION

The utilization of the chemical energy of the glucose molecule for the production of ATP will be examined as an example of the relationship between biological oxidations and ATP synthesis. Most of the material discussed will be applicable in principle to the mechanisms for the oxidation of other compounds in biological systems.

Let us consider first the quantitative aspects of energy transfer during the complete oxidation of glucose. When a mole of glucose is burned in air, 686 kilocalories (Kcal) of energy appear as heat, light, and pressure-volume work. The equation for the oxidation of glucose under these conditions is:

$$\text{glucose} + 6\,O_2 \rightarrow 6\,CO_2 + 6\,H_2O + 686\,\text{Kcal}$$

The production of ATP from ADP and inorganic phosphate under biological conditions requires about 10 Kcal of energy per mole of ATP formed.

$$\text{ADP} + P_i + 10\,\text{Kcal} \rightarrow \text{ATP} + H_2O$$

Obviously, the oxidation of 1 mole of glucose can supply energy sufficient for the formation of about 68 moles of ATP. In the oxidation of glucose to carbon dioxide (CO_2) and water by the most common metabolic pathway, about 38 moles of ATP are actually produced by cells per mole of glucose oxidized. The biological oxidation of glucose might therefore be summarized as:

$$\text{glucose} + 6\,O_2 + 38\,\text{ADP} + 38\,P_i \rightarrow$$
$$6\,CO_2 + 6\,H_2O + 38\,\text{ATP} + \text{heat (about 310 Kcal)}$$

You should realize that this equation cannot possibly represent a single chemical reaction, but must be a summary of many reactions. As written, the equation implies that 83 molecules collide simultaneously and are converted in one step to the products. In actuality, very few reactions exist which involve the simultaneous participation of more than three or four molecules. Therefore, the production of ATP in conjunction with the oxidation of glucose must occur in a stepwise fashion.

This means that only one molecule of ATP can be synthesized in any single reaction, ADP being one reactant, and an inorganic phosphate ion (indirectly) being a second. If the biological oxidation of glucose *could* take place in one step, we would anticipate the production of only one molecule of ATP, the rest of the energy being lost as heat. Because 38 molecules of ATP are actually produced upon the oxidation of one molecule of glucose, the conclusion must unavoidably be that the oxidation does not occur in one step, but in many steps. In the stepwise process, the energy of the glucose molecule can be released in a number of small portions rather than all in one burst. In this way a number of ATP molecules can be synthesized. Theoretically one ATP could be made in each step which liberates at least 10 Kcal of energy.

The sequential reactions necessary for the biological oxidation of glucose with the concurrent production of ATP make up a major portion of the metabolic activities of living cells. These reactions will be scrutinized in some detail in Chapter 9. For our present purposes it is necessary to note that among the sequential reactions needed for the complete oxidation of the carbon atoms of glucose to carbon dioxide, only six oxidation reactions actually occur. Again we are faced with a problem: How is it possible to produce 38 molecules of ATP using only six oxidation reactions?

In order to answer this question let us consider one example of the six oxidations, the oxidation of malic acid to oxalacetic acid. These compounds are two of the intermediates of the metabolic oxidation of glucose. First we shall give the reaction as if it were a single step:

$$
\begin{array}{c}
\text{OH} \\
\diagup \\
\text{C}=\text{O} \\
| \\
\text{HCOH} \\
| \\
\text{CH}_2 \\
| \\
\text{C}=\text{O} \\
\diagdown \\
\text{OH}
\end{array}
\quad + \quad \tfrac{1}{2}\,O_2 \quad \rightarrow \quad
\begin{array}{c}
\text{OH} \\
\diagup \\
\text{C}=\text{O} \\
| \\
\text{C}=\text{O} \\
| \\
\text{CH}_2 \\
| \\
\text{C}=\text{O} \\
\diagdown \\
\text{OH}
\end{array}
\quad + \quad H_2O \quad + \quad 47\ \text{Kcal}
$$

The reaction pictured is the minimum degree of oxidation of an organic compound which gives a stable product. Two electrons and two hydrogen atoms have been removed and accepted by the oxygen atom (in O_2 the oxidation state or net valence is zero, in H_2O the oxygen has an oxidation state of minus 2). Single electron changes would give unstable free radicals as products.

Note that even though the malic acid has been subjected to the minimum possible oxidation, the energy released is sufficient to form four molecules of ATP. As indicated above, we could actually expect only one ATP to be formed if the reaction occurred in the single step pictured. Again this would be wasteful of energy because most of it would be lost as unavailable heat. Biological systems are considerably more efficient; they form three molecules of ATP per molecule of malic acid which is oxidized. This implies that a sequence of stepwise reactions occurs, three of which are coupled with the synthesis of ATP. But we have stated that the oxidation of malic acid to oxalacetic acid, a two-electron change, is the minimum possible.

The answer to this apparent impasse, and to the question posed earlier, lies with the electrons. Rather than passing the electrons directly to oxygen, they are passed through a series of oxidation-reduction reactions and only in the last step to oxygen. In the course of this stepwise transfer of electrons, three of the steps are coupled to ATP formation, thus making use of most of the energy of the oxidation.

THE ELECTRON TRANSPORT SYSTEM

The preceding section led to the conclusion that the oxidation of malic acid to oxalacetic acid was accompanied by a series of reactions which passed electrons to oxygen in stepwise fashion. The same situation occurs with most biological oxidations. Each of these involves the loss of two electrons by the original organic compound, and these electrons are passed to oxygen only indirectly. Obviously it would be more efficient if there existed a single system for the utilization of the electrons from all these different oxidations. This ideal is actually approached in living cells. Electrons are funneled from a variety of sources, such as the six oxidation reactions in the metabolism of glucose, to a single sequence of oxidation-reduction reactions which passes them eventually to oxygen.

This common metabolic pathway for the channeling of electrons to oxygen is termed the *electron transport system*, the *respiratory chain*, or the *cytochrome system*. Most of the ATP used by animals is formed as the result of the operation of this sequence of reactions. In certain reactions, the electrons do go directly from the organic metabolite to oxygen rather than through the electron transport system. Most of the energy of these processes appears as heat.

The details of the electron transport system have proved to be difficult to determine. A major reason is that the enzymes of the system occur in the mitochondria in multi-enzyme aggregates which are called electron transport particles. Apparently one unit of each necessary component is bound in a specific spatial orientation with respect to the other components. This greatly facilitates the transfer of electrons through the various steps to oxygen and also the formation of ATP, giving in effect the greater efficiency of an assembly-line process. Substrates such as malic acid or other oxidizable compounds (as well as ADP, P_i and O_2) continually enter the mitochondria, and the reaction products, including ATP, continually leave the mitochondria and are further metabolized in other parts of the cell.

This high degree of structural organization is fine for the cell, but it makes the task of unravelling the system a difficult one for the biochemist. He can never be quite sure that a compound isolated from a solution of broken electron transport particles actually was present in the same form in the intact particle. Also, the properties of an isolated component of the system may be considerably different from those of the component bound in place in the particle.

For these reasons some details of the electron transfer system remain to be elucidated. Chief among these is the nature of the reactions in which ATP is formed. As yet these cannot be given even as good guesses.

The electron transport systems of different organisms, even of different tissues of the same organism, may also differ somewhat in details, further complicating the situation. Nevertheless, it is clear that the major components of the electron transport systems are: (1) a diphosphopyridine nucleotide-containing enzyme, (2) a flavoprotein, (3) coenzyme Q, and (4) a number of compounds called cytochromes. Figure 8-2 presents the currently most popular view as to the nature of the sequential reactions which these compounds undergo as they accept electrons and pass them on to the other components.

Certain biological oxidations utilize a flavin rather than a pyridine nucleotide as the coenzyme for the dehydrogenation of the organic metabolite. In some of these cases the electrons of the reduced flavin are passed back to DPN and then through the electron transport system shown in Figure 8-2. In other cases, a notable example being the oxidation of succinic to fumaric acid—one of the six oxidation reactions of glucose metabolism—the electrons pass from the flavin to the cytochromes. DPN is thus bypassed. This eliminates one of the sites of ATP formation. Such reactions yield only two ATP molecules per molecule of original substrate, rather than the common three molecules of ATP for the entire system.

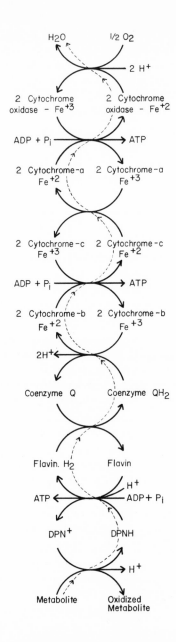

Figure 8-2. The Electron Transport System. The dashed line indicates the flow of electrons.

Figure 8-2 introduces a manner of representing chemical equations which may be new to you. However, the method has distinct advantages for the depiction of cyclical processes such as those of the respiratory chain, and accordingly is widely used in biochemical literature. To clarify this notation, let us examine the first reaction shown in the figure. This appears as:

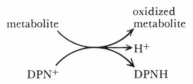

This equation would appear in the conventional manner as:

metabolite $+$ DPN$^+$ $\rightarrow$ oxidized metabolite $+$ DPNH $+$ H$^+$

Note also that the sites of formation of three ATP molecules are indicated in the figure. Again it must be emphasized that the reactions actually occurring at these points are unknown. Ultimately it will be necessary to add new reactions at these sites, either directly in the course of the electron transfer or as side-reactions. Among the compounds currently being considered as possible intermediates in the formation of ATP are a phosphorylated histidine unit of a protein and a phosphorylated derivative of Coenzyme Q, a quinone compound which can undergo readily reversible reduction to the hydroquinone.

At present all that is actually clear is that the phosphorylation of ADP (the addition of a phosphate group to ADP) is coupled with oxidation-reduction reactions near the positions indicated. The synthesis of ATP as the result of these reactions of the electron transport system is termed *oxidative phosphorylation*.

For the purpose of the examination of further aspects of the electron transport system, we will discuss certain reactions in more detail.

Substrate Dehydrogenation

The first step of the electron transport system is that of the oxidation of the organic substrate, in our example malic acid, with the simultaneous reduction of diphosphopyridine nucleotide. DPN$^+$ is used as the abbreviation for the oxidized form of this compound, DPNH for the reduced form, and DPN as a general term when the oxidation-reduction state is not specified.* The structural formulas of

*To prevent confusion in the reading of reference literature, we will use the well-established DPN nomenclature throughout this book. The reader should be aware, however, that the alternative terms NAD or NAD$^+$ and NADH$_2$ or NADH (see p. 83) have been accepted by international nomenclature agencies. They will undoubtedly find increased use in the future.

these compounds appear on p. 89. The formulas we shall use below will repeat only those portions of the molecule which are directly involved in the reaction.

It may also be recalled that DPN contains the vitamin, niacin, as part of the structure. It is this pyridine ring portion of the molecule which is actually reduced in this reaction and oxidized in other reactions. Its participation in the first step of the electron transfer system marks the major metabolic use of this vitamin by animals.

In order to emphasize certain aspects of this first step of the respiratory chain, we will present the reaction in conventional form, assuming the organic metabolite oxidized to be malic acid.

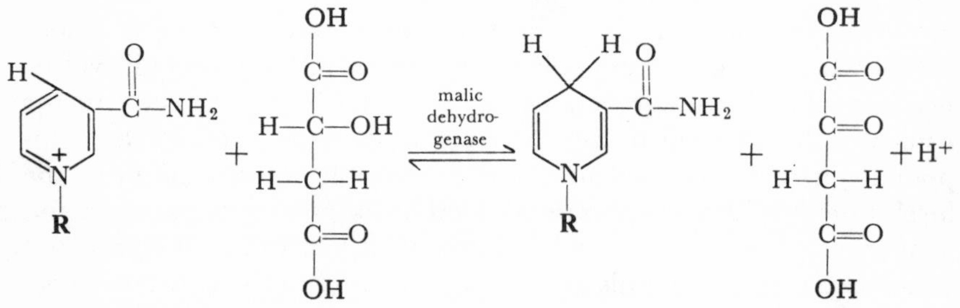

| DPN⁺ | malic acid | DPNH | oxalacetic acid |

In this reaction DPN⁺ is the oxidizing agent. It is reduced to DPNH by accepting two electrons and one hydrogen from the alcohol group of the malic acid as this is oxidized to the ketone. A second hydrogen is released to the solution as a hydrogen ion. Oxidation-reduction reactions of this type in which the molecule being oxidized loses hydrogen in addition to the mandatory loss of electrons are called *dehydrogenations*. The enzymes which catalyze this type of reaction are called *dehydrogenases*.

In this case DPN is the coenzyme for the dehydrogenase protein. Specific dehydrogenase proteins are required for each different organic substrate; however, DPN serves as the coenzyme for many of these enzymes. The specific enzyme required here is called *malic dehydrogenase*.

Reoxidation of DPNH by Flavins

Dehydrogenases bind DPNH relatively weakly. It seems likely in most cases that the further reaction of this compound requires its release from the protein and its use as one of the substrates of a second enzyme. For this reason the designation *cosubstrate* rather than coenzyme would seem preferable.

The DPNH formed in the electron transport system undergoes reoxidation to DPN+ by a reaction with a flavoprotein enzyme. The coenzyme here is a flavin, that is, a riboflavin derivative. The structures of the riboflavin coenzymes appear on p. 90. They should be consulted for review of the nature of these compounds. Again, in the equation which follows, we shall depict only the reactive portion of the coenzyme. In this case the reactive part of the molecule is the nitrogen-ring system of riboflavin, illustrating a major biological role of this vitamin.

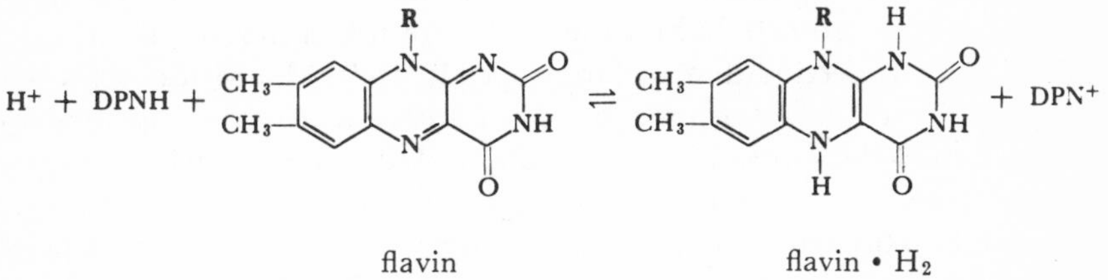

flavin   flavin • H_2

This reaction causes the oxidation of DPNH to DPN+ as the flavin accepts two electrons from the DPNH (and a hydrogen from DPNH and a proton from the solution). This completes the coenzyme cycle for the DPN+. The molecule is released to the solution where it will combine with a dehydrogenase protein which then will be able to catalyze the oxidation of another organic molecule.

Reoxidation of Flavin by Coenzyme Q

The oxidation of the reduced flavin is accomplished by the transfer of two electrons (and two hydrogens) to a molecule of Coenzyme Q. This compound is a substituted benzoquinone having a long isoprenoid side-chain. The number of isoprene units in the side-chain varies with the source of the compound—that having 10 isoprene units is the common form found in animal mitochondria. The hydrocarbon side-chain in particular gives the compound the properties of a lipid. In common with all quinones, Coenzyme Q is subject to readily reversible reduction to the hydroquinone form.

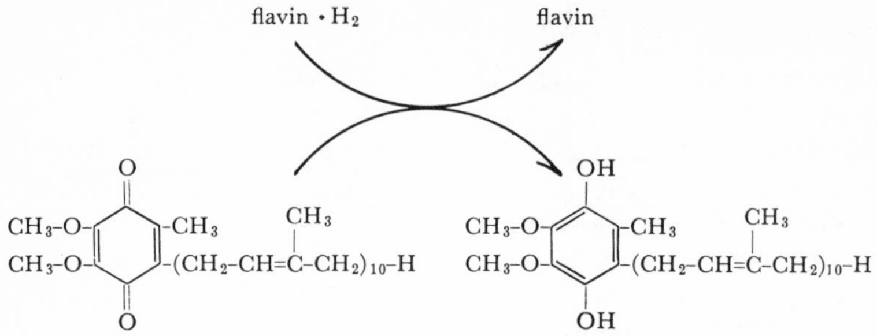

coenzyme Q_{10} (quinone)   coenzyme Q_{10} (hydroquinone)

Reoxidation of Coenzyme Q by Cytochromes

The compounds called *cytochromes* were probably the first components of the electron transfer system to be associated with oxidation-reduction reactions. As the name cytochrome (cell-color) indicates, each of these compounds is colored. Furthermore, the oxidized and reduced forms absorb light differently, giving different absorption bands when viewed with a spectroscope. In 1886 MacMunn observed that certain strong absorption bands of a cell suspension appeared as the oxygen of the solution was used up, and disappeared when oxygen was admitted to the system. This suggested that the compound was alternately oxidized and reduced. The term "cytochrome" was later coined for the substance involved, even though the precise structure was unknown.

We now know that there are a number of these compounds, at least four of which occur in the common mitochondrial electron transport system. Each of these substances is a conjugated-protein enzyme. The tightly bound coenzyme or prosthetic group is an iron porphyrin compound similar to the heme of hemoglobin. The various cytochromes differ with respect to the protein portion, and in the manner in which the porphyrin is bound to the protein, and in some cases with respect to the substituents on the porphyrin ring. The structure of the prosthetic group of cytochrome-c is given in Figure 8-3 for comparison with that of the heme portion of hemoglobin.

Owing to the differences of structure of the different cytochromes, they differ in reactivity, particularly in their ability to accept and to donate electrons. One of these compounds, thought to be cytochrome-b, is capable of accepting an electron from reduced Coenzyme Q. The oxidized form of cytochrome-b has a ferric ion at the center of the porphyrin system; the reduced form a ferrous ion. The reduction of cytochrome-b involves only the transfer of a single electron. Two of

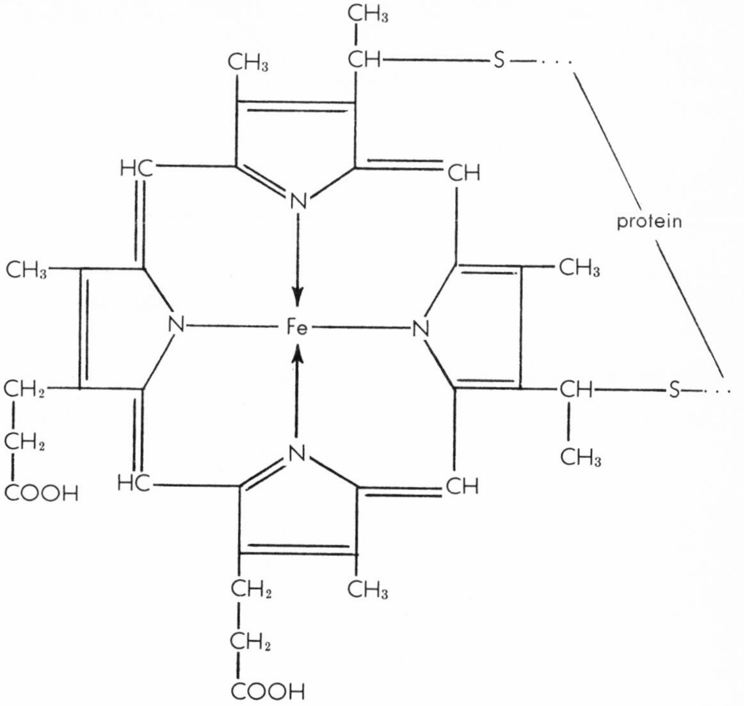

Figure 8-3. The Prosthetic Group of Cytochrome-c.

these molecules are therefore necessary to complete the reoxidation of the Coenzyme Q. Note that the hydrogens of the reduced Coenzyme Q are not transferred to cytochromes; they are released as hydrogen ions to the medium.

Reoxidation of Cytochromes

An electron is next passed from reduced cytochrome-b to one cytochrome after another with alternate oxidation and reduction of the iron atom. Finally a cytochrome called cytochrome-a₃, or more commonly *cytochrome oxidase*, is reached. This cytochrome is distinguished by its ability to undergo direct oxidation by molecular oxygen, a property rarely found in biological systems. As a class, enzymes catalyzing reactions involving oxygen are termed *oxidases*. It has been estimated that as much as 95 per cent of the oxygen utilized by cells reacts in this single process, the oxidation of the reduced form of cytochrome oxidase to the oxidized form. The reaction is not completely understood. In addition to the iron-porphyrin prosthetic group, the enzyme contains a copper ion. There are indications that the cupric ion receives an electron from the ferrous-porphyrin portion of the enzyme, being reduced to cuprous ion, and that it is the enzyme-bound cuprous ion which is oxidized in the final step by molecular oxygen.

Whatever the details of the reaction mechanism, cytochrome oxidase is an exceedingly important enzyme. Inactivation of this enzyme, as occurs by its combination with carbon monoxide or cyanide ion in rather low concentrations, leads to the rapid death of the cells of most organisms. Their utilization of oxygen is prevented, in turn prohibiting the formation of ATP in sufficient quantities to meet the energy demands.

In contrast to all the other steps of the electron transport system, the cytochrome oxidase reaction with oxygen is not reversible. In the presence of oxygen, therefore, the system will continually transport electrons in only one direction—from the organic metabolite to oxygen.

Perhaps we should again emphasize that the reactions of the electron transport system are catalytic in nature. Each of the components is present only in small amounts. The compounds are used over and over again, alternately undergoing oxidation and reduction, so that the net effect is the oxidation of the organic substrate, the reduction of oxygen, and the synthesis of ATP.

PHOTOSYNTHESIS

The biochemical processes usually included under the topic of photosynthesis may be divided into two main groups. The first of these involves those chemical reactions necessary for the conversion of the radiant energy of the sun into the chemical energy of compounds which plant cells are able to use as energy sources for the synthesis of organic compounds. These reactions are appropriately known as the *light reactions.*

The second division of the field of photosynthesis includes the reactions by which the chemical energy of each of the compounds formed in the light reactions is utilized to promote the formation of organic substances from inorganic materials. These processes are termed the *dark reactions.*

The dark reactions are closely related to the general processes of carbohydrate metabolism. Accordingly, we will postpone their examination until the groundwork for the metabolic transformations of carbohydrates can be laid in Chapter 9.

The light reactions of green plants and other photosynthetic organisms constitute the chief characteristic which distinguishes them from other living cells. Plants can live and grow in the absence of light provided they are supplied with an energy source such as glucose. In so doing they carry out metabolic transformations very similar to those of animals, obtaining ATP via the mitochondrial electron transport system. But only the photosynthetic organisms can directly use light energy when it is available, obviating the necessity for oxidative reactions as energy-supplying processes.

The photosynthetic reactions occur in the chloroplasts of plant cells. Like mitochondria, these relatively large particulate components of the cytoplasm have complex internal structures. Chlorophyll molecules are concentrated within the chloroplasts, in small bodies known as *grana*. Each of these appears to consist of an intricately folded lipoprotein membrane, resulting in a many-layered structure. The chlorophyll molecules are sandwiched between layers of the lipoprotein. Probably the long hydrocarbon chain of the chlorophyll molecule (see p. 77) is associated with the lipid portion of the membrane protein, while the remainder of the molecule is linked with a water-soluble portion of the protein. Relatively large amounts of carotenoid compounds such as β-carotene and Vitamin K also occur in the grana, perhaps as part of the lipoprotein membranes.

The light reactions of photosynthesis by green plants are based on the absorption of light from both the red and blue regions of the visible spectrum. The remaining, non-absorbed components of the original white light are seen as green by the human eye. The compound which absorbs the light was formerly believed to be only chlorophyll *a*. This substance has absorption peaks in the appropriate areas of the spectrum, near 430 and 680 mμ, which match reasonably well with the light capable of promoting photosynthesis. However, careful studies of photosynthetic efficiency as a function of wavelength have now shown that optimum performance is obtained only when light of wavelengths somewhat shorter than 680 mμ is *also* present.

This indicates that *two* photosynthetic pigments are required. One of these is chlorophyll *a*; the second pigment varies widely with the organism, but is thought to be chlorophyll *b* in higher plants. This compound differs from chlorophyll *a* by having a methyl group attached to the porphyrin ring system replaced by a formyl group. The methyl group involved in this change is the one at the top of the formula on page 77.

The absorption of light by the photosynthetic pigments increases the energy content of the pigments above the usual level, yielding molecules which are said to be *activated* or *excited*. These molecules are very reactive in processes by which their extra energy can be transferred to other compounds.

The reactions involved in the transfer of energy from the chlorophylls to other substances remain poorly known in spite of intensive research efforts. Regardless of the precise mechanisms and of the nature of the intermediates, it appears that the excitation energy of the chlorophyll is utilized in the formation, in rather direct fashion, of ATP and of reduced pyridine nucleotide. In plants, triphosphopyridine nucleotide (TPN) is used more extensively than is DPN as the coenzyme for many oxidation-reduction reactions. Apparently it is the reduction of TPN^+ to TPNH that occurs in the energy transfer process of photosynthesis.

A highly simplified view of these processes, ignoring the probability of the participation of other substances as intermediates, is that the light energy acting through chlorophyll causes the disruption of each water molecule to an oxygen atom and two hydrogen atoms (or more probably hydrogen ions and electrons). The oxygen atoms then combine to give molecular oxygen, much of which is liberated to the atmosphere. The hydrogen atoms, or at least their electrons, bring about the reduction of TPN^+ to TPNH. In the course of this electron transfer from water to TPN, ATP is synthesized. This simplified version of the light reactions of photosynthesis is summarized in Figure 8-4.

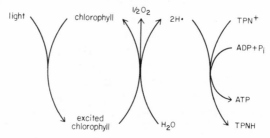

Figure 8-4. A Simplified Version of the "Light Reactions" of Photosynthesis.

This simplified picture leaves many questions unanswered. What are the roles of the *two* photosynthetic pigments? What sort of electron transfer processes, culminating in the reduction of TPN, occur in response to light? What reactions produce ATP? How are the components of the water molecule utilized?

The answers to these questions are not yet available with any degree of certainty. One of the schemes currently being tested for its ability to provide answers of the necessary kind is presented in Figure 8-5. This is probably correct in essence, although detailed mechanisms and almost certainly additional intermediates remain to be found.

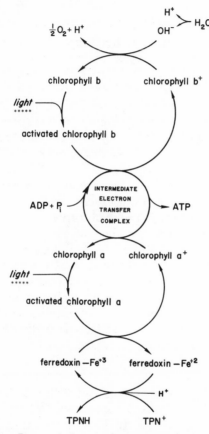

Figure 8-5. A Summary of the Light Reactions of Photosynthesis.

If we rewrite the reactions shown in Figures 8-4 and 8-5 to emphasize the net change irrespective of the reaction mechanisms, we obtain the following:

$$TPN^+ + ADP + P_i + HOH \xrightarrow{\text{chloroplast}} TPNH + ATP + \tfrac{1}{2}O_2 + H^+$$

In Figure 8-5 the starting materials of this process are encircled;

the products are enclosed in rectangles. Perhaps it should again be mentioned that in these equations, as in other similar cases in this book, we have omitted in the interests of clarity the water molecules formed when ADP and P_i condense to form the anhydride bond of ATP.

Let us look briefly at some of the major features of this scheme. Essentially it is a mechanism for the transfer of an electron from a hydroxyl ion to chlorophyll *b*, then on to chlorophyll *a* through an electron transfer complex, and finally to TPN. Basically, the electrons of water molecules are used to reduce TPN as we have previously indicated, but only through the participation of a number of electron carriers as intermediates. It should be clear that this view of photosynthesis requires that the chlorophyll molecules act as electron carriers themselves. They differ from the cytochromes and other such compounds involved in electron transport only in that they must be excited by absorption of light energy before they can become oxidized by loss of an electron. In the absence of light, the equilibrium must lie far toward the normal reduced forms.

The intermediate electron transfer complex which links the two chlorophyll systems is probably composed of at least two cytochromes, cytochromes *f* and b_6; at least one quinone related to Vitamin K, commonly called plastoquinone; and a copper-containing protein called plastocyanin. Other compounds, such as flavin nucleotides, may also be required. Electrons are transferred sequentially from one of these compounds to the other and on to cytochrome *a*. In the course of these electron transfer reactions, at least one and probably two ATP molecules are produced. The specific reactions which yield ATP are not yet known.

The production of ATP in chloroplasts at the expense of light energy and in mitochondria at the expense of chemical energy are probably very similar processes. In both cases the energy for ATP synthesis is derived directly from electron transfer reactions, although the original energy sources are different.

The process of ATP synthesis in chloroplasts is termed *photophosphorylation* or *photosynthetic phosphorylation* to distinguish it from oxidative phosphorylation in mitochondria.

Note also in Figure 8-5 that a compound called ferredoxin is an intermediate in the transfer of electrons from chlorophyll *a* to TPN. This recently discovered compound is an iron-protein; it is by no means certain that ferredoxin is reduced by accepting an electron directly from chlorophyll *a*. Many workers believe that a flavin is involved as an intermediate in this process.

Perhaps the least understood aspect of this whole complex set of "light reactions" is the production of oxygen. Certainly the oxygen released is derived from water molecules. The above scheme would require some process of oxidation of hydroxyl ions, although the nature of the first product of this reaction is still a mystery. It has been suggested that this product may be a hydroxyl free radical, which could react further to produce compounds similar to peroxides. In any case the further steps to the production of free oxygen are not known, although it has been established that manganese ions are required for oxygen evolution.

It is worth emphasizing that the various compounds required for the light reactions of photosynthesis are organized into operational units within the grana of chloroplasts in a specific physical relationship which facilitates these processes.

FREE ENERGY

The preceding discussion of energy changes accompanying chemical processes has been primarily descriptive in order to avoid going deeply into areas of physical chemistry necessary for proper understanding of more precise considerations. The following discussion of "free energy" changes is presented to introduce a little of the terminology and concepts of simplified thermodynamics.

The concept of free energy arose as a result of the search by physical chemists for a means of predicting whether a particular reaction or series of reactions could occur spontaneously. At first it was thought that the heat of reaction provided the desired criterion. Generally, reactions which evolve heat are spontaneous; those which absorb heat are not. However, exceptions were found—certain spontaneous reactions in which the reacting molecules absorbed heat from the solution.

The desired criterion was found only when a different kind of energy—called *entropy*—was also taken into account. The total entropy content (S) of a system is related to its relative degree of order or disorder. A system that can exist in many possible forms is more disordered (or more random) than is one that can exist only in a few different forms or patterns. The higher the degree of order, the lower the entropy; the more random the system, the higher the entropy. Thus a protein molecule will have a lower entropy content than will the system of all of its constituent amino acids in the free state. In considering energy changes in going from a set of amino acids to a specific protein, it is necessary to consider both the heat of reaction and the change in entropy.

In quantitative terms, the criterion of thermodynamic spontaneity was found to be $\Delta H - T\Delta S$, where ΔS is the entropy change, T is the absolute temperature, and ΔH is the heat of reaction. The $T\Delta S$ represents that part of the total energy of a reaction which is not available for the performance of work (at a constant temperature). The change in available energy was then called *free energy change*, and designated as ΔF. Thus we have the equation

$$\Delta F = \Delta H - T\Delta S$$

If ΔF for a given reaction is negative, the reaction is spontaneous and is said to be *exergonic;* that is, free energy is released. For a reaction which is not spontaneous, free energy must be supplied to the system if the reaction is to occur. Thus ΔF will have a positive value and the reaction is said to be *endergonic*. Technically, these terms should replace those of "energy-yielding" and "energy-requiring" reactions used earlier in this chapter.

Let us consider a solution of two compounds, A and B, each of which is present in a standard concentration of 1 mole per liter of solvent (1 molal). Assume that these compounds can react completely to form compounds C and D, which will again be at unit concentrations, i.e.,

$$A + B \longrightarrow C + D$$

Under these particular conditions of concentration, the change in free energy is termed the *standard free energy change* and is indicated as ΔF^0.

If we further assume that the ΔF^0 for this process is a negative value, we will be dealing with a conversion that *could* occur spontaneously. However, this does not mean that on mixing A and B the products C and D are formed immediately in unit concentrations. First, neither the sign nor the magnitude of the free energy change has anything to do with the reaction rate. For example, the ΔF^0 for the complete oxidation of glucose is a very large negative value, yet a sample of glucose may quite safely be exposed to air without fear of an explosion. The free energy change is simply a measure of the usable energy involved *if* the reaction does occur as it is written.

Secondly, the reaction will usually go only to equilibrium, not to completion. For any process the equilibrium point is the lowest energy level. Any reaction will proceed spontaneously to equilibrium (ΔF is always negative) but will be able to proceed from the equilibrium position to completion (ΔF is always positive) only if energy can be made available in some suitable way. The ΔF^0 for the over-all process tells us whether the free energy released in going to equilibrium is greater or less than that needed to go from equilibrium to completion.

In essence, the over-all free energy change is simply an expression (in terms of energy) of the relative distances from the starting point to equilibrium and from the end-point to equilibrium. To go back to our example of the reaction $A + B \rightarrow C + D$, let's assume that going from $A + B$ to equilibrium involves 10 Kcal of free energy, while going from equilibrium to $C + D$ involves 5 Kcal. The first step is capable of supplying all of the energy required for the second step,

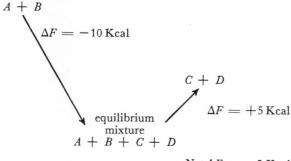

plus an extra 5 Kcal. On the other hand, if we were to start with $C + D$, the reaction will again proceed to the same equilibrium point, with the release of 5 Kcal of free energy. This is not enough to carry the reaction to completion, since this would require 10 Kcal.

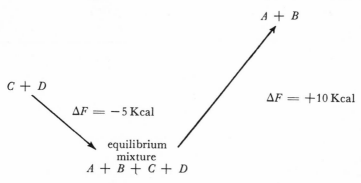

We can therefore say that the conversion of $A + B$ to $C + D$, with a ΔF of -5 Kcal, is a spontaneous reaction, while the conversion of $C + D$ to $A + B$, with a ΔF of 5 Kcal is not. Be sure to note that if we start with $C + D$, appreciable formation of A and B will always occur in spontaneous fashion, but the equilibrium will lie toward the side of C and D.

The free energy change of a reaction can be viewed simply as an indication of where the equilibrium point lies. This should be kept in mind. Otherwise it may be forgotten that reactions with positive ΔF's can nevertheless proceed to equilibrium. In fact the standard free energy change has a very simple relation to the equilibrium constant for a reaction:

$$\Delta F^0 = -4.6 \times T \times \log K$$

In this equation T is the absolute temperature and K is the equilibrium constant.

The application of free energy values to biological systems is fraught with difficulties. Among other problems, the concentrations (more properly the activities) of the reactants and products are rarely known with much precision. These values must be known in order to correct the standard free energy changes, which may be obtained from tables in the chemical literature, for the exact situation being considered. It should be apparent that the free energy change will vary with concentration of the reactants, because the equilibrium point will change.

Secondly, the thermodynamic considerations upon which ΔF values are based require that the processes involved be conducted under reversible conditions. Yet biological systems continually excrete compounds such as carbon dioxide, eliminating their effect on the chemical reactions of the system.

Furthermore, in any sequence of reactions such as characterize metabolism, an individual reaction may have a large positive ΔF. It is necessary only that the ΔF of the *entire sequence* have a negative value. The step with the unfavorable equilibrium proceeds spontaneously because the products are continually removed by succeeding reactions. For example, the oxidation of malic acid by DPN^+ has a very large positive ΔF, yet the reaction proceeds readily in cells, primarily because the DPNH is reoxidized by the electron transport system, a process with a large negative ΔF.

The finding that a reaction has a positive ΔF, therefore, does *not* mean that the reaction does not occur in the living cell. Any reaction, regardless of the free energy change, can occur provided it is followed by reactions with a net release of free energy. These considerations apply particularly to reactions which lead to products which are excreted from the cell.

However, processes which lead to end-products which are retained in the cell in large quantities pose special problems. Examples of such end-products are the polysaccharides and the proteins. The ΔF for the condensation of sugar units to give a polysaccharide or of amino acids to give a protein is a very large positive value. Here there are no following reactions to remove the products. Technically some polysaccharide and polypeptide would be formed by equilibrium processes, but the concentrations of glucose or of amino acids would have to be very high to obtain even a trace of the polymeric substances. In cells, the opposite situation occurs—the polymer content is very high compared with the concentrations of free glucose or of amino acids.

In cases such as this a positive free energy change is clear evidence that the reactions cannot occur to a significant extent by the simple condensation of monomers to give polymers. But polymers such as proteins, nucleic acids and polysaccharides are certainly synthesized by cells. The answer to this apparent puzzle is that the polymers are synthesized by mechanisms *other* than the condensation of monomers— mechanisms which *do* have an overall negative change in free energy.

SUGGESTED ADDITIONAL READING

Lehninger, A. L., "How Cells Transform Energy," *Scientific American*, **205**, No. 3, 62 (September 1961).

Green, D. E., "The Mitochondrion," *Scientific American*, **210**, No. 1, 63 (January 1964).

Rabinowitch, E. I. and Govindjee, "The Role of Chlorophyll in Photosynthesis," *Scientific American*, **213**, No. 1, 74 (July 1965).

Rosenberg, J. L., "Photosynthesis," Holt, Rinehart and Winston, Inc., New York, 1965.

Pardee, A. B. and Ingraham, L. L., "Free Energy and Entropy in Metabolism"; and

Green, D. E., and Fleischer, S., "Mitochondrial Systems of Enzymes," both in D. Greenberg, Ed., "Metabolic Pathways," Vol. 1, pp. 1-91, Academic Press, New York and London, 1960.

Singer, T. P., Ed., "Biological Oxidations," Interscience Publishers, New York, 1965.

Metabolism of Carbohydrates

9

The great bulk of carbohydrates which occur in biological materials serve structural roles. These are mainly the celluloses, pentosans (pentose polymers), and related compounds of higher plants. They comprise a very high percentage of the organic compounds on the earth. In contrast to the relatively inert structural carbohydrates, other polysaccharides can readily be interconverted to their monosaccharide components. These are the storage polysaccharides, the amyloses and amylopectins of plant seeds and tubers and the glycogens of animal muscle and liver tissues. Disaccharides, such as sucrose of plant juices and lactose of milk, may also, to some extent, act as reserve stores of sugar units—although a good reason for their presence in place of monosaccharides escapes us.

The final group of carbohydrates includes those which are by far the most interesting in an active, metabolic sense. These are the monosaccharides and their various derivatives, chiefly those related closely to glucose. These compounds are central to the formation of all di- and polysaccharides. They provide, via their oxidation, most of the available energy used by living cells for the whole variety of synthetic reactions carried out by the cell, and they serve as sources of carbon atoms for the production of most of the other compounds of the cell—the amino acids, sterols, nucleotides, etc. Furthermore, in green plants a monosaccharide derivative is the organic compound first formed from inorganic CO_2.

It should be evident that the monosaccharides in general and those related to glucose in particular are very important components of the metabolic economy of the cell. The reactions usually included in carbohydrate metabolism have significance far beyond that of the transformation of carbohydrates. They provide the basic framework of metabolic machinery upon which all of the cell's activities, either directly or indirectly, depend.

For this reason it is well to begin our discussions of metabolic activities with the carbohydrates. For the same reason we will examine many of the reactions of carbohydrate metabolism in greater detail than will be the case with other processes in later sections. This also reflects the fact that in the metabolism of carbohydrates we will find our first examples of many of the general kinds of biochemical reactions which are employed in specific instances throughout the cell's metabolic activities.

Before we turn to consider the mechanisms of the metabolic transformations of carbohydrates, we will first discuss briefly the chemical reactions utilized by living cells in the hydrolysis of complex carbohydrates to simple sugars. Only monosaccharides can be absorbed through cell membranes at appreciable rates, while most of the carbohydrates found in the biological materials which constitute the foods of animals or the nutrients of microorganisms are di- and polysaccharides. It is thus necessary that these substances be hydrolyzed before their sugar units are available for absorption and subsequent metabolism. Hydrolysis reactions of this type are catalyzed by *exoenzymes*, enzymes liberated into the extracellular environment. These reactions are known as digestive processes.

DIGESTION OF CARBOHYDRATES

The hydrolysis or digestion of the complex carbohydrates is catalyzed by exoenzymes commonly called *carbohydrases*. There are two major subclasses of carbohydrases: (1) the polysaccharidases, which have as their common substrates compounds of high molecular weight, and (2) the glycosidases, which catalyze the hydrolysis of relatively small compounds such as simple glycosides and disaccharides.

There are, of course, many different kinds of polysaccharides. Our discussion will be restricted to the important polymers of glucose such as glycogen and the amylose and amylopectin of starch. Most other polysaccharides can be hydrolyzed only by microorganisms. Polysaccharidases which catalyze the hydrolysis of starch or of glycogen are generally termed *amylases*. There are two types of amylases, both of which catalyze the hydrolysis of the α-1,4-glucosidic linkages of glucose polymers. One of these, occurring chiefly in plant seeds and tubers (where starch is stored), is called *β-amylase*. It acts on glucose polymers to cleave maltose units from the nonreducing ends of the molecules. The continued action of this enzyme, freeing one maltose unit at a time, results in the degradation of α-1,4-glucoside chains to maltose.

α-Amylase is the common polysaccharidase of animals. It is present in the secretion of the pancreas and, in the case of the omnivores, also in saliva. In contrast to β-amylase, α-amylase catalyzes the cleavage of α-1,4-glucosidic bonds at almost any location in the molecule. Should the first attack of the enzyme occur near the middle of a straight-chain glucose polymer, the two molecules which would result as products would be still of rather high molecular weight. Such oligo- and polysaccharide degradation products of native polysaccharides are called *dextrins*. The continued action of α-amylase on straight-chain glucose polymers eventually results mainly in the production of maltose.

Neither of the amylases has activity toward the α-1,6-glucosidic linkages constituting the branch points of glycogen and amylopectin. Furthermore, the hydrolysis of α-1,4-linkages near the branch points proceeds rather slowly, probably because of interference of the side-chain with the formation of the enzyme-substrate complex. Consequently the action of the amylases on the branched polysaccharides gives a final mixture of maltose and a variety of branched dextrins, sometimes called *limit dextrins*.

Another type of enzyme is necessary for further hydrolysis of the limit dextrins. Perhaps the best known of these is *oligo-α-1,6-glucosidase*, found in the secretion of the cells of the intestinal mucosa of animals. As its name indicates, this enzyme catalyzes the hydrolysis of the α-1,6-glucosidic branch points of oligosaccharides such as those produced by amylase action. The products normally are small straight-chain oligosaccharides which are subject to further hydrolysis to maltose by amylase action.

In animals at least, the usual glucose polysaccharides of the diet are hydrolyzed chiefly to maltose units as the result of α-amylase and oligo-α-1,6-glucosidase acting together in the digestive tract. As a

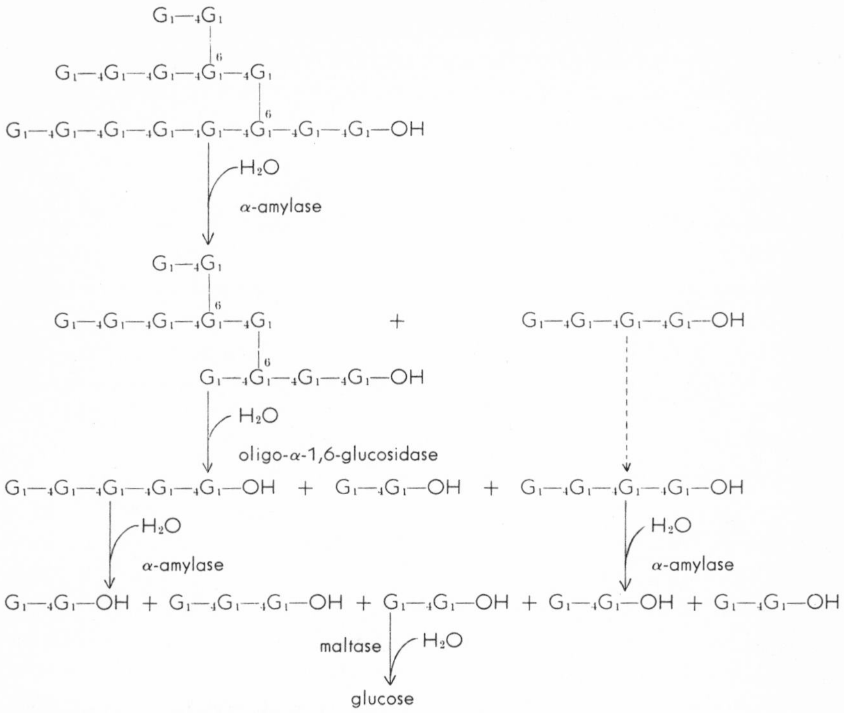

$$G_1-_4G_1$$
$$|^6$$
$$G_1-_4G_1-_4G_1-_4G_1-_4G_1$$
$$|^6$$
$$G_1-_4G_1-_4G_1-_4G_1-_4G_1-_4G_1-_4G_1-_4G_1-OH$$

$$\downarrow\!\!\!\curvearrowright\!-H_2O$$
$$\alpha\text{-amylase}$$

$$G_1-_4G_1$$
$$|^6$$
$$G_1-_4G_1-_4G_1-_4G_1-_4G_1 \qquad + \qquad G_1-_4G_1-_4G_1-_4G_1-OH$$
$$|^6$$
$$G_1-_4G_1-_4G_1-_4G_1-OH$$

$$\downarrow\!\!\!\curvearrowright\!H_2O$$
$$\text{oligo-}\alpha\text{-1,6-glucosidase}$$

$$G_1-_4G_1-_4G_1-_4G_1-_4G_1-OH \; + \; G_1-_4G_1-OH \; + \; G_1-_4G_1-_4G_1-_4G_1-OH$$

$$\downarrow\!\!\!\curvearrowright\!-H_2O \qquad\qquad\qquad\qquad\qquad\qquad\qquad \downarrow\!\!\!\curvearrowright\!H_2O$$
$$\alpha\text{-amylase} \qquad\qquad\qquad\qquad\qquad\qquad\qquad \alpha\text{-amylase}$$

$$G_1-_4G_1-OH \; + \; G_1-_4G_1-_4G_1-OH \; + \; G_1-_4G_1-OH \; + \; G_1-_4G_1-OH \; + \; G_1-_4G_1-OH$$

$$\text{maltase}\;\downarrow\!\!\!\curvearrowright\!H_2O$$
$$\text{glucose}$$

Figure 9-1. Typical Steps Involved in the Hydrolysis of a Polysaccharide to Glucose During Animal Digestion.

final step the glycosidase, *maltase*, catalyzes the hydrolysis of each maltose molecule to two glucose units, completing the digestive process. A representation of these processes appears in Figure 9-1.

Two additional glycosidases merit mention. These are *lactase* and *sucrase* which catalyze the hydrolysis of the disaccharides lactose and sucrose to their constituent monosaccharides. These enzymes are widely distributed in microorganisms and in the intestinal juices of animals. The reactions catalyzed by maltase, lactase, and sucrase are:

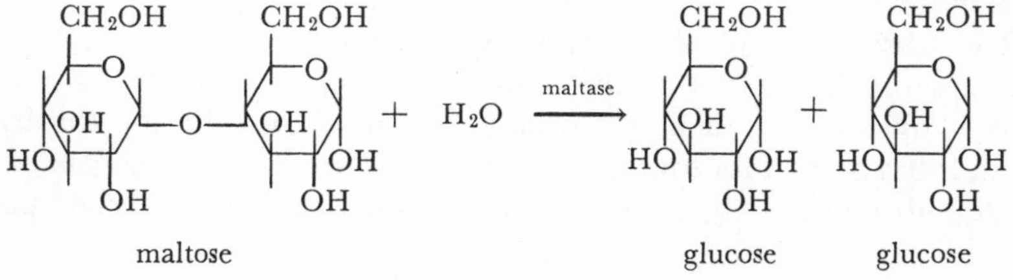

maltose $\quad + \quad H_2O \xrightarrow{\text{maltase}}$ glucose $\quad + \quad$ glucose

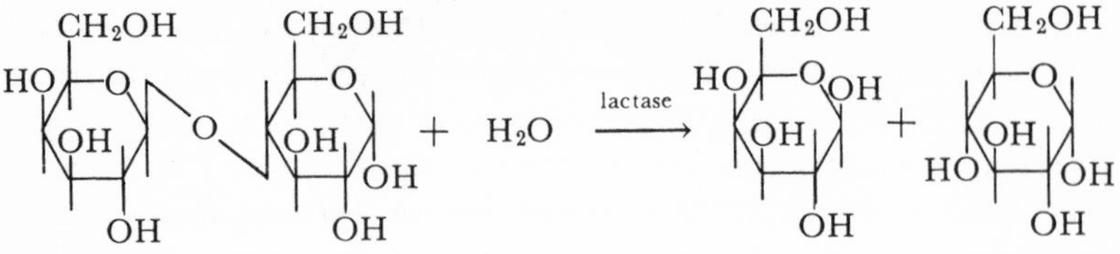

lactose

galactose   glucose

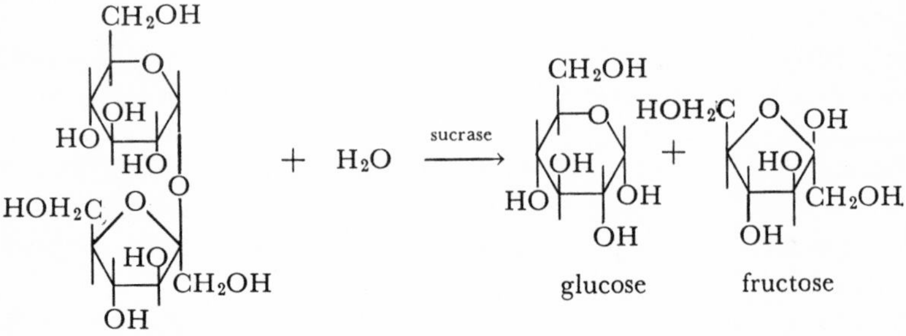

sucrose

glucose   fructose

Note that maltase is a specific α-glucosidase for which maltose, a glucose-α-glucoside is the common substrate. Similarly lactase is a specific β-galactosidase. Relatively nonspecific glucosidases and galactosidases, able to act on almost any small glucoside or galactoside, are also quite widely distributed among living organisms.

The polysaccharidases which have been described are specific for α-glucosidic linkages, and accordingly cannot catalyze the hydrolysis of cellulose, a polymer of β-glucose units. Various microorganisms and other lower organisms such as snails utilize enzymes called *cellulases* which facilitate the hydrolysis of cellulose. Herbivorous animals, for which cellulose is a major dietary component, are dependent for cellulose digestion upon enzymes liberated by bacteria present in their digestive tracts.

Absorption of Sugars

The absorption of the monosaccharides, glucose, fructose, and galactose, in common with the absorption of most materials by living cells, is by no means a simple process of osmosis or diffusion through an indifferent membrane. Cell membranes are not thin sheets of a single substance with holes or pores through which materials pass freely in either direction. Instead they are mosaics of many different substances, perhaps chiefly lipids and proteins, and display remarkable abilities in facilitating the passage of certain compounds while rejecting others. Cell membranes are selective in their action, implying that they play active roles in the absorption process. Indeed, the absorption of many substances can be accomplished against a net concentration gradient. Obviously, energy must be spent to carry out this operation. The term *active transport* is used to designate such energy-utilizing absorption processes.

Although no details of the cellular absorption of any compound are yet available, it appears that the membrane contains a number of different specific types of areas (absorption sites), each of which is concerned with the entrance of only one compound. Furthermore, in some well-established cases (and perhaps generally), the absorption of a compound involves its temporary combination with a specific enzyme-like protein called a *permease*.

The situation with respect to monosaccharide absorption has not yet been clarified. It seems likely that permeases specific for each sugar are necessary.

In this connection we may also note that a major effect of the hormone, insulin, is the facilitation of glucose absorption. The mechanism of its action is unknown. The insulin molecule may be a part of the permease system specific for glucose. This is consistent with the fact that in insulin-deficiency the cellular absorption of fructose appears to be unimpaired.

METABOLISM OF SUGARS

Once the sugars reach the cell interior their metabolism begins. The first step is their conversion to phosphate esters. This seems to occur almost immediately after absorption, so that free sugars do not exist within living cells to any appreciable extent. Carbohydrate metabolism is therefore almost entirely the metabolism of sugar phosphates. Among these compounds, glucose-6-phosphate is perhaps most important because it stands at a point in the metabolic activities which can be regarded as the direct intersection of a number of different metabolic pathways. These include the production of glucose polymers, the production of pentoses, oxidation to CO_2 and H_2O with ATP formation, and even hydrolysis to yield glucose once again. Indirectly, the carbon atoms of glucose-6-phosphate can be converted via intermediates of one or another of these processes to fatty acids, to glycerol, to sterols, to amino acids, and to other cell constituents. The reverse is also true; lipids and amino acids in particular are commonly degraded to substances which can enter the pathway for carbohydrate oxidation. These processes are diagrammed in Figure 9-2.

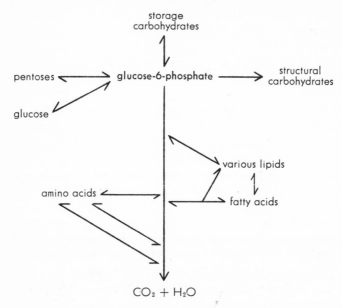

Figure 9-2.   Possible Metabolic Fates of Glucose-6-phosphate.

In particular, then, a glucose-6-phosphate molecule is faced with a number of competing reaction sequences. One molecule can follow only one of these possible paths. In general, some of the glucose-6-phosphate molecules present in the cell at any particular time will proceed down one path, some down each of the others. The quantitative distribution of the molecules among the various metabolic paths will be determined to a major extent by the activities of the various enzymes. These in turn will be governed by the physiological state of the cell.

Under conditions wherein glucose molecules are available to the cell in large quantities and there is little demand for ATP generation for synthetic or physical activities, many of the glucose-6-phosphate molecules will be converted to storage polysaccharide–glycogen in the animal. At the same time a greater percentage of the intermediates of the oxidation of the glucose-6-phosphate will be diverted from further oxidation to the synthesis of lipids. As some of us have reason to rue, animals are capable of storing almost unlimited amounts of lipids, while storage of glycogen, except by liver cells and to a lesser extent by muscle cells, is very limited.

On the other hand, when there is a continuing demand for relatively large amounts of ATP for various purposes, the balance of activities shifts so that a greater percentage of the available glucose units undergo oxidation. At the same time, storage polysaccharides are converted back to glucose-6-phosphate and lipids are transformed in larger quantities into compounds which can enter oxidative pathways.

We will describe each of the metabolic processes involved in the formation and utilization of glucose-6-phosphate in some detail in separate sections. You must bear in mind, however, that the whole metabolic pattern diagrammed in Figure 9-2 represents a single unified system in which each reaction is intimately related to every other reaction, not only those indicated here but every other metabolic process of the cell.

For the reasons previously indicated we will emphasize the metabolic interconversions of glucose. The other monosaccharides commonly available to cells, fructose and galactose, are rather directly converted to glucose phosphate and therefore the metabolic pathways of all these compounds quickly merge.

Phosphorylation of Glucose

The formation of a phosphate ester of a sugar such as glucose cannot be accomplished by the simple reaction of the sugar with phosphate ion, because the equilibrium is exceedingly unfavorable. The synthesis of the sugar phosphates in biological systems actually requires the donation of a phosphate group by ATP. The reaction involves the cleavage of a phosphate anhydride with the formation of a phosphate ester of an alcohol group of the sugar.

$$\text{ROH} \; + \; \text{ATP} \; \rightarrow \; \text{R}-\text{O}-\overset{\displaystyle O}{\overset{\displaystyle \|}{\underset{\displaystyle \underset{\textstyle OH}{|}}{\text{P}}}}-\text{OH} \; + \; \text{ADP}$$

The equilibrium for this reaction lies far toward the formation of the ester. In effect the chemical energy of ATP is utilized to overcome the unfavorable equilibrium for the direct reaction of the alcohol and the phosphate ion. Note that this is accomplished by making possible a different route to the ester. This is the first of many examples we will encounter in which the energy of ATP is utilized in the formation of compounds otherwise difficult to synthesize.

Since the phosphorylation of the alcohol involves phosphate transfer, the reaction is properly termed *transphosphorylation*. Enzymes catalyzing transphosphorylations are best termed transphosphorylases but are commonly called *kinases*. In animals, glucokinase, fructokinase, and galactokinase catalyze reactions of similar nature for their obvious substrates. Some organisms (such as yeast) produce a single enzyme, hexokinase, which catalyzes the phosphorylation of both glucose and fructose. The equation for the glucokinase reaction follows.

$$
\begin{array}{c}
\underset{\text{C}}{\overset{\text{H} \quad \text{OH}}{\diagdown \diagup}} \\
| \\
\text{HCOH} \\
| \\
\text{HOCH} \quad \text{O} \\
| \\
\text{HCOH} \\
| \\
\text{HC} \\
| \\
\text{H}_2\text{COH}
\end{array}
\; + \; \text{ATP}
\xrightarrow[\text{Mg}^{++}]{\text{glucokinase}}
\begin{array}{c}
\underset{\text{C}}{\overset{\text{H} \quad \text{OH}}{\diagdown \diagup}} \\
| \\
\text{HCOH} \\
| \\
\text{HOCH} \quad \text{O} \\
| \\
\text{HCOH} \\
| \\
\text{HC} \\
| \\
\text{H}_2\text{C}\!-\!\text{O}\!-\!\underset{\text{OH}}{\overset{\text{O}}{\text{P}}}\!-\!\text{OH}
\end{array}
\; + \; \text{ADP}
$$

α-D-glucose $\qquad\qquad\qquad$ α-D-glucose-6-phosphate

In connection with the glucokinase reaction, two general comments may be made: First, this is the first specific example of the general participation of Mg^{++} as a cofactor in reactions involving phosphorylated compounds. Second, it is important to note that the glucokinase reaction is essentially irreversible. This is true of all such reactions in which anhydride bonds are cleaved as ester bonds are formed. Thus ATP can never be formed in any appreciable amount by a reaction of ADP with a simple phosphate ester.

Similarly, the phosphorylation of fructose by fructokinase yields fructose-6-phosphate. However, the galactokinase reaction gives galactose-1-phosphate as the product.

Sugar phosphates cannot be released directly from living cells. Highly ionized substances in general cannot pass through cell membranes. In order for sugars to be returned to the environment, as exemplified by the release of glucose to the blood from liver cells, the phosphate group must be removed. This is accomplished by hydrolysis of the ester linkage in the presence of an enzyme of a type called *phosphatase*. Many cells, including muscle cells of animals, lack glucose-6-phosphatase and therefore cannot liberate glucose. Naturally the release of glucose to the environment is useless for all cells except those of specialized tissues (such as the liver of an animal) which are responsible for maintaining a supply of glucose to other tissues.

The products of phosphatase action are the alcohol and inorganic phosphate ion, as is shown for the case of glucose-6-phosphatase in the following equation:

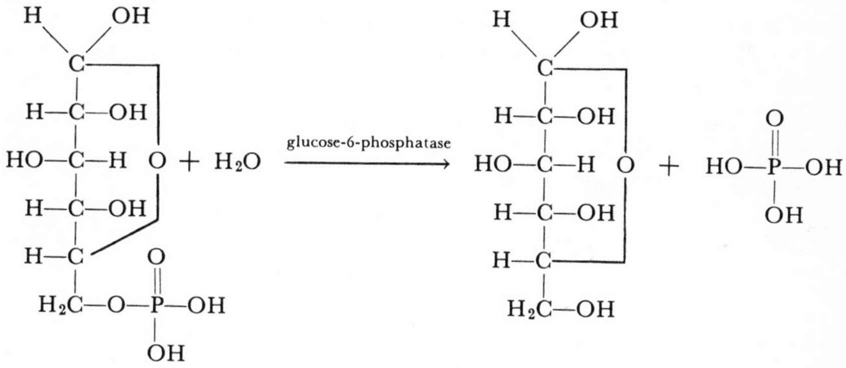

glucose-6-phosphate   glucose

For simplicity, phosphate groups in general will be indicated in formulas as being un-ionized. Actually, however, you should remember that under neutral conditions these groups will be highly, though not completely, ionized.

Polysaccharide Formation

The synthesis of disaccharides and polysaccharides is based on the use of sugar phosphates, rather than free sugars, as the starting material. Also, the conversion of these compounds back to the monosaccharide stage within living cells, in contrast to the hydrolytic processes of digestion, yields sugar phosphates directly instead of free sugars.

For all of the various compounds, regardless of the particular sugars involved, or the size of the molecules, the fundamental reactions are simply those of the formation and cleavage of glycosidic bonds linking sugar units. It should not be surprising that different organisms use remarkably similar mechanisms for these processes.

For simplicity we will consider mainly the formation and breakdown of glycogen in animal cells, using this as a model for the production of di- and polysaccharides in general.

The production of glycogen is a process which generally involves for each step only the addition of a single glucose unit to the end of a pre-existing glycogen chain. It will be recalled that glycogen is composed of glucose units linked as glucosides (acetals). Therefore, the reaction by which a new glucose unit is incorporated into glycogen must involve the reaction of its hemiacetal group with an alcohol group of another glucose unit. The direct reaction of an alcohol group with a hemiacetal does not proceed readily because the equilibrium is very unfavorable. Accordingly, glycoside formation in general requires that the hemiacetal group be "activated," that is, converted to a more reactive group which is capable of glycoside formation. In the present case two steps are needed. First, the glucose-6-phosphate is transformed into glucose-1-phosphate, a readily reversible reaction catalyzed by the enzyme, phosphoglucomutase.

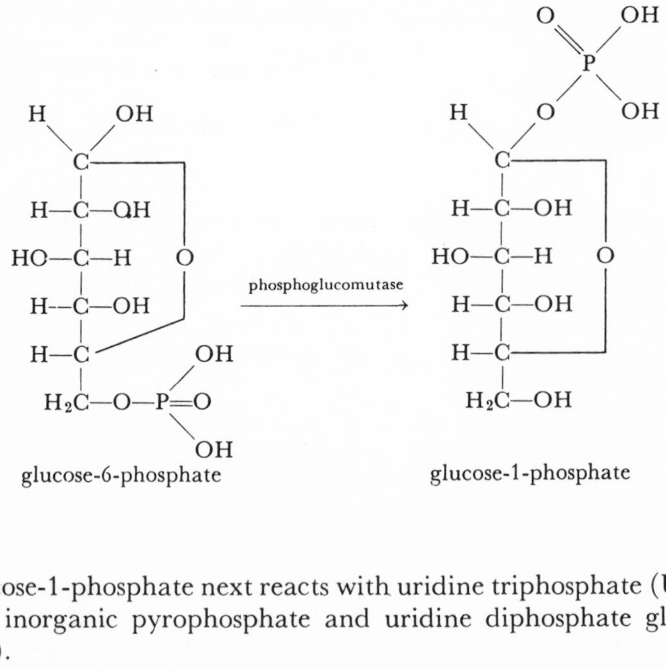

glucose-6-phosphate   glucose-1-phosphate

The glucose-1-phosphate next reacts with uridine triphosphate (UTP) to yield inorganic pyrophosphate and uridine diphosphate glucose (UDPG).

glucose-1-phosphate   uridine triphosphate (UTP)

uridine diphosphate glucose (UDPG)   pyrophosphoric acid (PP$_i$)

UDPG (and glucose-1-phosphate as well) is more reactive than the free hemiacetal with respect to glucoside formation. The glucose unit of UDPG in particular is then capable of being transferred to a glycogen molecule.

$$\text{UDPG} \;+\; \underset{(n \text{ glucose units})}{\text{glycogen}} \;\rightarrow\; \text{UDP} \;+\; \underset{(n+1 \text{ glucose units})}{\text{glycogen}}$$

Note that this reaction is not freely reversible, necessitating that the degradation of glycogen proceed by a route different from the synthetic one. The first step in the degradation process is that of *phosphorolysis* catalyzed by the enzyme, phosphorylase.

*In this and in many succeeding reactions the names of enzymes will be omitted for simplicity. Remember, however, that a specific enzyme is necessary for each biochemical reaction unless otherwise stated.

$$\text{glycogen} \underset{(n \text{ units})}{} + P_i \xrightleftharpoons{\text{phosphorylase}} \underset{(n-1 \text{ units})}{\text{glycogen}} + \text{glucose-1-}\mathbf{P}^*$$

This is a reaction equivalent to that of hydrolysis, with the water molecule being replaced by a phosphate ion. It is a reversible process to some extent, but not sufficiently so to account for glycogen formation in the living cell.

The glucose-1-$\mathbf{P}$ is then transformed into glucose-6-$\mathbf{P}$ by reversal of the previously mentioned phosphoglucomutase reaction.

The processes of glycogen formation (glycogenesis) and glycogen degradation (glycogenolysis) are summarized in Figure 9-3.

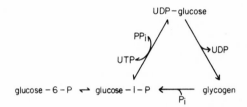

Figure 9-3. The Interconversion of Glucose-6-phosphate and Glycogen.

The energy required for the synthesis of the glycosidic linkage is supplied directly through the participation of uridine triphosphate rather than adenosine triphosphate as is perhaps most common in synthetic reactions. However, the resynthesis of UTP for subsequent reuse is brought about by direct reaction with ATP.

$$\text{UDP} + \text{ATP} \rightleftharpoons \text{ADP} + \text{UTP}$$

Other metabolic transformations of sugars are also carried out through the intermediate production of a UDP-sugar. For example, galactose-1-phosphate, formed upon the absorption of galactose, enters the glucose metabolic machinery in the following way:

$$\text{galactose-1-}\mathbf{P} + \text{UDP-glucose} \rightleftharpoons \text{UDP-galactose} + \text{glucose-1-}\mathbf{P}$$

$$\text{UDP-galactose} \rightleftharpoons \text{UDP-glucose}$$

---

*In this and in numerous following examples, phosphate groups of compounds often will be shown in equations and formulas as —$\mathbf{P}$ rather than $-P\!\!\!<^{\text{OH}}_{\text{OH}}=O$.

The second of these reactions involves the change of configuration of the sugar around the number 4 carbon atom. The reverse of this reaction also makes galactose units available from general carbon sources. These units can be used for lactose synthesis or can be converted to galacturonic acid derivatives for polysaccharide formation.

It should be realized that the term "glycogen" refers to a group of molecules of different sizes, not to a single, specific structure. A glycogen molecule in a cell must be regarded as being in a state of constant flux; under some circumstances it increases in size as glucose units are added one at a time to chain ends, and in other circumstances these glucose units are removed one at a time to provide glucose phosphate for metabolic purposes.

Starch synthesis and breakdown in plants proceeds by mechanisms similar to those shown for glycogen. Indeed, as a general rule the formation of glycosidic bonds of di- and polysaccharides requires the intermediate formation of a nucleoside diphosphate sugar as an "activation" step. The nucleoside need not be uridine; starch synthesis is thought to require ADP-glucose and cellulose production, GDP-glucose.

The finding that glycogen is synthesized and degraded by different mechanisms is perhaps surprising. However, this is a common situation in biological systems, allowing for greater possibilities of metabolic control. It must be recalled that an enzyme catalyzes both the forward and the reverse reactions of any single process. An activator or inhibitor of the enzyme will affect both processes to the same degree, achieving little. However, if the synthesis proceeds by one mechanism and the breakdown by another, then the presence of an activator or inhibitor can change the rate of one process without affecting the other. In the case at hand, for example, it appears that the hormone epinephrine (adrenalin) leads to an increase in glycogenolysis by stimulating the production of an activator of phosphorylase. In emergency situations this brings about the rapid production of glucose-6-phosphate, which can be oxidized for energy.

Glycolysis

The biochemical process by which glucose is oxidized is commonly considered to consist of two consecutive sections. The first series of reactions results in the production of two molecules of pyruvic acid. The second set of reactions leads to the complete oxidation of the pyruvic acid to carbon dioxide.

The formation of pyruvic acid from a glucose unit, either free glucose, glucose phosphate, or a component of glycogen, is known as *glycolysis*. Sometimes the designation "Emden-Meyerhof-Parnas pathway" is also used, to honor those scientists who worked out many of the details. The term "anaerobic phase" of glucose oxidation is also common. This term owes its origin to the fact that these reactions can occur in the absence of oxygen.

The reactions of glycolysis are summarized in Figure 9-4, assuming that the starting point is a molecule of glucose-6-phosphate which has been derived either from the phosphorylation of a glucose molecule which has just entered the cell or from the phosphorolysis of glycogen.

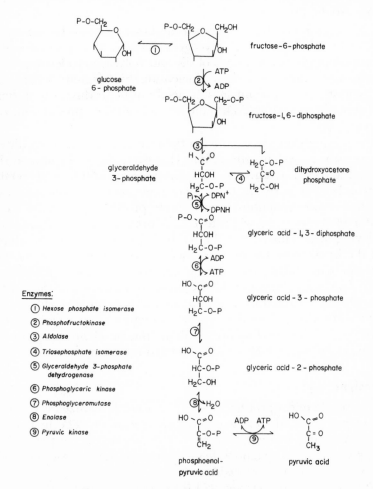

Figure 9-4.   The Glycolytic Pathway.

Certain significant aspects of each of these reactions will be considered.
The first step is the isomerization of glucose-6-phosphate to fructose-6-phosphate.

$$\text{glucose-6-}\mathbf{P} \underset{}{\overset{\substack{\text{hexose-phosphate}\\ \text{isomerase}}}{\rightleftharpoons}} \text{fructose-6-}\mathbf{P}$$

Obviously, any fructose entering the cell as fructose-6-phosphate will be indistinguishable from the compound formed from glucose-6-phosphate. This accounts, therefore, for the entrance of fructose into carbohydrate metabolism.

The next reaction is another transphosphorylation involving ATP and a kinase.

$$\text{fructose-6-}\mathbf{P} \;+\; \text{ATP} \xrightarrow{\substack{\text{phosphofructo-}\\ \text{kinase}}} \text{fructose-1,6-di-}\mathbf{P} \;+\; \text{ADP}$$

Note that this reaction is a typical ester formation and is not reversible.
However, fructose-1,6-diphosphate can be converted to fructose-6-phosphate by a specific phosphatase.

The fructose-1,6-diphosphate is then cleaved into two molecules of *triosephosphate*. The reaction is the reverse of a type called "aldol condensation" which involves the addition of an active methylene group to a carbon-oxygen double bond. Accordingly, the enzyme is termed *aldolase*.

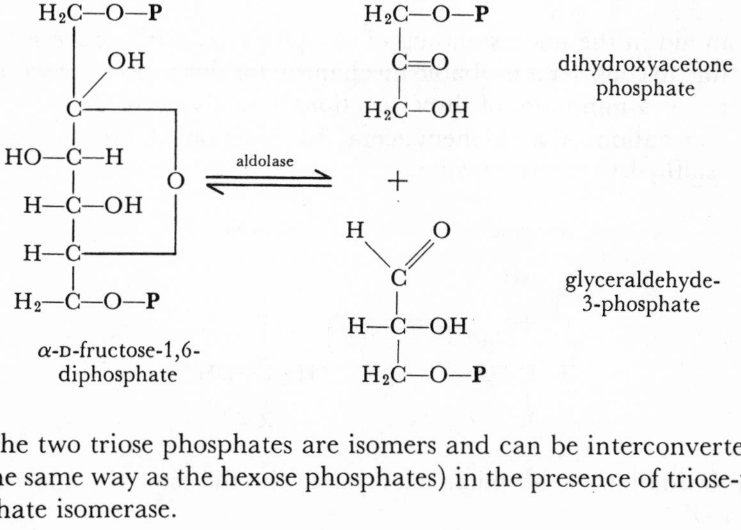

α-D-fructose-1,6-diphosphate

dihydroxyacetone phosphate

glyceraldehyde-3-phosphate

The two triose phosphates are isomers and can be interconverted (in the same way as the hexose phosphates) in the presence of triose-phosphate isomerase.

$$\text{glyceraldehyde-3-P} \xrightleftharpoons[\text{isomerase}]{\text{triose-phosphate}} \text{dihydroxyacetone-P}$$

The equilibrium lies to the right; that is, toward dihydroxyacetone-phosphate. Although this compound is important for the formation of the glycerol portion of triglycerides and other lipids, further carbohydrate metabolism is mainly concerned with glyceraldehyde-3-phosphate. Two molecules of this compound can be formed from one hexose because of the interconversion of the triose phosphates. This should be recalled when we attempt a quantitative view of the over-all sequence of reactions.

The next reaction is the first oxidation-reduction step of this pathway of carbohydrate metabolism. It is a rather unusual reaction in which a number of changes occur although only a single enzyme, glyceraldehyde-3-phosphate dehydrogenase, is involved. The aldehyde group is oxidized to a carboxyl which then forms a carboxylic acid-phosphoric acid anhydride.

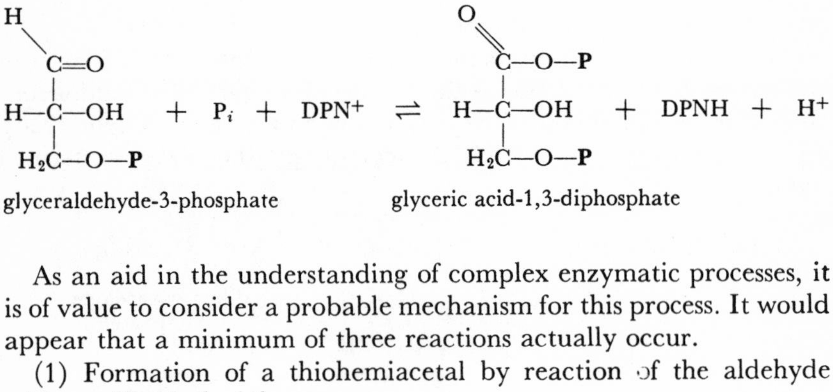

$$
\begin{array}{l}
\text{H} \\
\quad \diagdown \\
\qquad \text{C}{=}\text{O} \\
\qquad | \\
\text{H}{-}\text{C}{-}\text{OH} \\
\qquad | \\
\text{H}_2\text{C}{-}\text{O}{-}\text{P}
\end{array}
\;+\; \text{P}_i \;+\; \text{DPN}^+ \;\rightleftharpoons\;
\begin{array}{l}
\text{O} \\
\quad \diagdown\!\!\diagdown \\
\qquad \text{C}{-}\text{O}{-}\text{P} \\
\qquad | \\
\text{H}{-}\text{C}{-}\text{OH} \\
\qquad | \\
\text{H}_2\text{C}{-}\text{O}{-}\text{P}
\end{array}
\;+\; \text{DPNH} \;+\; \text{H}^+
$$

glyceraldehyde-3-phosphate   glyceric acid-1,3-diphosphate

As an aid in the understanding of complex enzymatic processes, it is of value to consider a probable mechanism for this process. It would appear that a minimum of three reactions actually occur.

(1) Formation of a thiohemiacetal by reaction of the aldehyde with a sulfhydryl of the enzyme:

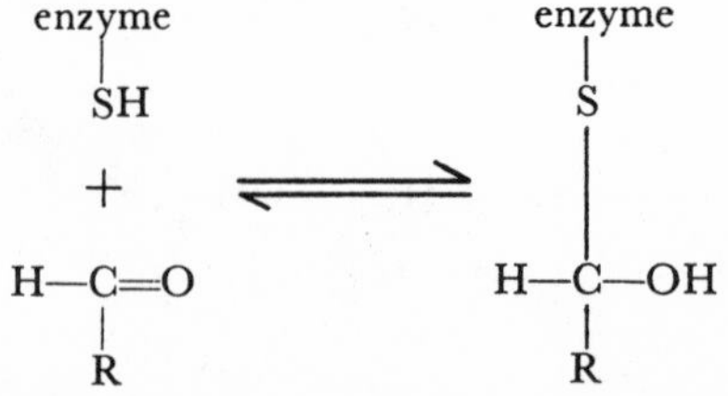

$$
\begin{array}{c}
\text{enzyme} \\
| \\
\text{SH} \\
+ \\
\text{H}{-}\text{C}{=}\text{O} \\
| \\
\text{R}
\end{array}
\quad \rightleftharpoons \quad
\begin{array}{c}
\text{enzyme} \\
| \\
\text{S} \\
| \\
\text{H}{-}\text{C}{-}\text{OH} \\
| \\
\text{R}
\end{array}
$$

(2) Oxidation of the thiohemiacetal to the thioester (by enzyme-bound DPN^+):

$$
\begin{array}{c}
\text{enzyme} \\
| \\
\text{S} \\
| \\
\text{H—C—OH} \\
| \\
\text{R}
\end{array}
\ + \ \text{DPN}^+ \ \rightleftharpoons \
\begin{array}{c}
\text{enzyme} \\
| \\
\text{S} \\
| \\
\text{C}{=}\text{O} \\
| \\
\text{R}
\end{array}
\ + \ \text{DPNH} \ + \ \text{H}^+
$$

(3) Phosphorolysis of the thioester, giving the anhydride:

$$
\begin{array}{c}
\text{enzyme} \\
| \\
\text{S} \\
| \\
\text{O}{=}\text{C} \\
| \\
\text{R}
\end{array}
\ + \ \text{HO—P—OH} \ \rightleftharpoons \
\begin{array}{c}
\text{enzyme} \\
| \\
\text{SH}
\end{array}
\ + \
\begin{array}{c}
\text{O} \quad \text{OH} \\
\backslash \, / \\
\text{O—P} \\
| \quad \backslash \\
\text{O}{=}\text{C} \quad \text{OH} \\
| \\
\text{R}
\end{array}
$$

This reaction is significant with respect to energy-transfer in two ways. First, note that DPNH is formed from DPN$^+$. The reoxidation of DPNH to DPN$^+$ by the electron transfer system can lead to the synthesis of three molecules of ATP. Secondly, the reaction produces an acid anhydride which is capable of reacting directly with ADP to yield ATP. This is the next metabolic step. Reactions of this type are known as "substrate-level" phosphorylations to distinguish them from oxidative and photosynthetic production of ATP.

$$
\begin{array}{c}
\text{O} \\
\backslash \\
\text{C—O—P} \\
| \\
\text{R}
\end{array}
\ + \ \text{ADP} \ \rightleftharpoons \ \text{ATP} \ + \
\begin{array}{c}
\text{O} \\
\backslash \\
\text{C—OH} \\
| \\
\text{R}
\end{array}
$$

glyceric acid-   glyceric acid-
1,3-diphosphate   3-phosphate

The glyceric acid-3-**P** is next converted to glyceric acid-2-**P**, in effect a migration of the phosphate group.

glyceric acid-3-**P** $\rightleftharpoons$ glyceric acid-2-**P**

A dehydration reaction then gives phosphoenolpyruvic acid:

$$
\begin{array}{c}
\text{O} \\
\backslash \\
\text{C—OH} \\
| \\
\text{H—C—O—P} \\
| \\
\text{H}_2\text{C—OH}
\end{array}
\ \xrightarrow[\text{enolase}]{} \
\begin{array}{c}
\text{O} \\
\backslash \\
\text{C—OH} \\
| \\
\text{C—O—P} \\
|| \\
\text{CH}_2
\end{array}
\ + \ \text{H}_2\text{O}
$$

glyceric acid-2-phosphate   phosphoenolpyruvic acid

The hydrogen atom of an enolic hydroxyl is an ionizable or acidic hydrogen. Therefore, the enolphosphate resembles a true acid anhydride in reactivity and is capable of a readily reversible reaction involving the transfer of the phosphate group to ADP. This is another example of a "substrate-level phosphorylation."

$$
\begin{array}{ccc}
\overset{\displaystyle O}{\diagdown} & & \overset{\displaystyle O}{\diagdown} \\
\text{C—OH} & & \text{C—OH} \\
| & & | \\
\text{C—O—P} \;+\; \text{ADP} \;\rightleftharpoons\; \text{ATP} \;+ & & \text{C=O} \\
|| & & | \\
\text{CH}_2 & & \text{CH}_3 \\
\text{phosphoenolpyruvic acid} & & \text{pyruvic acid}
\end{array}
$$

Presumably the enol form of pyruvic acid is formed first, but immediately rearranges to give the keto form as the major component of an equilibrium mixture.

All of the reactions of glycolysis are reversible (as long as we begin with glucose-6-phosphate) except that fructose-1,6-diphosphate cannot yield fructose-6-phosphate by reaction with ADP. However, the same effect is achieved by phosphatase action, and pyruvic acid may therefore be converted to glucose-6-phosphate (and thence to glycogen).

The glycolysis process is capable of operation either in the presence of oxygen (aerobically) or in the absence of oxygen (anaerobically). However, it must be emphasized that the amount of DPN$^+$ in a cell is very small. The number of molecules of glyceraldehyde-3-phosphate which can be oxidized will therefore be critically dependent on the DPN$^+$ supply. As the DPN$^+$ is converted to DPNH, the whole process will be blocked at the oxidation step unless some mechanism is available which will permit the resynthesis of the oxidized form, DPN$^+$. This ability each living cell must possess for itself; DPNH cannot traverse cell membranes. We have already seen, in the description of the electron transport system, how DPNH can be oxidized to DPN$^+$ provided that oxygen is available.

ANAEROBIC REOXIDATION OF DPNH

In *anaerobic glycolysis*, the electron transport system cannot function, since oxygen is absent. Therefore some other process must operate to regenerate DPN$^+$ Muscle cells of animals, which often operate under conditions of low oxygen supply (oxygen is utilized more rapidly than it can be brought to the cell), accomplish this feat by the use of pyruvic acid to oxidize the DPNH, yielding DPN$^+$ and lactic acid.

$$DPNH + H^+ + \underset{\text{pyruvic acid}}{\overset{\overset{\displaystyle O}{\underset{\displaystyle\parallel}{}}}{\underset{\underset{\displaystyle CH_3}{\overset{\displaystyle |}{\underset{\displaystyle C=O}{\overset{\displaystyle |}{}}}}}{C-OH}}} \underset{\text{dehydrogenase}}{\overset{\text{lactic acid}}{\rightleftharpoons}} DPN^+ + \underset{\text{lactic acid}}{\overset{\overset{\displaystyle O}{\underset{\displaystyle\parallel}{}}}{\underset{\underset{\displaystyle CH_3}{\overset{\displaystyle |}{\underset{\displaystyle H-C-OH}{\overset{\displaystyle |}{}}}}}{C-OH}}}$$

Many microorganisms often live with limited access to oxygen, and indeed can live in the complete absence of oxygen. This they manage to do by the use of reactions similar to the one given above. The lactic acid bacteria, in fact, reoxidize DPNH anaerobically in exactly the same manner as animal cells. However, some yeasts and other microorganisms have solved the same problem in a slightly different fashion.

$$\underset{\text{pyruvic acid}}{\overset{\overset{\displaystyle O}{\underset{\displaystyle\parallel}{}}}{\underset{\underset{\displaystyle CH_3}{\overset{\displaystyle |}{\underset{\displaystyle C=O}{\overset{\displaystyle |}{}}}}}{C-OH}}} \xrightarrow[\underset{\text{(TPP)}}{\text{thiamine pyrophosphate}}]{\overset{\text{pyruvic}}{\text{decarboxylase}}} CO_2 + \underset{\text{acetaldehyde}}{\overset{\overset{\displaystyle H}{\underset{\displaystyle |}{}}}{\underset{\underset{\displaystyle CH_3}{\overset{\displaystyle |}{}}}{C=O}}}$$

$$\underset{\text{acetaldehyde}}{\overset{\overset{\displaystyle H}{\underset{\displaystyle |}{}}}{\underset{\underset{\displaystyle CH_3}{\overset{\displaystyle |}{}}}{C=O}}} + DPNH + H^+ \underset{\text{dehydrogenase}}{\overset{\text{alcohol}}{\rightleftharpoons}} DPN^+ + \underset{\text{ethanol}}{CH_3-CH_2OH}$$

The first step is the decarboxylation of pyruvic acid, producing carbon dioxide from the carboxyl group. The coenzyme for the decarboxylase is *thiamine pyrophosphate* (TPP), a compound produced from the vitamin thiamine. One major biological role of thiamine is its participation as a portion of a coenzyme in a variety of decarboxylation reactions involving α-keto acids.

It should be realized that the formation of ethanol or of lactic acid in the absence of oxygen is not a process which the cell can turn on or off at will. Instead, the change in the metabolic pathway followed by the carbon atoms of pyruvic acid is entirely automatic. As the oxygen supply dwindles, DPNH will tend to accumulate. At the same time the concentration of pyruvic acid will be elevated since, as we shall soon see, its further metabolism is highly dependent upon the availability of oxygen. Naturally there will then be a much greater likelihood that

DPNH and pyruvic acid, for example, can interact to form DPN⁺ and lactic acid. As oxygen again is available, the DPN⁺ concentration rises, the pyruvic acid concentration drops, and the equilibrium shifts toward the oxidation of any lactic acid remaining in the cell back to pyruvic acid and then on to carbon dioxide.

An abbreviated summary of the reactions of glycolysis and of the various procedures for the reoxidation of DPNH appears in Figure 9-5.

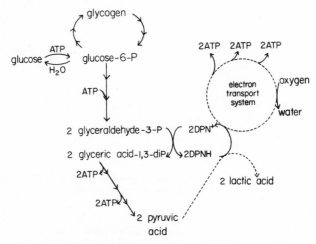

Figure 9-5. An Abbreviated Summary of Glycolysis and Some Related Processes.

We must here emphasize that anaerobic glycolysis is an inefficient process with respect to ATP production; only microorganisms can satisfy completely their energy needs by this process. Anaerobic glycolysis is important for animals only during relatively brief periods, until oxygen can again be made available. The end-products of anaerobic glycolysis—lactic acid or ethanol—are rather toxic substances and their continued production will halt the metabolic activities of the cells involved. For yeast, the ethanol concentration at which this occurs is about 14 per cent.

ENERGY YIELD OF GLYCOLYSIS

At this point it is perhaps well to take stock of the energy-transfer processes of glycolysis in a quantitative sense. Using ATP synthesis and utilization as the criteria, we find, starting with one glucose molecule outside the cell:

(1) Aerobic glycolysis:

	Change in ATP
ATP used:	
(a) glucose → glucose-6-**P**	—1
(b) fructose-6-**P** → fructose-1,6-**P**	—1
ATP formed:	
(a) 2 glyceric acid-1,3-di-**P** → 2 glyceric acid	+2
(b) 2 pyruvic acid-enol-phosphate → 2 pyruvic acid	+2
(c) 2 pairs of electrons through the electron transport system	+6
Net gain in ATP	+8

Thus, there is a net synthesis of eight molecules of ATP for each glucose molecule converted to two molecules of pyruvic acid.

(2) Anaerobic glycolysis:

Here the same processes must operate as in the aerobic case, except that the electron transfer system is inoperative. The energy available from the oxidation of DPNH is used, not for ATP production, but for lactic acid production. A net gain of only 2 ATP's per glucose molecule will then be possible. Obviously, the aerobic process is four times as efficient as the anaerobic one with respect to ATP production.

Aerobic Metabolism of Pyruvic Acid

Under anaerobic conditions, carbohydrate metabolism ends with lactic acid (or ethanol). However, if oxygen is freely available, most of the pyruvic acid is oxidized to CO_2 and H_2O, with the further production of ATP, rather than being reduced to lactic acid. This occurs by a sequence of reactions which can conveniently be separated into two groups. The first of these is known as the *oxidative decarboxylation* of pyruvic acid; the second as the *tricarboxylic acid cycle*.

THE OXIDATIVE DECARBOXYLATION OF PYRUVIC ACID

The first step in the oxidation of pyruvic acid is a very complex one in which a series of reactions undoubtedly occurs. This can be seen simply by examining the over-all process indicated below. For the complete structure of the compound called *coenzyme A*, see p. 91.

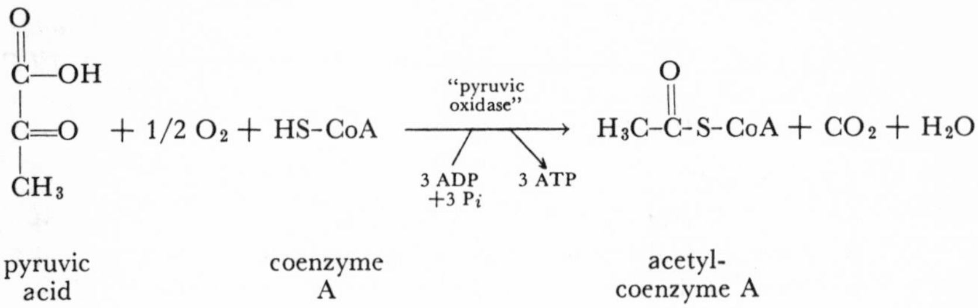

$$
\begin{array}{c}
\overset{\displaystyle O}{\overset{\|}{C}}\!\!-\!OH \\
|\\
C\!\!=\!\!O \\
|\\
CH_3
\end{array}
+ 1/2\ O_2 + HS\text{-}CoA
\quad\xrightarrow[\substack{3\ ADP\\ +3\ P_i}]{\text{``pyruvic oxidase''}\atop 3\ ATP}\quad
H_3C\text{-}\overset{\displaystyle O}{\overset{\|}{C}}\text{-}S\text{-}CoA + CO_2 + H_2O
$$

| pyruvic acid | coenzyme A | | acetyl-coenzyme A |

The term "pyruvic oxidase" is used here to represent an entire complex of enzymes and cofactors required for the complete conversion shown; that is, for decarboxylation of the pyruvic acid, oxidation of the resulting aldehyde to the acid level, and reoxidation of a reduced cofactor by the electron transport system. The final effect of the action of the electron transport system will appear, of course, as the reduction of one oxygen atom to water and the synthesis of three molecules of ATP.

Thiamine pyrophosphate is the coenzyme involved in the first phase of this process, the decarboxylation reaction. The sequence of reactions which has been postulated for its action may be represented as:

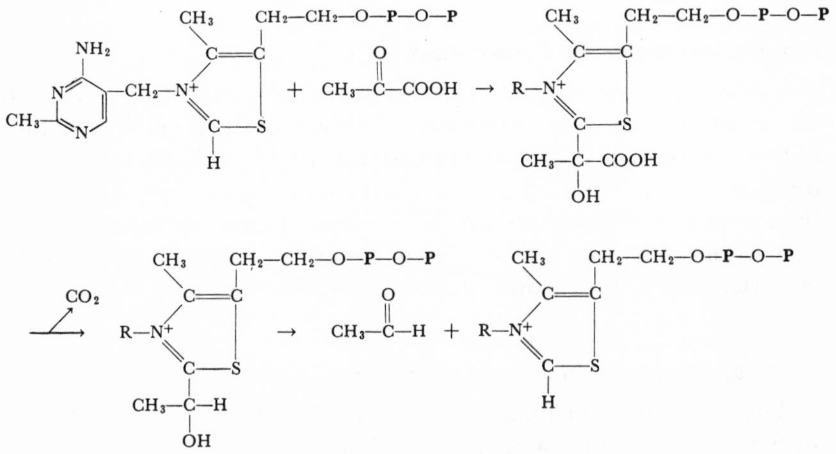

The addition of thiamine pyrophosphate to the carboxyl group of pyruvic acid is analogous to the addition of cyanide ion to a carboxyl function, i.e.,

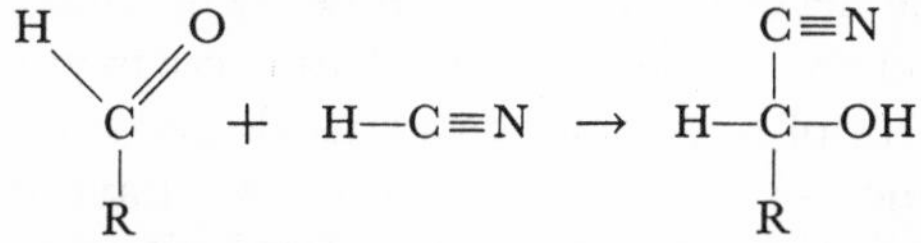

$$\underset{R}{\underset{|}{C}}\overset{\displaystyle H}{\overset{\diagup}{\underset{\diagdown}{}}}\overset{\displaystyle O}{\overset{\diagup\!\!\!\diagup}{}} \;+\; H\!\!-\!\!C\!\equiv\!N \;\rightarrow\; H\!\!-\!\!\underset{\underset{R}{|}}{\overset{\overset{C\equiv N}{|}}{C}}\!\!-\!\!OH$$

The product of the first step of pyruvic acid oxidation is shown to be acetaldehyde, although it may never be released from the enzyme— going instead directly to the next reaction.

At this point we encounter a most unusual coenzyme (or cosubstrate), namely *lipoic acid* (the cyclic disulfide form of 6,8-dithiooctanoic acid). This compound is capable of undergoing a reaction with the "acetaldehyde" unit in which the aldehyde is both oxidized to the acid and made into a thioester; at the same time the lipoic acid molecule is reduced to the equivalent of the dithiol form.

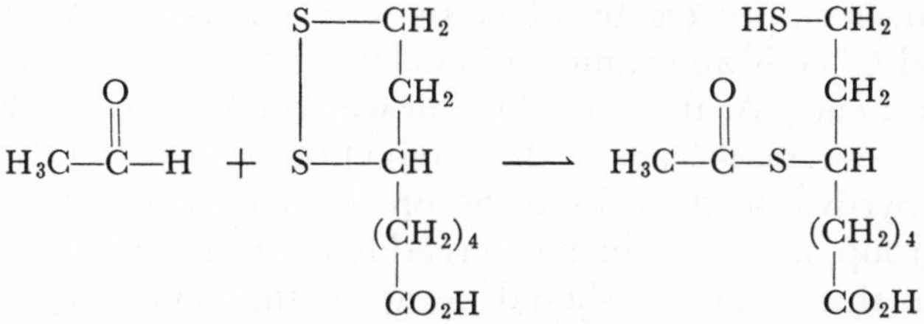

$$H_3C\!-\!\overset{\overset{\displaystyle O}{\|}}{C}\!-\!H \;+\; \begin{matrix} S\!-\!-\!CH_2 \\ | \quad\;\; | \\ |\quad\;\; CH_2 \\ S\!-\!-\!CH \\ | \\ (CH_2)_4 \\ | \\ CO_2H \end{matrix} \;\longrightarrow\; H_3C\!-\!\overset{\overset{\displaystyle O}{\|}}{C}\!-\!S\!-\!\begin{matrix} HS\!-\!CH_2 \\ | \\ CH_2 \\ CH \\ | \\ (CH_2)_4 \\ | \\ CO_2H \end{matrix}$$

Since the acetyl group is now in the form of a thioester, it may readily be transferred to another sulfhydryl compound, coenzyme A, to yield acetyl-coenzyme A and reduced lipoic acid.

This leaves only the reoxidation of the reduced lipoic acid (called dihydrolipoic acid) back to the cyclic disulfide form still to be achieved to complete the reaction sequence. For this purpose, there is a special enzyme which carries out the reaction:

$$DPN^+ + \text{dihydrolipoic acid} \rightleftharpoons DPNH + H^+ + \text{lipoic acid}$$

The DPNH thus formed may then be reoxidized aerobically, utilizing the services of the electron transport system (and producing energy in the form of ATP in the process).

Several additional points may be mentioned with regard to coenzyme A, the final acceptor of the acetyl group in this system. This compound was found in early work to be generally involved in biological reactions involving the production or transfer of acetyl groups, particularly "acetylation" reactions, reactions in which an acetyl group is added to another compound. The letter "A" in coenzyme A is derived from the necessity of the compound in these acetylation processes. More recently we have realized that coenzyme A is important in the metabolism of fatty acids in general, not simply of acetic acid.

This coenzyme, as are many of those we have encountered, is a nucleotide with adenosine monophosphate as part of the structure. Much of the remainder of the structure consists of the vitamin, pantothenic acid. Organisms needing pantothenic acid as an essential nutrient require it for coenzyme A synthesis. In addition, it should be noted that the coenzyme possesses a sulfhydryl group and that this is the reactive group of the molecule in acetyl-transfer reactions. Since the sulfhydryl group of the molecule is so important, attention is often drawn to it by abbreviating coenzyme A as CoA-SH, and acetyl-coenzyme A as acetyl-S-CoA. Alternatively, the abbreviation CoA may be used to designate the entire molecule. In any event, you should realize that the —SH group is part of the coenzyme molecule.

This over-all process, by which pyruvic acid is converted to acetyl-CoA and CO_2, is an example of *oxidative decarboxylation*. It serves two important ends. As it is an oxidation which is coupled to the electron transport system, it leads to the production of three ATP's per molecule of pyruvic acid oxidized. Secondly, it provides an "activated" acetyl group, a group which can readily be transferred to other molecules. In this regard, it should be noted that sulfhydryl groups are somewhat acidic in nature and therefore the thioester group of acetyl-CoA gains some of the reactivity generally associated with acid anhydrides. Acetyl-CoA was called "active acetate" before its structure was known.

THE TRICARBOXYLIC ACID CYCLE

The process just described may be regarded as a connecting link between glycolysis and an important cyclical process in which acetyl groups are oxidized to CO_2 and water. This process is called variously the *Tricarboxylic Acid* or *Citric Acid Cycle* after certain intermediate compounds, or the *Krebs Cycle* after H. A. Krebs, an English biochemist who played a major role in its elucidation.

The reactions of the cycle are presented in Figure 9-6. The first step is the transfer of an acetyl group from acetyl-CoA to oxalacetic acid to give citric acid. This is fundamentally the addition of an activated methyl group across the carbonyl double bond. The coenzyme A is

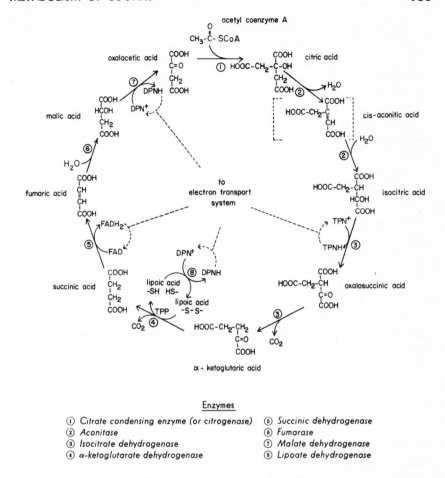

Figure 9-6. The Tricarboxylic Acid Cycle.

then released for further metabolic service. The next two reactions are
a dehydration, followed by a hydration in the opposite sense to yield
isocitric acid. The dehydration of an alcohol is a common biochemical
mechanism for the production of a double bond, just as the addition
of a water molecule across a double bond is a common biological
mechanism for the formation of an alcohol group. In the present case,
these two reactions are catalyzed by the same enzyme, and there is
some evidence that *cis*-aconitic acid may not be absolutely necessary
as a free intermediate in the synthesis of isocitric acid. Instead, the
conversion may be achieved with this intermediate bound to the enzyme. Of course, the result will be the same in either case.

The stage is now set for the dehydrogenation of isocitric acid to oxalosuccinic acid. The coenzyme serving as the immediate electron acceptor is of special interest in that it is triphosphopyridine nucleotide (TPN) rather than DPN. It differs from DPN solely by the presence of an extra phosphate group attached to the ribose component of the adenylic acid portion of the dinucleotide. Some dehydrogenases are specific for DPN, some for TPN, and some can utilize either. In general, DPN is used to a greater extent by animal cells, TPN by plant cells.

Oxalosuccinic acid is a β-keto acid and is subject, therefore, to the ready decarboxylation typical of this class of compounds. This reaction requires Mn^{++} ion as a cofactor and is apparently catalyzed by the same enzyme that is utilized for the dehydrogenation of isocitric acid.

The α-ketoglutaric acid which is the product of this reaction is then subjected to oxidative decarboxylation in a manner analogous to the conversion of pyruvate to acetyl-CoA. CoA, TPP, and lipoic acid are again necessary coenzymes. However, the succinyl-CoA which is formed is difficult to isolate in that it is rapidly cleaved to succinic acid and free CoA in a complex reaction which also, in somewhat indirect fashion, leads to the synthesis of one molecule of ATP. Probably this is what occurs:

$$\text{succinyl-CoA} \;+\; P_i \;\rightharpoonup\; \text{succinyl-P} \;+\; \text{CoA}$$
$$\text{succinyl-P} \;+\; \text{GDP} \;\rightharpoonup\; \text{GTP} \;+\; \text{succinic acid}$$
$$\text{GTP} \;+\; \text{ADP} \;\rightharpoonup\; \text{ATP} \;+\; \text{GDP}$$

(GDP and GTP are the di- and triphosphates of the nucleoside guanosine.)

The oxidation of succinic to fumaric acid is catalyzed by succinic dehydrogenase, an enzyme which contains firmly bound FAD as the coenzyme. The reduced flavin passes electrons on to coenzyme Q and the cytochromes of the electron transport system. In contrast with the more common dehydrogenations involving DPN or TPN as the immediate electron acceptor, only two molecules of ATP can be formed per pair of electrons, because the site of formation of one ATP has been bypassed.

The addition of a water molecule to the double bond of fumaric acid yields malic acid. This is then followed by the oxidation of malic acid by DPN^+ to oxalacetic acid, completing the cycle and regenerating an oxalacetic acid molecule for subsequent use in accepting another acetyl group.

The net effect of the cycle is the entrance of an acetyl group, its oxidation to CO_2 and H_2O by four different oxidation reactions, and the synthesis of ATP, chiefly via the electron transport system. Quantitatively this may be summarized as:

$$H_3C\text{-}\underset{\underset{O}{\|}}{C}\text{-}SCoA + 2\,O_2 + 12\,ADP + 12\,P_i \rightarrow 2\,CO_2 + 12\,ATP + 13\,H_2O + HSCoA$$

One molecule of CO_2 is produced in each of the two decarboxylation reactions. Water molecules are produced and used in a number of reactions. No accounting of these will be attempted here, except to note that twelve water molecules are released in conjunction with the formation of the phosphoanhydride bonds of ATP. Each of the three oxidations involving TPN, lipoic acid, and DPN, respectively, as the immediate electron acceptor, yields three ATP's through the reactions of the electron transport system. Reoxidation of the flavin of the succinic dehydrogenase reaction yields only two ATP's; however, the cleavage of succinyl-CoA produces a single ATP, accounting for the total of twelve.

The energy yields of various divisions of the process of glucose oxidation may now be compared, balancing the various steps only with respect to the carbon atoms.

Process			Net Gain of ATP
1 glucose	$\rightarrow$	2 pyruvic acid (aerobic glycolysis)	8
2 pyruvic acid	$\rightarrow$	2 acetyl-CoA + 2CO₂	6
2 acetyl-CoA	$\rightarrow$	4 CO₂ (Krebs cycle)	24
Summary: glucose	$\rightarrow$	6 CO₂	38

The yield of 38 ATP's possible under aerobic conditions should be contrasted with the two possible by the usual pathways of metabolism under anaerobic conditions.

A simplified version of glycolysis and the citric acid cycle is presented in Figure 9-7 as an aid in visualizing the relationship of the various individual oxidation reactions to the over-all process of glucose oxidation.

GLUCOSE AS A CARBON SOURCE

The emphasis on ATP production in this discussion of carbohydrate oxidation should not hide the importance of many of the intermediate compounds as starting points for the synthesis of many other cell metabolites. It must be realized that glucose serves not only as an

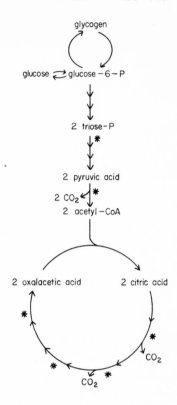

Figure 9-7. A Simplified View of Glycolysis and the Tricarboxylic Acid Cycle.

Each of the six starred reactions is an oxidation which passes electrons to the electron transport system with the subsequent formation of ATP and the reduction of oxygen to water.

energy source, but also as a major carbon source. We will see later, for example, that a number of the α-keto acids (pyruvic, oxalacetic, and α-ketoglutaric acids) can be converted readily to amino acids (alanine, aspartic, and glutamic acids, respectively) and that acetyl-CoA molecules supply all the carbon atoms required for the synthesis of both fatty acids and steroids.

The diversion of compounds of the tricarboxylic acid cycle to other metabolic ends leads to the loss of oxalacetic acid and the decreased ability of the cycle to accept acetyl groups for oxidation. New oxalacetic acid molecules must therefore be formed to restore the original metabolic balance. A variety of sources exists. Aspartic acid can readily be deaminated to yield oxalacetic acid. Glutamic acid can similarly yield α-ketoglutaric acid, which can be converted to oxalacetic acid by reactions of the cycle.

In addition there are several reactions which can generate oxalacetic acid by the introduction of a CO_2 molecule into a three-carbon acid. The reaction which is apparently most important in the quantitative sense is the conversion of pyruvic acid to malic acid, which can then be dehydrogenated to oxalacetic acid.

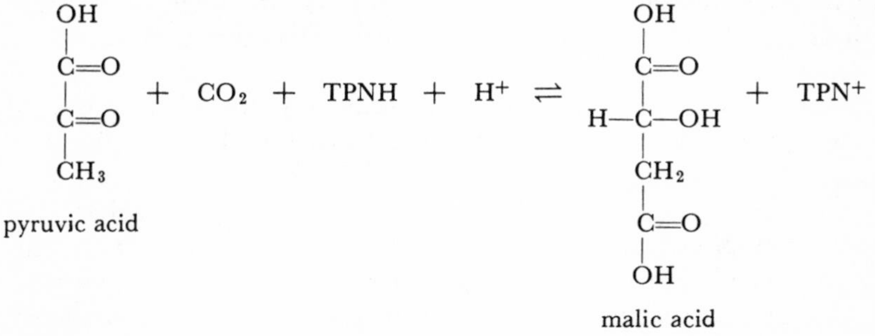

$$
\begin{array}{c}
\text{OH} \\
| \\
\text{C=O} \\
| \\
\text{C=O} \\
| \\
\text{CH}_3
\end{array}
\quad + \quad CO_2 \quad + \quad TPNH \quad + \quad H^+ \quad \rightleftharpoons \quad
\begin{array}{c}
\text{OH} \\
| \\
\text{C=O} \\
| \\
\text{H—C—OH} \\
| \\
\text{CH}_2 \\
| \\
\text{C=O} \\
| \\
\text{OH}
\end{array}
\quad + \quad TPN^+
$$

pyruvic acid

malic acid

CONVERSION OF CYCLE INTERMEDIATES TO GLUCOSE

Most of the reactions of the tricarboxylic acid cycle are individually reversible. However, the decarboxylation steps are essentially irreversible. The cycle as a whole can therefore turn only in one direction. Nevertheless, the compounds of the cycle can be used to form glucose units, essentially by the reversal of glycolysis. In particular, the carbon atoms of various amino acids can be converted directly or indirectly to intermediates of the cycle and ultimately to carbohydrates.

As compounds enter the tricarboxylic acid cycle from other metabolic sources they are oxidized to oxalacetic acid. One might guess that this would react to give pyruvic acid and CO_2 (a reaction which occurs spontaneously in the test tube), followed by reversal of the kinase reaction to give phosphoenolpyruvic acid and then on to glucose-6-phosphate. However the kinase reaction is poorly reversible and limits the formation of glucose units by this path. Instead, much of the oxalacetic acid is apparently converted directly to phosphoenolpyruvic acid by a reaction which bypasses this poorly reversible step.

oxalacetic acid $+$ ITP $\rightleftharpoons$ CO_2 $+$ IDP $+$ phosphoenolpyruvic acid

The compound designated as ITP is inosine triphosphate, a compound closely related to ATP. The NH_2 group of the adenine portion is replaced by an OH group to give a new purine, hypoxanthine. Note that this reaction can also *yield* oxalacetic acid by acting in the opposite direction.

The Phosphogluconate Pathway

The sequential processes of glycolysis and the tricarboxylic acid cycle probably account for the bulk of the glucose oxidized by most cells. However, a number of alternative mechanisms for the oxidation of glucose units occur in many organisms. In some cases these may make major contributions to the ATP supply; in other cases these reactions may be chiefly important as sources of compounds useful in other metabolic processes.

The sequence of metabolic reactions known as the *phosphogluconate pathway* is one of these alternate mechanisms for glucose oxidation which is of importance in a wide variety of organisms. Because this pathway can be considered to metabolize glucose-6-phosphate by reactions which bypass those of glycolysis, it is also known as the *hexose monophosphate shunt*. In animal tissues such as liver, or in various microorganisms, 30 per cent or more of the glucose units oxidized probably follow this route. An abbreviated version of this metabolic pathway is provided in Figure 9-8 to indicate the general nature of the process and of some of the key intermediates.

Note that there are two oxidation reactions for each carbon atom that is evolved as CO_2—the oxidation of the hexose phosphate to the gluconic acid derivative and the oxidation of phosphogluconic acid to ribulose phosphate. These oxidations can be coupled to the reactions of the normal electron transport system, with the usual synthesis of three molecules of ATP per pair of electrons. To make this possible

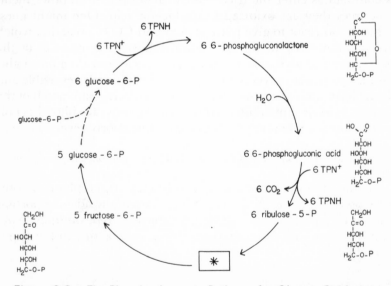

Figure 9-8. The Phosphogluconate Pathway for Glucose Oxidation.
The asterisk replaces a complex series of reactions involving the intermediate formation of 4- and 7-carbon sugars.

it is only necessary that electrons be first transferred from the TPNH formed in the oxidations to DPN$^+$. The resulting DPNH can then be reoxidized in the usual manner.

The reactions of this pathway for glucose oxidation proceed without the need for ATP as an essential reactant, in contrast to the reactions of glycolysis. Accordingly, stored glucose units of starch or glycogen can be oxidized readily by the phosphogluconate pathway (with the synthesis of ATP) under conditions of low ATP concentration in the cell. Under these same conditions, the oxidative reactions of the glycolytic pathway would be seriously hindered.

The participation of TPN rather than DPN in the oxidation steps merits further comment. We will later see that the synthesis of fatty acids in particular requires relatively large amounts of TPNH. Probably much of the reduced TPN used in these processes is derived (in animals at least) from the phosphogluconate pathway.

Also note that ribulose-5-phosphate is a major intermediate of the phosphogluconate pathway. Ribulose is the 2-keto sugar related to ribose. Ribulose-5-phosphate can be isomerized to ribose-5-phosphate by a reaction analogous to the fructose-6-phosphate isomerization to glucose-6-phosphate. Thus this pathway provides a metabolic source of ribose units for the synthesis of ribonucleic acids and of the nucleotide coenzymes. Also, we shall see in a later section of this chapter that ribulose-1,5-diphosphate plays a major role in the photosynthetic reactions of plants. This compound can be formed from ribulose-5-phosphate by a reaction with ATP which is analogous to fructose-1,6-phosphate formation from fructose-6-phosphate. The production of these important pentose phosphates must certainly be considered a major role of the first few reactions of the pathway.

Although many of the hexose units entering the phosphogluconate pathway find their metabolic fate to be that of the formation of pentose units of nucleic acids or other complex molecules, it should not be overlooked that the operation of the entire cyclical process can, in effect, accomplish the complete oxidation of a hexose unit. In conjunction with Figure 9-8, we can most readily visualize this process by starting with six molecules of glucose-6-phosphate. In the first three reactions these are oxidized to six molecules of CO_2 and six of ribulose-5-phosphate. The remaining reactions of the pathway result in the formation of five glucose-6-phosphate molecules from the six pentose units. Thus five of the original six hexose units have been resynthesized. If another hexose unit now becomes available, such as from glycogen breakdown, another turn of the cycle can occur, again with the net effect being the complete oxidation of one hexose unit. In a crude sense the five glucose-6-phosphate molecules can be used over and over again to facilitate the oxidation of numerous other glucose units.

Actually, as we shall soon see, the five glucose-6-phosphates which are reformed are not five of the original six molecules. Instead, considerable redistribution of the carbon atoms occurs in the reactions which have been omitted from the figure. The detailed examination of these reactions is beyond the scope of this book but an introduction to their nature seems appropriate.

The conversion of six ribulose-5-phosphate molecules to five fructose-6-phosphate units involves a complex system of interlocking reactions, including a number of isomerizations of the sugars. In particular, ribulose-5-phosphate is isomerized on the one hand to ribose-5-phosphate and on the other to xylulose-5-phosphate. But the novel reactions of the system are those which entail the transfer of a two- or three-carbon portion of one sugar unit to another. Triose, tetrose, and heptose phosphates result as intermediates.

Two subclasses of these transfer reactions are found. In the first of these, catalyzed by *transketolases*, the group transferred is the two-carbon ketol or glycolaldehyde group. In the second, *transaldolases* catalyze the transfer of the three-carbon dihydroxyacetone group.

The transketolase reaction may be represented in the general sense as:

$$\begin{array}{ccccccc}
\text{CH}_2\text{OH} & & \text{H} \quad \text{O} & & \text{H} \quad \text{O} & & \text{CH}_2\text{OH} \\
| & & \diagdown\diagup & & \diagdown\diagup & & | \\
\text{C}=\text{O} & + & \text{C} & \rightleftharpoons & \text{C} & + & \text{C}=\text{O} \\
| & & | & & | & & | \\
\text{CHOH} & & \text{R}' & & \text{R} & & \text{CHOH} \\
| & & & & & & | \\
\text{R} & & & & & & \text{R}'
\end{array}$$

A particular example would be:

$$\begin{array}{ccccccc}
& & \text{H} \quad \text{O} & & & & \text{CH}_2\text{OH} \\
\text{CH}_2\text{OH} & & \diagdown\diagup & & \text{H} \quad \text{O} & & | \\
| & & \text{C} & & \diagdown\diagup & & \text{C}=\text{O} \\
\text{C}=\text{O} & & | & & \text{C} & & | \\
| & + & \text{H}-\text{C}-\text{OH} & \rightleftharpoons & | & + & \text{HO}-\text{C}-\text{H} \\
\text{HO}-\text{C}-\text{H} & & | & & \text{H}-\text{C}-\text{OH} & & | \\
| & & \text{H}-\text{C}-\text{OH} & & | & & \text{H}-\text{C}-\text{OH} \\
\text{H}-\text{C}-\text{OH} & & | & & \text{CH}_2-\text{O}-\text{P} & & | \\
| & & \text{H}-\text{C}-\text{OH} & & & & \text{H}-\text{C}-\text{OH} \\
\text{CH}_2-\text{O}-\text{P} & & | & & & & | \\
& & \text{CH}_2-\text{O}-\text{P} & & & & \text{H}-\text{C}-\text{OH} \\
& & & & & & | \\
& & & & & & \text{CH}_2-\text{O}-\text{P} \\
\text{xylulose-5-P} & & \text{ribose-5-P} & & \text{glyceral-} & & \text{sedoheptulose-7-P} \\
& & & & \text{dehyde-3-P} & &
\end{array}$$

The transaldolase reaction may be generalized as:

$$
\begin{array}{c}
\text{CH}_2\text{OH} \\
| \\
\text{C}{=}\text{O} \\
| \\
\text{CHOH} \\
| \\
\text{CHOH} \\
| \\
\text{R}
\end{array}
\;+\;
\begin{array}{c}
\text{H} \quad \text{O} \\
\diagdown \;/ \\
\text{C} \\
| \\
\text{R}'
\end{array}
\;\rightleftharpoons\;
\begin{array}{c}
\text{H} \quad \text{O} \\
\diagdown \;/ \\
\text{C} \\
| \\
\text{R}
\end{array}
\;+\;
\begin{array}{c}
\text{CH}_2\text{OH} \\
| \\
\text{C}{=}\text{O} \\
| \\
\text{CHOH} \\
| \\
\text{CHOH} \\
| \\
\text{R}'
\end{array}
$$

A corresponding specific example is:

$$
\begin{array}{c}
CH_2OH \\
| \\
C{=}O \\
| \\
HO{-}C{-}H \\
| \\
H{-}C{-}OH \\
| \\
H{-}C{-}OH \\
| \\
H{-}C{-}OH \\
| \\
CH_2{-}O{-}\mathbf{P}
\end{array}
\;+\;
\begin{array}{c}
H \quad O \\
\diagdown \;/ \\
C \\
| \\
H{-}C{-}OH \\
| \\
CH_2{-}O{-}\mathbf{P}
\end{array}
\;\leftrightharpoons\;
\begin{array}{c}
H \quad O \\
\diagdown \;/ \\
C \\
| \\
H{-}C{-}OH \\
| \\
H{-}C{-}OH \\
| \\
CH_2{-}O{-}\mathbf{P}
\end{array}
\;+\;
\begin{array}{c}
CH_2OH \\
| \\
C{=}O \\
| \\
HO{-}C{-}H \\
| \\
H{-}C{-}OH \\
| \\
H{-}C{-}OH \\
| \\
CH_2{-}O{-}\mathbf{P}
\end{array}
$$

sedoheptulose   glyceral-   erythrose-4-**P**   fructose-6-**P**
-7-phosphate   dehyde-3-**P**

Transketolase enzymes require thiamine pyrophosphate as a co-enzyme (no coenzyme seems to be involved with the transaldolases). Presumably the ketol group is bound in an intermediate stage to the thiamine, much as is the acetaldehyde fragment formed in oxidative decarboxylation of pyruvic acid.

It is chiefly through the transfer of the two or three carbon units that hexose production from the pentose stage occurs. Two pentose phosphates interact, for example, to give a triose phosphate and a heptose phosphate (sedoheptulose-7-phosphate) by a transketolase reaction. The heptose phosphate reacts with a triose phosphate in a transaldolase reaction to give a tetrose phosphate (erythrose-4-phos-phate) and fructose-6-phosphate. The tetrose phosphate can then accept a ketol group from another pentose to form another fructose-6-phosphate and a triose phosphate. Finally, two triose phosphates can react to give fructose-1,6-diphosphate. These processes may be summarized as follows:

$$\begin{array}{c} \text{isomerases} \\ 6 \text{ ribulose-P} \xrightarrow{\hspace{3cm}} 2 \text{ ribose-P} + 4 \text{ xylulose-P} \\ (5C) \hspace{3cm} (5C) \hspace{1cm} (5C) \end{array}$$

$$\begin{array}{c} \text{transketolase} \\ 2 \text{ ribose-P} + 2 \text{ xylulose-P} \xrightarrow{\hspace{2.5cm}} 2 \text{ glyceral-} + 2 \text{ sedohep-} \\ (5C) \hspace{1cm} (5C) \hspace{3cm} \text{dehyde-P} \hspace{0.5cm} \text{tulose-P} \\ (3C) \hspace{1cm} (7C) \end{array}$$

$$\begin{array}{c} \text{transaldolase} \\ 2 \text{ sedohep-} + 2 \text{ glyceral-} \xrightarrow{\hspace{2.5cm}} 2 \text{ erythrose-P} + 2 \text{ fructose-P} \\ \text{tulose-P} \hspace{0.5cm} \text{dehyde-P} \hspace{3cm} (4C) \hspace{1cm} (6C) \\ (7C) \hspace{1cm} (3C) \end{array}$$

$$\begin{array}{c} \text{transketolase} \\ 2 \text{ xylulose-P} + 2 \text{ erythrose-P} \xrightarrow{\hspace{2.5cm}} 2 \text{ glyceral-} + 2 \text{ fructose-P} \\ (5C) \hspace{1cm} (4C) \hspace{3cm} \text{dehyde-P} \hspace{0.5cm} (6C) \\ (3C) \end{array}$$

$$\begin{array}{c} \text{1. aldolase} \\ 2 \text{ glyceraldehyde-P} \xrightarrow{\hspace{2.5cm}} \text{fructose-P} \\ (3C) \hspace{2cm} \text{2. phosphatase} \hspace{0.3cm} (6C) \end{array}$$

$$6 \text{ ribulose-5-P} \xrightarrow{\hspace{3cm}} 5 \text{ fructose-6-P}$$

Note that the reactions shown above are those which were replaced by an asterisk in Figure 9-8.

The Path of Carbon in Photosynthesis

Our rather meager knowledge of the reactions by which a photosynthetic organism utilizes radiant energy for the synthesis of TPNH and ATP was summarized in Chapter 8. There remains for us the examination of the "dark reactions" of photosynthesis—the incorporation (or "fixation") of carbon dioxide into organic compounds.

Until recently it had been generally assumed that glucose was a rather direct product of the "dark reactions." This belief was due in part to the easily demonstrated accumulation of starch in the leaves of plants kept in the light, and in part to the rather simple equations which could be written for the reduction of CO_2 to HCHO and the polymerization of the formaldehyde to glucose. We now know that these early ideas were in error and that the major reaction of photosynthesis yields glyceric acid-3-phosphate as the first stable product of carbon dioxide fixation. Other reactions which result in the conversion of carbon dioxide to organic compounds undoubtedly exist. As yet we have little information as to their quantitative significance. We shall therefore emphasize the reactions involved in the production and utilization of glyceric acid-3-phosphate.

The identification of the major product of CO_2 fixation awaited the development of tracer techniques and of two-dimensional paper chromatography, which took place shortly before, during, and after World War II. With these techniques a research group headed by Melvin Calvin was able to show in the late 1940's that glyceric acid-3-phosphate was probably the direct product of the CO_2-incorporation reaction.

In these experiments a photosynthetic alga was supplied carbon dioxide labeled with carbon-14 and was allowed to photosynthesize for varying periods of time in the light. The cells were then killed by immersion in hot alcohol. Two-dimensional paper chromatograms were prepared from extracts of the cells. It was found that radioautographs of the chromatograms, upon development of the film, contained numerous dark spots, demonstrating that a number of organic compounds had been formed from the radioactive CO_2. As the time of exposure to the light was decreased, fewer compounds contained C^{14}. With very short photosynthetic periods, most of the isotope was found to occur in a single spot on the chromatogram. This spot was shown to consist of glyceric acid-3-phosphate in which most of the C^{14} was located in the carboxyl group.

In the next step it was demonstrated (as the result of the efforts of a number of laboratories) that the formation of phosphoglyceric acid occurred by the following reaction:

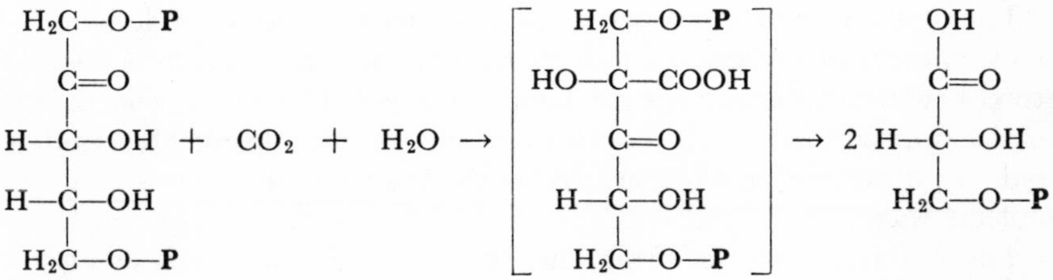

$$
\begin{array}{l}
H_2C-O-P \\
\ \ \ | \\
\ \ C=O \\
\ \ \ | \\
H-C-OH \\
\ \ \ | \\
H-C-OH \\
\ \ \ | \\
H_2C-O-P
\end{array}
+ CO_2 + H_2O \rightarrow
\left[
\begin{array}{l}
H_2C-O-P \\
\ \ \ \ \ | \\
HO-C-COOH \\
\ \ \ \ \ | \\
\ \ \ C=O \\
\ \ \ \ \ | \\
H-C-OH \\
\ \ \ \ \ | \\
H_2C-O-P
\end{array}
\right]
\rightarrow 2
\begin{array}{l}
OH \\
\ | \\
C=O \\
\ | \\
H-C-OH \\
\ \ \ | \\
H_2C-O-P
\end{array}
$$

ribulose-1,5-diphosphate   glyceric acid-3-phosphate

It appears that this reaction may involve the intermediate formation of a highly unstable six-carbon compound which almost immediately decomposes to two molecules of the three-carbon compound.

One further point remains to be explained—the dependence of this reaction upon the TPNH and ATP formed in the light reactions. Certainly this dependence must be indirect in nature, because neither of these compounds participates in the CO_2-fixation step. Actually the compounds are required chiefly for resynthesis of the ribulose diphosphate needed as the CO_2 acceptor, and for the formation of glucose units. These processes are accomplished by reactions which are

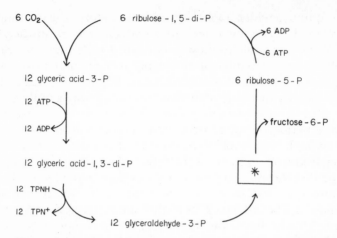

Figure 9-9. An Abbreviated Version of the Photosynthetic Cycle.

The transaldolase, transketolase, and related reactions have been replaced by an asterisk for simplicity.

the reversal of certain reactions of glycolysis and of the hexose monophosphate shunt. They are summarized in abbreviated form in Figure 9-9.

The first phase of the process, the production of glyceraldehyde-3-phosphate from glyceric acid-3-phosphate, should be readily understood because the reactions are simply those of glycolysis proceeding in the opposite direction. Naturally twelve molecules of glyceraldehyde-3-phosphate can be formed as the result of the fixation of six molecules of CO_2.

The reactions omitted from the figure permit the synthesis of six molecules of ribulose-5-phosphate and of a single "extra" hexose unit from every twelve molecules of glyceraldehyde-3-phosphate. In part this entails the further reversal of glycolysis to yield fructose-6-phosphate and in part the reversal of the reactions of the phosphogluconate pathway.

Again, this is basically the redistribution of carbon atoms of the sugar phosphates by aldolase, transaldolase, and transketolase reactions (through the tetrose and heptose phosphates as intermediates) to produce ribulose-5-phosphate and hexose phosphate. The ribulose-5-phosphate may then be phosphorylated to the diphosphate, completing the cycle.

The over-all effect of the cycle is the reaction of six molecules of CO_2 with six of ribulose diphosphate at the expense of 18 molecules of

ATP and 12 molecules of TPNH to regenerate six molecules of ribulose diphosphate and form one molecule of hexose phosphate. The requirement for high concentrations of ATP and TPNH supplied by the light reactions should now be obvious.

Each turn of the photosynthetic cycle can theoretically produce one molecule of hexose phosphate, which could then be stored as a glucose unit of starch. However, some of the intermediates of the cycle will almost always be drained off into other metabolic pathways. The amino acid serine can be formed rather directly from glyceric acid-3-phosphate. Triose phosphates will be used for triglyceride and phospholipid production and ribulose-5-phosphate for nucleotide synthesis; and the phosphoglyceric acid can also be oxidized directly by the glycolytic and citric acid cycle mechanisms. Therefore the yield of glucose units will normally be only a fraction of the possible yield.

The major effect of the light reactions on carbohydrate metabolism is to control the direction of the reactions of glycolysis and of the hexose monophosphate shunt. In the presence of sufficient light, chlorophyll, and other accessory factors, the ATP and TPNH concentrations will be high. This will promote those reactions leading toward the formation of hexose units from CO_2. On the other hand, when the plant is in the dark, the concentrations of ATP and TPNH are constantly being lowered by the usual energy-requiring metabolic processes. Under these conditions, the plant metabolizes the stored carbohydrate in essentially the same manner as does the animal. The hexose units are oxidized by the glycolytic and tricarboxylic acid pathways and by the hexose monophosphate shunt with the ultimate formation of CO_2.

SUGGESTED ADDITIONAL READING

Bassham, J. A., "The Path of Carbon in Photosynthesis," *Scientific American*, **206**, No. 6, 88 (June 1962).

Greenberg, D. M., Ed., "Metabolic Pathways," Vol. 1, pp. 97–295, Academic Press, New York and London, 1960.

Noggle, G. R., "Photosynthesis and Metabolism of Carbohydrates," in W. Pigman, Ed., "The Carbohydrates," pp. 733–777, Academic Press, New York, 1957.

Metabolism of Lipids

10

TYPES OF LIPIDS

The wide variety of lipid compounds found in living organisms was described in Chapter 4. Of these materials, the triglycerides are quantitatively the most important, comprising as much as 10 per cent of the body weight of a normal animal, even more in obese individuals. Because the triglycerides are insoluble in water, they may be stored in almost unlimited quantities without disturbing osmotic pressure relationships. The normal biological role of these compounds is, quite simply, that of serving as a store of organic material which can be readily oxidized with the concomitant synthesis of ATP.

In the qualitative sense, other types of lipids perform roles which are more vitally essential to the organism with respect to the maintenance of normal structure and function. The steroid hormones, the fat-soluble vitamins, and the plant pigments are only a few obvious examples. A major addition to this list is the phospholipids. These substances are unusual lipids in that each molecule contains a hydrophobic hydrocarbon (or fat-soluble) portion and a hydrophilic, ionic (or water-soluble) portion. This is the type of structure necessary for a compound to be an emulsifying agent. In all probability the phospholipids of plant and animal cells are important in both structural and metabolic contexts primarily because they are emulsifying agents.

Emulsification

The necessity for the presence of emulsifying agents in biological systems must be emphasized. Lipids, of course, are insoluble in water. On the other hand, enzymes are mainly water-soluble substances. A mixture of an enzyme and a lipid in water would be expected to separate into two mutually exclusive phases. Any possible catalytic activity of the enzyme would then be restricted to the interface, the boundary between the insoluble lipid phase and the aqueous phase containing the enzyme. Obviously the digestion and metabolism of lipids involve difficulties in bringing the lipid and enzyme molecules into intimate contact so that reactions can proceed at reasonable rates.

Any emulsifying agent aids in the production of a finely divided suspension of a lipid in an aqueous medium—a suspension known as an "emulsion." The hydrocarbon portions of the emulsifier and the lipid tend to associate (as we discussed in connection with hydrophobic bonding of hydrocarbon side-chains of proteins). This leaves the water-soluble group of the emulsifying agent projecting into the aqueous phase. A lipid droplet will associate with a number of molecules of emulsifier, in effect producing a new water-soluble surface. The water-soluble groups are those which are capable of forming hydrogen bonds with water molecules. Water molecules therefore tend to be held in a cloud or layer around each lipid droplet, thus interfering with the aggregation of the droplets. This process is illustrated in Figure 10-1.

The presence of the emulsifying agent permits the transformation of a single, separate lipid mass into a number of small lipid droplets.

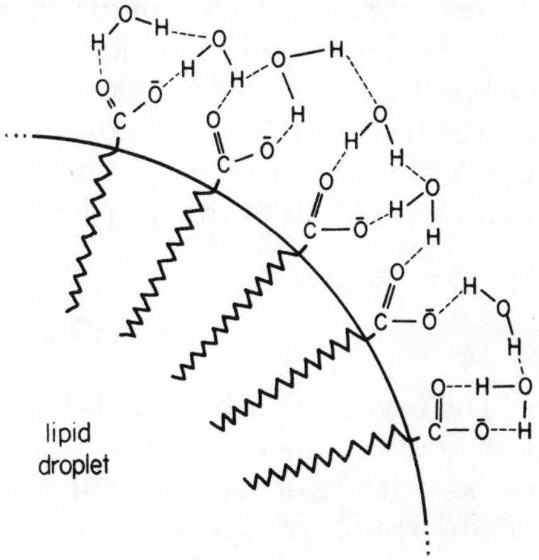

Figure 10-1. The Surface of an Emulsified Fat Globule.

In this case, the emulsifier chosen is a simple anion of a fatty acid (i.e., a soap). A portion of the surface of the globule is shown with the projecting carboxyl groups hydrogen-bonded to water molecules. Further hydrogen bonding among the water molecules leads to further stability of the resulting water "cloud" around the droplet.

The size of the droplets produced from a given lipid will vary with the chemical nature of the emulsifier. In any case, as a large mass of a lipid is converted to a large number of small droplets, the surface area of the lipid, the interfacial area between lipid and aqueous medium, is greatly increased.

The biologically important emulsifying agents are chiefly the phospholipids, proteins, and bile salts. The bile salts, or more properly the anions of the bile acids, function primarily in emulsification of lipids in the digestive tracts of animals, facilitating the digestion and absorption of these materials.

The emulsifying roles of the proteins and phospholipids are not so clear-cut as those of the bile salts. Lipoprotein complexes of all sorts may be considered to be emulsification phenomena. These complexes may be nonspecific, as in the case of the giant lipoprotein aggregates of the blood which transport absorbed lipids from the digestive tract to the liver and other storage areas. On the other hand, specific lipoprotein molecules occur as major components of the membranous structures of cells. In part these may result from the interaction of nonionic lipids with hydrocarbon side-chains of the proteins, and in part emulsified lipids may be bound to proteins through the charged groups of the phospholipids. Mitochondria, for example, contain large amounts of phospholipids. These compounds probably assist in the integration of the lipid and protein components of the electron transport system into a functional unit.

In addition, the phospholipids, particularly the lecithins, are of metabolic importance with respect to utilization of stored triglycerides. A dietary deficiency of lecithins or of substances such as choline or methionine which can be used in the synthesis of lecithins, is followed by the condition known as "fatty liver"—the accumulation of lipids in the liver in massive amounts. The related fundamental role of the lecithins is unknown. They may be concerned with transport of lipids from the liver to other storage areas or with mobilization of the lipids of the liver for oxidative metabolism.

HYDROLYSIS OF LIPIDS

The necessity for hydrolysis of dietary lipids as a prelude to absorption of the compounds into cells is not so clearly defined as it is for the carbohydrates or for the proteins. To a considerable extent the rate of absorption of lipids appears to be a function of the degree of emulsification which has been achieved. Lipids emulsified into very small droplets by a very efficient synthetic detergent can be absorbed without hydrolysis. The bile salts released into the digestive tract in the bile are not nearly as efficient, and alone are not capable of producing an emulsion that can pass through cell membranes. However, the bile salts acting in conjunction with other emulsifying agents such as dietary phospholipids and the di- and monoglycerides produced by partial hydrolysis of triglycerides, apparently can facilitate the absorption of much undigested lipid material. The degree to which this occurs is not clear. We will simply assume that the lipids absorbed by animals are an emulsified mixture of mono-, di-, and triglycerides, phospholipids, sterols, sterol esters, and fatty acids in unknown proportions.

In the over-all process of digestion and absorption, the bile salts are of major significance in a number of ways. They emulsify the dietary lipids, thereby increasing the rate at which digestive enzymes can act, and with other agents they assist in producing emulsions for absorption. Also, excess cholesterol is excreted in the bile as an emulsion with bile salts.

These compounds are a group of closely related steroids. The proportion of each of the different compounds varies somewhat with the animal. The major bile salt of humans is sodium glycocholate.

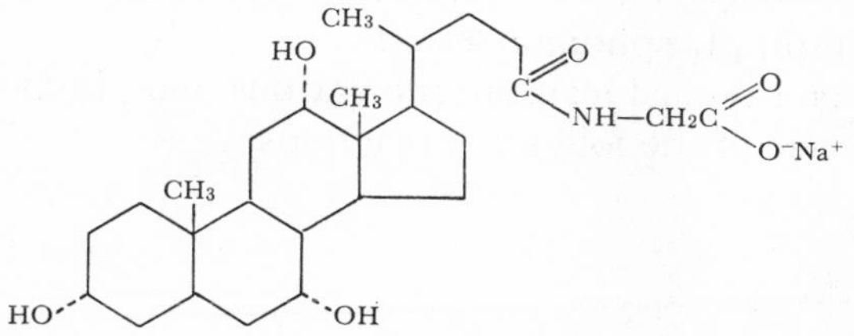

sodium glycocholate

Regardless of the somewhat questionable necessity for enzymes capable of the hydrolysis of all dietary lipids, the digestive tracts of animals receive enzymes in the pancreatic and intestinal cell secretions which are capable of catalyzing the hydrolysis of these substances to their simple components. The major ones are described in the following sections.

LIPASES

These are enzymes which catalyze the hydrolysis of the ester linkages at the α- positions of a tri-, di-, or monoglyceride. Thus a triglyceride will first be converted to an α, β-diglyceride, and then to a β-monoglyceride. These enzymes will catalyze the hydrolysis of the third fatty acid linkage also, but at a very greatly reduced rate.

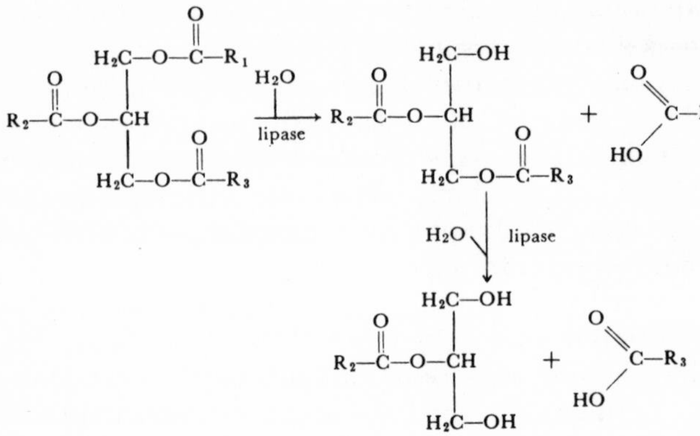

PHOSPHODIESTERASES

These enzymes catalyze the hydrolysis of a phosphate ester linkage only when it is part of a phosphodiester grouping. They normally have no action on phosphomonoesters.

In the case of a typical lecithin, the various phosphodiesterases will each catalyze one of the following reactions:

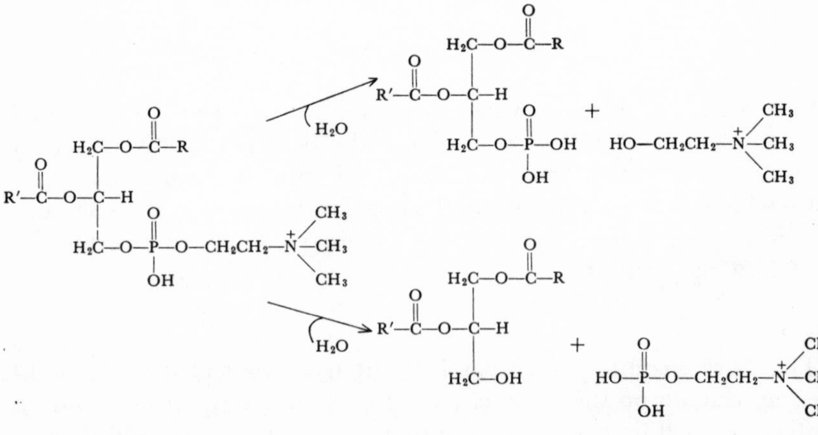

PHOSPHOMONOESTERASES

These enzymes catalyze the hydrolysis of monoesters of phosphoric acid and are commonly called "phosphatases." They may be either nonspecific (i.e., the rate of reaction does not greatly depend upon the alcohol group involved) or highly specific for one particular phosphate ester or group of esters. The phosphomonoesterases usually found in the digestive tracts of animals are generally nonspecific in nature. Among other reactions they will catalyze the removal of the phosphate groups from the products of phosphodiesterase action above, to yield a diglyceride, phosphoric acid, and choline (in the case shown). Of course, the diglyceride may be further acted upon by lipase.

CHOLESTEROL ESTERASE

Much of the cholesterol in an animal's diet is in the form of fatty acid esters. A special enzyme known as "cholesterol esterase" exists, which is capable of catalyzing the hydrolysis of these esters to release the free sterol and fatty acid.

Plant tissues commonly contain at least the first three of these types of enzymes. They are found in particularly high concentration in seeds, and function to release stored materials during the germination process.

Enzymes capable of removing a fatty acid from an intact glycerol phospholipid are generally missing from both plant and animal systems, perhaps due to the toxicity of the lysophosphatides which would be the products of their action. Certain snake venoms, however, contain rather high concentrations of "phospholipase A," which does remove one fatty acid from a phospholipid. When injected into a blood stream, this enzyme causes the release of lysophosphatides (e.g., lysolecithins), which are very potent surface-active agents, thus bringing about the extensive rupture of red blood cells.

METABOLISM OF FATTY ACIDS

Since the major storage forms of lipids in most organisms are those that contain as part of their structure one or more fatty acids, it would appear only reasonable to begin our discussion of lipid metabolism with a consideration of the metabolism of these acids. We will consider first the process of fatty acid oxidation.

Fatty Acid Oxidation

Before a fatty acid can be oxidized, it must first be "activated," i.e., converted to the more suitably reactive thioester of coenzyme A. This activation requires energy, which is supplied by a molecule of ATP. First, the ATP reacts to produce an anhydride of AMP and the fatty acid. This anhydride can then react with the sulfhydryl group of the coenzyme A molecule to yield the fatty acyl CoA derivative and release free AMP:

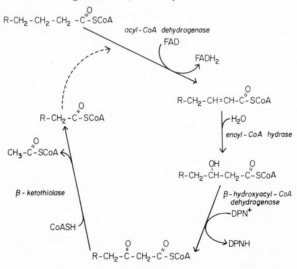

The fatty acyl CoA derivative may now enter into the sequence of reactions shown in Figure 10-2, usually referred to as the "Beta Oxida-

Figure 10-2. The Fatty Acid β-Oxidation System.

tion" pathway for fatty acids. First, there is a FAD-requiring dehydrogenation reaction, followed by the addition of water to the double bond in such a way as to yield a β-hydroxy compound. Oxidation of the β-hydroxyacyl CoA derivative to the keto form is catalyzed by an enzyme which requires DPN as its coenzyme. The β-keto ester so formed may then be "thiolyzed" with the addition of another molecule of coenzyme A to yield one molecule of acetyl-CoA and one molecule of a fatty acyl CoA derivative having two fewer carbon atoms than the fatty acid with which we started. The over-all reaction for one turn of the cycle may then be summarized as follows:

$$CH_3-(CH_2)_{n+2}-\overset{\overset{\displaystyle O}{\|}}{C}-S-CoA \ + \ FAD \ + \ DPN^+ \ + \ CoASH \ \rightarrow$$

$$CH_3-(CH_2)_n-\overset{\overset{\displaystyle O}{\|}}{C}-S-CoA \ + \ FADH_2 \ + \ DPNH \ + \ H^+ \ + \ \text{acetyl-CoA}$$

From the point of view of energy production, if we assume that reoxidation of the reduced DPN yields three ATP's and the reoxidation of the reduced FAD yields two ATP's, we obtain a net yield of five ATP's for each two carbon atoms that are removed from the fatty acid. Of course it would be necessary to subtract from the total for the whole fatty acid the one ATP required for activation to the original CoA ester derivative.

The acetyl-CoA units are normally further oxidized by the usual processes of the citric acid cycle. We have seen in Chapter 9 that the complete oxidation of one molecule of acetate results in the production of 12 molecules of ATP. Thus the complete oxidation of a 2-carbon fragment of a fatty acid (ignoring the activation step for the moment) will yield on the order of 17 molecules of ATP.

Thus the energy yields *per carbon* for complete oxidation of a polysaccharide and a triglyceride are approximately equal. However, the lipid materials contain many more carbon atoms per unit *weight*, and thus represent a more efficient way of storing a given amount of reserve energy supply in a minimum weight. For plants, which do not have to move around, this is presumably of little importance, whereas for most other organisms additional weight means additional energy requirements. Whether this type of reasoning is sound or not, it remains a fact that most plants store their reserve energy supplies chiefly in the form of polysaccharides, while most other organisms utilize some form of lipid as the major storage compound.

FATTY ACID BIOSYNTHESIS

The biosynthesis of the fatty acids might well be expected to proceed by the reversal of the β-oxidation pathway, but this definitely does not occur to any appreciable extent. It is true that the carbon atoms of a fatty acid are derived, two at a time, from the acetyl groups of acetyl-CoA molecules and that many of the reactions leading to the fatty acids resemble closely those of the degradative process. However, the synthetic process is an energy-consuming one and must accordingly involve mechanisms that can overcome the energy barrier. Present ideas concerning these mechanisms are summarized in Figure 10-3. You should be aware that our knowledge is not yet complete and that the scheme given here may well not be the complete answer, at least in all organisms.

With regard to the over-all process of formation of fatty acids from acetyl groups, one must realize that two major chemical events are involved. The first of these is the formation of new carbon-to-carbon bonds between acetyl radicals, and the second is the reduction of ketone groups to the hydrocarbon stage. Both of these are energy-requiring processes. The energy requirement for the reduction steps is supplied rather directly by TPNH. The condensation step is a more difficult hurdle. Under biological conditions, the methyl group of one acetyl-CoA is apparently not sufficiently reactive for combination with another acetyl group, so that acetyl-CoA units cannot directly condense to produce longer carbon chains. The difficulty has been overcome in living systems by a process which involves the formation of malonyl-CoA as a more reactive intermediate, with ATP furnishing the required energy.

The synthesis of malonyl-CoA, shown as the first step in Figure 10-3, is a complex process which results in the addition of a molecule of CO_2 (actually as HCO_3^-) to a molecule of acetyl-CoA. At least two steps can be demonstrated to occur. In the first, CO_2 reacts with a molecule of biotin bound to an enzyme to yield a carboxybiotinyl-enzyme. In the second stage, the "bound CO_2" is transferred to acetyl-CoA, producing malonyl-CoA and biotinyl-enzyme.

biotinyl-enzyme $+$ CO_2 $+$ ATP $\rightarrow$ carboxybiotinyl-enzyme $+$ ADP $+$ P_i

carboxybiotinyl-enzyme $+H_3C$—$\overset{\overset{\textstyle O}{\|}}{C}$—S—CoA$\rightarrow$biotinyl-enzyme$+HO$—$\overset{\overset{\textstyle O}{\|}}{C}$—$CH_2$—$\overset{\overset{\textstyle O}{\|}}{C}$—S—CoA

Note that these reactions are "CO_2-fixation" processes in which

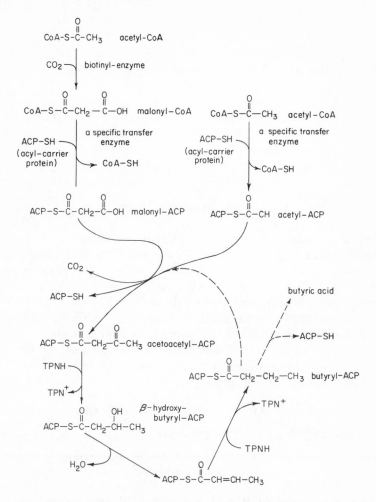

Figure 10-3. The Malonyl CoA - Acyl Carrier Protein Pathway for Fatty Acid Synthesis.

inorganic CO_2 is used, even by animals, to form organic compounds. Several such reactions are known which involve the participation of biotin, one of the water-soluble vitamins, as a coenzyme. In this case the term prosthetic group is probably preferable to that of coenzyme because the biotin molecule is strongly bound to the protein by an amide linkage between the carboxyl group of biotin and an ϵ-amino group of a lysine unit of the protein. The structures of biotin and carboxybiotin appear on the following page.

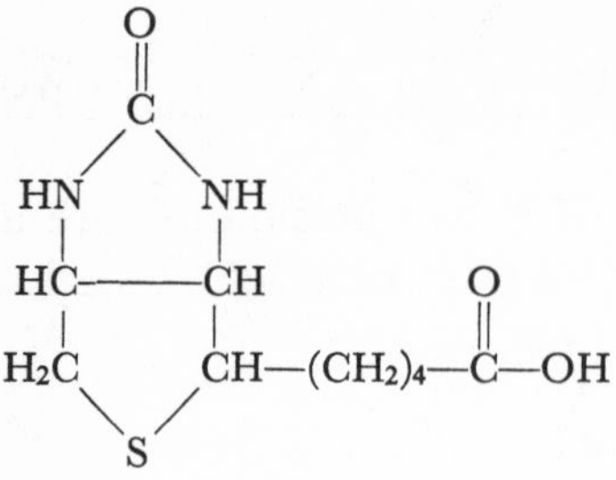

biotin

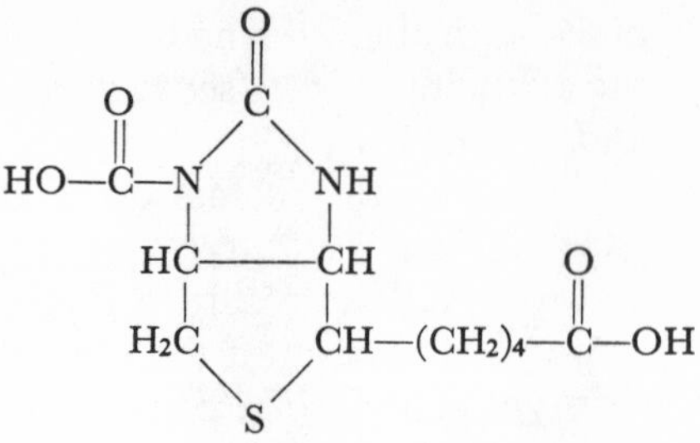

N-carboxybiotin

The reactions that bring about the elongation of the fatty acid chain are not yet completely clear. Apparently there are differences among the mechanisms used by different organisms. However, it is rather certain that in many cases, if not in most, the acetyl and malonyl groups are transferred from CoA in independent reactions to a small protein called acyl-carrier protein (ACP). The prosthetic group of this protein is phosphopantetheine, shown below. Note that this molecule is identical to a major portion of coenzyme A (p. 91). The phosphopantetheine is bound to the protein in ester linkage through its phosphate group and a hydroxyl group of a serine unit. As with CoA, the sulfhydryl group is the reactive part of the molecule in the acceptance and transfer of acyl groups.

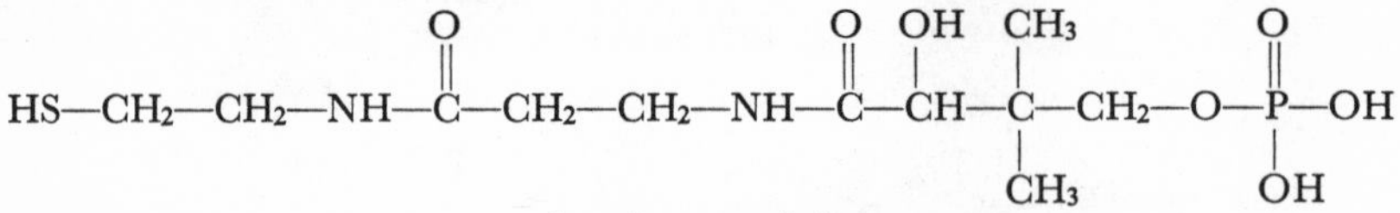

phosphopantetheine

Once the acetyl-ACP and malonyl-ACP molecules have been formed by the transfer of the acyl groups from CoA units, the chain-elongation step can occur. As is shown in Figure 10-3, the acetyl radical is transferred to the malonyl group, the carboxyl group of the malonyl residue is lost as carbon dioxide, and the major product is acetoacetyl-ACP. Note that CO_2 plays essentially a catalytic role in fatty acid synthesis. It is first fixed at the expense of ATP to provide a reactive malonyl derivative and is then released as the condensation step or chain-elongation reaction occurs.

The remaining reactions of Figure 10-3 are similar, in the reverse direction, to those of the β-oxidation sequence. The reactions take place with the intermediates bound to ACP rather than to CoA, and the reducing agents seem generally to be TPNH rather than DPNH and $FADH_2$.

Following the formation of butyryl-ACP two possibilities are apparent. First the butyryl group can react with another molecule of malonyl-ACP to result in further elongation of the fatty acid chain. Continued cycling of this nature forms the long-chain fatty acid derivatives. The second possible reaction of the fatty acid-ACP molecule at any stage is the release of the free fatty acid. Usually this does not occur until the chain-length is in the C_{16} to C_{18} range. The factors responsible for the release of these fatty acids from the cycle are unknown. We should also mention that in some organisms the free fatty acid is not released from the cycle. Instead the fatty acid group is transferred to a CoA molecule. The fatty acid-CoA unit can then be used directly for the formation of glyceryl esters.

At this point it should be noted that the existence of these separate processes for the synthesis and breakdown of fatty acids is analogous to the situation we have already discussed in connection with the synthesis and breakdown of glycogen (and other glucose polymers). In the present case, the separate pathways permit automatic but essentially independent regulation of the rates of oxidation and synthesis by the general metabolic state of the cell. To illustrate this point, let us consider first a situation in which energy (in the form of ATP) is being rapidly consumed by some other cellular process.

The increase in the concentrations of ADP and P_i which accompanies this use of ATP will shift the relative concentrations of all of the oxidation-reduction coenzymes in the direction of the oxidized forms. This is a simple mass-law type of effect which will be more clearly appreciated if we recall that one ATP is formed from ADP and P_i concomitant with the reoxidation of DPNH in the electron transport system. Thus we can write a very real, albeit partial, reaction

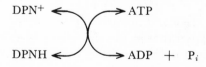

which illustrates the fact that high concentrations of ADP will tend to accelerate the reaction in the direction of more DPN^+ formation. Of course, another partial reaction can be written coupling this process to substrate oxidation

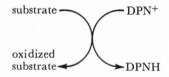

Thus the use of ATP will tend to increase the rate of the oxidative reactions of the β-oxidation pathway and in this way move metabolism in the direction of meeting the increased energy requirements of the cell. At the same time, the lowering in levels of ATP and of TPNH will drastically curtail the synthetic pathway.

On the other hand, when ATP concentrations within the cell are high (usually as a result of carbohydrate oxidation or photosynthesis) DPNH and TPNH levels will also rise, and net synthesis of fatty acids may proceed.

In photosynthesizing plants, as described earlier, the process of photosynthesis itself yields a net excess of both ATP and TPNH, and fatty acid synthesis may proceed at a rate which is independent of the oxidation of other compounds within the cell (provided of course that acetyl-CoA is available). In other organisms, however, and in plant cells during dark periods, both the synthesis and the oxidation of fatty acids are intimately related to and dependent upon carbohydrate metabolism. First, it should be noted that in order to carry out complete oxidation of a fatty acid, the acetyl-CoA units which are split off must be capable of being passed through the citric acid cycle to yield CO_2. In order for this to occur there must be a supply of oxalacetic acid available for condensation with the acetyl-CoA units. As we mentioned in Chapter 9, it is necessary that this compound be made from an intermediate of glycolysis.

In the event that carbohydrate metabolism is impaired (as in diabetes mellitus or certain types of cellular poisoning) the production of oxalacetate is reduced and acetyl-CoA tends to accumulate. This is aggravated by the fact that in the absence of carbohydrate oxidation, the rate of fatty acid oxidation tends to increase to meet the energy requirements of the cell. Under these circumstances there is a reversal of the β-oxidation pathway, at least far enough to produce acetoacetyl-CoA. This particular compound is rather readily hydrolyzed by enzymes occurring in many organisms and tissues, yielding free acetoacetic acid and free coenzyme A. To a lesser extent, the reduced compound, β-hydroxybutyric acid, is also produced.

Both the condensation of acetyl-CoA units and the hydrolysis of the resulting acetoacetyl-CoA structures release more free CoA, which can then be used to continue the process of oxidation of the fatty acids, with a continuing buildup in concentration of free acetoacetic acid (and β-hydroxybutyric acid). Since these acids are usually excreted in the form of the neutral sodium salt, this process soon leads to a serious depletion of the sodium content of the tissues. In animals, there is eventual interference with the pH of the blood and consequently with the transport of oxygen. The presence in the blood of excess acetoacetic acid (or acetone—see below) is called "ketosis." Ketosis is usually accompanied by "acidosis," the lowering of the ability of the blood to buffer against acids. Ketosis occurs not only in diabetes but also in any situation, such as high fat consumption or early starvation, in which lipid oxidation is not balanced by carbohydrate oxidation.

An interesting side reaction of this process may also be mentioned: Since acetoacetic acid is a free β-keto acid, it is rather easily decarboxylated, yielding CO_2 and acetone. Certain microorganisms are capable of producing rather high concentrations of acetone by essentially this process. (This was an important commercial source of acetone during World War I.) In animals, this reaction gives rise to the "acetone breath" found as one of the symptoms of ketosis.

Unsaturated Fatty Acids

The dehydrogenation of a saturated fatty acid to introduce a double bond between carbons 9 and 10 (e.g., to form oleic acid from stearic acid, palmitoleic from palmitic, etc.) is a reaction common to most organisms. The introduction of a second double bond between carbon atoms 12 and 13 (e.g., to form linoleic from oleic acid) appears to be restricted to plants and to certain microorganisms. On the other hand, the insertion or removal of the third double bond (as in the conversion of linoleic to linolenic acid) and the rather complex reactions necessary to form the 20-carbon tetra-unsaturated arachidonic acid from linoleic (or linolenic) acid occur commonly in animals, plants, and various microorganisms.

Since most animals appear to require some one of the polyunsaturated fatty acids for maintenance of normal structure and function, and since they are incapable of making the polyunsaturated fatty acids from saturated or monounsaturated derivatives, some of the polyunsaturated materials must be included in the diet. These are thus often referred to as "essential fatty acids." However, owing to the interconvertibility of linoleic, linolenic, arachidonic, and similar polyunsaturated structures, any one of these will meet the requirements.

BIOSYNTHESIS OF GLYCEROL LIPIDS

Carbohydrate and lipid metabolism are tied together not only in the synthesis and oxidation of fatty acids but also in the process of biosynthesis of the glycerol portion of the glycerol lipids. The starting compound in this case is dihydroxyacetone phosphate, which is of course formed during the process of glycolysis. This compound is reduced to an α-glycerol phosphate by a DPN-dependent enzyme system. It should be apparent at this point that α-glycerol phosphate is an optically active compound and can exist in either the D- or L-form. The isomer which is formed in this reaction (and which is specifically required for the synthesis of the glycerol lipids) is the L- isomer,

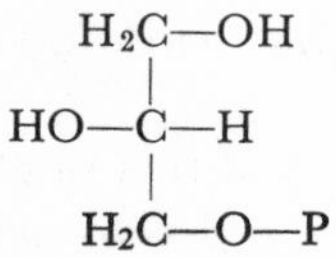

$$H_2C—OH$$
$$HO—C—H$$
$$H_2C—O—P$$

L-α-glycerophosphoric acid

formally designated as L-α-glycerol phosphate or L-α-glycerophosphoric acid. Having thus established that all of the glycerol lipids are based upon the L- structure, we will proceed to ignore the matter during the rest of this discussion.

The α-glycerol phosphate can then react with several fatty acids, in the form of their coenzyme A esters, to form a *phosphatidic acid:*

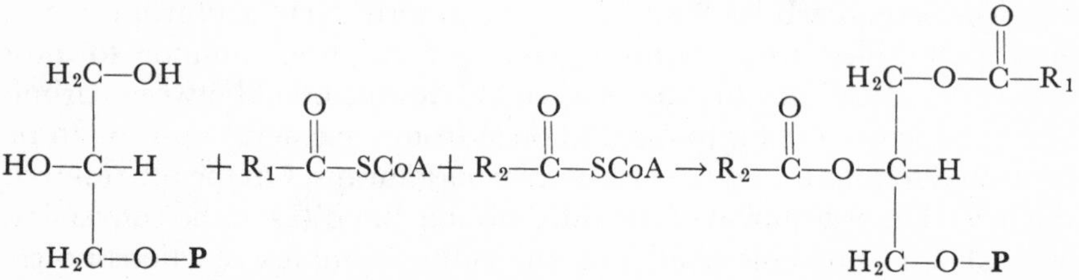

$$
\begin{array}{l}
H_2C—OH \\
HO—C—H \quad + R_1—\overset{\displaystyle O}{\overset{\|}{C}}—SCoA + R_2—\overset{\displaystyle O}{\overset{\|}{C}}—SCoA \rightarrow R_2—\overset{\displaystyle O}{\overset{\|}{C}}—O—\begin{array}{c} H_2C—O—\overset{\displaystyle O}{\overset{\|}{C}}—R_1 \\ C—H \\ H_2C—O—P \end{array} \\
H_2C—O—P
\end{array}
$$

We can proceed one step further by removing the phosphate ester group under the influence of very specific phosphatidic acid phosphatases. The product of this reaction is, of course, a diglyceride. This whole process may appear a rather long way around to get to a diglyceride, since it would obviously be much simpler to combine the fatty acyl-CoA's with free glycerol in the first place. However, if this latter type of reaction does occur at all, it appears to proceed at a very much slower rate than does the reaction with α-glycerol phosphate.

In any case, the diglyceride will react, under the influence of a quite different enzyme, with a third fatty acyl-CoA molecule to yield a triglyceride. Needless to say, a wide variety of triglycerides may be formed simply by varying the fatty acids inserted at each step.

Phospholipids

The syntheses of the phosphatidyl cholines, serines, and ethanolamines are very closely related. We will use the synthesis of a phosphatidyl choline (lecithin) to illustrate the reactions involved. Choline is first made into the phosphate ester by transfer of a phosphate group from ATP to the free alcohol group. The choline phosphate then undergoes a sort of exchange reaction with cytidine triphosphate (CTP), yielding cytidine-diphosphate-choline and inorganic pyrophosphate. The cytidine-diphosphate-choline then takes part in another transfer reaction, with a diglyceride, this time transferring the

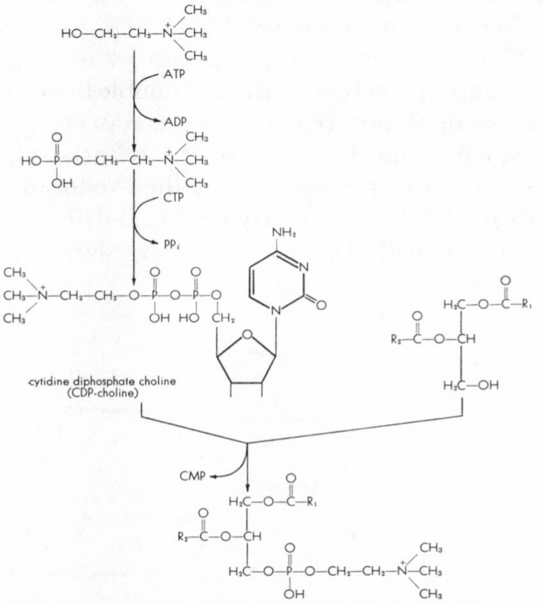

Figure 10-4. Biosynthesis of a Lecithin.

phosphorylcholine portion to the diglyceride and releasing a molecule of cytidine monophosphate (CMP) as shown in Figure 10-4.

The cytidine monophosphate can be readily reconverted to cytidine triphosphate (CTP) by successive transfers of a phosphate group from each of two molecules of ATP.

$$CMP + ATP \rightarrow CDP + ADP$$

$$CDP + ATP \rightleftharpoons CTP + ADP$$

BIOSYNTHESIS OF CHOLESTEROL

In animal systems, cholesterol occupies a central position in the biosynthesis of all of the steroids. Essentially all the other compounds can be formed metabolically from cholesterol, as we will see in the next section. Thus the pathway of *de novo* biosynthesis of steroids becomes first the pathway of biosynthesis of cholesterol. We may add here that similar reactions occur in plants and some microorganisms, but yield closely related compounds rather than cholesterol.

All of the carbons of the cholesterol molecule, like those of the fatty acids, are derived directly from acetyl-CoA. In fact, the first few reactions of cholesterol synthesis and of fatty acid synthesis are identical, namely those necessary for the production of acetoacetyl-CoA. At this point the steroid pathway diverges by way of a condensation reaction between the acetoacetyl-CoA and another molecule of acetyl-CoA. This is, of course, a special case of addition of an "activated methylene group" across a carbonyl double bond. It is somewhat similar to the condensation reaction between acetyl-CoA and oxalacetic acid, which is the first step of the tricarboxylic acid cycle. The thioester portion of the molecule is then reduced to an alcohol function (with release of free coenzyme A), and the compound thus formed is mevalonic acid. These reactions are shown in Figure 10-5.

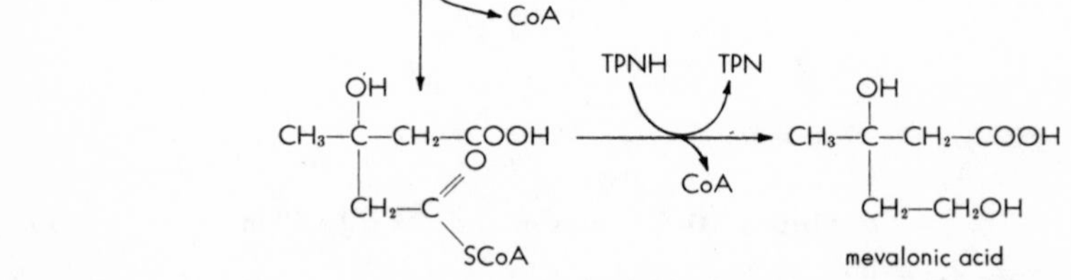

Figure 10-5. Conversion of Acetyl-CoA to Mevalonic Acid.

Mevalonic acid is next subjected to a series of reactions, in the course of which: (1) a pyrophosphate group is attached to the primary alcohol position, (2) the tertiary alcohol group is removed by dehydration, and (3) the carboxyl group is lost by a nonoxidative decarboxylation. The product is a relative of isoprene called isopentenyl pyrophosphate. We may regard this compound as an "activated iso-prene unit."

A "head to tail" condensation of three of these units yields a 15-carbon intermediate that still possesses a pyrophosphate group. Two of these 15-carbon molecules can then come together in a "head to head" reaction to produce the terpenoid hydrocarbon "squalene." The sequence of reactions from mevalonic acid to squalene is shown in abbreviated form in Figure 10-6.

At first glance, we might appear to be still a long way from choles-terol. However, when we rewrite the squalene molecule with some-

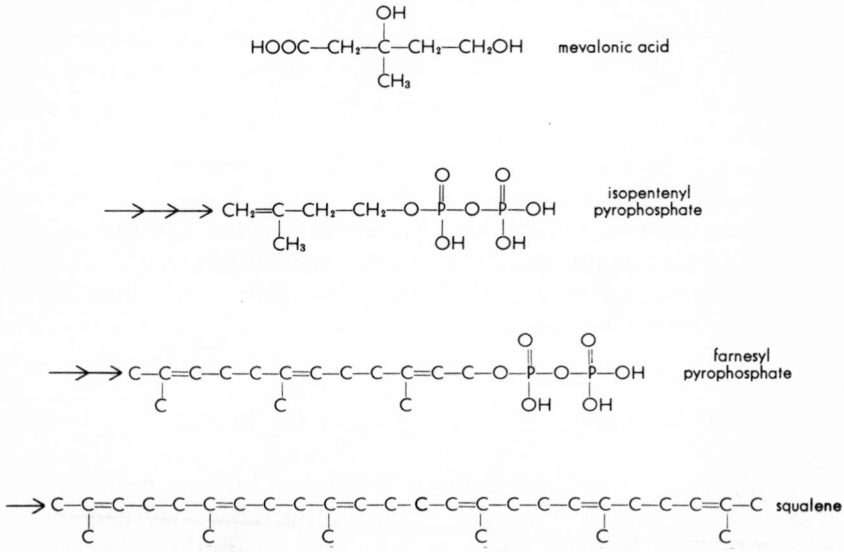

Figure 10-6. Conversion of Mevalonic Acid to Squalene.

what more realistic bond angles, we obtain the following as one possible configuration:

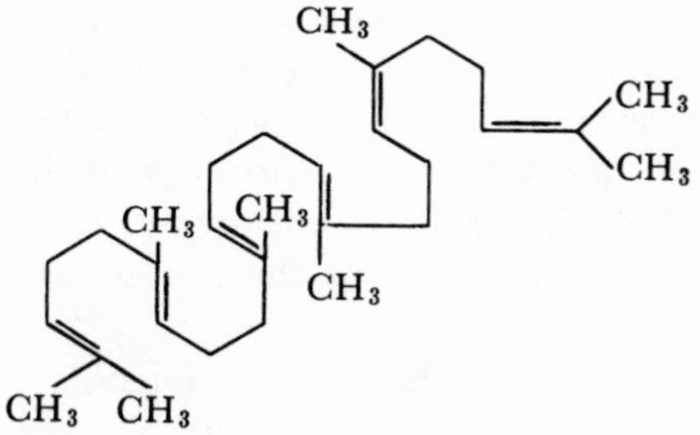

squalene

The compound in this form undergoes a reaction or sequence of reactions involving multiple shifting of electrons, methyl group migration, and the insertion of a hydroxyl group. The result is a molecule (lanosterol) having the basic steroidal ring structure and the side chain characteristic of cholesterol. Conversion of this molecule to cholesterol is a relatively simple enzymatic process:

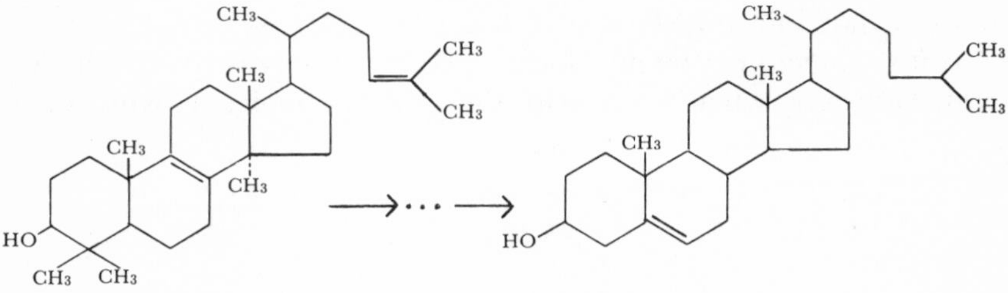

lanosterol   cholesterol

A number of compounds are capable of being fed into this biosynthetic pathway without first being converted to acetyl-CoA. These include some of the branched-chain amino acids from which mevalonic acid can be formed.

METABOLIC INTERCONVERSIONS OF STEROIDS

In Figure 10-7 the metabolic relationships among a number of representative steroids are shown, indicating how they can all be formed from cholesterol. The number of arrowheads shown represents approximately the number of reactions needed for a given conversion.

The relatively small number of reactions necessary to convert one steroid hormone to another reflects the tremendous physiological significance of relatively minor changes in the steroid molecule. Thus, for example, progesterone (a female hormone important during pregnancy) can be converted to testosterone (one of the male sex hormones) in about three steps, or to cortisone in about five or six steps. Of course, not all of these conversions are possible in all tissues, but it is usually control of the balance among them, rather than the lack of one or more reactions, that governs the pattern of steroid hormone activity in an organism.

In any case, it is clear that the steroid molecule is one of the most versatile small compounds in a cell. Cholesterol can even be converted to bile acids, in turn forming bile salts, which are absolutely necessary

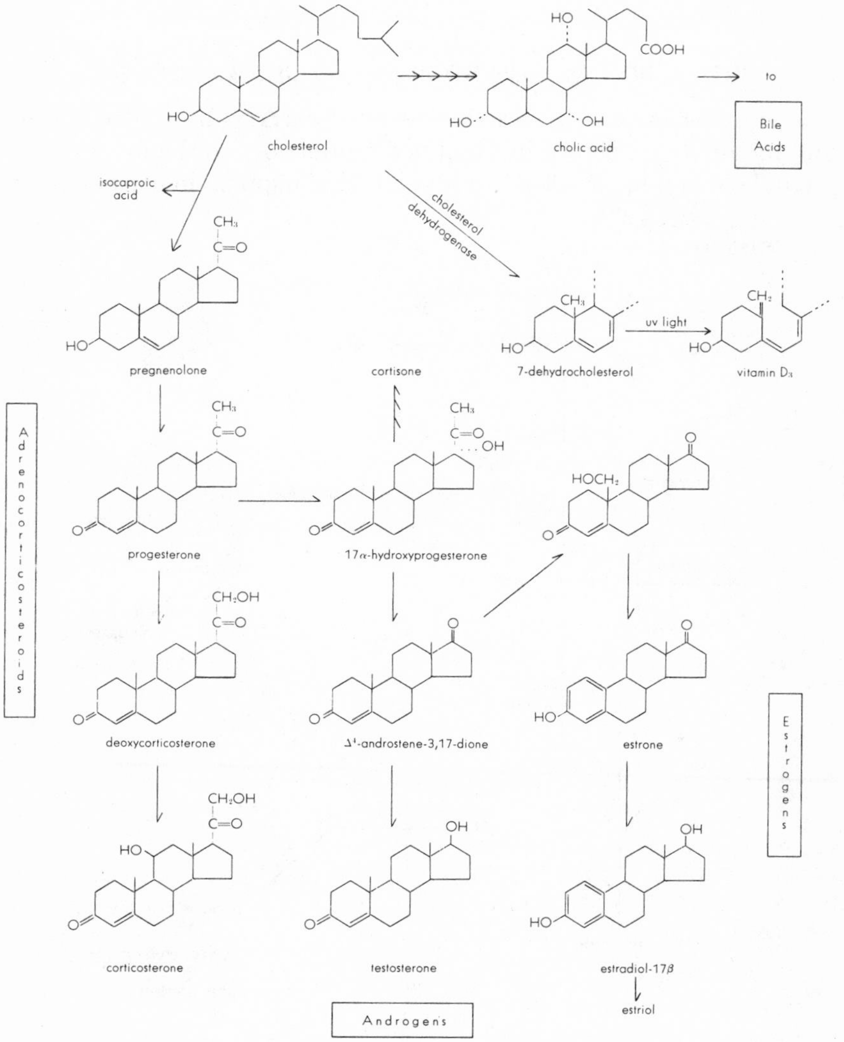

Figure 10-7. Some Metabolic Relationships Among the Steroids.

Most of the reactions shown with single-headed arrows are reversible, leading to ready interconversions among the different types of steroids.

in animals if cholesterol (and, of course, other lipid material) is to be absorbed from the intestine. This may be viewed as roughly equivalent to pulling itself up by its own boot straps.

INTERACTION OF CARBOHYDRATE AND LIPID METABOLISM

The major areas of interaction between carbohydrate metabolism and the lipids are shown in simplified outline form in Figure 10-8. It might be useful to consider at this point what happens in most animals

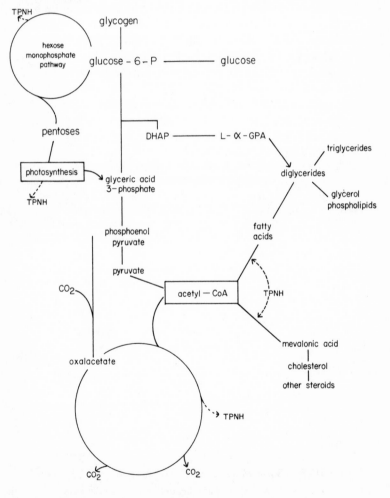

Figure 10-8.   Interactions of Carbohydrate and Lipid Metabolism.

when an excess of glucose is available to the cells. Under these conditions, some of the glucose will always be oxidized, maintaining a relatively high concentration of ATP and reduced forms of coenzymes such as DPNH and TPNH. This in turn will favor glycogen synthesis on the one hand, and on the other the reduction of dihydroxyacetone phosphate to α-glycerol phosphate and the reductive coupling of acetyl groups (from acetyl-CoA) to yield fatty acids and sterols. The maximum amount of glycogen which can be stored in a cell is soon reached, leaving the remaining carbohydrate to be converted chiefly to triglycerides.

Going in the other direction, while it is true that carbons from fatty acids can be converted to carbons of glycogen, there is a very limited *net* conversion of fatty acids to carbohydrates. This is because the pyruvic oxidase system is essentially irreversible. Thus an acetyl-CoA unit arising from oxidation of a fatty acid cannot be converted directly to pyruvic acid. The carbons of the acetyl-CoA unit *can* be incorporated into carbohydrate indirectly by going once around the TCA cycle to oxalacetate, then up the glycolytic pathway. It should be readily apparent that this type of conversion does not really result in a *net* synthesis of carbohydrate.

SUGGESTED ADDITIONAL READING

Green, D. E., "The Metabolism of Fats," *Scientific American*, **190,** No. 1, 54 (January, 1954); also "The Synthesis of Fat," *ibid.*, **202,** No. 2, 46 (February, 1960).

Greenberg, D. M., Ed., "Metabolic Pathways," Vol. 1, Academic Press, New York and London, 1960.

Bloch, K., Ed., "Lipide Metabolism," John Wiley & Sons, New York, 1960.

Metabolism of Nitrogen Compounds

11

Biological materials contain a remarkably diverse array of nitrogenous organic compounds. These range in complexity from the simple amino acids through a host of nucleotides, porphyrins, alkaloids, and similar compounds to the exceedingly complex proteins and nucleic acids. To a major degree the biosynthesis of the more complex substances is based on the use of amino acids as precursors. Not only are the nitrogen atoms of the compounds commonly derived directly or indirectly from the amino groups of amino acids, but in addition the carbon chains of the amino acids often accompany the amino groups as they are built into more complicated structures. The metabolic role of the amino acids is commonly thought of as being only that of building blocks of proteins. Certainly this is a very important role, but in the light of the statements above, it should be clear that the amino acids occupy a central position in the field of metabolism of nitrogenous compounds in general. Accordingly, most of the material of this chapter relates to the mechanisms by which amino acids are synthesized and to those processes by which they are used in the synthesis of other compounds.

SOURCES OF AMINO ACIDS

Each living cell must have a supply of amino acids constantly available for a variety of synthetic processes of which protein synthesis is quantitatively the most important. These amino acids may be derived by synthesis from simple substances or by their absorption from the surrounding environment. Often, in order to obtain amino acids from the environment, the cell must liberate enzymes which catalyze the hydrolysis of protein compounds originally formed by other cells.

In the first case, where there is *de novo* synthesis of the compounds from simple substances, they are often described as being of *endogenous* origin. The second case, where the compounds are obtained preformed from the environment, would be termed an *exogenous* source. Respectively, these two terms mean literally "formed within" and "formed without."

SYNTHESIS OF AMINO ACIDS

Higher plants, as well as many microorganisms, are capable of the synthesis of all the natural amino acids from inorganic substances. The synthetic reactions for most of the amino acids may be divided into the following steps: (1) synthesis of the α-keto acids corresponding in structure to each of the α-amino acids, i.e., synthesis of the carbon chains; (2) the production of ammonia; (3) formation of glutamic acid by the reaction of ammonia with α-ketoglutaric acid; and (4) transfer of the amino group from glutamic acid to another α-keto acid.

FORMATION OF α-KETO ACIDS

We have already examined the reactions by which plants form glyceric acid-3-phosphate, and carbohydrates in general, from inorganic carbon dioxide. These compounds can yield, directly via glycolysis and the citric acid cycle, three of the α-keto acids required for amino acid synthesis—pyruvic, oxalacetic, and α-ketoglutaric acids. The α-keto acid needed for serine production can be formed readily from glyceric acid-3-phosphate by an oxidation reaction and a dephosphorylation step. The syntheses of most of the other α-keto acids are also closely related to intermediates of the oxidation of carbohydrates. We will make no attempt here to provide the details of each of these processes.

Ammonia can, of course, be formed in the degradation of nitrogenous organic compounds. Much of the ammonia used by plants and microorganisms is derived in this way. We shall restrict our discussion at this point to the formation of ammonia from two other inorganic substances, atmospheric nitrogen and nitrate ion.

The reduction of nitrogen to ammonia can be accomplished only by certain microorganisms such as the *Azotobacter*. This process and the subsequent incorporation of the ammonia into organic compounds is known as *nitrogen fixation*. The chemical events of the production of NH_3 from N_2 are still unknown, although some progress is currently being made.

Green plants possess enzymes which catalyze the reduction of nitrate ion through nitrite ion and several other compounds of uncertain nature to ammonia. Hydroxylamine appears to be one of the intermediates in this process. Two of the enzymes needed for the reduction of nitrate ion to ammonia, nitrate reductase and nitrite reductase, seem to be flavoproteins which contain a molybdate ion as an essential component. The metal ion may be involved in the electron transfer processes accompanying the reduction reactions. This apparently explains the need for traces of molybdenum in fertilizers.

The introduction of ammonia into organic compounds can occur by a variety of reactions. One of these, which leads to the formation of carbamyl phosphate, we will examine later in another context. Most of the other reactions are limited in extent or appear only in a few organisms. However, the single reaction of ammonia with α-ketoglutaric acid to yield glutamic acid probably accounts for most of the "fixation" of ammonia into organic compounds. This reaction can be characterized as a *reductive amination*. The reducing power is supplied by DPNH or TPNH in different organisms. The enzyme is termed L-glutamic dehydrogenase. The α-keto acid is, of course, a familiar component of the tricarboxylic acid cycle. This is therefore the first specific example that we have encountered of a mechanism linking amino acid and carbohydrate metabolism.

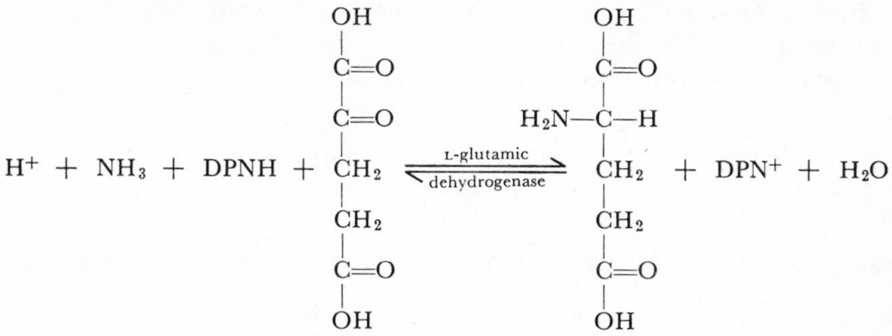

$$H^+ + NH_3 + DPNH + \begin{array}{c} OH \\ | \\ C=O \\ | \\ C=O \\ | \\ CH_2 \\ | \\ CH_2 \\ | \\ C=O \\ | \\ OH \end{array} \underset{\text{dehydrogenase}}{\overset{\text{L-glutamic}}{\rightleftharpoons}} \begin{array}{c} OH \\ | \\ C=O \\ | \\ H_2N-C-H \\ | \\ CH_2 \\ | \\ CH_2 \\ | \\ C=O \\ | \\ OH \end{array} + DPN^+ + H_2O$$

α-ketoglutaric
acid   L-glutamic
acid

TRANSFER OF AMINO GROUPS

The amino group of glutamic acid can be transferred to other α-keto acids by a type of reaction which is of general importance in amino acid metabolism. This is called *transamination;* the enzymes are *transaminases.*

The transaminases require pyridoxal phosphate as a coenzyme, in part explaining the metabolic importance of pyridoxine, the vitamin from which the coenzyme is formed. Pyridoxal phosphate also serves as a coenzyme in a number of other reactions involving amino acids, in particular amino acid decarboxylation and the dehydration of β-hydroxy amino acids. Any one of three compounds satisfies the dietary need for vitamin B_6: pyridoxine, pyridoxal, or pyridoxamine. These compounds differ only in that they have as part of their structure either a primary alcohol group, an aldehyde, or a primary amine, respectively. Pyridoxal phosphate and pyridoxamine phosphate occur in tissues, and are the functioning forms of the coenzyme. In common with most phosphorylated compounds, they do not readily pass through cell membranes and must be dephosphorylated by phosphatase action before they can be absorbed.

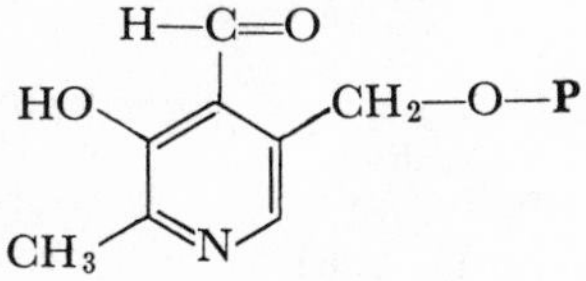

pyridoxal phosphate 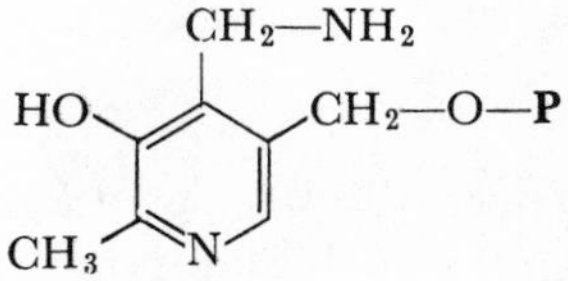   pyridoxamine phosphate

Present ideas concerning the mechanism of the transamination step are summarized in the equations given below. The **R** group in each case represents the remainder of the coenzyme molecule.

$$
\begin{array}{cccc}
& \text{OH} & \text{OH} & \text{OH} & \text{OH} \\
& | & | & | & | \\
\text{H} & \text{C}{=}\text{O} & \text{C}{=}\text{O} & \text{C}{=}\text{O} & \text{C}{=}\text{O} \\
| & | & \xrightarrow{-\text{H}_2\text{O}} & | & | & \xrightarrow{+\text{H}_2\text{O}} & | \\
\text{C}{=}\text{O} + \text{H}_2\text{N-C-H} & \rightleftharpoons & \text{HC}{=}\text{N-C-H} \rightleftharpoons \text{H}_2\text{C-N}{=}\text{C} & \rightleftharpoons & \text{C}{=}\text{O} + \text{H}_2\text{N-CH}_2 \\
| & | & | & | & | & | \\
\text{R} & \text{CH}_2 & \text{R} \;\; \text{CH}_2 & \text{R} \;\; \text{CH}_2 & \text{CH}_2 & \text{R} \\
& | & | & | & | \\
& \text{CH}_2 & \text{CH}_2 & \text{CH}_2 & \text{CH}_2 \\
& | & | & | & | \\
& \text{C}{=}\text{O} & \text{C}{=}\text{O} & \text{C}{=}\text{O} & \text{C}{=}\text{O} \\
& | & | & | & | \\
& \text{OH} & \text{OH} & \text{OH} & \text{OH} \\
\end{array}
$$

pyridoxal   glutamic   Schiff's   α-keto-   pyridox-
phosphate   acid   bases   glutaric   amine
                                                acid   phosphate

This process occurs with the compounds all bound to the transaminase. It accomplishes the removal of the amino group from the amino acid and its transfer for the formation of pyridoxamine phosphate. In a second set of reactions which are in form simply the reverse of those given above, the amino group of pyridoxamine phosphate is transferred to another keto acid, for example, pyruvic acid. In simplified form, omitting the Schiff's bases:

$$
\begin{array}{ccccc}
& & \text{OH} & & \text{OH} \\
& & | & & | \\
& & \text{C}{=}\text{O} & & \text{C}{=}\text{O} \\
& & | & \xrightarrow{\text{transaminase}} & | \\
\text{H}_2\text{C-NH}_2 & + & \text{O}{=}\text{C} & \rightleftharpoons \;\; \text{HC}{=}\text{O} + \text{H}_2\text{N-C-H} \\
| & & | & \;\;\;\; | & | \\
\text{R} & & \text{CH}_3 & \;\;\;\; \text{R} & \text{CH}_3 \\
\end{array}
$$

pyridoxamine   pyruvic   pyridoxal   α-alanine
phosphate   acid   phosphate

The over-all effect of these two reactions occurring in sequence is the transfer of the amino group from glutamic acid to pyruvic acid, yielding α-ketoglutaric acid and alanine. This may be indicated as:

$$
\text{glutamic acid} + \text{pyruvic acid} \underset{\text{pyridoxal phosphate}}{\overset{\text{transaminase}}{\rightleftharpoons}} \text{α-ketoglutaric acid} + \text{alanine}
$$

Probably there are a large number of different transaminases, each specific for a different amino acid-keto acid pair of substrates. Not all of these have been purified; however, glutamic-oxalacetic acid transaminase (yielding aspartic acid), and glutamic-pyruvic acid transaminase (giving alanine) are well known.*

Other transaminases catalyze the transfer of amino groups from aspartic acid and from alanine to other α-keto acids. The amino group of a particular amino acid may, therefore, be derived from glutamic acid in a somewhat indirect manner.

Lysine and threonine are exceptions to the rule that α-amino acids are formed by direct transamination of their α-keto analogs. Threonine is formed from aspartic acid by reactions which preserve all four carbon atoms as well as the amino group.

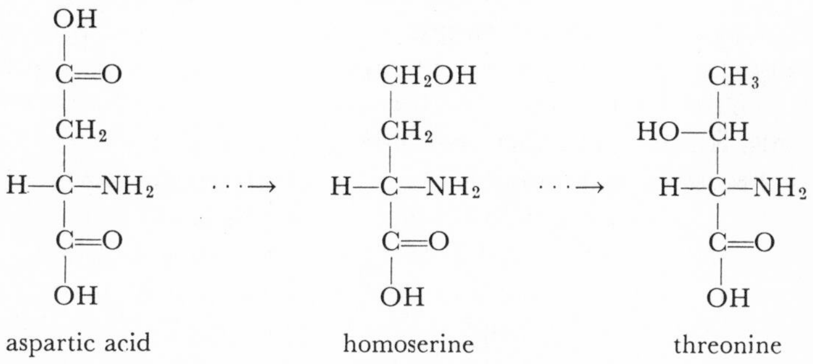

$$
\begin{array}{ccc}
\text{OH} & & \\
| & & \\
\text{C=O} & \text{CH}_2\text{OH} & \text{CH}_3 \\
| & | & | \\
\text{CH}_2 & \text{CH}_2 & \text{HO—CH} \\
| & | & | \\
\text{H—C—NH}_2 \dashrightarrow & \text{H—C—NH}_2 \dashrightarrow & \text{H—C—NH}_2 \\
| & | & | \\
\text{C=O} & \text{C=O} & \text{C=O} \\
| & | & | \\
\text{OH} & \text{OH} & \text{OH} \\
\text{aspartic acid} & \text{homoserine} & \text{threonine}
\end{array}
$$

Lysine synthesis occurs by different routes in molds, bacteria, and higher plants. In all cases the α-amino group appears to be added before the structure of the rest of the molecule is completed.

Of course, proline too cannot be formed by transamination. This "imino acid" is synthesized by reactions which preserve all the carbon atoms and the amino group of glutamic acid.

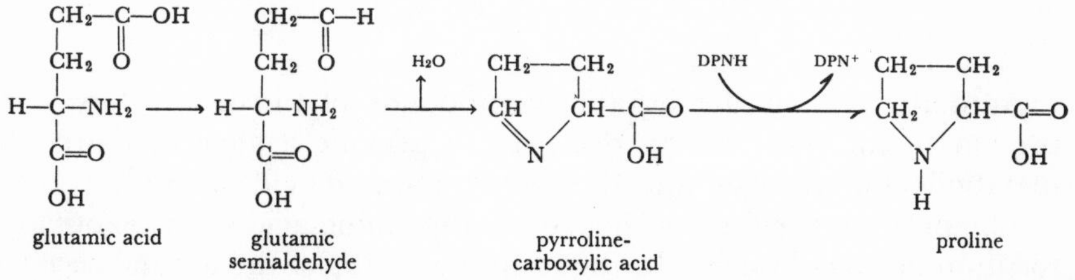

glutamic acid   glutamic semialdehyde   pyrroline-carboxylic acid   proline

---

*Determinations of the blood concentrations of these two enzymes are clinically important in estimating damage to heart and liver tissue, respectively; for with damage to these tissues the enzymes are released from the cells to the blood.

The net effect of ammonia fixation and amino group transfer is summarized below:

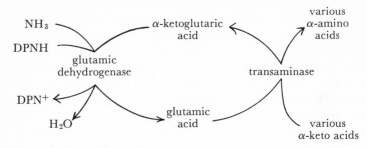

ABSORPTION OF PREFORMED AMINO ACIDS

In contrast to green plants and many microorganisms, animals do not utilize ammonia to any major extent in amino acid production. This is not the result, as you might expect, of a lack of either glutamic dehydrogenase or transaminases; these enzymes are commonly present in animals. Rather, there are two other factors which generally act to prevent the use of ammonia as a general nitrogen source. The first of these is the fact that ammonia is not a significant component of animal diets. Secondly, animals and certain microorganisms lack enzymes needed for the production of a number of the α-keto acids required as acceptors of the amino groups in amino acid formation. Obviously, certain amino acids cannot then be produced by transamination processes. Those amino acids which cannot be synthesized at a rate commensurate with normal growth are called "essential" or "indispensable" amino acids for the organism concerned. The amino acids which are "essential" for humans are:

Lysine	Threonine
Leucine	Tryptophan
Isoleucine	Valine
Methionine	Phenylalanine

Animals rely on the organic compounds of nitrogen which are present in the diet, chiefly proteins, to provide a general source of metabolizable nitrogen and the essential amino acids as well.

The proteins are first hydrolyzed to the amino acid stage before absorption occurs. As a result, the individual cells of the animal receive a grand mixture of all the amino acids present in the dietary proteins. Some of these the animal could synthesize easily; however, there is comparatively little need to do so as a rule, for the diet will usually provide all the amino acids, not just the essential ones. The synthesis of nonessential amino acids will normally require only transamination reactions to reshuffle the amino groups of the dietary amino acids to supply each compound in the quantities demanded by the metabolic activities of the cell at the particular time. If the diet contains only the essential amino acids, as might be the case with a synthetic diet, a major portion of these molecules will be used to provide amino groups for the synthesis of the nonessential amino acids, which are metabolic essentials but not dietary essentials.

HYDROLYSIS OF PROTEINS

The importance of dietary proteins as amino acid sources for animal cells has been mentioned in the previous section. For a variety of reasons these dietary proteins must be completely hydrolyzed or digested to the amino acids prior to the entrance of any component into the cells of the animal organism. Large molecules such as proteins are, of course, poor candidates for the absorption process. Of major importance, however, is the condition of "anaphylactic shock" which is likely to result from the presence of intact foreign proteins in the blood or tissues of an animal. This is a condition in which the normal mechanisms of defense against bacterial invasions respond in overly enthusiastic fashion. Among other effects, histamine, the product of decarboxylation of the amino acid, histidine, is released in excess amounts. Histamine causes dilation of the capillaries and loss of blood fluid to the tissue spaces, effects which are counteracted by the "antihistamines." The rather common pollen and food allergies present examples, comparatively minor in nature, of the results of absorption of foreign proteins by cells.

You might reasonably expect small peptides to be capable of absorption. However, as we noted previously, it appears that the absorption process for most materials is not accomplished simply by diffusion, but rather through the mediation of specific enzyme-like components of the cell membrane called *permeases*. Apparently a separate permease or specific absorption site is available for each common amino acid, but it would not be possible for such sites to exist for each of the great numbers of different small peptides.

Finally, you should realize by now that the proteins made by a given cell will contain sequences of amino acids which are not likely to be duplicated by proteins of other organisms. Hence, the "foreign" dietary proteins must be degraded and the amino acids reassembled to provide the specific "native" proteins.

You will also recall that the amino acids of a protein are joined primarily through the secondary amide linkages commonly called peptide bonds. The digestion of proteins to amino acids must therefore entail the hydrolysis of peptide linkages. Disulfide bonds occur commonly in proteins, but digestive fluids do not contain enzymes capable of cleaving these linkages. Consequently proteins with disulfide linkages yield cystine upon hydrolysis. However, proteins such as the keratins of skin and hair which are highly cross-linked by disulfide bridges, are usually resistant to digestion and are of little food value.

Because protein digestion requires the hydrolysis only of a single kind of linkage, we might expect that a single enzyme would suffice. However, the actual *peptidases*, the enzymes which catalyze the hydrolysis of peptide bonds, display specificities of varying degree with respect to the individual amino acids involved. Consequently, the rapid, quantitative conversion of a protein to amino acids requires a number of different peptidases with different hydrolytic abilities. In higher animals, at least six digestive peptidases are used.

Endopeptidases: Three of the peptidases of higher animals, pepsin, trypsin, and chymotrypsin, are termed *endopeptidases* in that they can catalyze the hydrolysis of peptide bonds in interior positions of a peptide chain, cleaving it into large fragments. They are sometimes termed *proteinases* or *proteolytic enzymes* because intact proteins form a major portion of their normal substrates. The peptide linkages which are most susceptible to hydrolysis under the action of pepsin are those formed from amino groups of the aromatic amino acids, phenylalanine and tyrosine. Chymotrypsin, on the other hand, is most active toward bonds involving carboxyl groups of these same two acids, and trypsin toward bonds involving the carboxyls of basic amino acids such as lysine or arginine. This specificity is illustrated in Figure 11-1, using a hypothetical peptide as substrate for each of these enzymes.

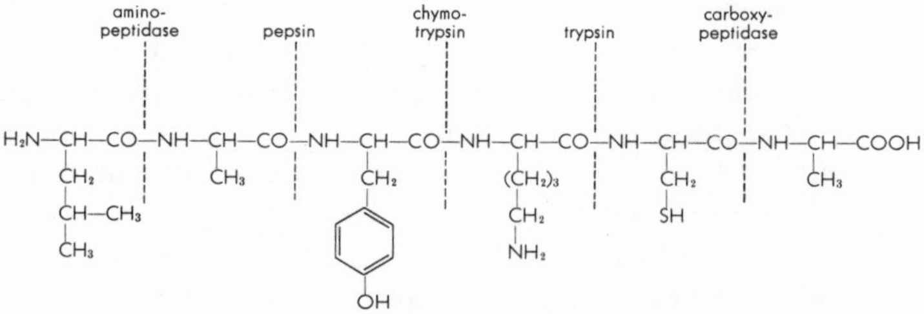

Figure 11-1. Specificity of Action of Peptidases.

Each of the peptidases shown will catalyze hydrolysis at the points indicated. Each is assumed to be acting independently on the whole intact peptide.

Were the three endopeptidases to act on proteins in the absence of other peptidases, mixtures of peptides of a wide size-range would be produced. These would be peptides lacking bonds susceptible to rapid hydrolysis in the presence of these enzymes. A few amino acids would be liberated from susceptible linkages occurring at chain ends.

Exopeptidases: The remaining enzymes of the animal which catalyze the digestion of proteins are termed *exopeptidases* owing to their catalytic activity solely toward external or terminal peptide bonds. Carboxypeptidase is active toward the peptide bond nearest the free carboxyl end of a peptide chain, and aminopeptidase toward the bond nearest the free amino end. Either of these enzymes acts to release one amino acid after another from the appropriate end of a peptide chain. Accordingly, these enzymes catalyze the rapid production of amino acids from the peptides presented to them as a result of endopeptidase action on proteins. Neither of these enzymes will cleave a dipeptide. Another enzyme, a dipeptidase, is necessary for this final step. Of course, this yields two amino acids from each dipeptide.

It should be noted that several aminopeptidases and dipeptidases of different specificity occur in intestinal juices, and that a separate enzyme, prolidase, is required for the hydrolysis of bonds involving the nitrogen atom of the prolines, in that these are not typical α-amino nitrogens.

It may be of interest that the exopeptidases are generally metal-ion enzymes. Presumably the metal functions in the binding of the peptide to the protein portion of the enzyme. Metal ions such as Zn^{++}, Mn^{++}, Co^{++}, and Mg^{++} are necessary for different exopeptidases.

Peptidase Activation: The endopeptidases, and carboxypeptidase as well, are produced by cells as proteins which lack peptidase activity. Activity appears only after chemical modification of these inactive substances, usually the hydrolysis of a peptide bond with the liberation of a small peptide. The remaining protein probably undergoes changes in three-dimensional structure to yield an active enzyme. The inactive enzyme precursors are termed either *zymogens* or *proenzymes*, and the process of their conversion to catalytic proteins is termed "activation." The activation of the zymogens occurs in the digestive tract after their liberation from the cells, a mechanism which prevents the exposure of cell proteins to possible destructive effects of the enzymes.

The hydrolysis of pepsinogen to yield pepsin is catalyzed by hydrogen ion. The normally high acidity of the stomach juices, therefore, favors the activation of this enzyme. Once some pepsin is formed, these molecules assist in the activation of the remaining pepsinogen. This is an example of *autocatalysis*, the catalysis of a reaction by one of the products.

The activation of the remaining zymogens is initiated by *enterokinase*, an enzyme liberated by the intestinal mucosa. This catalyzes the conversion of trypsinogen to trypsin. Trypsin is then the activator for chymotrypsin formation from chymotrypsinogen as well as for carboxypeptidase formation from procarboxypeptidase. The activation of trypsin itself is again an autocatalytic process.

Finally, it should be mentioned that cells of animal tissues contain a variety of peptidases called *cathepsins*. Apparently these are counterparts of the enzymes of the digestive tract with respect to specificity, although differing in other aspects. The function of the cathepsins is unknown. They are responsible for protein hydrolysis (autolysis) after the death of an organism. Many of the cathepsins are active only in acidic conditions and only in the presence of compounds with free sulfhydryl groups. Both of these conditions are favored by the death of the cells of higher organisms because of the resulting deficiency of oxygen.

SPECIFIC METABOLIC ROLES OF INDIVIDUAL AMINO ACIDS

We have already noted that the amino groups of the amino acids are utilized by cells in the formation of almost all other nitrogen-containing compounds, such as nucleic acids and porphyrins. In many cases the carbon chain is incorporated into the newly formed molecule along with its nitrogen atom. In others, processes akin to transamination occur, so that only the nitrogen is utilized in the particular synthetic process. There are a great number of such metabolic interconversions involving amino acids, including reactions of very diverse chemical nature. We shall examine only a few examples to illustrate the general nature of some of these processes.

Amino Acid Amides

Amino acids are not stored in cells—neither in a free form which would lead to osmotic pressure problems, nor as "storage protein." Neither can ammonia (actually ammonium ion) be stored, since it is quite toxic, even in low concentrations. However, nitrogen can be stored to a limited extent as the amide groups of glutamine and asparagine. These are formed from ammonia and glutamic and aspartic acids, respectively, by reactions requiring ATP.

Both of these amino acid amides occur in relatively high concentrations in plant tissues. In animals glutamine predominates, and is

$$
\begin{array}{cc}
\text{OH} & \text{OH} \\
| & | \\
\text{C}{=}\text{O} & \text{C}{=}\text{O} \\
| & | \\
\text{H}_2\text{N}{-}\text{C}{-}\text{H} & \text{H}_2\text{N}{-}\text{C}{-}\text{H} \\
| & | \\
\text{CH}_2 & \text{CH}_2 \\
| & | \\
\text{CH}_2 & \text{C}{=}\text{O} \\
| & | \\
\text{C}{=}\text{O} & \text{NH}_2 \\
| & \\
\text{NH}_2 & \\
\text{glutamine} & \text{asparagine}
\end{array}
$$

a major component of the pool of compounds which have nitrogen atoms readily available for general metabolic purposes. The amide groups of these two compounds may be used for the synthesis of other nitrogenous substances in three major ways: In the first process, the amide is hydrolyzed, giving ammonia, which can then be used to form the amino group of glutamic acid. This amino group in turn can be transaminated to yield other substances. Secondly, the NH_2 portion of the amide group may be transferred directly, by reactions akin to transamination, to suitable acceptor molecules. Finally, intact glutamine and asparagine are used, along with the usual amino acids, in the formation of many proteins.

Single-Carbon Metabolism

The reactions necessary for synthesis of many important biochemical compounds include one or more steps in which a single carbon atom is introduced into the metabolic machinery. At first glance this topic seems to be thoroughly divorced from the area of amino acid metabolism; however, as we shall see, the single-carbon units are formed from amino acids and are often incorporated into metabolic processes by reactions which involve amino acids.

We have already described several examples of metabolic processes in which a carbon dioxide molecule is incorporated into an organic compound. This obviously is the metabolism of a single carbon atom; however, the area of single-carbon metabolism is usually taken to include those reactions involving units which can readily be transferred from one compound to another and transformed from one oxidation state to another. These units, generalizing somewhat for simplicity, are essentially the methyl group, $-CH_3$, the hydroxymethyl group, $-CH_2OH$, and the formyl group, $-CHO$.

The metabolism of these single-carbon units takes place chiefly through intermediates in which the carbon atom is bound to either a nitrogen or a sulfur atom of a compound of coenzyme nature. The binding of the units to the coenzymes occurs in a manner which enhances their reactivity in certain kinds of reactions. They are therefore "activated" single-carbon units. The terms "active formaldehyde" and "active formate" have long been used to designate certain of these intermediates.

These terms also draw attention to the fact that a hydroxymethyl group bound to a nitrogen or sulfur atom would yield formaldehyde on hydrolysis (in the hydrated form), a formyl group would similarly yield formic acid, and a methyl group would yield methanol. The free single-carbon units are quite poisonous; their metabolism in bound form obviates this difficulty.

ORIGIN OF SINGLE-CARBON UNITS

In all probability the major endogenous source of single-carbon units is the amino acid serine. This compound can readily be synthesized by standard reactions from glyceric acid-3-phosphate of the glycolytic pathway, and a suitable donor of an amino group.

$$
\begin{array}{ccccc}
\text{OH} & & \text{OH} & & \text{OH} & & \text{OH} \\
| & & | & & | & & | \\
\text{C}{=}\text{O} & \xrightarrow[\text{DPN}^+]{\text{dehydrogenase}} & \text{C}{=}\text{O} & \xrightarrow[\substack{\text{pyridoxamine}\\\text{phosphate}}]{\text{transaminase}} & \text{C}{=}\text{O} & \xrightarrow[\text{H}_2\text{O}]{\text{phosphatase}} & \text{C}{=}\text{O} \\
| & & | & & | & & | \\
\text{H-C-OH} & & \text{C}{=}\text{O} & & \text{H}_2\text{N-C-H} & & \text{H}_2\text{N-C-H} \\
| & & | & & | & & | \\
\text{H}_2\text{C-O-}\mathbf{P} & & \text{H}_2\text{C-O-}\mathbf{P} & & \text{H}_2\text{C-O-}\mathbf{P} & & \text{H}_2\text{C-OH}
\end{array}
$$

glyceric acid-   serine
3-phosphate

The β-carbon atom of serine, the hydroxymethyl group, serves as an immediate precursor of "active formaldehyde" by reactions of complex nature in which the —CH$_2$OH group is transferred from the amino acid to a nitrogen atom of a coenzyme named *tetrahydrofolic acid* (abbreviated as THFA or FH$_4$). This coenzyme is formed by the addition of four hydrogen atoms to folic acid, a compound which is

$$
\begin{array}{ccccccc}
\text{OH} & & & & \text{OH} & & \\
| & & & & | & & \\
\text{C}{=}\text{O} & & & & \text{C}{=}\text{O} & & \\
| & & & & | & & \\
\text{H}_2\text{N-C-H} & + & \text{FH}_4 & \rightleftharpoons & \text{H}_2\text{C-NH}_2 & + & \text{FH}_4\text{-CH}_2\text{OH} \\
| & & & & & & \\
\text{H}_2\text{C-OH} & & & & & &
\end{array}
$$

serine   tetrahydro-   glycine   "active
                  folic acid   formaldehyde"

one of the water-soluble vitamins of animal nutrition. The biochemical role of folic acid is thus related to its conversion to a coenzyme required in single-carbon metabolism.

The structure of FH_4 is depicted below. The asterisks indicate the nitrogen atoms to which a single-carbon unit may be linked in one or another of the various "activated" compounds. We must emphasize that several simplifying generalizations have been made in the following discussion with respect to the precise structures of the FH_4-single carbon compounds.

For example, FH_4—CH_2OH probably does not exist in appreciable amounts because it undergoes a reaction with the second nitrogen atom starred in the FH_4 formula to eliminate a water molecule and give a FH_4=CH_2 compound. In this compound the methylene group (—CH_2—) forms a bridge between the two nitrogens. The single carbon unit would still give formaldehyde upon hydrolysis and is therefore an "active formaldehyde."

Similarly, three "active formate" compounds are known. One of these has the formyl group bound to one of the starred nitrogens, while in the second case it is linked to the other nitrogen. In a third case, the formyl group is converted to a methenyl group (—CH=) bound to *both* nitrogens.

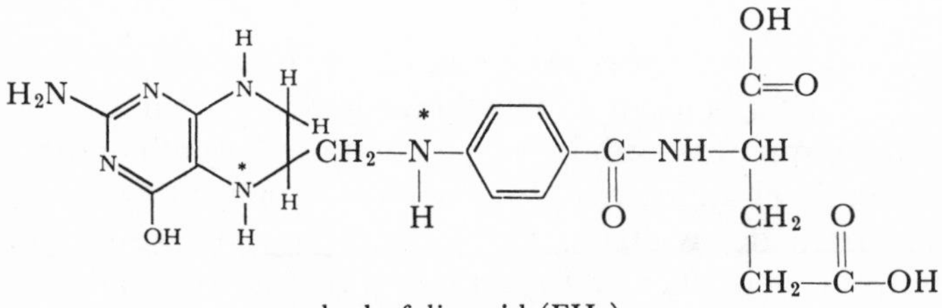

tetrahydrofolic acid (FH_4)

"Active formaldehyde," the formaldehyde-FH_4 compound, occupies a central role in the metabolism of single-carbon units. On one hand the —CH_2OH group can be reduced to a methyl group, or on the other oxidized to a formyl group yielding an "active methanol" or an "active formate." It might appear that this trio of compounds could satisfy all metabolic needs for single-carbon units. The formaldehyde and formate compounds do function in known reactions requiring the addition of a hydroxymethyl or formyl group.

However, for many reactions in which a methyl group is transferred from one compound to another, the actual participant as a coenzyme or cosubtrate is an activated form of the amino acid methionine. This amino acid is formed in plants by a series of reactions which culminate in the transfer of a methyl group from a folic acid coenzyme. Methionine itself does not possess an activated methyl group. But the methyl group can be rendered more reactive with respect to transfer reactions by a reaction with ATP, giving a compound usually called "active methionine." The details of these processes are not yet known. A simplified version of the formation of "active methionine" is given below to illustrate the nature of the various compounds.

```
  SH                                  S—CH₃        adenine-ribose—S⁺—CH₃
  |          FH₄—CH₃   FH₄            |            ATP              |
(CH₂)₂                              (CH₂)₂                        (CH₂)₂
  |          \        /               |                             |
H—C—NH₂       \      /        →     H—C—NH₂      →         H—C—NH₂
  |              (ATP)                |          Pᵢ + PPᵢ           |
  C=O                                 C=O                          C=O
  |                                   |                            |
  OH                                  OH                           OH

homocysteine                       methionine           adenosyl methionine
                                                                  or
                                                        "active" methionine
```

Vitamin B_{12} is also involved in single-carbon metabolism. It apparently functions as a coenzyme in a reaction necessary for the production or the further metabolism of the methyl derivative of tetrahydrofolic acid.

Animals cannot synthesize homocysteine from simple C, N, and S sources as can plants, nor does homocysteine occur in the diet in appreciable quantities under usual conditions. Methionine is therefore an essential amino acid for these organisms. However, if homocysteine is made available to animals they are quite capable of synthesizing methionine by the process described above.

However, animals must usually depend on exogenous methionine, not only for incorporation into proteins, but also as a major source of "active" methyl groups. Indeed, a rather high percentage of the "active" hydroxymethyl and formyl groups utilized by animals are probably formed from the methyl groups of dietary methionine, even though they can be derived from serine.

Active single-carbon units can also be formed from any substance which can be degraded to formaldehyde or formic acid. These compounds react rapidly with FH_4 to give the active derivatives. The metabolic conversion of glycine to NH_3, CO_2, and formic acid is the most significant of these processes.

The various reactions of single-carbon metabolism are drawn together in summarized form in Figure 11-2.

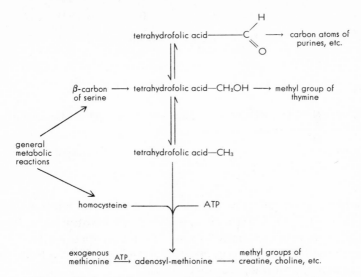

Figure 11-2. A Summary of Single-carbon Metabolism.

USES OF "ACTIVE" SINGLE-CARBON UNITS

Creatine Synthesis: An example of the donation of the methyl group of "active" methionine in a synthetic process is provided by the biogenesis of creatine. This example is useful also as an illustration of the manner in which certain amino acids are incorporated into other substances.

The synthesis of creatine begins with a reaction between glycine and arginine in which the guanidino group of arginine is transferred to glycine.

$$H_2N—CH_2—COOH \quad + \quad H_2N—\overset{\overset{\displaystyle NH}{\|}}{C}—N—(CH_2)_3—\overset{\overset{\displaystyle NH_2}{|}}{CH}—COOH \quad \leftrightarrows$$

$$\underset{H}{|}$$

glycine   arginine

$$H_2N—\overset{\overset{\displaystyle NH}{\|}}{C}—N—CH_2—COOH \quad + \quad H_2N—(CH_2)_3—\overset{\overset{\displaystyle NH_2}{|}}{CH}—COOH$$

$$\underset{H}{|}$$

guanidoacetic acid   ornithine

The next step involves the transfer of a methyl group from "active methionine" to guanidoacetic acid. The products are creatine and adenosylhomocysteine (and a hydrogen ion).

$$H_2N-\underset{\underset{H}{|}}{\overset{\overset{NH}{||}}{C}}-N-CH_2-COOH \; + \; adenosyl-\overset{\overset{CH_3}{|}}{\underset{+}{S}}-CH_2-CH_2-\overset{\overset{NH_2}{|}}{CH}-COOH \; \rightarrow$$

$$H_3C-\underset{\underset{H}{|}}{\overset{\overset{H}{|}}{N}}-\overset{\overset{NH}{||}}{C}-N-CH_2-COOH + adenosyl-S-CH_2-CH_2-\overset{\overset{NH_2}{|}}{CH}-COOH + H^+$$

creatine   S-adenosylhomocysteine

Reactions such as this are termed "transmethylations." The example given here is typical of many methyl-transfer reactions in which the donor of the methyl group is adenosylmethionine.

Note that *all* of the atoms of creatine have been derived from amino acids—glycine, arginine, and methionine.

The biological significance of creatine merits some attention. This compound participates in muscle metabolism by virtue of the freely reversible reaction with ATP.

$$creatine \; + \; ATP \; \rightleftharpoons \; ADP \; + \; creatine\ phosphate$$

In this regard it should be realized that the ATP concentration in cells is relatively low. Furthermore, ATP is involved in many reactions of very diverse nature. Accordingly, any sudden depletion of the ATP, such as would occur with sudden muscle action, would have marked effects of undesirable nature on the general metabolic balance. The reverse of the reaction as written above is usually able to maintain normal supplies of ATP until the stimulation of glycolysis can result in increased ATP formation. Naturally, at times when the ATP concentration is high, the balance is shifted toward the formation of creatine phosphate. This compound may thus be regarded as a quickly available store of utilizable energy. Compounds of this type are sometimes called phosphagens. The phosphagen of invertebrate muscle appears to be arginine phosphate rather than creatine phosphate. In both of these compounds the phosphate is combined with a nitrogen atom of the guanidino group as a special kind of phosphoamide. This structure, like that of the more common phosphoanhydrides, is highly reactive with respect to phosphate group transfer.

Purine and Pyrimidine Synthesis: The single-carbon derivatives of tetrahydrofolic acid are of particular importance in the synthesis of the nitrogenous bases required for nucleic acid formation. Examples are provided in Figure 11-3 for the participation of these units as well

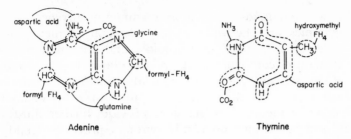

Figure 11-3. Sources of Atoms Built into Purine and Pyrimidine Bases.

as certain amino acids in the production of adenine—a typical purine, and thymine—a typical pyrimidine.

In these diagrams the compounds which serve as the ultimate sources of each of the various atoms of the ring structures are indicated. It should be understood that the compounds are formed by stepwise metabolic pathways in which only one of the groups at a time becomes part of the growing molecule.

Purine synthesis actually occurs with all the intermediate compounds being nucleotides. Thus it is the purine nucleotides that are synthesized directly, rather than the free bases. The bases arise only from degradation of the nucleotides.

For those interested in the details of nucleotide biosynthesis, the reactions leading to adenylic and thymidylic acids are summarized in Figures 11-4 and 11-5. Guanylic acid, like adenylic acid, is formed rather directly from inosinic acid; cytidylic acid is produced from uridylic acid. Furthermore, as indicated in the formation of thymidylic acid, the deoxyribotides are formed from the ribotides. Thus all the purine nucleotides are derived from inosinic acid, all the pyrimidine nucleotides from uridylic acid.

Phenylalanine Metabolism

Compounds containing benzene rings are comparatively rare components of animal tissues. The major examples are the aromatic amino acids (and several closely related compounds such as epinephrine, thyroxine, and melanin), riboflavin derivatives, vitamin B_{12} compounds, and the steroidal female sex hormones such as estradiol. Of these only the steroids can be synthesized by animals from simple compounds. However, exogenous phenylalanine can be used as the starting point for the production of a number of other aromatic compounds.

Benzenoid compounds are of more common occurrence in plants. Major examples are the wide variety of plant pigments such as anthocyanidins, a number of alkaloids, and the high-molecular-weight structural components of woody plants known as lignin. Plants, of course, can synthesize phenylalanine. As with animals, it is the starting point for the synthesis of numerous other compounds.

Phenylalanine metabolism therefore provides further illustrations of the utilization of an amino acid in synthetic processes. In addition it is the source of many of the benzenoid compounds in nature. Certain examples will be described in the following sections. How-

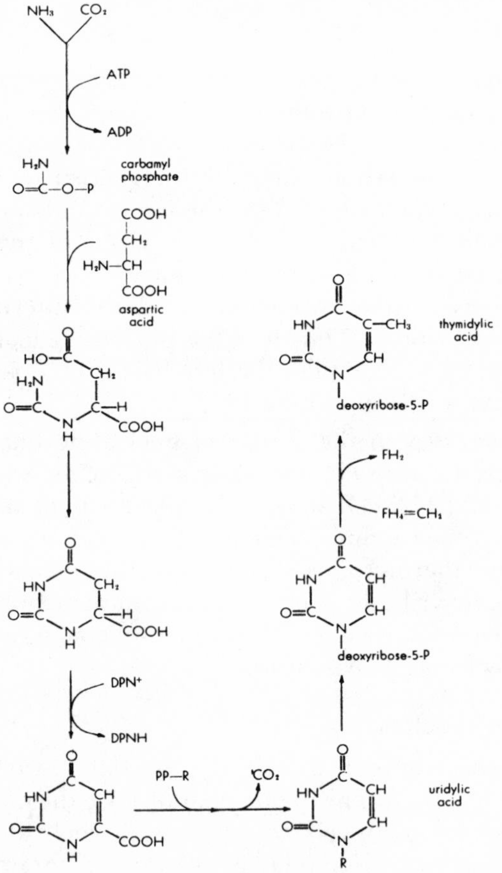

Figure 11-4. **A Summary of the Reactions of Thymidylic Acid Synthesis.** The "R" stands for ribose-5-phosphate; "PP—R" for ribose-5-phosphate-1-pyrophosphate. The reduction of uridylic acid to uracil deoxyriboside-5-phosphate probably occurs at the UDP stage.

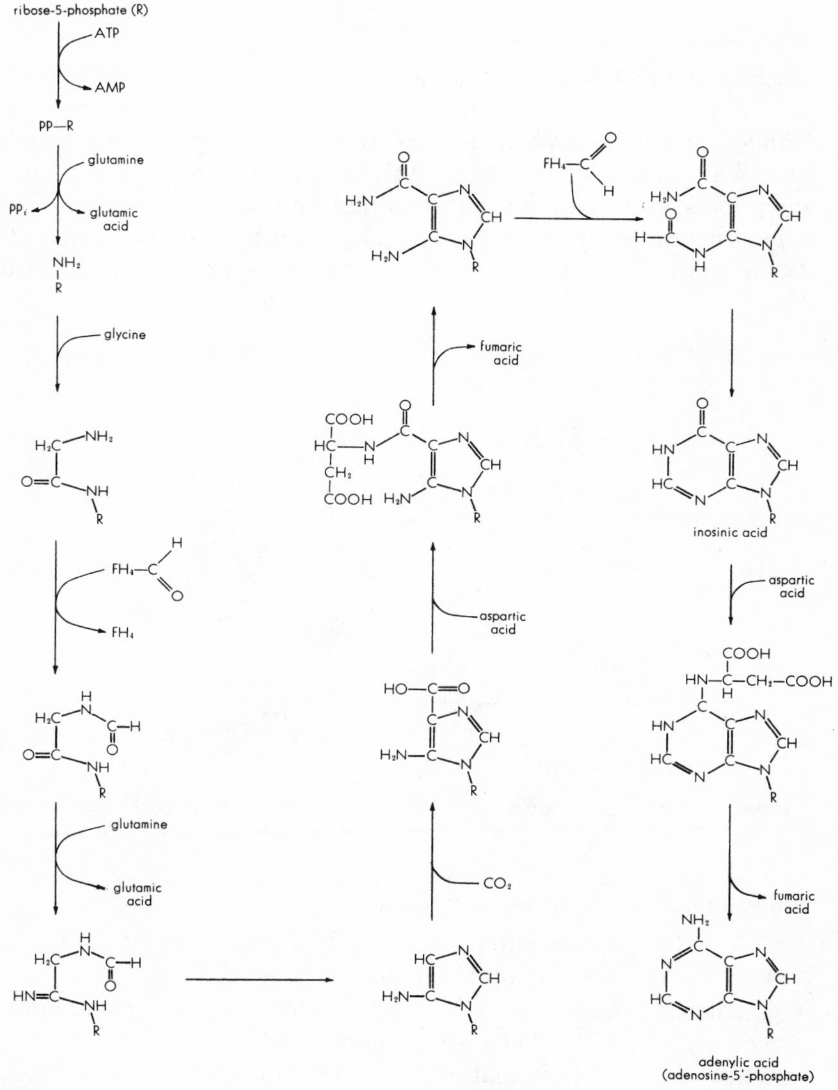

Figure 11-5.   A Summary of the Reactions of Adenylic Acid Biosynthesis.

The "R" stands for ribose-5-phosphate; "PP—R" for ribose-5-phosphate-1-pyro-phosphate. ATP (or GTP) has been shown to be required in a number of the reactions; the detailed mechanisms for most of these steps are not known.

ever, it seems desirable to first sketch the mechanisms used by plants in the production of this amino acid.

BIOSYNTHESIS OF PHENYLALANINE

The details of the biosynthetic pathway leading to phenylalanine are by no means fully known. However, the carbon atoms of the compound are apparently derived from one molecule of erythrose-4-phosphate (you will recall that this is formed as an intermediate in the photosynthetic cycle), and two molecules of phosphoenolpyruvic acid. The amino group is, as usual, supplied by transamination. The major steps of the synthesis of phenylalanine are shown in Figure 11-6.

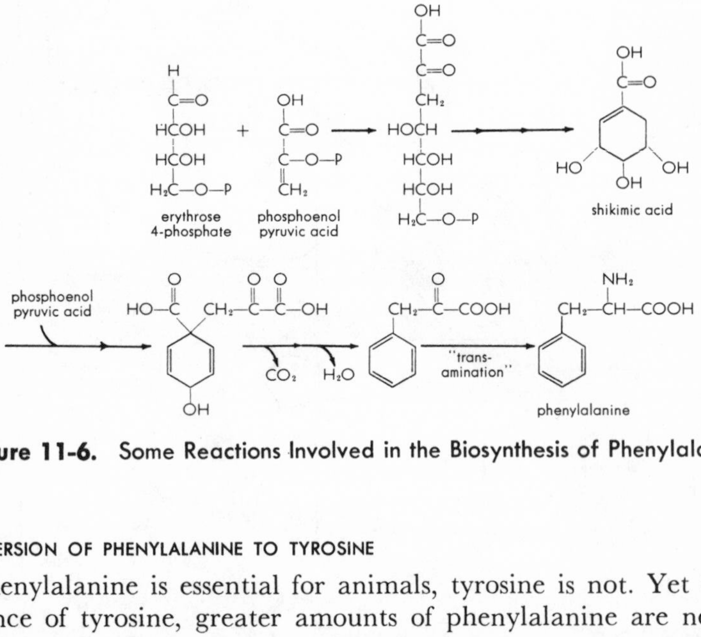

Figure 11-6. Some Reactions Involved in the Biosynthesis of Phenylalanine.

CONVERSION OF PHENYLALANINE TO TYROSINE

Phenylalanine is essential for animals, tyrosine is not. Yet in the absence of tyrosine, greater amounts of phenylalanine are needed. This suggests that tyrosine can be formed from phenylalanine, a suggestion which has been amply confirmed.

Although tyrosine formation from phenylalanine would appear to be a simple process requiring only the addition of a hydroxyl group to the benzene ring, the mechanism of the reaction is not yet completely known. Enzymes catalyzing this type of oxidation are termed *hydroxylases*. The coenzyme is apparently a compound with a structure similar to that of the ring system of folic acid. No attempt will be made to give a complete equation.

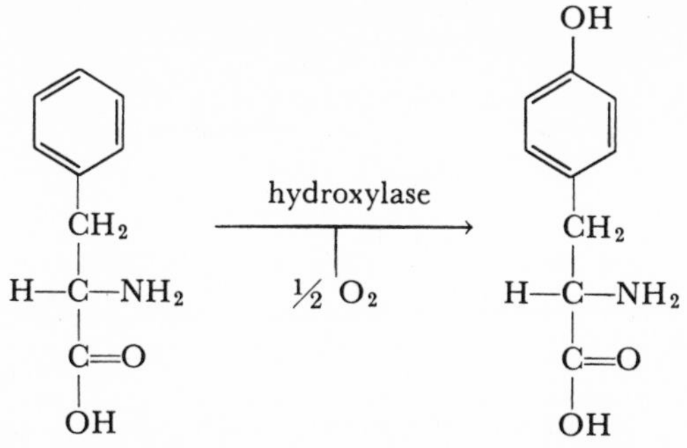

phenylalanine   tyrosine

This reaction is of historical interest in that it led to one of the first instances in which a genetic alteration could be shown to result in the loss of a chemical ability. The original finding was that a number of individuals of certain families excreted large quantities of phenylpyruvic acid in the urine. This compound is the α-keto acid corresponding to phenylalanine. It was therefore suggested (and later confirmed) that the inherited deficiency was a block in the production of tyrosine. Excess phenylalanine therefore accumulated, some of which was converted to the α-keto acid.

This condition, which is known as *phenylketonuria*, is also of practical importance. Unless victims of the deficiency are detected in infancy and placed on a special diet low in phenylalanine, serious mental impairment results.

EPINEPHRINE SYNTHESIS

The first step in the utilization of phenylalanine in synthetic reactions is usually its conversion to tyrosine. This is the case in the synthesis of epinephrine, a hormone produced by the adrenal medulla. A hydroxyl group is then added to the tyrosine structure, a decarboxylation reaction removes the carboxyl group, and another hydroxyl is added, yielding a compound called *nor-epinephrine*. A methyl group is transferred to this substance from "active" methionine producing epinephrine.

One of the intermediates in the conversion of tyrosine to nor-epinephrine, the compound dihydroxyphenylalanine, is interesting from another standpoint. This substance, formed from tyrosine, is the starting point for a series of reactions which culminate in the polymeric compound, melanin—the dark pigment of hair and skin. Albinos lack an enzyme necessary for the catalysis of one of these reactions.

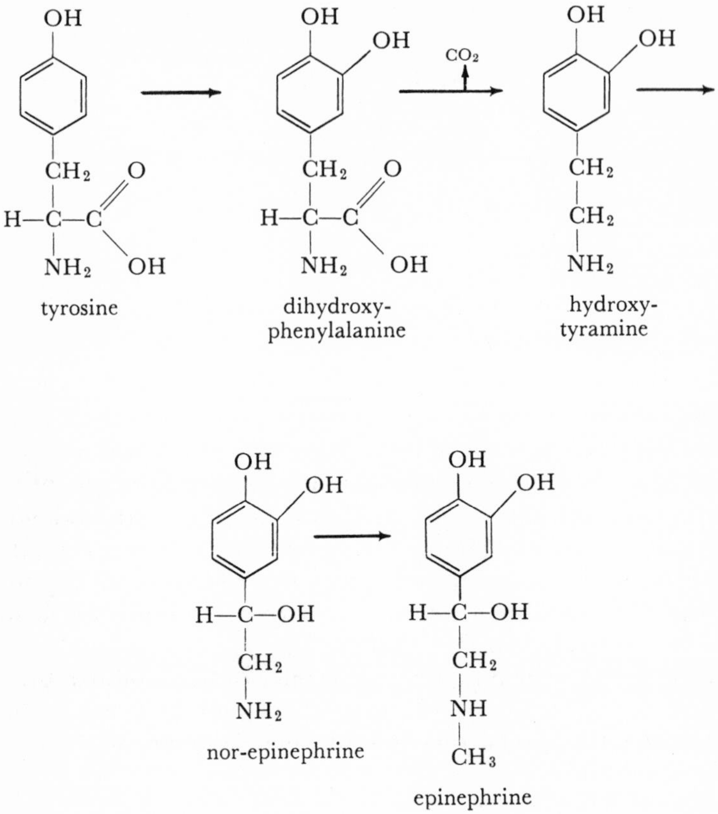

tyrosine — dihydroxy-phenylalanine — hydroxy-tyramine

nor-epinephrine — epinephrine

The conversion of dihydroxyphenylalanine to dihydroxytyramine is a decarboxylation. Enzymes catalyzing decarboxylations of α-amino acids are common in nature and are appropriately called *amino acid decarboxylases*. The coenzyme is pyridoxal phosphate, the same compound which is necessary for transaminase activity.

SYNTHESIS OF THYROXINE

Thyroxine production from tyrosine requires iodination reactions which are not thoroughly understood. The first known product is diiodotyrosine. Two molecules of this substance condense to form thyroxine. A dietary deficiency of I^- naturally results in a thyroxine deficiency. The reactions shown probably occur with the compounds bound to protein. The compound which circulates in blood is thyroglobulin, a thyroxine-protein.

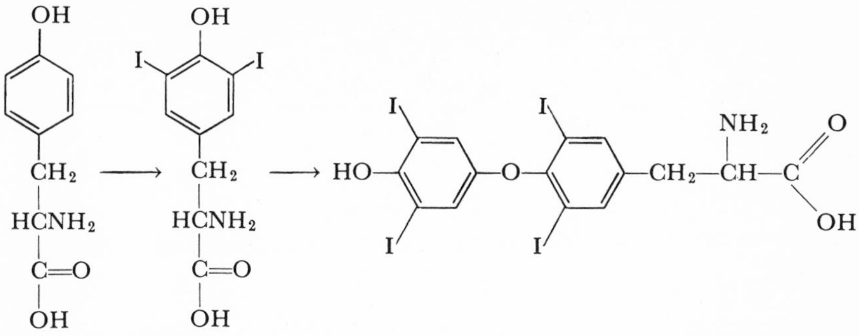

tyrosine   diiodotyrosine   thyroxine

SYNTHESIS OF LIGNIN

The exact structure of lignin is unknown. The compound appears to be a random polymer of several compounds closely related chemically to coniferyl alcohol. The structure of this compound follows;

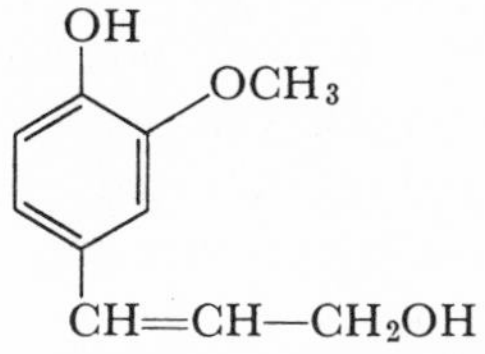

coniferyl alcohol .

note its similarity to dihydroxyphenylalanine. Probably the methyl group arises by transmethylation from "active methionine."

BIOSYNTHESIS OF AN ALKALOID FROM TYROSINE

The compounds known as *alkaloids* are a group of basic, nitrogen-containing compounds which may be viewed as end-products of nitrogen metabolism in plants. Most of these substances have marked physiological effects on animals.

The metabolism of most alkaloids is poorly known. Examination of their chemical structures in many cases indicates their close relationship to amino acids such as phenylalanine or tyrosine, tryptophan, lysine, or proline. As an example, the structure of papaverine, one of the alkaloids of opium, is given below. Note that this compound could be formed rather simply from two molecules of dihydroxyphenylalanine with the elimination of both carboxyls and one amino group. The actual biosynthetic pathway is not known.

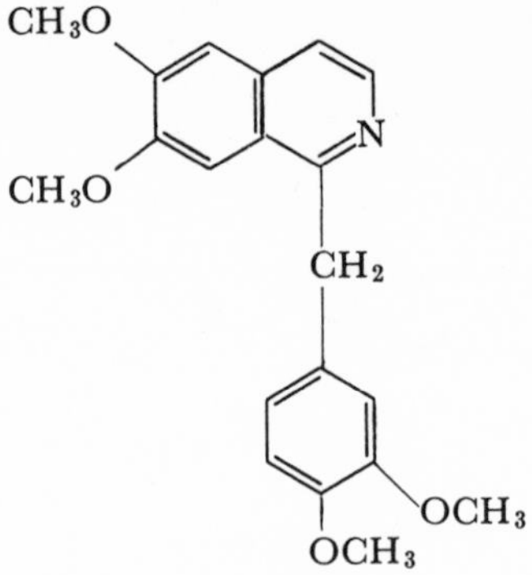

papaverine

AMINO ACID DEGRADATION

Amino acids, in common with other compounds of low molecular weight, are not stored by cells. Moreover, there is no evidence for the existence in cells of storage proteins which can yield amino acids for metabolic purposes. Amino acids present in excess of the immediate metabolic demands are, on the other hand, utilized as a general source of carbon atoms and of energy by reactions which destroy the amino acid molecule.

The major route of amino acid degradation involves as a first step the release of the amino group as ammonia, with the concurrent oxidation of the carbon skeleton to an α-keto acid. The various keto acids then enter the general metabolic mills. Some of these compounds —pyruvic acid from alanine or serine, oxalacetic acid from aspartic acid, and α-ketoglutaric acid from glutamic acid—are themselves intermediates of glucose oxidation. Other keto acids are converted into intermediates of carbohydrate or lipid metabolism by various special pathways.

The branch-chain amino acids provide excellent examples of this process, and in Figure 11-7 we have shown for purposes of illustration the pathway of degradation leading from leucine to acetoacetic acid and acetyl-CoA. Note that one of the intermediates in this process, β-hydroxy–β-methylglutaryl CoA, is very readily converted to mevalonic acid, which in turn is an excellent precursor of cholesterol.

Thus it should be clear that the carbon chains of the amino acids can, in general, be oxidized by the normal pathways of oxidative metabolism, with the attendant production of ATP, or they can be used for synthetic purposes under appropriate conditions. Many of

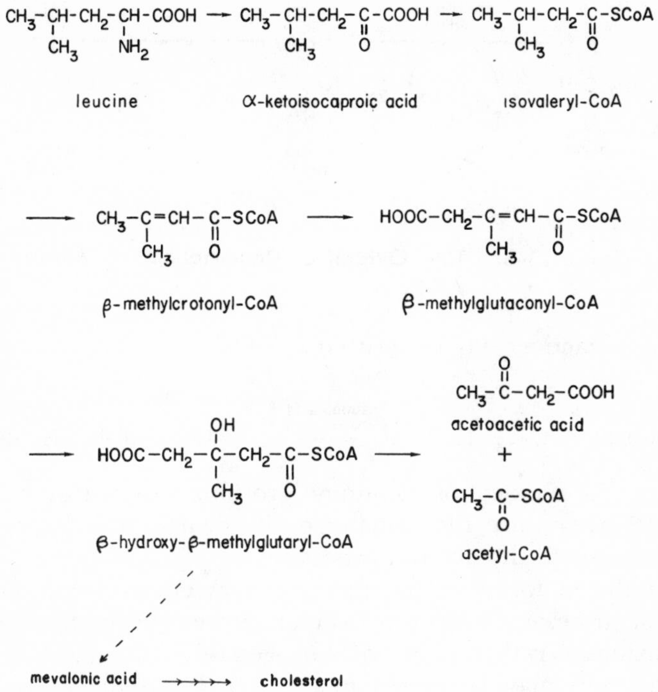

$$CH_3-CH-CH_2-CH-COOH \rightarrow CH_3-CH-CH_2-C-COOH \rightarrow CH_3-CH-CH_2-C-SCoA$$

leucine   α-ketoisocaproic acid   isovaleryl-CoA

$$\rightarrow CH_3-C=CH-C-SCoA \rightarrow HOOC-CH_2-C=CH-C-SCoA$$

β-methylcrotonyl-CoA   β-methylglutaconyl-CoA

$$CH_3-C-CH_2-COOH$$

acetoacetic acid

+

$$CH_3-C-SCoA$$

$$\rightarrow HOOC-CH_2-C-CH_2-C-SCoA \rightarrow$$

β-hydroxy-β-methylglutaryl-CoA

acetyl-CoA

mevalonic acid $\rightarrow\rightarrow\rightarrow\rightarrow$ cholesterol

Figure 11-7. Metabolic Degradation of Leucine.

them can even give rise to storage polysaccharides by the reversal of carbohydrate metabolism.

AMINO ACID OXIDASES

In lower organisms this first step of amino acid degradation is accomplished by the action of enzymes called *amino acid oxidases*. Each of these enzymes possesses a flavin compound as the oxidation-reduction coenzyme, and is accordingly a *flavoprotein*. The oxidation of the amino acid is accomplished by the dehydrogenation of the amino group to yield an imino acid,

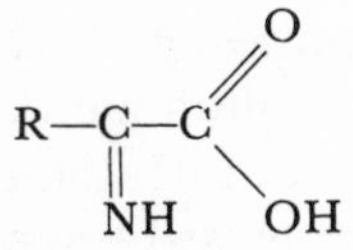

$$R-C-C\begin{smallmatrix}O\\\\OH\end{smallmatrix}$$
$$\underset{NH}{\parallel}$$

α-Imino acids react spontaneously with water, so rapidly that no enzyme is needed for the next step—hydrolysis to the keto acid and ammonia. These reactions are summarized in Figure 11-8.

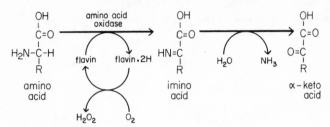

Figure 11-8. The Oxidative Deamination of Amino Acids.

The net reaction may be written as:

$$\alpha\text{-amino acid} + O_2 + H_2O \xrightarrow{\text{amino acid oxidase}} \alpha\text{-keto acid} + NH_3 + H_2O_2$$

Because the removal of the amino group is initiated by a reaction of an oxidative nature, the term "oxidative deamination" is frequently used to designate the over-all process.

The reduced forms of the flavin coenzymes of the amino acid oxidases can be oxidized by molecular oxygen; hence the use of the term "oxidase" rather than "dehydrogenase." In intact cells, however, electrons may be passed first to DPN and then through the electron transport system, rather than directly to oxygen.

Note that a product of the direct oxidation of the flavoprotein is hydrogen peroxide, a substance with toxic properties. The compound is, however, removed rapidly by reactions catalyzed by peroxidases and catalases. These enzymes are iron-porphyrin proteins, closely related in structure to hemoglobin and to the cytochromes. Both enzymes catalyze oxidation-reduction reactions in which H_2O_2 is the oxidizing agent, being reduced to water as some organic compound is oxidized. In addition, as a sort of safety valve, the catalases catalyze the decomposition of H_2O_2 to yield H_2O and O_2. This reaction becomes important only in the presence of rather high concentrations of hydrogen peroxide, and may have little biological significance.

Most of the L-amino acid oxidases of animal tissues, in contrast to those of lower organisms, appear to be rather ineffectual enzymes. It seems likely that in animals glutamic dehydrogenase is the most important enzyme for amino acid deamination. Amino groups of other amino acids are channeled toward the amino group of glutamic acid by transamination reactions. The glutamic acid then yields ammonia and α-ketoglutaric acid by the readily reversed glutamic dehydrogenase reaction. The over-all process is simply the reverse of the incorporation of ammonia into various amino acids by the processes previously described.

The Ammonia Problem

Ammonia is produced in relatively large amounts by the deamination of amino acids. The compound is quite poisonous, and its accumulation in cells or in extracellular fluids in appreciable concentrations is incompatible with life. Organisms living in aqueous environments such as the sea, can without difficulty excrete the ammonia directly. Organisms living on land, however. are prevented from doing so by the relative lack of the water necessary to dilute the ammonia to nontoxic levels.

For most land animals the solution provided by evolutionary changes lies in the formation of urea (H_2N—C—NH_2), a compound

$$\overset{\|}{O}$$

which can be tolerated in much higher concentrations than ammonia. The urea can therefore be allowed to accumulate in the organism until conditions are favorable for its excretion.

Even urea is too toxic to permit its continued accumulation in the water-poor environment faced by developing embryos in the eggs of birds and reptiles. Here evolutionary pressure has resulted in the use of waste nitrogen for the production of the purine, uric acid.

This compound is quite insoluble, so that even saturated solutions do not lead to difficulties. The continued production and excretion of uric acid is simply accompanied by the deposition of uric acid crystals in the egg space.

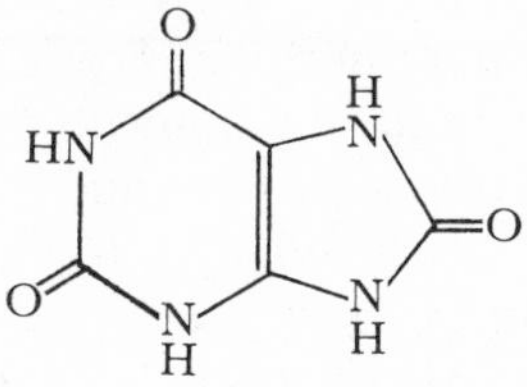

uric acid

The formation of uric acid follows very closely the mechanisms previously indicated for the formation of the purine components of the nucleic acids. The need for glycine for uric acid production in the chick is so great that this becomes an essential amino acid for this organism and probably for other birds as well.

THE ORNITHINE CYCLE

The mechanisms for the production of urea from ammonia merit further discussion in that most of the reactions are the same as those by which all living organisms synthesize arginine. In addition, these reactions illustrate processes of general importance in nitrogen metabolism.

The synthesis of urea can be summarized as:

$$2\,NH_3 \;+\; HO\!-\!\underset{\underset{O}{\|}}{C}\!-\!OH \;\rightarrow\; H_2N\!-\!\underset{\underset{O}{\|}}{C}\!-\!NH_2 \;+\; 2\,H_2O$$

$$\text{carbonic acid} \qquad\qquad \text{urea}$$

It should be apparent from this presentation that urea is the di-amide of carbonic acid. As we have noted several times, the biological synthesis of amides cannot proceed to a significant extent in the absence of mechanisms which couple the process to an energy source such as ATP. Therefore, the actual pathway for urea synthesis must be a more complex one than that suggested above.

Urea formation actually occurs in a cyclical process involving the stepwise synthesis of arginine from ornithine, followed by the hydrolysis of arginine to yield ornithine and urea. This set of reactions is named variously the *Ornithine, Arginine, Urea,* or *Krebs-Henseleit Cycle.* Since it is ornithine which actually travels the cyclical path, the term "Ornithine Cycle" is perhaps the most logical one. The reactions of the cycle, and certain related reactions, appear in Figure 11-9 in somewhat simplified form.

Certain aspects of this process deserve particular attention. First, the production of carbamyl phosphate from NH_3, CO_2 (or H_2CO_3), and ATP represents an additional mechanism for the fixation of inorganic nitrogen into organic compounds. The details of the reaction are incompletely known. Somewhat different reactions produce the same compound in bacteria, certain mushrooms, and mammals.

Secondly, one of the nitrogen atoms necessary for urea synthesis is supplied, not by ammonia, but by the amino group of aspartic acid. Here we must emphasize that the fumaric acid released in the succeeding step can be converted by reactions of the tricarboxylic acid cycle to oxalacetic acid. This compound in turn can be transaminated to yield aspartic acid. Thus the amino groups of the general amino acids enter the cycle in two ways: (1) deamination to ammonia, followed by carbamyl phosphate and then citrulline production, and (2) transamination to give aspartic acid, followed by use of this compound for arginine synthesis from citrulline. (See Figure 11-10.)

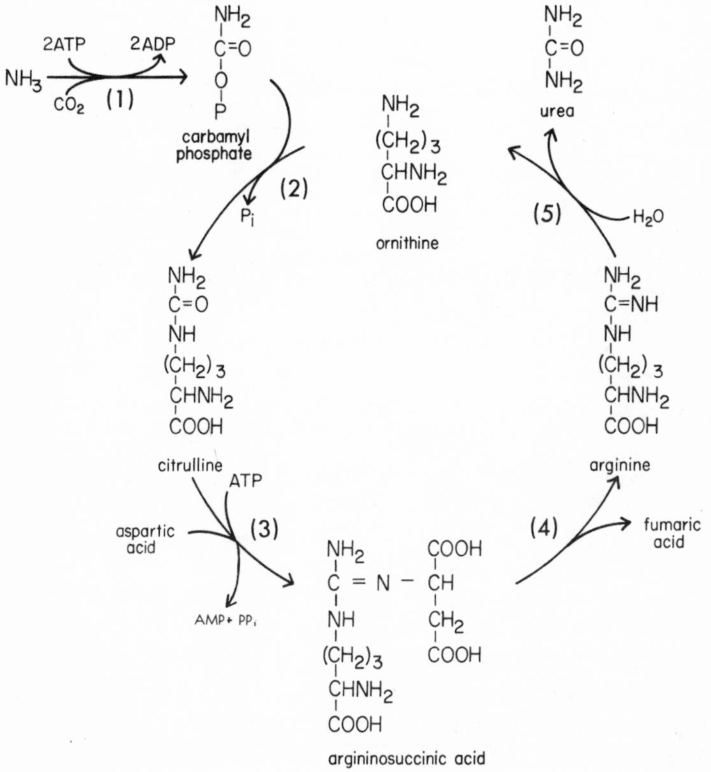

Figure 11-9. The Ornithine Cycle. Enzymes: (1) carbamyl phosphate synthetase, (2) ornithine transcarbamylase, (3) argininosuccinate synthetase, (4) argininosuccinase, (5) arginase.

In connection with our discussion of the ammonia problem, we should also point out that the solutions represent an evolutionary diversion of two basic biochemical processes of importance to all

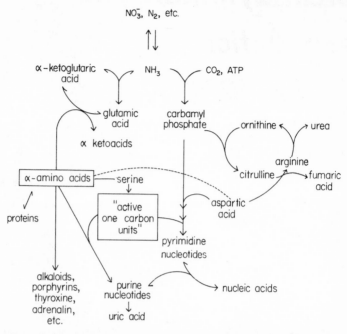

Figure 11-10. A Summary of the Major Processes of Nitrogen Metabolism.

cells, arginine synthesis and purine synthesis, to meet the new demands imposed by environmental changes as organisms left the sea for dry land.

SUGGESTED ADDITIONAL READING

Meister, A., "Biochemistry of the Amino Acids," Academic Press, New York, 1957.

Greenberg, D. M., "Metabolic Pathways," Vol. 2, Academic Press, New York and London, 1961.

Huennekens, F. M., and Osborn, M. J., "Folic Acid Coenzymes and One-carbon Metabolism," *Advances in Enzymology*, **21**, 369 (1959).

Protein Synthesis and Gene Action

12

The mechanisms by which living cells synthesize specific protein molecules are processes basic to life as we know it. The properties of a cell at any given time are chiefly determined by the kinds of proteins present and by the amount of each kind. We have previously seen that the chemical activities of the cell, and accordingly all the compounds that the cell can make, are directly related to the enzymes available. In addition, the structural components of the cell—membranes, mitochondria, chloroplasts and the like—are also composed of specific proteins interacting with each other and with other substances to form specific multimolecular aggregates. The physical properties of these components, indeed of the whole cell, are therefore also dependent directly on the types of proteins the cell has produced.

Differences existing among a variety of cells in terms either of physical structure or of chemical activities must then reflect differences in protein synthesis. But fundamental differences among cells of different organisms are inherited! This leads to a key concept: *the inheritance of characteristics must involve the inheritance of the ability to synthesize specific proteins.*

The concept was first clearly seen by Beadle and Tatum as an outgrowth of their work on radiation-produced mutants of the mold, *Neurospora crassa*. Their experiments demonstrated conclusively that many of the genetically altered strains of the mold failed to synthesize one of a number of enzymes. Each strain could be shown to be a single-gene mutant and to lack one particular enzyme. This work led to the *single gene–single enzyme hypothesis*, now more precisely termed the *single gene–single peptide chain hypothesis*. Each gene is thought to provide the organism with the ability to produce one particular kind of peptide chain.

Research conducted on human hemoglobin in the laboratories of Pauling and of Ingram has provided a most striking illustration of the relation between genes and proteins and between proteins and cell characteristics.

Normal hemoglobin is composed of four peptide chains that interact to give a compact, grossly spherical molecule. The peptide chains are of two types, which are called the α and β chains. The complete molecule is thus formed of two α and two β chains, each bound to a heme unit.

Abnormal hemoglobins are manufactured in a variety of hereditary conditions. One of these is termed *sickle-cell anemia*. At low oxygen concentrations, the hemoglobin-containing red blood cells of persons with this disease are elongated or sickle-shaped rather than the usual spherical shape. Oxygen transport is also affected, resulting in relative anoxia or oxygen deficiency in the tissues.

The hemoglobin from sickle cells was found to differ from normal hemoglobin in electrophoretic behavior, suggesting a difference in one or more of the ionizable side-chains of the amino acid residues. Chromatographic separations of peptides produced by partial hydrolysis and amino acid sequence analyses finally traced the difference to the sixth amino acid from the N-terminus of the β chain. Here a normal glutamic acid has been replaced by a valine. This is the sole difference between normal and sickle-cell hemoglobin—one amino acid of the 146 amino acids in each of the β chains.

Two major conclusions can be drawn from these and many similar experiments. First, a gene must provide the cell with the ability to assemble amino acid units into a precise sequence giving a specific peptide chain. Gene mutations lead to the production of proteins with altered amino acid sequences. Some changes may not alter the protein's properties significantly; others may be either deleterious or advantageous with respect to biological function. Evolutionary changes should then be seen as changes in proteins. Indeed, the more closely related two organisms are, the greater will be the similarities in the amino acid sequences of their proteins. In effect, one can trace the evolution of a protein such as hemoglobin or any of the enzymes if one knows the amino acid sequences of the compound isolated from numerous species of organisms.

The second major conclusion from the hemoglobin work is that the physical attributes of cells can be altered by seemingly minor changes in a protein. In this case, sickle-cell hemoglobin molecules tend to assemble side-by-side in the red cell in long aggregates, which distort the cell into the sickle shape. The change in amino acid sequence has presumably resulted in a change in conformation of the protein and thereby in the manner in which it interacts with others of its kind.

DNA AND GENES

Along with the development of the concepts relating gene action to protein biosynthesis, evidence accumulated that genes are units of deoxyribonucleic acid (DNA). Each gene is thought to be a portion of a DNA double helix. The genetic information is believed to reside in coded form as the nucleotide sequence of each DNA unit.

There is much evidence for the conclusion that genes are DNA units. Most significant, perhaps, are the results of experiments with the transformation of bacteria. This is a phenomenon in which bacteria gain the ability to synthesize a new protein solely by virtue of their growth in a medium containing certain DNA molecules. These molecules must be DNA which has been isolated from a related strain of organisms, organisms which have the genetic ability to produce the protein in question. In effect, a genetic change in protein-synthesizing capabilities is brought about by the addition of the right kind of DNA molecule. Presumably the DNA enters the cell and becomes part of the normal genetic complement. This experiment is shown diagrammatically in Figure 12-1. Such experiments have not yet been performed successfully with higher organisms; yet they offer much promise that eventually man may be able in this way to produce desirable changes in domestic plants and animals and even to repair genetic deficiencies in himself. These deficiencies may well become more common in this nuclear age.

Pertinent too are experiments with virus infection. Virus particles are nucleoprotein aggregates. Upon the infection of a suitable host cell, practically all of the virus protein remains outside the cell while all of the nucleic acid enters the cell. Indeed, virus infections can be obtained with preparations of the viral nucleic acids which are devoid of protein. The events following infection must then be ascribed to

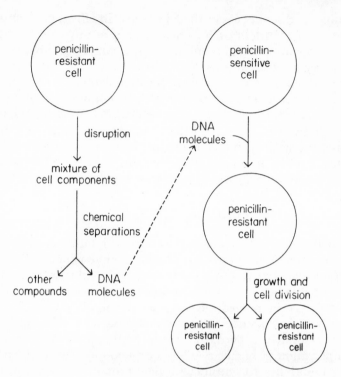

Figure 12-1. A Schematic Representation of an Experiment Demonstrating Bacterial Transformation.

A strain of cells sensitive to inhibition by penicillin is shown to acquire resistance to the antibiotic in the presence of DNA isolated from a resistant strain. The acquired characteristic, which is then a new inheritable property of the transformed cells, has been shown to result from the synthesis of a new protein which catalyzes a reaction converting penicillin to an inactive product.

the presence in the cell of new kinds of nucleic acid units. Among these events are the synthesis of new enzymes, the replication of the new nucleic acids, and finally the production of new virus particles complete with their normal proteins.

In both transformation and virus action the necessary attributes of a gene, the property of replication and the ability to induce the formation of a protein, are seen to reside in the chemical and physical properties of nucleic acid molecules.

DNA DUPLICATION

The most dramatic aspect of the Crick-Watson model of DNA structure was the possible mechanism for the duplication of DNA that was readily apparent. Obviously, the genetic information must be precisely duplicated prior to cell division. A molecule better suited to this purpose than DNA is hard to imagine. You will recall that each DNA unit is a double helix composed of two polynucleotide chains held together by very specific hydrogen bonding among the nitrogenous bases (see p. 86). The size of the various units and their capacities to form strong hydrogen bonds insure that only certain base-pairings are possible. If one chain has an adenine nucleotide at a certain point, the other chain must have a thymine nucleotide. Similarly, one chain must have a guanine unit corresponding to a cytosine unit of the second chain. It should be apparent that the nucleotide sequence of one chain determines the nucleotide sequence of the second chain; that is, the two chains have complementary structures.

Should these two chains of the double helix be separated, each one could form hydrogen bonds with free mononucleotide units. The specific nature of such bonding would insure that each chain would align the nucleotides in complementary fashion. The formation of internucleotide linkage would result in the creation of two new DNA units identical to the original one. This process is represented in diagrammatic form in Figure 12-2. The capital letters are the initial letters of each of the different DNA bases.

Present evidence indicates that DNA duplication does not involve as an initial step the complete separation of the double helix into single strands. Rather, a separation of only a few base pairs at one end of the helix is followed almost at once by base-pairing with free nucleotide units and formation of the phosphodiester bonds. This process continues one nucleotide pair at a time along the entire length of the helix. The two new chains are formed as the old chain separates. Single-stranded DNA cannot be detected in the cells at any time.

Considerable evidence has accumulated that the basic mechanism for DNA duplication by living cells is indeed founded on base-pairing of nucleotide units with pre-existing DNA. This mechanism is diagrammed in Figure 12-2. One strand (one-half of the duplex) of each

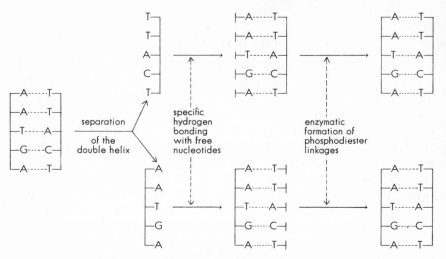

Figure 12-2. Replication of a Portion of a DNA Molecule.

new DNA unit is assumed to be derived from the original DNA and the other strand is newly formed.

Meselson and Stahl were the first to show that the duplication of bacterial DNA conforms to this assumption.

These workers made use of the heavy isotope of nitrogen, N^{15}, to trace DNA chains through duplication. Bacteria were grown for several generations in culture media containing, as the sole nitrogen source, ammonium ion formed from N^{15}. This produced organisms whose DNA was almost completely labeled with the heavy isotope. This we can indicate as DNA-N^{15}. This DNA was, as we would expect, of geater density than normal DNA-N^{14} prepared from the same kind of bacteria.

Some of the bacteria containing DNA-N^{15} were transferred to a medium with normal N^{14} as the nitrogen source and allowed to duplicate once. The DNA of these new cells was found to have a density *halfway between* the densities of the DNA-N^{15} and DNA-N^{14}. This we can indicate as DNA-N^{15}, N^{14}.

When the bacteria were permitted to pass through two duplications before the DNA was isolated and examined, *two* kinds of DNA were found. One of these was again the DNA-N^{15}, N^{14}; the other was like the normal DNA-N^{14}.

The results of these experiments are diagrammed in Figure 12-3. Clearly they are in agreement with the expectations arising from the Crick-Watson model.

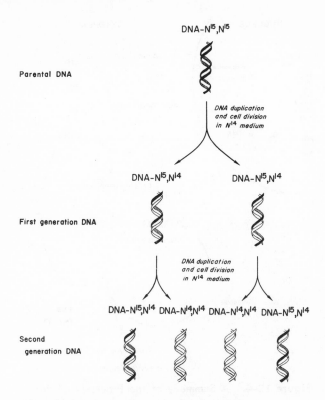

DNA-N^{15},N^{15}

Parental DNA

DNA duplication
and cell division
in N^{14} medium

DNA-N^{15},N^{14} DNA-N^{15},N^{14}

First generation DNA

DNA duplication
and cell division
in N^{14} medium

DNA-N^{15},N^{14} DNA-N^{14},N^{14} DNA-N^{14},N^{14} DNA-N^{15},N^{14}

Second
  generation DNA

Figure 12-3. The Meselson-Stahl Experiments on DNA
Duplication.

The dark helices indicate strands of DNA which were present
in the original cell before DNA duplication. The light
helices represent DNA strands formed in the processes leading to cell division.

DNA AND PROTEIN SYNTHESIS

Our information pertinent to the basic processes of protein synthesis is summarized in Figure 12-4. We can divide these processes
into four stages: (1) the transcription stage, (2) the activation stage,
(3) the adaptor stage, and (4) the translation stage.

Transcription of the Genetic Information

In the *transcription stage* the genetic information of the DNA is
copied as RNA molecules are formed. Riboside triphosphate units
are assembled into molecules whose nucleotide sequence is determined
by base-pairing mechanisms with *one* of the DNA strands. Recall that

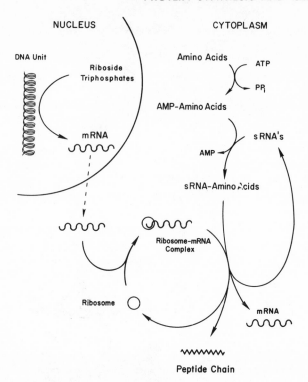

**Figure 12-4.   A Summary of the Processes of Pro-
tein Synthesis.**

cytosine, adenine, and guanine are common to both DNA and RNA.
The fourth base of RNA, uracil, closely resembles the thymine of DNA
and forms base-pairs with adenine in the same manner. The nucleotide sequence of the RNA will be complementary to one of the DNA
strands (and identical to the other), always with a uracil unit in
place of a thymine unit. Thus the genetic information is available in
the RNA, still coded as a nucleotide sequence.

Once formed and released from the DNA, the RNA moves into the
cytoplasm and combines with ribosomal particles, long known to be
involved with protein formation.

As we shall see, this means that DNA does not participate directly
in protein synthesis. The situation is much as if the master copy of the
hereditary information—the DNA—is retained in the safe environs of
the nucleus with working copies—the RNA—being struck off for
distribution and general use by the cell. Because this kind of RNA
carries a copy or transcript of the genetic data from the DNA to the

site of protein synthesis, it has been widely designated as *messenger RNA*, abbreviated as *mRNA*.

Amino Acid Activation

In the *activation stage*, free amino acids are converted to more reactive compounds, the *amino acid adenylates*. Recall that the equilibrium for the condensation of amino acids to form peptides lies far toward the amino acid side. In cellular conditions with low concentrations of amino acids, it is not thermodynamically possible for the free amino acids to condense directly to form large quantities of protein. The energetically favorable route to protein synthesis that cells have developed requires that the amino acids be "activated" by ATP. In this reaction a "high-energy" acid anhydride linkage is formed between the carboxyl group of the amino acid and the phosphate group of adenosine monophosphate, AMP.

$$
\text{ATP} + \underset{\substack{| \\ \text{NH}_2 \\ \text{amino acid}}}{\text{HO—C—CH—R}}^{\overset{\overset{\text{O}}{\|}}{}} \longrightarrow \underset{\substack{| \\ \text{OH} \quad \text{NH}_2 \\ \text{"activated" amino acid} \\ \text{(amino acid adenylate)}}}{\text{adenosine—O—P—O—C—CH—R}}^{\overset{\overset{\text{O} \quad\quad \text{O}}{\| \quad\quad \|}}{}} + \text{PP}_i
$$

In this way the carboxyl group of the amino acid gains increased reactivity at the expense of the cleavage of one of the phosphate anhydride bonds of ATP. This process should be compared with that utilized for the activation of fatty acids.

The Adaptation Process

A major problem still remains—that of ordering the amino acid units according to the coded information of the mRNA. Apparently there is no direct way for amino acid adenylates to interact with nucleic acid bases in order to provide sufficient specificity for amino acid alignment. Instead, the activated amino acids are first transferred to sRNA molecules which act as "adaptors." This we have termed the *adaptation step*.

Remember that sRNA molecules (sometimes called transfer RNA) are rather small nucleic acids that occur free in the cytoplasm of cells. There is at least one kind of sRNA molecule for each of the twenty kinds of amino acids incorporated into proteins. Each sRNA molecule is specific in two ways.

First, it will react only with one kind of amino acid adenylate as shown below.

$$
\underset{\substack{\text{amino acid} \\ \text{adenylate}}}{\text{AMP}-\overset{\overset{\text{O}}{\|}}{\text{C}}-\underset{\text{NH}_2}{\text{CH}}-\text{R}} \quad + \quad \text{sRNA} \quad \rightleftharpoons \quad \text{AMP} \quad + \quad \underset{\substack{\text{amino acid-sRNA} \\ \text{compound}}}{\text{sRNA}-\overset{\overset{\text{O}}{\|}}{\text{C}}-\underset{\text{NH}_2}{\text{CH}}-\text{R}}
$$

In the amino acid-sRNA compound shown above, the acid remains in reactive or "activated" form. The carboxyl group of the amino acid is bound as an ester with an alcohol group at either the 2' or 3' positions of the ribose of the nucleotide unit at the end of the poly-nucleotide chain.

Translation of the Genetic Information

The second specific feature of each kind of sRNA molecule is its capacity to form base pairs with mRNA molecules at certain sites. Recall from Chapter 5 that many of the bases of an sRNA molecule are paired internally with other bases of the same chain. This is possible because the single polyribotide molecule is folded back on itself. But at the loops or bends of the chain, bases remain free. The evidence indicates that it is a sequence of three nucleotides located at one of the loops of sRNA that forms base pairs with complementary sequences of the mRNA. Accordingly, each kind of sRNA-amino acid complex will bind with mRNA only at sites determined by the nucleotide sequence of the mRNA, i.e., by the genetic information. In this way, through base-pairing mechanisms, the amino acids attached to sRNA molecules are brought into the correct sequence for the assembly of a polypeptide.

In the final stage of synthesis of a peptide chain, the nucleotide language of mRNA is *translated* into the amino acid language of the peptide—the nucleotide sequence specifies an amino acid sequence. In this process, a ribosomal particle combines in some manner with one end of an mRNA chain. Amino acids bound to sRNA molecules are also aligned on the mRNA. Peptide bonds are formed one step at a time between the aligned amino acids as the ribosomes move along the mRNA. The synthesis of the polypeptide begins at the end of the chain which has a free amino group and proceeds linearly toward the end with the free carboxyl group. sRNA molecules are released from the mRNA for further use after the discharge of their amino acids.

When the polypeptide chain is completed, it and the messenger RNA are released from the ribosome. The folding of the peptide chain into the "native" conformation is believed to occur spontaneously.

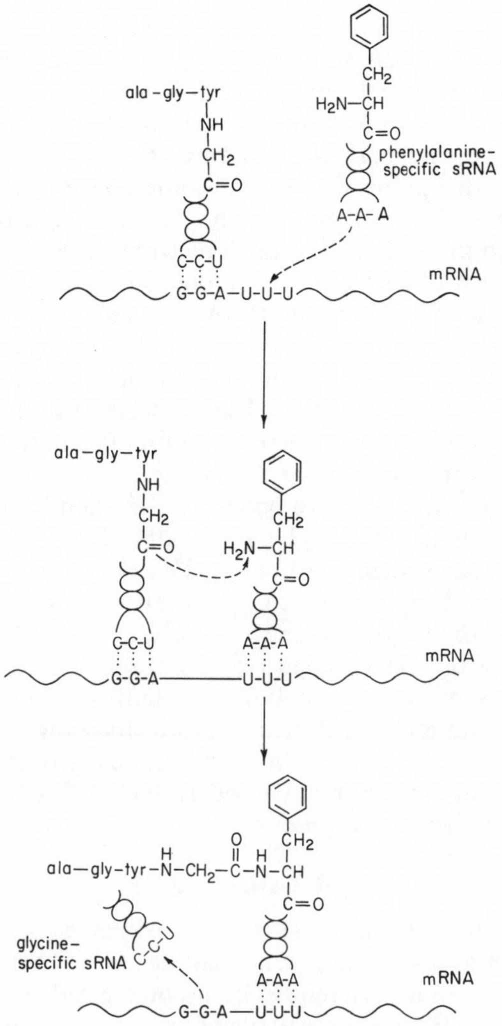

Figure 12-5. Growth of a Peptide Chain.

All processes take place in association with a ribosome system which moves along the mRNA from left to right (in the orientation of this figure) as the peptide is formed.

The mRNA now is free for attachment to another ribosome. In bacteria at least, a particular mRNA molecule persists only a short time before it is degraded, probably by hydrolysis to the nucleotides. In higher organisms, some mRNA molecules may be used for protein synthesis numerous times before being destroyed.

With this as an overview of the translation stage, let us examine the mechanism of addition of each amino acid to the peptide chain in more detail. Figure 12-5 summarizes much of our present information. Here an mRNA molecule is shown lying across a ribosomal particle. In the first part of the figure, peptide chain synthesis has proceeded to the point where four amino acids have been linked together. The fourth of these, glycine, is still attached to its adaptor sRNA through the carboxyl group. The whole peptide-sRNA complex is bound to the mRNA by hydrogen bonds between three consecutive bases of each RNA. A second sRNA molecule carrying a phenylalanine unit is shown about to bind to the mRNA at an adjacent site.

In the second part of the figure, the binding of the phenylalanine-sRNA has been accomplished. The carboxyl group of the glycine has begun to shift its allegiance from an OH group of its sRNA to the amino group of the nearby phenylalanine.

Finally the glycine becomes bound to the phenylalanine through a typical peptide linkage. The glycine-specific sRNA has been released. The ribosome has shifted position on the mRNA by three nucleotide units. The scene is now ready for a new sRNA-amino acid.

As one ribosome moves along the mRNA away from the starting point, it is possible for a second ribosomal particle to combine at the end of the messenger and also begin to synthesize the peptide chain. In fact, it is common to find five or more ribosomes at a time strung along a messenger RNA, each busily synthesizing protein and moving in step toward the end of the messenger. Such mRNA-multiribosomal aggregates are termed *polysomes*.

THE GENETIC CODE

We have indicated that the genetic information for protein synthesis is coded as a sequence of nucleotides in mRNA and, of course, in DNA. There must, therefore, be a correspondence between each kind of amino acid and a particular nucleotide sequence. In that 20 amino acids are necessary for protein synthesis while only four kinds of nucleotides occur in the nucleic acids, it is apparent that the code for an amino acid must consist of at least three nucleotides. There are only sixteen combinations possible for four items taken two at a time, but sixty-four combinations for four items taken three at a time. The present evidence agrees that it is this *triplet code* that cells do utilize.

Each set of three nucleotides in an mRNA molecule that represents one of the twenty amino acids is termed a *codon* for the particular amino acid. Each codon presumably forms base pairs with three complementary nucleotides of the sRNA specific for the same amino acid. The portion of the sRNA molecule that combines with the mRNA is called an *anticodon*.

In Figure 12-5 the codon for phenylalanine was shown to be three consecutive uridylic acid units, shown as U-U-U. Similarly, the codon for glycine was guanylic acid, guanylic acid and adenylic acid, G-G-A. The codons for all of the amino acids are now known and are thought to be the same for all organisms. The genetic code is accordingly said to be a universal code, although insofar as we know it is limited to earthly organisms.

Recalling that there are sixty-four possible codons and only twenty amino acids requiring coding, one is not surprised that each of a number of amino acids has more than one codon.

The research leading to the information on the identity of the coding triplets for the various amino acids was initiated by Nirenberg and Matthei. These workers made the striking discovery that synthetic polyribotides of known composition could be utilized by ribosomes as if they were messenger RNA. The test system was composed of a mixture of ribosomes, the twenty amino acids, the various sRNA molecules, the various amino acid activating enzymes, and the synthetic polyribotide. Under these conditions, the kinds of amino acids incorporated into peptides were found to be determined by the kind of polyribotide present. For example, polyuridylic acid having only U-U-U as possible codons, gave rise to peptides containing only phenylalanine. Continued efforts of this type, notably by Nirenberg and by Ochoa, have led to the identification of all of the amino acid codons. These are provided in Figure 12-6.

In this context, it may be of interest to mention that the infection of cells with RNA viruses may be viewed simply as supplying the cells with a new kind of messenger RNA, the viral RNA. The ribosomes, sRNAs and various enzymes of the cell simply proceed to synthesize proteins according to the sequence of codons in the new RNA. Some of these proteins are viral coat proteins, others are enzymes needed for the replication of the viral RNA.

A final major problem of protein synthesis is that of the control of the *amount* of each protein actually formed. These aspects will be

		Second	Base	of	Codon	Triplet	
		U	C	A	G		
U		phe	ser	tyr	cys	U C	
		leu	ser	c.t.[1]	try	A G	
C		leu	pro	his	arg	U C	
		leu	pro	glu-NH$_2^2$	arg	A G	
A		ileu	thr	asp-NH$_2^2$	ser	U C	
		met	thr	lys	arg	A G	
G		val	ala	asp	gly	U C	
		val	ala	glu	gly	A G	

First Base of Codon Triplet / Third Base of Codon Triplet

Figure 12-6.   The Genetic Code.

The amino acids corresponding to each codon are designated by the first three letters of their names. The "c.t." indicates that this is believed to be one of the codons responsible for "chain termination," that is, indicating when a polypeptide chain is finished and should be released without further elongation. The designations "glu-NH$_2$" and "asp-NH$_2$" have been used to represent glutamine and asparagine, respectively.

considered under the general heading of metabolic control processes in Chapter 13.

SUGGESTED ADDITIONAL READING

Benzer, S., "The Fine Structure of the Gene," *Scientific American*, **206**, No. 1, 70 (January, 1962).

Fraenkel-Conrat, H., "The Genetic Code of a Virus," *Scientific American*, **211**, No. 4, 46 (October, 1964).

Hurwitz, J., and Furth, J. J., "Messenger RNA," *Scientific American*, **206**, No. 2, 41 (February, 1962).

Nirenberg, M. W., "The Genetic Code: II," *Scientific American*, **208**, No. 3, 80 (March, 1963).

Rich, A., "Polyribosomes," *Scientific American*, **209**, No. 6, 44 (December, 1963).

Spiegelman, S., "Hybrid Nucleic Acids," *Scientific American*, **210**, No. 5, 48 (May, 1964).

Sutton, H. E., "Genes, Enzymes, and Inherited Diseases," Holt, Reinhart, and Winston, New York, 1961.

The Control of
Metabolic Activities

13

The basic chemical activities of living cells have been discussed in preceding chapters. In these discussions we have necessarily been concerned with the examination of a rather large number of individual chemical reactions. Nevertheless, we have attempted to emphasize that the individual processes are organized into a variety of sequential metabolic pathways, such as glycolysis or the process of protein synthesis. In addition, the interlocking of the various pathways has repeatedly been noted. The view of metabolism which we have attempted to establish is one of many different kinds of molecules following a precisely controlled pattern of chemical interconversions.

At this point it would be redundant for us to repeat that the metabolic activities of a cell are primarily reactions involving enzymes and their substrates. However, we can now add that the control of such activities must necessarily entail the control, directly or indirectly, of the *rates* of enzyme-catalyzed reactions. We have seen in Chapter 6 that the rate of an enzymatic process is determined mainly by the concentration of the substrate (or substrates, including coenzymes) and by the concentration of the active form of the enzyme. The rate of a particular metabolic process might accordingly be altered in three major ways:

(1) by changing the concentration of the substrates;
(2) by altering the concentration of cofactors, inhibitors, or activators, thereby affecting the activity of the existing enzyme molecules; or
(3) by changing the rate of synthesis or of the degradation of the enzyme, leading to differences in the total number of enzyme molecules present in the cell at different times.

Each of these three possibilities is actually known to operate as a mechanism for the control of metabolic activities. The remainder of this chapter will be concerned primarily with the discussion of these processes and with specific examples of their occurrence in living systems.

SUBSTRATE CONCENTRATION EFFECTS

We have already seen a variety of examples of effects upon the course of metabolism which occur as the result of changes in the concentration of an essential metabolite. The most obvious cases are found with the coenzymes, preferably the cosubstrates, such as ATP and DPN. Recall that glycogen formation from glucose-1-phosphate requires uridine triphosphate which is generated by the reaction of uridine diphosphate with ATP. Glycogen cleavage to glucose-1-phosphate on the other hand involves inorganic phosphate ion. Accordingly as the ATP concentration tends to increase, the rate of glycogen formation will also increase. At the same time, as the ATP concentration rises, that of the phosphate ion will fall as phosphate groups are incorporated into organic molecules. The rate of degradation of glycogen will therefore also decrease. Both factors operate in the same direction, giving a higher net formation of glycogen at the expense of ATP. As this occurs, the ATP concentration will in time be brought back to "normal." On the other hand, a decrease in ATP concentration (and the accompanying increase in ADP and P_i) will favor the net conversion of glycogen to glucose-1-phosphate. This will in turn increase the rate of glycolysis and the rate of ATP formation. These situations are depicted in Figure 13-1.

The effect of the oxygen concentration on the course of the metabolism of pyruvic acid by muscle cells is another obvious example of substrate concentration effects. Recall that pyruvic acid can be metabolized in two major directions, oxidation to acetyl-CoA and CO_2,

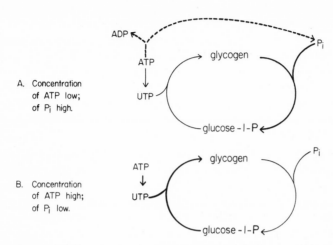

Figure 13-1. Substrate Concentration Effects on Glycogen Synthesis and Breakdown.

and reduction to lactic acid. The first of these reactions requires DPN$^+$ to reoxidize reduced lipoic acid; the second needs DPNH as the reducing agent. The distribution of pyruvic acid molecules between these two fates will be chiefly determined by the ratio of the concentrations of DPN$^+$ and DPNH. Naturally the rate of oxidation of DPNH by the electron transport system will in part be determined by the availability of oxygen.

Numerous similar examples could be provided. There seems to be no doubt that interlocking effects of substrate concentration changes are exceedingly important in the second-to-second balancing of metabolic activities, particularly with respect to the synthesis and utilization of stored nutrients.

EFFECTS ON ENZYME ACTIVITY

Theoretically, any compound in a cell might be an inhibitor or an activator of one or more of the enzymes present. Opportunities for competitive inhibition would appear to be particularly likely because any cell metabolite is necessarily a structural analog of several other compounds of the cell. Numerous metabolic control mechanisms involving the alteration of enzyme activity by variations in the concentrations of normal metabolites are therefore possible.

Specific, well-documented examples of the regulation of metabolic activities by the inhibition or activation of enzymes are relatively rare, probably because biochemists have barely begun to look for them rather than because of their infrequent occurrence. However, a number of examples of a phenomenon termed *feedback inhibition* are known —sufficient to suggest that this is a mechanism of major importance.

"Feedback" is a term widely used to refer to an effect of a product of a process on one or more of the steps required for its own production. In biochemistry, *feedback inhibition* is the phenomenon in which a compound is an inhibitor of one of the steps in its own synthesis. Often the inhibited reaction is the first metabolic process unique to the synthesis of the particular end-product. The terms end-product inhibition and retroinhibition are also used to denote this phenomenon.

A specific example may help to clarify the nature of feedback inhibition. Cytidine triphosphate (CTP), as we have seen, is one of the precursors of the ribonucleic acids. Its biosynthesis begins with a reaction between aspartic acid and carbamyl phosphate catalyzed by aspartic transcarbamylase and continues via the reactions shown in Figure 11-4 until uridylic acid is reached. Recall here that uridylic acid is the precursor of all of the pyrimidine nucleotides needed for nucleic acid production. Part of the uridylic acid is converted to CTP by amination and two consecutive phosphorylations.

In a variety of organisms, CTP is a potent inhibitor of aspartic transcarbamylase. In this case, not only does CTP inhibit its own production, but also that of all other pyrimidine nucleotides and, in turn, nucleic acid synthesis as well. These relationships are diagrammed in Figure 13-2.

Kinetic analysis of the inhibition indicates that a competition exists between aspartic acid and CTP. However, in this case, competition for an active site is not involved. Aspartic transcarbamylase

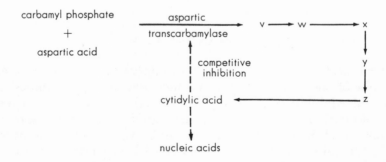

Figure 13-2.   An Example of Feedback Inhibition.

consists of six peptide chains. Only two of these have catalytic sites. The remaining four chains have binding sites for CTP. The binding of CTP to these chains brings about a conformational change of the intact protein which in turn results in the inhibitory effects. CTP is, therefore, an allosteric inhibitor of aspartic transcarbamylase. An explanation of the factors leading to competitive inhibition in this case is beyond the scope of this book.

Regardless of the details of the inhibitory mechanism, consideration of Figure 13-2 should lead one to realize that the rate of the aspartic transcarbamylase reaction will be controlled by the *ratio* of the intracellular concentrations of aspartic acid and CTP. Let us assume that at a given moment in a cell, aspartic acid and CTP are both present in "normal" amounts. Aspartic transcarbamylase will be partly inhibited under these conditions and pyrimidine nucleotide production will continue at a "normal" rate. However, if the CTP concentration should fall below normal, a lower degree of inhibition would exist and pyrimidine synthesis, including that of CTP, would increase. Naturally the reverse effects would take place if the CTP concentration should rise above normal. Any disturbance of the normal balance initiates events that tend to restore the initial condition.

Feedback inhibition, therefore, provides cells with a very sensitive mechanism for coupling, on a moment-to-moment basis, the rate of production of cell constituents with the rate of their utilization. Undoubtedly, it is of great metabolic importance.

In the example of feedback inhibition that we have described, the enzyme was a multiunit one, and the inhibition resulted from an allosteric interaction. It should be clear that allosteric inhibition or activation of any enzyme need not be restricted to end-products of the reaction sequence in which the enzyme participates. Almost any compound could conceivably exert such effects. In particular, evidence exists that hormonal control of certain processes is mediated through effects on the interaction of the sub-units of multiunit enzymes.

EFFECTS ON ENZYME SYNTHESIS

In previous discussions we have emphasized the importance of DNA units in providing the cell with the hereditary abilities needed to manufacture a variety of proteins, including specific kinds of enzymes. We have suggested that these genetic units control metabolism by determining which enzymes a cell can produce. In the large view this is correct; but it is an oversimplification. One might conclude that all cells with the same genes would display identical metabolic patterns. But a young, rapidly growing cell is markedly different from the same cell in the mature stage. And the metabolic reactions of a cell vary in amount and even in kind depending on the substances it absorbs from its environment. Therefore, the presence of a certain set of genes does not establish a single, definite metabolic pattern.

The genes do provide the cell with the *potential* abilities for the production of certain enzymes. However, it is becoming clear that the activities of the genes in enzyme synthesis are subject to metabolic control just as are the other cell activities. The genes, important as they are, are still chemical substances involved in certain metabolic processes. To an extent which is uncertain as yet, these processes are subject to inhibition and perhaps to activation just as are the cell processes of more plebeian nature. Genes in this view are involved in a mutual interaction with their environment, including other genes, the various metabolic and structural compounds within the cell, and the compounds of the medium surrounding the cell. Just as the results of gene action alter the environment, so does the environment modify gene action.

Examples of the control of gene action by other compounds of the cell are few in number at the present time and are limited mainly to microorganisms. Again this represents our comparative ignorance. In all probability effects of this nature are of general importance.

In particular, evidence has been accumulating that suggests that some hormones bring about physiological changes by affecting gene action.

Enzyme Repression

Numerous examples are now known in which the presence of unusually high concentrations of a normal cell metabolite prevents the synthesis of an enzyme. This is the phenomenon known as *enzyme repression*. In one of the major types of repression, the end-product of a sequence of metabolic reactions interferes with the production of one or more of the enzymes utilized in its own synthesis. The result is much like that of feedback inhibition.

Repression does not affect existing enzyme molecules, only the replacement of those which are lost in the normal degradation reactions of the cell. Accordingly, the decrease in total enzyme activity occurs more slowly in the case of repression than in that of feedback inhibition, where the effect is an immediate one.

The mechanism of repression is by no means clear. Particularly puzzling in early work was the finding that often *all* of the enzymes of a whole reaction sequence were repressed *simultaneously* in the presence of the end product. Work based on this finding has led to the concept of an *operator gene*, a gene that figuratively switches on or off the activity of a number of *structural genes* responsible for enzyme synthesis. The operator gene and the structural genes under its control are all closely linked on the chromosome. Presumably the operator normally provides the starting point for the production of messenger-RNA molecules corresponding to its structural genes.

Logically, repression must relate directly to the operator gene rather than to the structural genes so that the simultaneous repression of a number of related enzymes can be accounted for. The nature of the effect on the operator gene remains hazy. Monod, chiefly responsible for the operator gene concept, has suggested that yet a third type of gene is involved—a *regulatory gene*. This gene, in contrast with the operator gene, may be far removed from the structural genes which it ultimately controls. It may even be on a different chromosome.

In Monod's view, diagrammed in Figure 13-3, each regulatory gene is responsible for the synthesis of a specific compound, possibly

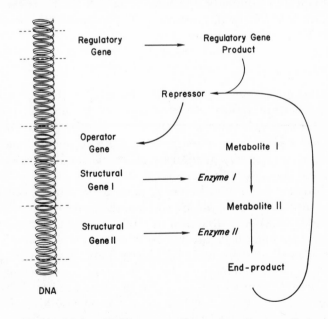

Figure 13-3. Multi-enzyme Repression by an End-Product.

a protein. This compound combines with a *regulatory metabolite*, a substance such as an end-product of a reaction sequence. The resulting complex, here called a *repressor*, binds to the operator gene and prevents initiation of the synthesis of mRNA molecules corresponding to the structural genes. In turn, the production of the pertinent enzymes (or other proteins) will cease as the existing mRNA molecules are destroyed by normal processes. Finally, the synthesis of the product of the whole reaction sequence will be slowed, or even halted completely, until such time as the concentration of the regulatory metabolite is again reduced to a normal level. As this occurs, presumably the processes described above are all reversed and the operator gene again is free to act.

Repression is most easily demonstrated by growing certain microorganisms in a culture medium containing large amounts of a compound that they will normally synthesize—an amino acid or a purine, for example. With the compound available from the medium, there is no need for the cell to produce it. Under these conditions, the enzymes normally required for synthesis of the compound will be found to be lacking or greatly reduced in amount. Repression of the production of mRNA (and consequently of certain specific proteins) thus provides an automatic mechanism by which the energy of the cell is conserved for useful purposes rather than being wasted on the synthesis of unnecessary compounds.

Enzyme Induction

The phenomenon known as enzyme induction is the increase in the rate of synthesis of an enzyme in response to the increase in concentration of a specific compound. Often the enzyme is not formed in detectable amounts in the absence of the active compound, the *inducer*. The inducer is generally a substrate of, or chemically similar to the substrate of, the induced enzyme.

The simple illustrations of enzyme induction again come from microorganisms. For example, many bacteria grown in a medium with glucose as the carbon source form no detectable β-galactosidase and are therefore unable to hydrolyze lactose, a process required before the disaccharide can be utilized. However, if these same cells are placed in a medium containing lactose as the source of carbon atoms, β-galactosidase synthesis begins, and soon the organisms are able to metabolize the sugar. The synthesis of the galactosidase has been induced by the presence of lactose.

The mechanisms of enzyme induction appear to be closely related to those of enzyme repression. Presumably the effect of the inducer is to overcome existing repression. Monod has suggested that for an inducible enzyme the product of the regulatory gene acts directly as a repressor and that the inducer combines with this repressor to inactivate it. The evidence for this hypothesis is still quite limited.

Note that there are two possible ways to overcome repression. One of these is by the introduction of an inducer; the other is simply by a decrease in the concentration of a regulatory metabolite. This latter process is called *de-repression* to differentiate it from induction. It is also important to realize that in contrast to repression, the effects of induction of enzyme synthesis can appear quite rapidly. Cells are capable of producing detectable amounts of induced enzymes within a very few minutes after addition of the inducer.

Similar considerations may apply to the enzymes which are apparently usual cell constituents. These are called *constitutive enzymes* in contrast to the induced enzymes. This distinction may be somewhat artificial. Constitutive enzymes may simply be those enzymes whose substrates are normally present in the cell to act as inducers. Only in those cases where the substrate is rarely present can the phenomenon of induction be easily detected. However, a number of experiments have demonstrated that large increases in the amounts of certain compounds fed to animals are followed by increases in the concentrations of the constitutive enzymes required to metabolize the compounds. The concentration of the substrate may therefore be of general importance in controlling the rate of synthesis of an enzyme.

In these discussions of repression and induction of enzyme synthesis, our attention has been focussed on the activity of end-products and of substrates. These are the cases most easily observed, but we should not overlook the possibility that other cell metabolites, such as hormones, may function in the same roles.

OTHER ASPECTS OF METABOLIC CONTROL

Cell Membrane Permeability

Another possible mechanism of metabolic control involves variation of the permeability of the cell membrane. This may be of particular importance to higher organisms which can control the composition of the fluid medium bathing the cells. For example, many workers believe that insulin, a pancreatic hormone, interacts with cell membranes and increases their permeability to glucose. However, the absorption of many substances is now believed to require the participation of the enzyme-like substances, the permeases. If absorption is indeed an enzymatic process, the control of the rate of absorption can be mediated by one or several of the mechanisms previously described as applying to enzymes in general, rather than by a new and different means.

It is also possible that some of the metabolic changes occurring as cells grow in size are simply the result of the accompanying decrease in the surface area of the cell per unit of cell volume. The relative rates of absorption and of excretion of various substances may therefore change, leading to secondary changes in metabolic activities.

Cell Differentiation

All of the cells of the various tissues of higher organisms originate from a single fertilized egg cell and presumably have the same set of genes. The process of the development of different cell types from a common parent is termed *differentiation*. Obviously the various cells do not express all of the potentialities inherent in their genetic units. The biochemical basis of differentiation is unknown; however, it is attractive to postulate that enzyme repression and enzyme induction play major roles. It may even be that small differences in the chemical environment of each of the cells of a developing embryo—differences in the availability of oxygen or nutrients or differences in concentrations of substances excreted or secreted by neighboring cells—determine the future course of the cell's career by influencing gene action.

Even though we know very little, these suggestions are not entirely pipedreams. If tissue cells are removed from their usual environment in the organism and grown artificially in tissue culture, they tend to de-differentiate; that is, they change to some extent toward an embryonic, nondifferentiated cell. Complete reversion does not occur, however, indicating that irreversible changes in gene action take place once a cell has proceeded a given distance toward the differentiated state.

The freshwater polyp, hydra, offers a more direct example of the influence of environmental substances on the development of specialized cells. This organism normally reproduces by budding, an asexual process. However, if the carbon dioxide concentration of hydra's aqueous environment is significantly elevated, as occurs naturally in stagnant ponds, sex cells develop and sexual reproduction begins. Apparently the carbon dioxide concentration in a hydra cell determines whether or not it will differentiate to become the source of sex cells.

Malignant Growth

Any discussion of metabolic control would be incomplete without reference to malignant or cancerous tissues. In a general sense, these tissues differ from the normal ones from which they are derived chiefly by their rapid, uncontrolled rate of cell division. Therefore, it seems logical to assume that cancerous tissues arise as the result of the failure of, or interference with, the normal metabolic control processes.

Diversion of the metabolic activities of a cell toward the cancerous state may be initiated by any of a wide variety of agents. Among these are high-energy radiations such as X-ray and ultraviolet, a variety of simple chemical compounds, and certain virus particles.

Presumably high-energy radiation leads to cancer by producing a chemical change, either directly or indirectly, in a nucleic acid molecule. For example, ultraviolet radiation absorbed by a cytosine portion of a DNA unit of an epithelial cell might result in the deamination of this compound to give a uracil molecule in place of the original cytosine. Uracil is of course not a normal component of DNA, but it would be expected to act in the processes of RNA synthesis and of DNA replication as if it were a thymine unit. You will recall that the functional groups of uracil and thymine are identical, providing the same possibilities for hydrogen-bonding.

The change in nucleic acid composition will in turn affect the synthesis of a protein, yielding a molecule with altered biological activity. The resulting deviation of the metabolic pattern from the normal situation probably causes in most cases the death of the cell, but in certain relatively rare instances the changes are such that a cancer appears. There is a definite correlation, for example, between exposure to the ultraviolet radiation of the sun and the frequency of skin cancer.

The activity of the cancer-causing or *carcinogenic* chemical is not entirely clear. Some of these compounds may react directly with nucleic acids to alter their composition in much the same way as was discussed above for radiation. Other compounds may themselves be incorporated into nucleic acid units in place of the normal nucleotides. Still others seem to interfere with nucleic acid synthesis from nucleotides by causing the omission of a nucleotide or the insertion of an extra nucleotide as the polynucleotide chains are being formed.

It should be apparent that these two possible means of altering cell activities toward the cancerous state actually involve mutation of a somatic or "body" cell as opposed to a sex cell. In both cases an altered form of a nucleic acid molecule is produced.

The generation of tumors in response to the presence of virus particles probably occurs in a different manner. In this case there may be no change in the composition of the original nucleic acids of the host cell. Instead, the alteration of the metabolic balance seems to result simply from the presence of the new kinds of nucleic acid units supplied by the virus. Whatever the mechanism, it is evident that a number of cancerous conditions of animals are caused by viruses. Indeed, some workers believe that viruses are responsible for the great majority of malignant growths. The point is one which is difficult to prove, because virus particles can exist in cells for long periods of time without causing untoward effects, only to be triggered into activity in an occasional cell by an unknown set of circumstances. Here, as in many other instances, we must admit that much remains to be learned.

Current treatment of cancer normally involves one or more of three procedures: surgical removal of the tumor tissues, killing of the tumor cells by high-energy radiation, or the use of chemical inhibitors of the growth of the tumor cells. The first two of these should require no comment here; however, the third method merits further discussion.

It is unfortunately true that the metabolic activities of cancer cells are qualitatively much the same as those of normal cells. The differences which exist are only of quantitative nature insofar as we know. A compound which would inhibit a process of a cancer cell would therefore be expected to inhibit the same process in normal cells. However, the rapid rate of cell division which is characteristic of cancer tissues requires in particular that the rate of nucleic acid synthesis be unusually high. Any compound which affects the synthesis of nucleic acids will accordingly have a more pronounced effect on a cancer cell than on a normal cell. Most of the chemotherapeutic agents in clinical use for cancer treatment are, therefore, structural analogs of nucleic acid constituents or analogs of compounds used in the synthesis of the nucleic acids. A few of these may be mentioned:

(1) *Amethopterin* is a folic acid analog which inhibits the enzymatic introduction of single-carbon units into the precursors of the nucleic acid bases.
(2) *6-Mercaptopurine*, which interferes with the use of normal purine compounds for synthetic processes, is closely related in structure to adenine.
(3) *5-Fluorouracil*, a rather recent development, is a compound similar to thymine, which inhibits the formation of the thymine nucleotide needed for DNA synthesis.

The chemotherapeutic agents alone do not generally cure cancer.

They simply prolong life by slowing the growth of the tumor. In time the tumor cells often adapt to the presence of the inhibitor, and rapid growth again begins. A different inhibitor may then prove useful for another period of time.

It should be clear that as a group the mechanisms which integrate the individual reactions into the complete metabolic pattern and which preserve or control the balance among these reactions constitute one of the basic problems encountered in the study of living things. Since very little is known compared to that which remains to be learned about metabolic control processes, the material which we have discussed in this chapter should be accepted as being only a fragmentary, preliminary picture. However, the available evidence which we have described does suggest that the major mechanisms of metabolic control involve automatic chemical responses to variations in the chemical composition of the cell.

SUGGESTED ADDITIONAL READING

Changeux, J.-P., "The Control of Biochemical Reactions," *Scientific American*, **212,** No. 4, 36 (April, 1965).

Davidson, E. H., "Hormones and Genes," *Scientific American*, **212,** No. 6, 36 (June, 1965).

Robertson, J. D., "The Membrane of the Living Cell," *Scientific American*, **206,** No. 4, 64 (April, 1962).

Frisch, L., Ed., "Cellular Regulatory Mechanisms," *Cold Spring Harbor Symposia on Quantitative Biology*, Volume XXVI, Long Island Biological Association, Cold Spring Harbor, New York, 1961.

Bonner, D. M., Ed., "Control Mechanisms in Cellular Processes," The Ronald Press Co., New York, 1961.

Spratt, N. T., Jr., "Introduction to Cell Differentiation," Reinhold Publishing Corp., New York, 1964.

Special Biochemistry of Higher Organisms

14

The previous chapters have dealt in the main with the biochemical processes common to all living cells. Within limits the material given has been sufficient to provide a general description of the biochemistry of single-cell organisms. However, the cells of multicellular organisms meet additional problems, problems which necessarily arise with the association of many individual cells into an organismal unit. This chapter will be concerned with these new problems and with the mechanisms which have developed for their solution.

THE PROBLEM OF INFORMATION TRANSFER

A major characteristic of multicellular organisms is the specialization of groups of cells (tissues) in terms of both physical and chemical activities. By such a division of labor the complex organism is able to perform more efficiently many of the biochemical processes which every independent cell must carry on for itself. But as cells minimize certain activities and specialize in others, they become very dependent upon one another. The advantages of specialization can be gained only when means are developed to control and to integrate the activities of the various types of cells. Such control and integration necessitate mechanisms for communication or information transfer among widely separated cells. The more complex the organism, the more precise and sensitive must be the communication system.

The transfer of information from one cell to others can occur in two main ways: (1) by direct cell-to-cell contact, and (2) by the release of a compound from one cell which can be transported by the intracellular fluids to cells at distant points in the organism.

Under the mechanisms designated as cell-to-cell contact, we shall include the liberation by one cell of substances which affect the activities of only a few closely neighboring cells. The nervous system of animals is the most specialized example of information transfer by this means. Nerve cells form a network throughout the organism so that most tissue cells are very close to one or more nerve endings. Plants and some primitive animals do not have a typical nervous system, yet a certain amount of information transfer can be accomplished by direct cell-to-cell contact.

The most dramatic examples of information transfer by chemical compounds which are transported away from the cells that produced them are provided by the hormones. The term "chemical messenger" is sometimes applied to hormones to emphasize their involvement in the communications system among cells.

A compound is usually not classed as a hormone unless the production of the substance is restricted primarily to one kind of cell, such as the cells of one of the endocrine glands. However, many other substances of more general occurrence are also involved in information transfer. For example, carbon dioxide is produced by all animal cells as an end-product of oxidative reactions. Yet the concentration of this compound in the body fluids is a major factor controlling the rate of breathing. As oxygen is utilized by the tissues and carbon dioxide is produced, the carbon dioxide content of the blood increases. The cells of a certain part of the brain (the respiratory center) are sensitive to the carbon dioxide concentration. As it rises, these brain cells increase the frequency of nervous impulses to the muscles of the chest and diaphragm, causing an increased rate of respiration. Naturally, as the carbon dioxide concentration falls the respiratory rate will also decrease.

Perhaps it should be repeated here that the effect of a hormone or other compound on the metabolic activities of a cell probably involves one or the other of the general mechanisms of control of the rate of a chemical reaction which we discussed in Chapter 13.

THE PROBLEM OF CONTROL OF ENVIRONMENT

The cells of a multicellular organism must face another major problem in addition to that of communication. In contrast with single-cell entities, most of these cells are far removed from contact with the outside world—the external environment. The immediate environment of the cells of the complex organism consists of the intercellular fluids. These fluids are present in rather small amounts, yet they must furnish the necessary nutrients to each cell and receive its wastes.

In the absence of mechanisms for the continual removal of the wastes and replacement of the nutrients, the composition of the intercellular fluids would soon become incompatible with life. Furthermore, even a rather minor change in the chemical composition of these fluids could be expected to alter in differing degrees the metabolic activities of the different kinds of cells. This would soon lead to an uncontrollable imbalance of activities, a failure of coordination, and rapid death of the organism. Obviously, multicellular organisms must have mechanisms for maintaining the composition of the intercellular fluids within very precise limits.

The material which follows will be concerned primarily with these two major problems of higher organisms: communication among cells, and control of the internal environment. Because a high proportion of the communications of cells is concerned with the maintenance of the internal environment, these two problems are inextricably interwoven. We will make no particular attempt to keep the discussions of these problems separate, trusting that you will recognize the pertinence of a particular discussion to one or the other or both.

We will not attempt to examine in any depth the extensive volume of data available regarding the various physiological adaptations and interrelationships related to the two basic problems involved. This information may be found in standard texts of animal or plant physiology or medical biochemistry. Instead, we will try to present only an introduction to the fundamental nature of the special biochemistry of higher organisms. Our discussions will be based mainly on the human organism. This is one of the most complex of biological systems, and at the same time—for obvious reasons—one about which we have the most information. Bear in mind that other organisms utilize similar mechanisms, differing chiefly in relatively small details.

HORMONES

No hormone has had its precise mode of action clearly defined. However, as we have previously suggested, most hormones probably act as either specific activators or inhibitors of enzymes, while others may bring about the induction or repression of enzyme synthesis. In considering that hormones may react directly with an enzyme to affect its catalytic activity, we must point out that, for this purpose at least, we will consider the "permeases" to be true enzymes. Thus some hormones may exert their effects by controlling entry of specific substances into cells.

The chief reason for our relative ignorance of the chemical basis of hormone action is the marked physiological activity displayed by very low concentrations of these substances. For example, a 5×10^{-10} molar solution of oxytocin (about 1 mg in 2000 liters of solution) will cause the contraction of isolated uterine muscle. Naturally, chemical processes occurring in these low concentrations are very difficult to detect and almost impossible to study. In most cases we are able to discern and to examine only the over-all physiological response, not the primary chemical event which ultimately leads to the response we see. In this regard, remember that a relatively minor effect on the rate of one enzymatic reaction will alter the rates of other reactions and may ultimately lead to a major shift in the metabolic activities of the cell. Accordingly it is difficult to determine which altered activities are primary ones and which are secondary. The secondary changes will also depend on the original metabolic pattern of the particular cell; hence a hormone may affect two different cells in appreciably different ways. Furthermore, there is no guarantee that a hormone affects only one enzymatic reaction. Although proof is lacking, in some cases it seems that the activities of two or more enzymes of widely different nature may be controlled by a single hormone. This situation may explain some of the experimental confusion concerning the basic effect of a hormone.

One further point must be made concerning the hormonal regulation of metabolic activities. The secretion of each of the hormones must also be controlled. The ultimate stimulus in each case will be the change in concentration of some compound of the extracellular fluids. In some cases the cells of an endocrine gland are affected directly. In others, the primary effect is upon brain cells which control by neural impulses the secretion of a gland. Finally, the hormonal secretion of one gland, controlled by either of the previous mechanisms, may affect the rate of secretion of a hormone of another gland.

Presumably a hormone could be almost any kind of organic molecule. Most known hormones are either steroids or peptides of a wide range of molecular weights. A third group is composed of a variety of compounds of relatively low molecular weight, most of which may be considered to be amino acid derivatives. Selected examples of these three groups of hormones will be presented in the following pages.

Steroid Hormones

Hormones of steroid nature are synthesized by mammals in either the testis or ovary and in the cortex (the outer layer) of the adrenal gland, as well as in the corpus luteum and the placenta. The various compounds may be divided into groups on the basis of their physiological effects; however, as biochemists we prefer a classification which has a chemical basis. Accordingly we shall classify the steroid hormones as either C_{18}, C_{19}, or C_{21} steroids, depending upon the number of carbon atoms in the molecule.

C_{18} STEROIDS

A distinguishing feature of the C_{18} group is the presence of a benzenoid ring. The usual hydroxyl group attached to carbon-3 of this ring is therefore a phenolic hydroxyl. The C_{18} steroid hormones are commonly called *estrogens*. They are produced chiefly by the ovary, but also in smaller amounts by the testis and perhaps by the adrenal cortex. The estrogens are responsible for the secondary sex characteristics of the female and have relatively specific effects during the ovarian cycle, stimulating, for example, the growth of the endometrium—the mucous membrane lining the uterus. However, the same hormones have roles of uncertain nature in both the male and female with respect to calcium and phosphorus metabolism and perhaps lipid metabolism.

Some workers believe that the primary effect of the estrogens is the activation of a transhydrogenase, an enzyme catalyzing the exchange of hydrogen (and electrons) between TPNH and DPN. As such, the hormones would affect the balance of energy production by the electron transport system.

Other workers believe as strongly that the estrogens induce the synthesis of a variety of enzymes and other proteins. If the ovaries of an experimental animal are removed and estrogens are supplied at a later time, the synthesis of proteins by the cells of the uterus increases by as much as 300 per cent. Also, supplying estrogens to a rooster has been found to result in the production of typical egg proteins in small quantities by *liver* cells.

There are three chief compounds with estrogenic activity—*estradiol, estrone*, and *estriol*. It is possible that only one of these is the functioning compound. The other two may be formed by accidental side-reactions which are freely reversible.

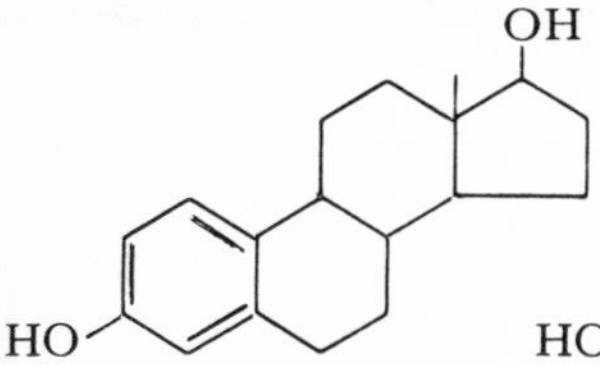

estradiol 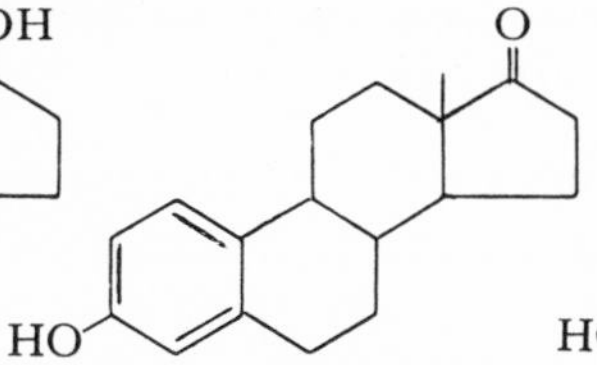 estrone 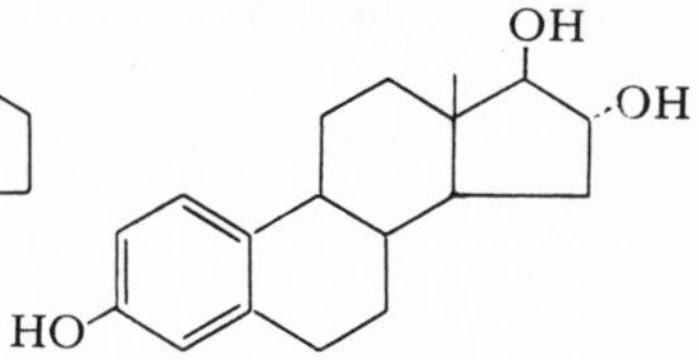 estriol

The synthetic compound, *stilbestrol*, is also a powerful estrogen even though the compound is not a steroid. The phenolic group is present, however, and the two OH groups are the same distance apart as in estradiol.

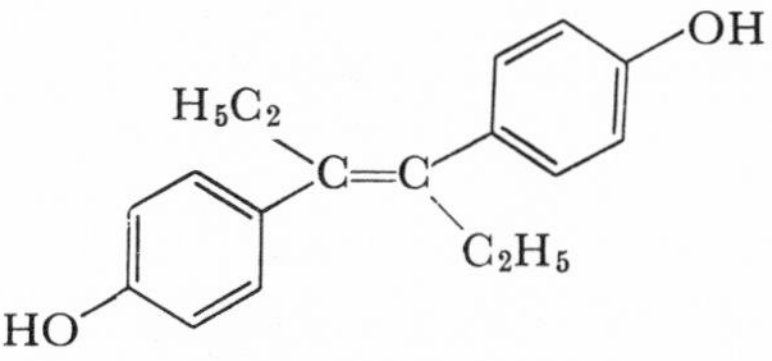

stilbestrol

C_{19} STEROIDS

The C_{19} steroids are chiefly the *androgens*, or the male sex hormones. The major androgen is *testosterone*, depicted below. Note its similarity to estradiol, particularly if the carbonyl group at carbon-3 were to be shown in the enolic form. The major site of production of androgens is the testis, but apparently the ovary and the adrenal cortex also synthesize compounds with androgenic activity. The androgens are responsible for the accessory sex characteristics of the male.

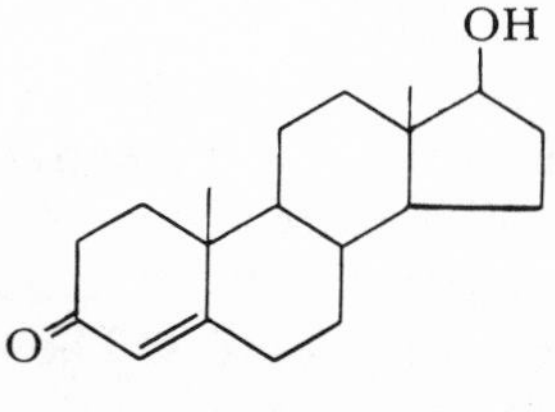

testosterone

Androgens and estrogens are present in both the male and the female, and may well serve essential roles in both. The relative balance of androgenic and estrogenic activities is of major importance with respect to the secondary sex characteristics.

C_{21} STEROIDS

The C_{21} steroids are chiefly hormones produced by the cortex portion of the adrenal gland, but *progesterone*, a hormone produced by the ovarian *corpus luteum*, also falls in this group.

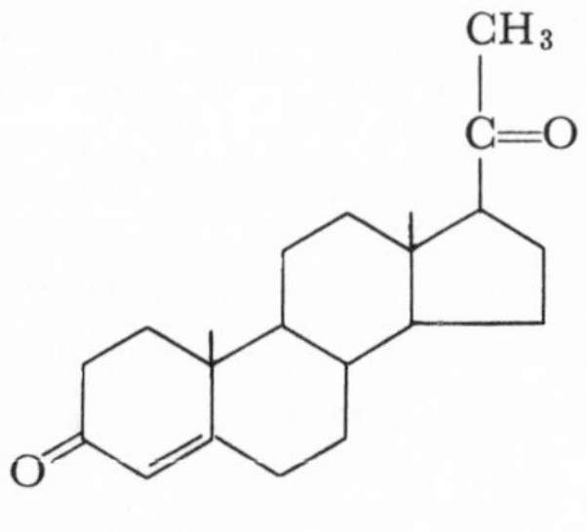

progesterone

Progesterone is secreted during the second half of the menstrual cycle. Among other effects, it acts to induce mucous secretory activity by the endometrium in preparation for implantation of the ovum.

A number of closely related C_{21} steroids, the *corticosteroids*, are apparently produced by the adrenal cortex. There is some uncertainty as to which of these compounds are primary products of cortex metabolism and which may be the result of metabolic side reactions.

As a group, these compounds have a variety of physiological effects. Any given C_{21} steroid, even progesterone, is likely to display all of these biological properties, but in widely differing degree. Slight changes in chemical structure can result in marked alteration of one or more of these activities. In fact, certain synthetic substances similar in structure to the natural C_{21} steroids are more potent in various ways than the natural compounds.

One group of the corticosteroids is primarily concerned with the regulation of the ionic constitution of the extracellular fluids. They are often stated to be involved in electrolyte or salt balance and water balance. The compounds apparently act by stimulating the reabsorption of sodium ion from the kidney tubules. The retention of negative ions, chiefly chloride ion, and of water naturally follows this primary process. The most potent compound with respect to sodium ion retention is *aldosterone*.

A second group of the corticosteroids exhibit greatest activity in increasing the conversion of amino acids to carbohydrates, a process termed *glyconeogenesis*. Most probably the compounds inhibit one of the steps of protein synthesis, diverting amino acids to the degradative reactions which lead to the citric acid cycle or to the glycolytic pathway. These hormones may also stimulate the breakdown of liver glycogen and thus increase the concentration of glucose in the blood stream. The C_{21} steroids with these effects are often called *glucocorticoids;* cortisone and cortisol are the best examples. In addition, both of these compounds are active anti-inflammatory substances, with cortisol being by far the most effective. The structures of the three major steroids of the human adrenal cortex appear below.

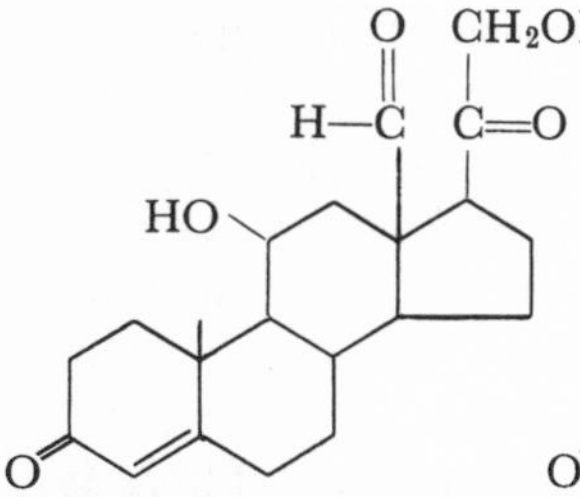

aldosterone 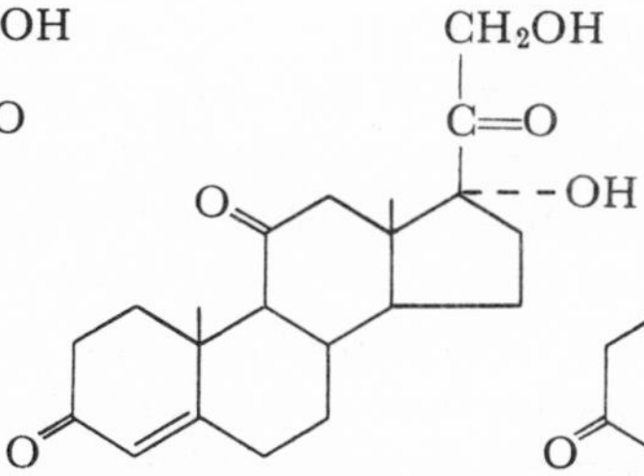   cortisone 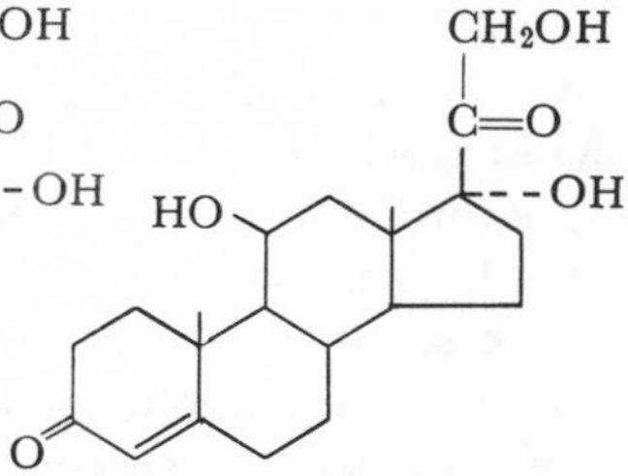   cortisol

Some Hormones of Insects

The processes of metamorphosis in the insect are under hormonal control. One of the hormones involved is a steroid. This is *ecdysone*, which promotes the transformation to the pupal stage. The so-called *juvenile hormone*, thought to be a terpenoid compound, tends to preserve the larval form of the organism. Obviously the balance between these two hormones is highly significant to the insect.

Peptide Hormones

Hormonal compounds of peptide nature are produced by a variety of endocrine glands. We will describe those of the pancreas, hypophysis, parathyroid, and gastrointestinal mucosa.

PEPTIDE HORMONES OF THE PANCREAS

The pancreas gland is composed of two distinct tissues. One of these is concerned with the production and liberation of digestive enzymes; the other, the "Isles of Langerhans," is composed of groups of three distinct cell types. One of these, the α-cells, produce the hormone *glucagon*. *Insulin* is synthesized and released by the β-cells of the islet tissue. These hormones are both peptides—insulin with a molecular weight of about 6000, glucagon of about 3500 (29 amino acids). Both hormones are involved with carbohydrate metabolism.

The injection of insulin into the blood stream of an animal leads to the removal of glucose from the blood, primarily by the muscle cells. Associated with this is the increased metabolism of glucose, both with respect to glycogen formation and to oxidation. Although insulin has been available in crystalline form since 1926 and its relation to the common disease, *diabetes mellitus*, has stimulated a high level of research activity, it cannot yet be said with certainty that its biochemical role is known. Much is known about the results of insulin deficiency or insulin excess in terms of gross physiological changes, but the basic chemical effect of the compound remains a mystery. Most workers feel that insulin is necessary for the absorption of glucose through the cell membrane, perhaps as an accessory factor for a specific glucose-transport system. There is also evidence that insulin decreases the activity of glucose-6-phosphatase, an enzyme needed for the release of glucose to the blood from liver cells.

Glucagon has been known for only a relatively few years. There is impressive evidence that it functions in liver cells to bring about the activation of phosphorylase, the enzyme which catalyzes the first step in glycogen metabolism. Under resting conditions this enzyme is chiefly present in an inactive form. The presence of glucagon will therefore result in an increase in the active form of the enzyme, and an increased phosphorolysis of glycogen to glucose-1-phosphate. We will see later that epinephrine (adrenalin) acts in the same manner as glucagon both in liver and muscle tissue.

The steps involved in the activation of phosphorylase illustrate the complexity of the task of assigning the physiological activity of a hormone to a specific metabolic effect. In this case the increased availability of glucose phosphate for oxidation or for release to the bloodstream as glucose is readily observed as the physiological effect. The primary site of action of glucagon or of epinephrine, however, is a reaction rather far-removed in a metabolic sense from that of glycogen breakdown. Figure 14-1 summarizes the actual chain of events as we now see them.

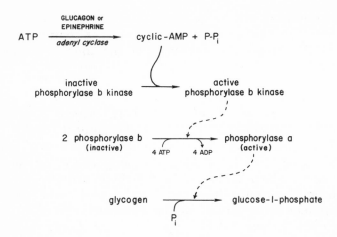

Figure 14-1. The Role of Glucogen in Glycogen Synthesis.

The direct effect of the hormones is apparently the activation of the enzyme that produces adenosine-3′, 5′-cyclic phosphate (cyclic AMP) from ATP. In turn the cyclic AMP combines with inactive phosphorylase b kinase, converting this enzyme to the active state. The kinase then catalyzes the phosphorylation of phosphorylase b, resulting in phosphorylase a, which catalyzes glycogen breakdown. Phosphorylase a is composed of four peptide chains and can be regarded as a phosphorylated dimer of phosphorylase b, which itself is a two subunit protein. Each chain of the phosphorylase a has a serine residue that has been converted to the phosphate ester by the kinase-catalyzed step. A specific phosphatase is present that continually acts to reconvert phosphorylase a to the inactive form. Only when one of the hormones is present will significant quantities of active phosphorylase be available.

PEPTIDE HORMONES OF THE HYPOPHYSIS

The hypophysis, or pituitary gland, is located just beneath the brain, with which it is connected by numerous nerve fibers. This provides a major connection between the nervous system and the system of hormones. This is particularly true in that a number of hypophyseal hormones act to affect the production and release of hormones by other tissues. Such hormones are called *tropins* or trophic hormones. This mechanism provides for nerve control of hormonal activities. The tropins are produced by the anterior portion of the hypophysis and include:

(1) *Thyrotropin*, which stimulates activity of the thyroid gland.

(2) *Adrenocorticotropic hormone* (ACTH), which stimulates the hormone-producing activity of the adrenal cortex.

(3) *Three gonadotropins*—follicle-stimulating hormone, luteinizing hormone, and luteotropin (formerly called lactogenic hormone), which stimulate the metabolic activity and development of certain cells of the ovary or testis responsible for the production of various steroid hormones.

(4) *Growth hormone*, which appears to act *directly* upon various tissues, to produce a variety of effects associated with increased metabolic activity, rather than through the intermediate action of another endocrine gland. Properly speaking it is not a tropic hormone although it is often called *somatotropin*.

All these hormones are peptides or proteins with molecular weights ranging from about 10,000 for thyrotropin to 100,000 for swine luteinizing hormone. Considerable variation in molecular weight of a particular hormone is found among different animal species, implying that different proteins can serve the same function or that some of these substances contain unnecessary portions. Most of the corticotropic hormones appear to contain 39 amino acid units. However, treatment of these hormones under proper conditions of hydrolysis gives a peptide fragment of 24 amino acids which retains essentially all of the hormonal activity of the original molecule. The peptide is derived from the N-terminal portion of the hormone. The amino acid sequence of this peptide is the same in all adrenocorticotropic hormones which have been examined, but there are differences in the remainder of the molecule. Furthermore, this peptide has been synthesized chemically and found to possess the full activity of the corticotropic hormones. The presence in the natural hormones of nonessential material, comprising as much as half of the molecule, is an unsolved puzzle. Apparently only the first twenty of the amino acids are actually necessary. Studies of this type have paved the way for many further experiments on the relationship of the chemical structure of these hormones to their biological function.

The chief hormones of the posterior portion of the hypophysis are the two similar octapeptides, *oxytocin* and *vasopressin*.

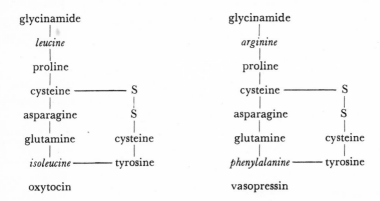

Note that these two compounds differ only in two respects, the second and seventh amino acids from the top in the representations provided (in vasopressin isolated from sheep, lysine replaces arginine). Yet these apparently minor structural differences lead to major differences in physiological effect, although there is some cross activity. Oxytocin stimulates contraction of the smooth musculature, in particular of the uterus, and is of importance in childbirth. Vasopressin, on the other hand, seems to have two major effects: (1) constriction of the arterioles and capillaries, leading to an increase in blood pressure, and (2) increased reabsorption of water from the kidney tubules. This second property has led to the use of the name *antidiuretic hormone* for the compound. Obviously it plays a role in water balance.

PARATHYROID HORMONE

Another peptide hormone is produced by the parathyroid tissue. This hormone is sometimes called *parathormone*. The compound inhibits the reabsorption of phosphate ion from the kidney filtrate and accelerates the release of calcium and phosphate from the skeleton. It has been suggested that the primary action in the bone cells is the stimulation of the production of citric acid. Increased citrate ion concentrations would then lead to displacement of phosphate ion from the mixed crystal matrix, primarily calcium phosphate, which constitutes bone. In effect this is an ion-exchange process, citrate ion replacing phosphate ion. Calcium citrate is more soluble than the usual bone material and tends to be released to the blood.

The control of secretion of parathyroid hormone is apparently vested in the calcium ion concentration of the blood. As the calcium ion concentration increases, parathormone secretion decreases, tending to restore the original condition. This is obviously a feedback mechanism of metabolic control at the organism level.

A number of hormones are elaborated by cells of the mucosa of the gastrointestinal tract. The structures of all of these are not known; however some of them are peptides, meriting their discussion here. These hormones are involved in the stimulation of release of digestive enzymes from the appropriate tissues in response to the presence of food compounds in the digestive tract. Among these hormones are:

(1) *Secretin*, a peptide of molecular weight 5000, produced by cells of the upper intestine, which stimulates the flow of pancreatic juice and bile

(2) *Cholecystokinin*, a compound also produced in the upper intestine, which stimulates contraction of the gall bladder

(3) *Pancreozymin*, another hormone of the upper intestine which stimulates the release of pancreatic enzymes

(4) *Gastrin*, produced by certain cells of the stomach, which stimulates the secretion of HCl by other stomach cells

Amino Acid Derivatives

THYROID HORMONES

The thyroid gland produces a variety of iodinated compounds, perhaps chiefly *thyroxine*, which have a profound influence on many metabolic activities. Principally because of the wide variety of these effects, it has been suggested that thyroid hormone has a single primary action to which all other effects are secondary. Such primary action, should it indeed be a single effect, probably involves some basic phase of energy-transfer reactions.

An attractive possibility seems to be that the thyroid hormone acts to increase the level of cytochrome-c in the tissue cells. This would result in the concentration of thryoid hormone functioning as a controlling factor in ATP production and hence affecting the rates of many metabolic processes. Much remains to be learned. There is no doubt, however, that the thyroid hormone acts to increase the over-all metabolic rate, regardless of the nature of its specific activity.

We have already described the production of thyroxine from tyrosine. Apparently thyroxine is bound in the thyroid gland in storage form as the protein *thyroglobulin*. Present evidence favors the view that under the influence of thyrotropin, enzyme-catalyzed hydrolysis of thyroglobulin occurs, releasing thyroxine to the blood stream. In turn, the release of thyrotropin is governed by the level of thyroxine in the blood.

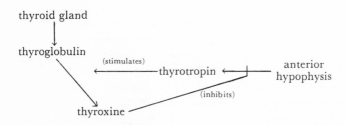

EPINEPHRINE

The central portion or the medulla of the adrenal gland is the major site of production of two substances with hormone activity. These are *epinephrine* (adrenalin) and *norepinephrine* (noradrenalin). The structures of these compounds and a sketch of their biosynthesis appear on p. 240. These compounds seem to exert similar effects in the regulation of carbohydrate metabolism and of blood pressure. It is possible that epinephrine is more closely related to carbohydrate metabolism, and norepinephrine to the control of blood pressure. At any rate, the release of epinephrine from the medulla is preferentially initiated as the concentration of glucose in the blood falls below normal. Presumably the deficiency of glucose stimulates particular cells of the brain which then trigger a nerve impulse to the adrenal medulla. Norepinephrine release, on the other hand, seems to be stimulated preferentially in response to a fall in blood pressure.

The major effect of epinephrine is closely allied to that of glucagon; that is, it stimulates the synthesis of the cofactor required for production of active phosphorylase. While glucagon effects are restricted to the liver, epinephrine appears to promote the synthesis of adenosine-3',5'-cyclic phosphate in both liver and muscle.

Norepinephrine also seems to be important in the transmission of nerve impulses in the sympathetic system, sometimes called the *adrenergic* system.

Plant Hormones

The hormonal control systems developed by plants are even less well understood than those of animals. Hormones serve essential roles in controlling the growth-rate of plants, the healing of wounds, the induction of flower formation, and quite possibly numerous other activities. Best known are the substances termed *plant growth hormones,* originally called "auxins."

INDOLEACETIC ACID

The best known plant growth hormone is *indoleacetic acid,* a compound closely related to the amino acid, tryptophan. This substance, and a number of closely related structural analogs, is found in particularly high concentration in rapidly growing tissues such as root tips or the tips of growing shoots. It seems to exert its growth-promoting effects through control of cellular growth and elongation, rather than through changes in cell division rates.

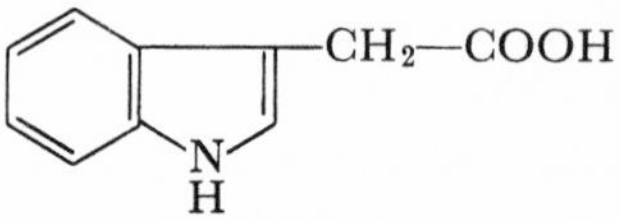

indoleacetic acid

Hormones of this type are involved in one way or another not only in simple plant growth, but also in the bending of plants toward light sources, in prevention of premature fruit drop, and—in part—in the initiation of flowering.

GIBBERELLIC ACIDS

The gibberellic acids are a group of closely related compounds, of which nine members have been isolated to date. The structure of a typical example is given below:

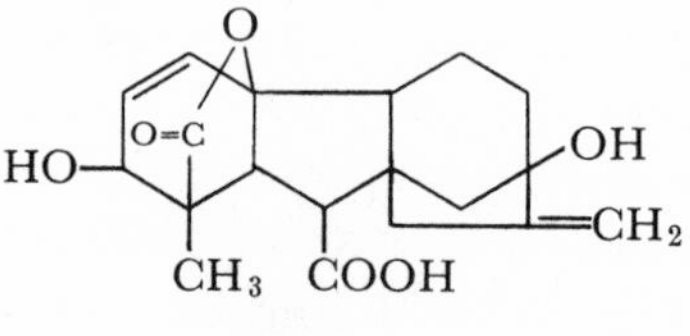

gibberellic acid A_1

The hormone action of these materials is in many ways similar to that of the indoleacetic acid group. That is, they cause elongation, of stems in particular, by cell elongation and enlargement rather than by cell proliferation. The gibberellins were originally isolated from a parasitic fungus, but have now been shown to be normal constituents of a number of flowering plants. In addition to linear growth-promotion, they are useful in the process of fruit "setting," and have a partial role in the onset of flowering.

PHYTOKININS

A group of purine derivatives which have hormone activity for plants are referred to as "kinins." In order to avoid confusion with the peptide hormones of animal gastrointestinal tracts, it would seem more appropriate to rename the plant hormones *phytokinins*. In any case, these compounds appear to promote cell division and multiplication rather than an increase in cell size or a change in shape. They are particularly active during the process of fruit development, and may play a role in seed germination.

SYNTHETIC PLANT HORMONES

There are a wide variety of synthetic compounds which have been found to exhibit various types of hormone activities in plants. We will mention only two examples: First, a compound which is similar in action to the indoleacetic acid group—2,4-dichlorophenoxyacetic acid (2,4-D). This material is often used as a weed-killer for certain broad-leafed species. In this capacity, it acts to stimulate uncontrolled and unbalanced growth, thus eventually destroying the plant. Grasses are more resistant to its effects, and are not normally affected. The close structural relationship between this compound and indoleacetic acid may be seen from the structures below:

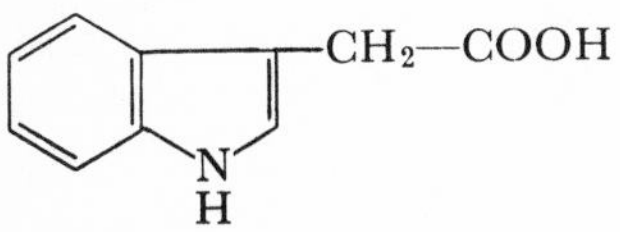

indoleacetic acid 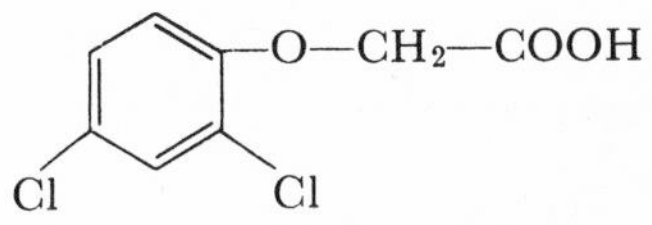   2,4-dichlorophenoxyacetic acid

Secondly, various compounds, of which (2-chloroethyl)trimethyl-ammonium chloride (CCC) is a good example, have been found recently to inhibit the vertical growth of certain plants. These compounds have some interesting potential uses, ranging from more efficient harvesting of grain crops to bushier shrubs and hedges that rarely have to be cut. The mechanism of action of these compounds is obscure at the present time.

A NOTE ON PLANT HORMONE BALANCE

Many of the physiological activities of plants—growth in general, flowering, leaf drop, fruit set and drop, phototropisms, etc.—appear to involve more than one of the hormones mentioned above. As in animal systems, the final effect noted is more a measure of the balance of all the activities present than an effect of a single causative agent.

BIOCHEMISTRY OF NERVE TRANSMISSION

The primary function of nerves is the transfer of information from one point to another in the organism. In part this is accomplished by the transmission of an electrical impulse along the nerve fiber. The biochemical processes associated with nerve impulses are very poorly understood in detail; however, two phenomena are clearly of major importance: (1) the movement of sodium and potassium ions through the nerve cell membrane, and (2) the production, release, and hydrolysis of acetylcholine.

We normally think of an electrical current as a flow of electrons; however, you should recall that in an aqueous solution electron transport occurs with the movement of ions. It should not be difficult, then, to realize that the movement of ions in and out of a nerve fiber can give rise to electrical impulses. The control of the movement of ions through the nerve cell membrane is another matter. Nerve cells, like all animal cells, have lower Na^+ and higher K^+ concentrations than the extracellular fluid. This situation is associated with a difference in electrical potential across the cell membrane. The maintenance of this nonequilibrium situation requires that work be continually performed at the expense of the usual metabolic energy. The mechanisms are unknown. Physiologists often speak of a "sodium pump," a hypothetical device for the elimination of Na^+ from cells, but it should be realized that any such mechanism must be based on chemical processes.

With the passage of a nerve impulse along a fiber, a net flow of sodium ions into the cell occurs, along with a flow of K^+ ions in the opposite direction, and the electrical polarity changes. This is what we would expect if the mechanisms maintaining the concentration differences were suddenly to be prevented from acting. Both ions move toward areas of lower concentration, hence work need not be done. As the nerve impulse passes, the original state is restored by the excretion of Na^+ and the absorption of K^+. These restorative processes occur against the concentration gradient and therefore necessitate the use of energy and of energy-coupling reactions. In simple terms, the nerve impulse involves rapid changes in the permeability of the cell membrane to ions, especially Na^+ and K^+.

Whatever the precise nature of the mechanisms involved in the transmission of an impulse along a nerve fiber, there remains another problem—the transmission of the impulse from one nerve cell to another or to a receptor such as a muscle fiber. Apparently this is accomplished by the release from the nerve ending of a compound which stimulates other cells with which it may come in contact. Basically this resembles hormone action, but the effect is a very local one and essentially provides only for cell-to-cell information transfer. Nevertheless the compounds involved are sometimes called *neurohormones*. Although other compounds may serve similar roles, two compounds are of general significance. These are *acetylcholine* and *norepinephrine*. These compounds are released at the endings of the "cholinergic nerves" and the "adrenergic nerves," respectively. Norepinephrine has been described on p.239. Practically nothing is known about its action.

Acetylcholine is the ester of choline with acetic acid. The compound is apparently formed by nerve cells from choline and acetyl-CoA and stored in small bundles near the nerve endings. With the arrival of an electrical impulse, acetylcholine is released into the small space between the nerve terminus and the surrounding cells. Upon contacting a cell membrane, the compound apparently combines with a protein of the membrane in much the manner that a substrate or a competitive inhibitor combines with an enzyme. This combination alters the permeability of the cell membrane to small ions, and presumably the subsequent changes in metabolic activity of the receptor cell follow automatically.

After the transmission of the impulse in this way, conditions must be restored to the initial state. This is accomplished with the hydrolysis of acetylcholine by *acetylcholinesterase*, an enzyme associated with nerve tissue. The reaction is given below.

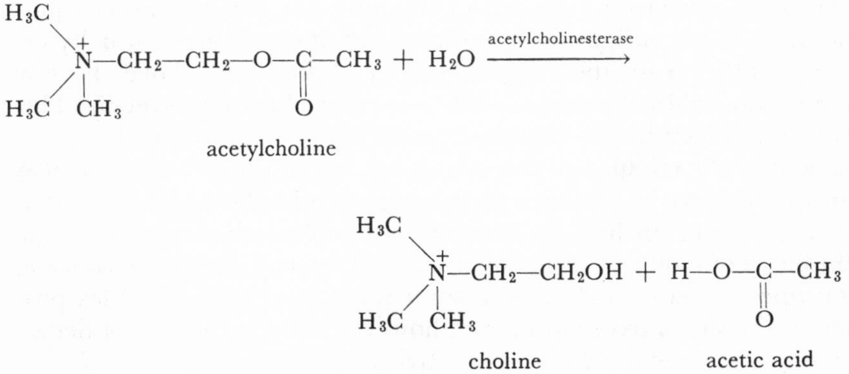

$$\underset{\text{acetylcholine}}{\overset{H_3C}{\underset{H_3C}{\diagdown}}\overset{+}{N}-CH_2-CH_2-O-\overset{\overset{\textstyle |}{C}}{\underset{\textstyle O}{\|}}-CH_3} \;+\; H_2O \;\xrightarrow{\text{acetylcholinesterase}}$$

$$\underset{\text{choline}}{\overset{H_3C}{\underset{H_3C\;\;CH_3}{\diagdown}}\overset{+}{N}-CH_2-CH_2OH} \;+\; \underset{\text{acetic acid}}{H-O-\overset{\|}{\underset{O}{C}}-CH_3}$$

As the free acetylcholine around the nerve ending is hydrolyzed, the bound acetylcholine with which it is in equilibrium is released and also hydrolyzed. The cell is then ready for another stimulus. In the nerve ending, acetylcholine will also be resynthesized from choline and acetyl-CoA.

It has also been suggested that the hydrolysis and reformation of acetylcholine *within* the nerve is associated with the changes in permeability occurring with the nerve impulse.

The transmission of nerve impulses can be inhibited in a variety of ways by different substances. Certain "nerve gases" such as diisopropylfluorophosphate combine in essentially irreversible fashion with the active site of acetylcholinesterase, preventing its action and thereby blocking nerve transmission. A number of insecticides also operate in this fashion. Drugs such as atropine are apparently competitive inhibitors of the enzyme. The active compound in curare, the South American Indian arrow poison, appears to combine, not with the enzyme, but with the substance of the cell membrane with which acetylcholine reacts.

OXYGEN TRANSPORT

Multicellular organisms require large quantities of oxygen to meet their relatively high demands for oxidative, energy-yielding reactions. Simple diffusion from the environment serves to bring oxygen to the cells of plants and simple animals at a rate sufficient for their needs. However, the cells of most animals are so far removed from the environment, and their utilization of oxygen is so rapid, that a mechanism for the transportation of this material from the surface to the interior of the organism is a necessity. In part, this mechanism involves the mechanical circulation of a fluid, the blood, between lungs or gills and the various tissue cells. In addition, means are usually required to increase the oxygen content of the fluid above the low limits imposed by the poor solubility of oxygen in aqueous media. This is accomplished by the chemical combination of oxygen with a component of the circulating fluid. In most organisms this component is an iron-porphyrin protein called *hemoglobin*. In the blood of certain marine worms an iron-protein complex replaces hemoglobin, while the blood of molluscs, cephalopods, and crustacea contains *hemocyanin*, a copper-protein. In all three cases the metal ion of the complex protein is the site of oxygen-binding; however, only in the case of hemoglobin is the metal held by a porphyrin structure.

Hemoglobin

The hemoglobins of most vertebrates have molecular weights near 68,000 and have four iron-porphyrin groups per molecular unit. Although the protein molecules differ somewhat from organism to organism, the iron-porphyrin prosthetic group of these proteins is a single compound, *heme*. Its structure appears on p. 77. Recall that a number of other heme proteins such as catalases, peroxidases, and cytochromes are of major biological importance. These substances are catalysts for a variety of oxidation-reduction reactions. Only hemoglobins and certain related compounds have the chemical property of binding oxygen in reversible fashion. Obviously the chemical reactivity of a heme unit (and its biological effect) is determined by the nature of the particular protein with which it is combined and by the nature of the binding forces.

It is important to note that the iron atoms of the heme units of hemoglobin remain in the ferrous state throughout the process of combining with and releasing oxygen. These processes are not oxidation and reduction reactions but are more properly termed *oxygenation* and *deoxygenation*. The oxidation of the iron atoms of hemoglobin to the ferric state gives *methemoglobin*, a compound lacking the property of reversible combination with oxygen.

If you find it difficult to reconcile the structure of heme with the usual concept of ferrous iron as a divalent ion, remember that iron, in common with certain other metals, is capable of forming two types of bonds, ionic and covalent. Often our attention is directed only to the ionic bonding, so that Fe^{++} would be considered to have a valency of two. But a ferrous ion can also form up to six covalent bonds; in fact, in water solution the ion is not Fe^{++} but $Fe(H_2O)_6^{++}$. Such ions are called *complex ions*, and are of major importance in biological systems in the binding of metals to proteins and other substances. The structure of heme, in simplified form, is shown in Figure 14-2, the N's representing the nitrogen atoms of the porphyrin ring system. Heme is a neutral molecule in that two of the bonds of the dipositive iron are to nitrogen atoms which can be viewed as having negative charges.

In hemoglobin at least one, and probably both, of the water molecules of the heme structure are replaced by groups of the protein, in all likelihood nitrogen atoms of histidine side-chains. The combination of hemoglobin with oxygen results in the replacement of one of these groups by the oxygen molecule. The oxygenated form is usually called *oxyhemoglobin;* the deoxygenated form, simply hemoglobin. A diagrammatic version of oxyhemoglobin appears in Figure 14-3.

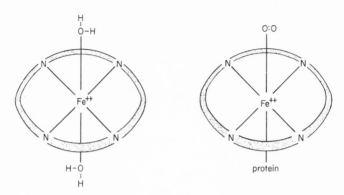

Figure 14-2.   **Figure 14-3.**

**Simplified Representations of the Heme Molecule
(left) and Oxyhemoglobin (right).**

Certain other substances are capable of binding with the iron atoms of hemoglobin in essentially the same manner as does oxygen. Carbon monoxide, for example, is held at least 100 times as strongly as oxygen, explaining the toxicity of this gas.

It has been indicated that the outstanding property of the hemoglobins is their reversible interaction with oxygen. This can be visualized in simplified fashion as occurring in the following way:

$$HHb \; + \; O_2 \; \rightleftharpoons \; H^+ \; + \; HbO_2^-$$

   hemoglobin   oxyhemoglobin

Oxyhemoglobin is a stronger acid than is hemoglobin, hence tends to ionize to a greater extent. The particular group (or groups) releasing the proton is unknown.

Consideration of this equilibrium should lead you to conclude that the percentage of the total hemoglobin which is present as oxyhemoglobin will vary both with the oxygen concentration and with the hydrogen ion concentration. In the tissues, O_2 is utilized and CO_2 is produced. The CO_2 combines with water to give carbonic acid and therefore an increase in hydrogen ions. The lower oxygen concentration and the greater concentration of hydrogen ion both favor the release of oxygen from oxyhemoglobin.

In the lungs the opposite situation prevails. The oxygen concentration of the inspired air is high and CO_2 is released, in effect removing hydrogen ion from the blood. Oxyhemoglobin formation is therefore enhanced. The major effect in these processes is that of the concentration of oxygen, the hydrogen ion effect being of lesser magnitude and normally of lesser biological importance.

Myoglobin

The red color of many animal tissues as seen in a meat market is not due to the hemoglobin of blood but to a related compound called *myoglobin*. This compound is located within the various cells and therefore is not involved in oxygen transport from place to place in the organism. Rather it seems to serve as an emergency store of oxygen. Generally, those cells which are more active in metabolic transformations have higher myoglobin contents.

Myoglobin has a molecular weight of about 17,000 and contains only one heme unit per molecule. It combines more strongly with oxygen than does hemoglobin, and releases the oxygen only when the free oxygen concentration drops to rather low levels. The brown color of meat which has been unduly exposed to oxygen, as in long storage or in cooking, is due to the oxidation of the iron to the ferric stage, giving *metmyoglobin*.

CARBON DIOXIDE TRANSPORT AND pH CONTROL

Any appreciable alteration in hydrogen ion concentration will change the rates of practically all metabolic reactions, chiefly by altering the catalytic activities of the enzymes. The maintenance of a specific metabolic pattern accordingly requires the preservation of the pH within narrow limits, which are characteristic of the organism but are usually close to neutrality.

Under normal conditions, the major factor tending to change the pH of the cell contents is the continual production of carbon dioxide (and therefore of carbonic acid) associated with the processes of oxidation of organic substances. Minor factors of importance to higher organisms include the production of sulfuric acid by the oxidation of organic sulfur compounds, and the formation of bases by the oxidation either of organic compounds which contain metal ions or of the sodium and potassium salts of organic acids.

Simple organisms and plants are able to excrete CO_2 to the environment as rapidly as it is formed, hence no special mechanisms are needed for CO_2 transport or pH control. Minor variations in pH can be handled by the selective excretion or retention of the hydrogen ion. However, the liberation of CO_2 into the relatively small volume of intercellular fluids of higher animals would lead to two serious problems in the absence of control mechanisms. Most obvious perhaps is that the pH of the fluids, in particular the blood, would decrease continually as the blood moved away from the lungs. In addition, the solubility of CO_2 in water is quite low, so that bubbles of CO_2 gas might be expected in the blood.

The solution to both of these problems lies in the presence in the extracellular fluids, again particularly in the blood, of various proteins. Proteins in general are buffers; that is, they tend to minimize changes in pH by combining with or liberating hydrogen ions as acids or bases are added.

In the present case the buffer action also leads to a major increase in the amount of CO_2 which can be dissolved in blood. A solution of CO_2 in water is composed of CO_2 gas, carbonic acid molecules, bicarbonate ions, and to a very minor extent carbonate ions—all in equilibrium with each other. This equilibrium lies far toward the CO_2 gas. We may depict it as:

$$CO_2 \;+\; H_2O \;\rightleftharpoons\; H_2CO_3 \;\rightleftharpoons\; H^+ \;+\; HCO_3^-$$

It should be apparent that if the hydrogen ion were to be removed, more H_2CO_3 would ionize and more CO_2 would dissolve. Carbon dioxide is readily soluble in a basic solution in which hydroxyl ions rapidly react with most of the hydrogen ions formed. The blood proteins accomplish the same end—various groups of these molecules combining with the hydrogen ion—thus minimizing the pH change and increasing the total carbon dioxide in solution (chiefly as bicarbonate ion).

The first reaction given above, the combination of water and CO_2, approaches equilibrium too slowly to meet the biological needs. However, red cells of the blood contain a zinc-requiring enzyme, *carbonic anhydrase*, which accelerates this interconversion.

The processes occurring as CO_2 is released by cells of the various tissues are summarized below. It can be seen that the net effect of the buffer action of the proteins is the enhanced formation of bicarbonate ion and of the hydrogen ion-protein adduct.

$$CO_2 \;+\; H_2O \;\xrightarrow{\text{carbonic anhydrase}}\; H_2CO_3 \longrightarrow H^+ \;+\; HCO_3^-$$
$$\downarrow\!\!\text{protein}$$
$$H^+\!\cdot\text{protein}$$

In the lungs, the blood is exposed to the inspired air which contains very little CO_2. Carbon dioxide therefore diffuses from the blood to the environment, and the other reactions proceed in the reverse direction to those shown above. In particular, note that a protein molecule will lose one or more hydrogen ions and will leave the lungs in a condition in which it can again accept hydrogen ions. These ions, of course, become parts of water molecules.

You should recognize that the H_2CO_3–HCO_3^- system is itself a buffer system. In fact, most of the buffering action of blood toward inorganic acids or bases is probably accomplished with an alteration in the ratio of H_2CO_3 to HCO_3^-. On the addition of H^+, some HCO_3^- will be converted to H_2CO_3. On the addition of a base, the H^+ concentration will tend to drop, leading to greater ionization of the H_2CO_3. Some buffering is also accomplished by the $H_2PO_4^-$ – HPO_4^{--} system.

The role of the lungs in the elimination of carbonic acid from the body fluids and in the restoration of the protein buffer systems has already been mentioned. To these processes must also be added those occurring in the kidney. Simplifying somewhat, we may regard these as the selective retention in the blood or excretion into the urine of hydrogen ions. These processes are chiefly responsible for the restoration of the normal balance of the inorganic buffer systems.

There remains to be discussed one further mechanism for CO_2 transport. This involves the reaction of CO_2 (quite possibly as H_2CO_3) with amino groups of proteins to form amides as indicated below. The resulting compounds are often called *carbamino proteins*. Although such

$$CO_2 \; + \; \text{protein—}NH_2 \; \rightleftharpoons \; \text{protein—}\overset{\displaystyle H}{\underset{}{N}}\text{—}\underset{\displaystyle O}{\overset{}{C}}\text{—OH}$$

reactions occur with all blood proteins, the carbamino derivatives of hemoglobin are of particular importance. First, hemoglobin comprises about 75 per cent of the total blood protein. Secondly, hemoglobin apparently binds CO_2 to a considerably greater extent than does oxyhemoglobin. Therefore CO_2 will tend to combine with hemoglobin in the tissues and to be released in the lungs. About 25 per cent of the carbon dioxide transported by blood is as *carbaminohemoglobin*, the remainder chiefly as *bicarbonate ion*.

BLOOD COAGULATION

The phenomenon of coagulation or clotting of the blood is of major importance as a mechanism of defense against the catastrophic loss of blood which otherwise would occur with even minor damage to the vessels of the circulatory system. The clotting process may be viewed as a series of chemical transformations of certain proteins of the blood. The final reaction of this series leads to the formation of *fibrin*, a highly polymerized, quite insoluble protein, which effectively plugs breaks in the blood vessel walls.

We will not examine the process of blood coagulation in detail, but shall restrict our attention to the fundamental reactions. We should point out, however, that the necessarily precise control of the clotting process involves a number of related reactions and accessory compounds which either accelerate or inhibit one or another of the basic steps. The over-all process is very complex and is not completely understood in detail.

The three basic steps in blood clotting are:

(1) The formation of active *thromboplastin* (or thrombokinase).
(2) The thromboplastin-catalyzed conversion of *prothrombin* to *thrombin*.
(3) The thrombin-catalyzed conversion of *fibrinogen* to *fibrin*.

A thromboplastin precursor, of lipoprotein nature, occurs in most tissue cells and outstandingly in the cell-like bodies in the blood which are called *platelets*. The presence of rough surfaces, such as a break in the normally smooth blood vessel wall, leads to the disintegration of platelets, releasing the thromboplastin precursor. Damaged tissue cells also release the compound. The thromboplastin precursor reacts with certain compounds of blood plasma to give thromboplastin. The nature of this process is unknown; the effect is the formation of an enzyme from an inactive precursor.

The substrate of thromboplastin is the plasma protein *prothrombin*. This glycoprotein is formed mainly by liver cells and released to the circulating blood. In the presence of thromboplastin and Ca^{++}, prothrombin is converted to *thrombin*. The exact reaction which occurs is not clear. Certainly a change in the structure of prothrombin must take place. This change confers upon the product a new property, that of being a catalyst of the formation of fibrin. This is reminiscent of the activation of various digestive proteases. Prothrombin is therefore a zymogen or proenzyme.

The substances discussed to this point have been either enzyme precursors, active enzymes, or cofactors of various kinds. Fibrinogen, the substrate of thrombin, is none of these, but simply a protein which can irreversibly be converted to the insoluble aggregate called fibrin. At least two steps appear to be necessary. The first of these is the specific

enzymatic cleavage of the fibrinogen molecule by thrombin to give a
small peptide or peptides and a large portion called fibrin monomer.
Accordingly thrombin may be regarded as a very specific proteolytic
enzyme. The fibrin monomer molecules rapidly interact with each
other to give aggregates of extremely great molecular weight. This
polymerization apparently involves the spontaneous formation of
cross-linkages from molecule to molecule. The resulting insoluble network of protein fibers traps red cells and other blood substances to give
the typical blood clot.

These processes may be summarized in chemical terms as:

(a) Thromboplastin precursor + accessory factors → thromboplastin

(b) Prothrombin $\xrightarrow{\text{thromboplastin-Ca}^{++}}$ thrombin

(c) Fibrinogen $\xrightarrow{\text{thrombin}}$ fibrin monomer + fibrino-peptide
$$\downarrow$$
fibrin

A number of substances block the coagulation of blood by interfering with one or another of the individual reactions. *Heparin* is often
considered to be a natural inhibitor of coagulation or a natural *anticoagulant.* This compound is a polysaccharide containing glucosamine
and glucuronic acid units partly esterified with sulfuric acid. Apparently heparin inhibits both the formation of thrombin and the catalytic
activity of thrombin upon fibrinogen. Presumably, low concentrations
of heparin in the circulating blood act under normal conditions to prevent clotting. Naturally, with the release of large amounts of thromboplastin at the sites of wounds, the inhibitory effects of heparin are
overcome and coagulation proceeds.

Any substance which can form an insoluble or poorly ionized compound with calcium ion will prevent coagulation by blocking the
formation of thrombin. Oxalate, fluoride, and citrate ions are examples of substances of this type which are used clinically to prevent
the clotting of blood samples under *in vitro* conditions. However, the
calcium ion concentration of the blood of living organisms rarely, if
ever, is sufficiently low to affect the rate of thrombin production *in
vivo.*

On the other hand, a deficiency of vitamin K does lead to impairment of the coagulation process. Such a deficiency is rarely found, ex-

cept during antibiotic treatment, because microorganisms of the intestinal tract usually synthesize the compound in amounts sufficient for the needs of their host. The relationship of vitamin K to the clotting reactions is not clear. Presumably it is required indirectly, not as a portion of the prothrombin molecule, but either as a cofactor for an enzyme used in the synthesis of prothrombin or as an inducer of prothrombin synthesis. Essentially all that is known is that prothrombin synthesis is decreased in vitamin K deficiency.

Certain compounds structurally related to vitamin K appear to act as metabolic antagonists to the action of the vitamin. They may

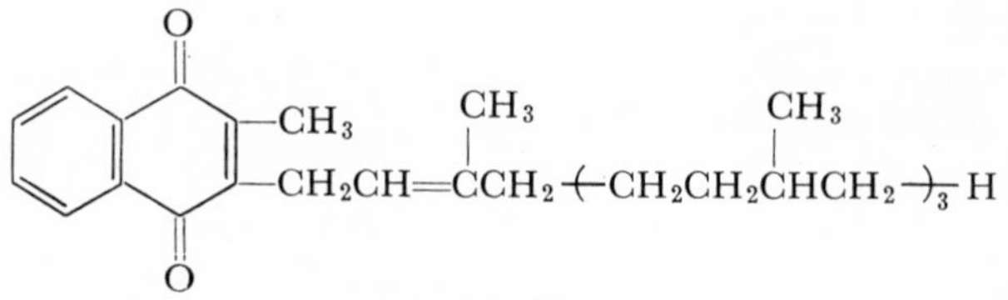

vitamin K₁

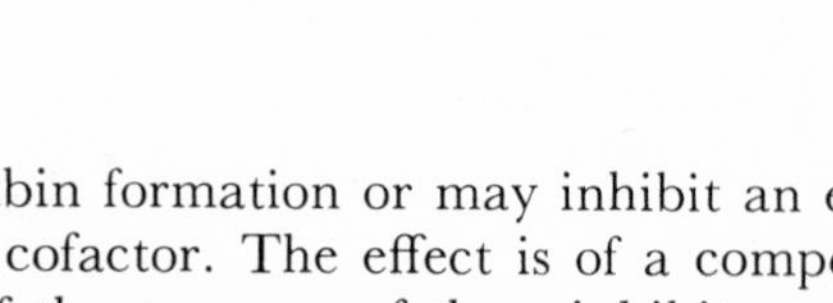

dicoumarol

repress prothrombin formation or may inhibit an enzyme for which the vitamin is a cofactor. The effect is of a competitive nature. By careful control of the amounts of these inhibitors and of vitamin K which are injected into the blood, almost any desired rate of blood clotting can be obtained. Dicoumarol is one of the compounds which has had much clinical use during surgery or after heart attacks to minimize the possibility of clot formation in the blood vessels. Warfarin, a related compound with greater anticoagulant activity, has recently gained favor for similar uses. The compound was developed as a rat poison. Larger amounts than would be used clinically cause extensive internal hemorrhaging from normal wear-and-tear damage to the vascular system.

SUGGESTED ADDITIONAL READING

Allen, J. M., "The Nature of Biological Diversity," McGraw-Hill Book Company, Inc., New York, 1963.

Bonner, J., and Galston, A. W., "Principles of Plant Physiology," W. H. Freeman and Co., San Francisco, 1959.

Heftmann, E., and Mosettig, E., "Biochemistry of Steroids," Reinhold Publishing Corp., New York, 1960.

Langley, L. L., "Cell Function," Reinhold Publishing Corp., New York, 1961.

Nachmanson, D., "Chemical and Molecular Basis of Nerve Activity," Academic Press, New York and London, 1959.

Pincus, G., and Thimann, K. V., "The Hormones: Physiology, Chemistry and Applications," Vol. I (1948) through Vol. III (1955), Academic Press, New York and London.

White, A., Handler, P., and Smith, E. L., "Principles of Biochemistry," Third Ed., McGraw-Hill Book Company, New York, 1964.

Index

The presence of illustrative material is indicated by page numbers in *italics*; structures of specific compounds appear on the pages whose numbers are shown in **boldface**.

Absorption (*see* Amino acids; Lipids; Monosaccharides; absorption of)
Acetaldehyde, from pyruvic acid, 177
Acetals, 6
Acetic acid, **8**
Acetoacetic acid, 208–209, 243
Acetoacetyl-coenzyme A, 208–209
Acetone, 209
Acetylcholine, **293**
Acetylcholinesterase, 293–294
Acetyl-coenzyme A
    conversion to mevalonic acid, *212*
    from leucine, *243*
    function in acetyl group transfers, 182
    production from pyruvate, 181
    role in cholesterol synthesis, 212
    role in fatty acid metabolism, *202–205–209*
    and tricarboxylic acid cycle, 182–183
N-Acetylglucosamine, **52**, 61, 70
N-Acetylneuraminic acid, **54**, 70
Acidosis, 209
Acids
    fatty (*see* Fatty acids)
    nomenclature, 8–9
    reactions of, 9–10

Aconitase, 183
cis-Aconitic acid, **183**
ACTH (*see* Adrenocorticotropic hormone)
Active acetate (*see* Acetyl-coenzyme A)
Active formaldehyde, 230–231
Active formate, 231–232
Active methanol, 231–232
Active methionine, 232–234 (*see also* Adenosyl methionine)
Active sites of enzymes, 101
Acyl-carrier protein, 204–*205*–207
Acyl-CoA dehydrogenase, 202
Adenine, **80**, 237
Adenosine, 83
Adenosine-3′,5′-*cyclic*-phosphate, 285
Adenosine-5′-diphosphate (ADP), 135
Adenosine monophosphates, 83
Adenosine-5′-phosphate, biosynthesis, *236*
Adenosine triphosphate
    production of, *136*
        and biological oxidation, 138–140
        photosynthetic, 149–152
    significance of, 135–137
    structure of, 87–**88**
S-Adenosyl methionine, **232**–234
Adenylic acid, 83

ADP (*see* Adenosine-5'-diphosphate)
Adrenal hormones, 282–283, 289
Adrenaline (*see* Epinephrine)
Adrenergic nerves, 293
Adrenocorticotropic hormone (ACTH), 286
Alanine, **17**
Albumins, 35
Alcohol dehydrogenase, 177
Alcohols, reactions of, 1–4
Aldehydes and ketones, reactions of, 5–7
Aldolase, 172, *173*, 192, 194
Aldonic acids, 53
Aldoses, 44–46
Aldosterone, 283
Alkaloids, 241–242
Allose, **46**
Allosteric inhibition, 114–115
Alpha-helix, *31*–32
Altrose, **46**
Amethopterin, 274
Amines, 10
Amino acid adenylates, **257**
Amino acid amides, 18, 228–229
Amino acid oxidases, 243–*244*
Amino acids
    absorption of, 224–225
    acidic and basic nature of, 20–24
    "activation" of, 257
    biosynthesis of, 219–224
    classification, 16–20
    degradation of, 242–244
    essential, 224
    ninhydrin reaction, 41
    sequence, in peptides, 114–115
    specific metabolic roles, 228–242
    structures of, 17–20
    transamination of, 221–224
    (*see also* individual amino acids)
Aminopeptidases, 227
Amino sugars, 52
Ammonia
    excretion of, 245–*247*–*248*
    in synthesis of amino acids, 220–*221*
    as a waste product, 245
AMP (*see* Adenosine monophosphates)
Amylases, 160
Amylopectin
    biosynthesis, 167–171
    digestion of, 159–*161*
    structure, **60**
Amylose
    digestion of, 159–161
    structure, **60**
    synthesis of, 167–171
Anaerobic glycolysis, 176–178

Androgens, 215, 281–282
Animal cell, structure of, *120*
Anthocyanins, 76, **78**
Anticoagulants, 301–302
Antidiuretic hormone (*see* Vasopressin)
Apoenzyme, 95
Arabinose, **45**
Arachidonic acid, **64,** 209
Arginase, 247
Arginine, **18,** 247
Arginine phosphate, 234
Argininosuccinate, in urea synthesis, **247**
Ascorbic acid, **54**
Asparagine, **229**
Aspartic acid
    function in ornithine cycle, *247–248*
    in purine and pyrimidine biosynthesis, *235–236*
    structure, **18**
ATP (*see* Adenosine triphosphate)
Auxins (*see* Plant growth hormones)

B vitamins, and coenzymes, 95–*97*
Bacterial transformation, *252*
Benedicts test, 55
Bile, 198, 199
Bile acids, 198–**199**
    biosynthesis of, 215
Bile salts, 198–**199**
Biotin, 97, **206**
    role in carboxylation reactions, 204–206
Biuret reaction, 41–42
Blood
    coagulation of, 299–302
    pH control in, 297–299
    (*see also* Hemoglobin)
Butyric acid, 8, 64

Calcium, in blood clotting, 300–301
Calcium utilization, and parathormone, 287
Cancer (*see* Malignant growth)
Carbaminohemoglobin, 299
Carbamyl phosphate
    in pyrimidine synthesis, **235**
    in transcarbamylase reactions, 266
    in urea synthesis, 246–*247*–*248*
Carbohydrate metabolism, interaction with lipid metabolism, *216*–217
Carbohydrates, digestion of, 159–*162*
Carbon, path of, in photosynthesis, 192–195
Carbon-14, use as a radioactive tracer, 127
Carbon dioxide
    addition to acetyl-coenzyme A, 204–205
    and carbonic anhydrase, 298
    fixation in photosynthesis, 192–195
    formation of carbamino proteins, 299

and purine synthesis, *235–236*
reactions with biotin, 204–205
transport in animals, 297–299
and urea biosynthesis, 246–*247–248*
Carbonic anhydrase, 298
Carbon monoxide, and hemoglobin, 296
Carboxypeptidase, 226–227
Carcinogens, 273–274
Carotenes, 74, **76**
Catalase, 244
Cathepsins, 228
Cell, structure of, *120*
Cellular differentiation, 272
Cellulose
    digestion of, 162
    structure, **61**
Cerebrosides, 70
Chaulmoogric acid, **65**
Chitin, 61
Chlorophyll
    function in photosynthesis, 149–153
    structure, **77**
Chloroplasts, 120
    role in photosynthesis, 149
Cholecystokinin, 288
Cholesterol
    absorption of, 198, 214–215
    biosynthesis of, *212–214*, 243
    conversion to other steroids, 214–*215*
    structure, **71**
Cholesterol esterase, 201
Cholic acid, **215**
Choline, **68**
    and one-carbon metabolism, 233
    in phospholipids, 68, *211*
    product of acetylcholinesterase, 293
Cholinergic nerves, 293
Chondroitin sulfate, 62
Chromatography
    ion-exchange, 37–40
    paper, 128–*129*–130
Chromosomes, 120
Chymotrypsin, 226
Chymotrypsinogen, 228
Citrate condensing enzyme, 183
Citric acid, 182–**183**
    and calcium metabolism, 287
Citric Acid Cycle (*see* Tricarboxylic Acid
    Cycle)
Citrulline, **247**
Coagulation, blood, 299–302
Cocarboxylase (*see* Thiamine pyrophos-
    phate)
Codons, 261
Coenzyme A
    importance of, 181–182

role in fatty acid activation, 202
role in fatty acid metabolism, 202–209
role in pyruvic oxidase reaction, 180, 182
structure, 90–**91**
Coenzyme Q, 143, 145–146
Coenzymes
    definition, 95
    in oxidation-reduction reactions, *103*
    relation to B vitamins, 95–98
Collagen, 35
Coniferyl alcohol, **241**
Corticosteroids, 215, 282–283
Cortisol, **283**
Cortisone, **215, 283**
Creatine, 233–**234**
Creatine phosphate, 234
Crotonase (*see* Enoyl-CoA hydrase)
Curare, 294
Cysteine, **17**
Cystine, **18**
Cytidine, 83
Cytidine-diphosphate-choline, **211**
Cytidine triphosphate, 87
    role in phospholipid biosynthesis, *211*
Cytidylic acid, 83
    biosynthesis, *235*
    feedback control of biosynthesis, *266*
Cytochrome *c*, structure of prosthetic
    group, **147**
Cytochromes, 131–*133*, 146–148
    role in electron transport, 146–148
Cytoplasm, 120
Cytosine, **80**

Deamination, of amino acids, 220–221,
    243–244
Decarboxylation
    of amino acids, 221, 225, 240
    of keto acids, 177, 179, 184–185, 187, 205
    oxidative (*see* Oxidative decarboxylation)
Denaturation, of proteins, 34
Deoxynucleotides, 81–**82**
Deoxyribonucleic acids, 79
    genetic function, 251–*252*, 255–*256*
    replication of, 253–*255*
    structure, 82, *83–86*
Deoxyribose, **52**
Diabetes mellitus, 284
2,4-Dichlorophenoxyacetic acid (2,4-D),
    291
Dicoumarol, **302**
Diethylaminoethyl cellulose, 37, 40
Differentiation of cells, 272
Digestion (*see* Proteins, Polysaccharides,
    Lipids)
Diglycerides, 66–67

Dihydrolipoic acid, 181
Dihydroxyacetone, **44**
Dihydroxyacetone phosphate, **172, 173**
Dihydroxyphenylalanine, 239–**240**
Diiodotyrosine, **241**
Dinucleotides, 88
Diphosphopyridine nucleotide, 88–**89**, 143–144
Disaccharides, structures of, 57–59
DNA (*see* Deoxyribonucleic acid)
DPN (*see* Diphosphopyridine nucleotide)

Electron transport system, 140–148
  cellular localization, 120, 123, 140–141
  diagram of, *142*
  reoxidation of $CoQH_2$, 146
  reoxidation of DPNH, 145
  reoxidation of Flavin.H_2, 145
  role of the cytochromes, 146–148
  substrate dehydrogenation, 143–144
Electrophoresis of proteins, 37, *38*
Embden-Meyerhof pathway (*see* Glycolysis)
Emulsification, *197*–198
Endergonic reactions, 154
Endopeptidases, 226
Endoplasmic reticulum, *120*–121
Enolase, 172
Enoyl-CoA hydrase, 202
Enterokinase, 228
Environment, control of, 278
Enzyme activation, 114, 227–228
Enzyme-catalyzed reactions
  effect of enzyme concentration, *105*–107
  effect of pH, *110*–111
  effect of substrate concentration, *99*
  effect of temperature, *107*–110
  role of metal ions, 98, *104*
Enzyme induction, 270–271
Enzyme inhibition, 111–118
  allosteric effects, 114–115
  and elucidation of metabolic pathways, 124–126
  Lineweaver-Burk plots, 116–118
Enzyme repression, 268–*269*–270
Enzymes
  chemical nature of, 95–98
  classification of, 94–95
  constitutive, 271
  factors affecting rates of enzymic reactions, 104–115
  induced, 270
  mechanism of action, 98–104
  nomenclature, 93
Enzyme-substrate intermediates, 100–104
Epinephrine, 289
  action of, 284–*285*

biosynthesis, 239–**240**
  in glycogenolysis, 171, *285*
Erythrose, **45**
Erythrose-4-phosphate
  in aromatic biosynthesis, *238*
  in phosphogluconate pathway, 191–192
  in photosynthesis, 194
Essential amino acids, 224
Essential fatty acids, 209
Estradiol, **215, 281**
Estriol, **215, 281**
Estrogens, 215, 280–281
Estrone, **215, 281**
Ethanolamine, **69**
Exergonic reactions, 154
Exopeptidases, 227

ΔF, definition, 154
ΔF^0, definition, 154
FAD (*see* Flavin-adenine-dinucleotide)
Fats, 63
Fatty acids, 63–65
  activation of, *202*
  biosynthesis of, 204–*205*–209
  classes of, 64–65
  definition, 63
  "essential," 209
  oxidation of, *202*–203
  unsaturated, metabolism of, 209
Fatty acyl CoA dehydrogenase, 202
Fatty livers, 198
Feedback control of metabolism, *266*–267
Fehlings test, 55
Fibrin, 300–301
Fibrinogen, 300–301
Fibroin, of silk, *31*
Flavin-adenine-dinucleotide
  in amino acid oxidation, 243–244
  in fatty acid oxidation, 203
  structure, **90**
  in succinic dehydrogenase, 184
Flavins
  role in amino acid oxidation, 243–244
  role in electron transport, 145
  structures of, **90**
Flavones, flavonols, flavonones, 76, **78**
5-Fluorouracil, 274
Folic acid, 97, 230 (*see also* Tetrahydrofolic acid)
Follicle-stimulating hormone, 286
Free energy, 153–157
Fructokinase, 166
Fructose, **47**, 166
Fructose-1,6-diphosphate, **172-173**
Fructose-6-phosphate, **172**-173, **188**, 194
Fumarase, 183

Fumaric acid
formation, in ornithine cycle, **247**
in Tricarboxylic Acid Cycle, *183*–184
Functional groups, reactions of, 1–11
Furanose rings, in sugars, 48
Furfural, formation from sugars, 55

Galactokinase, 166
Galactose, **46,** 166
Galactose-1-phosphate, 166
β-Galactosidase, induction of, 270
Gangliosides, 70
Gastrin, 288
Gastrointestinal hormones, 288
Gels, in protein purification, 36
Genes, 251–252
Genetic code, 260–*262*
Gibberelic acids, **290**–291
Globulins, 35
Glucagon, 284–*285*
Glucaric acid, **53**
Glucokinase, 166
Gluconic acid, **53**
Glucosamine, **52**
Glucose, **45**
as a carbon source, 185–187
equilibrium forms in water, *50*
phosphorylation of, 165–*166*
Glucose oxidation, energy yields, 185
Glucose-6-phosphatase, 167
Glucose-1-phosphate, **168**–170
Glucose-6-phosphate
formation from glucose, 165–*166*
in glycogen synthesis, 168–171
in glycolysis, *172*
in phosphogluconate pathway, 188
possible metabolic fates, *164*
Glucuronic acid, **53**
Glutamic acid, **18**
formation of, 220–221
L-Glutamic dehydrogenase, 221
Glutamic semialdehyde, 223
Glutamine, **229**
in purine biosynthesis, **236**
Glutathione, 25
Glyceraldehyde, 44
Glyceraldehyde-3-phosphate, **172**–174,
190–192
Glyceraldehyde-3-phosphate dehydrogenase, *172*, 174–175
Glyceric acid 1,3-diphosphate, **172**, **174**, 175, 190
Glyceric acid 2-phosphate, **172**, 175
Glyceric acid 3-phosphate, **172**, 175, 189, 190

Glycerides
nomenclature, 65–69
structures, 66–69
Glycerol lipids, biosynthesis, 210–*211*
α-Glycerol phosphate, **210**
Glycerol phospholipids, 67–69
biosynthesis of, 210–*211*
Glycine, **17**, 230, 233, 236, 245
Glycocholate, sodium, **199**
Glycogen
digestion of, 159–162
formation of, 167–171
structure, **60**
Glycolysis, 171–179
aerobic, 176
anaerobic, 176–178
diagram of, *172*
energy yields in, 178–179
reversal of, 187, 194
Glycosides, 56
Gonadotropins, 286
Growth hormone, 286
Guanine, **80**
Guanosine, 83
Guanosine diphosphate, in Tricarboxylic
Acid Cycle, 184
Guanosine triphosphate, 87
in Tricarboxylic Acid Cycle, 184
Gulose, **46**
Gums, plant, 62

Haworth projection formulas, *49–51*
α-Helix, *31*–32
Heme, **77**
Hemicelluloses, 62
Hemocyanin, 294
Hemoglobin
and CO_2 transport, 298–299
and oxygen transport, 294–297
structure of heme portion, 77
Heparin, 62, 301
Hexokinase, 165–*166*
Hexose monophosphate shunt (*see* Phosphogluconate pathway)
Hexose-phosphate isomerase, 172
Histamine, 225
Histidine, **19**, 225
Histones, 35
Holoenzyme, 95
Homocysteine, **232**
Homoserine, **223**
Hormones, 279–292
action of, 279–280
derivatives of amino acids, 288–289
peptide hormones, 283–288
plant growth hormones, 289–292

Hormones (*contin.*)
  steroid hormones, 280–283
  (*see also* individual hormones or physio-
    logical groupings)
Hyaluronic acid, 62
Hydra, 272
Hydrocarbons, in biological materials, 73,
  74
Hydrogen bonding
  in DNA, 85, 253
  in proteins, 28–29
Hydrogen ion concentration (*see* pH)
β-Hydroxyacyl-CoA dehydrogenase, 202
β-Hydroxybutyric acid, 209
Hydroxylases, 238
Hydroxyproline, **19**
Hypophysis, hormones of, 285–287

Idose, **46**
Imino acids, **243**
Indoleacetic acid, **290**
Inducer, of enzyme, 270
Induction of enzymes, 270–271
Information transfer
  in higher organisms, 276–277
  in protein synthesis, 251–252, 255–260
  in synthesis of RNA, 255–256
Inhibitors, 111–118, 124–126, 265–267
Inosine triphosphate, 187
myo-Inositol, **54, 69,** 70
Insulin
  amino acid sequence, **29**
  action of, 284
Ion-exchange, in protein separations, 36,
  38, 40
Ionization of carboxyl and amino groups,
  20–24
Isocitrate dehydrogenase, 183–184
Isocitric acid, **183**–184
Isoelectric point, 23
Isoleucine, **17,** 224
Isomerism, 11–13
Isomers, optical
  of amino acids, 15–16
  of sugars, 44–47
Isopentenyl pyrophosphate, 212–**213**
Isotopes, 127–128

Juvenile hormone, 283

α-Ketoglutarate dehydrogenase, 183–184
α-Ketoglutaric acid, **183**
  formation in Tricarboxylic Acid Cycle,
    183, 184
  and L-glutamic dehydrogenase, 221
"Ketone bodies," formation of, 209

Ketoses, 46–**47**
Ketosis, 209
β-Ketothiolase, 202
Kinins (*see* Phytokinins)
Krebs Cycle (*see* Tricarboxylic Acid Cycle)
Krebs-Henseleit Cycle (*see* Ornithine Cycle)

Lactase, *162*
Lactic acid, **177**
  formation in anaerobic glycolysis, 176–177
Lactic acid dehydrogenase, 177
Lactogenic hormone (*see* Luteotropin)
Lactose,**58**
  digestion of, 161–*162*
Lanosterol, **214**
Lecithins, **68**
  biosynthesis of, 210–*211*
  hydrolysis of, 200
Leucine, **17,** 224
  metabolic degradation of, *243*
Lignin, 241
Limit dextrins, 160
Lineweaver-Burk plots, 116–118
Linoleic acid, **64,** 209
Linolenic acid, **64,** 209
Lipases, 199–200
Lipids
  absorption of, 198–199
  classification, 65–78
  fatty acids in, 63–65
  hydrolysis of, 198–201
  metabolism of, 201–217
Lipoate dehydrogenase, 183
Lipoic acid, **181,** 183–185
Luteinizing hormone, 286
Luteotropin, 286
Lysine, **18,** 224
Lysophosphatides, 201
Lyxose, **45**

Malate dehydrogenase, 144, 183
Malic acid, **144, 183,** 184, 187
Malignant growth, 273–275
Malonyl-Coenzyme A, 204–**205**
Maltase, *161*–162
Maltose, **57**
Mannose, **46**
Menadione, **75**
6-Mercaptopurine, 274
Meselson-Stahl experiment, 254–*255*
Messenger RNA, 255–257, 258–260
  (*see also* Protein synthesis)
Metabolic control
  cell membrane permeability, 271–272
  effects of substrate concentration, 264–*265*
  enzyme induction, 270–271

enzyme repression, 268–*269*–270
feedback inhibition, 266–*267*
Metabolism
  carbohydrate and lipid interactions, 216–217
  definition, 93
  of glucose 6-phosphate, *164*, 170, *172*, 187–*188*
  of nitrogen compounds, summary, *248*
  organization of, 122–123
  of steroids, *215*
Methemoglobin, 295
Methionine, **18**, 224, 232–233
Methyl glycosides, 56
Methyl group transfers, 231–234
Metmyoglobin, 297
Mevalonic acid, **212**, 213
Michaelis equation, 115–116
Mitochondria
  ATP production in, 140–141
  location of electron transport system, 123, 140–141
  as multienzyme aggregates, 123
  as subcellular particles, *120*
Molecular sieves, in protein purification, 38
Monosaccharides
  cellular absorption of, 162–163
  cyclic forms, *47–50*
  Fischer projection formulas, 44
  Haworth projection formulas, *49–51*
  structures of, **44–47**
Mucopolysaccharides, 62
Mutation, biochemical, 126–127
Myoglobin, 32, 297
Myo-inositol, **54**, 69, 70
Myristic acid, 8, 64

NAD (*see* Diphosphopyridine nucleotide)
NADP (*see* Triphosphopyridine nucleotide)
"Nerve gases," and acetylcholinesterase, 294
Nerve impulse transmission, 277
  mechanism of, 292–294
Nicotinamide, 97
Nicotinamide-adenine-dinucleotide (*see* Diphosphopyridine nucleotide)
Ninhydrin reaction, **41**
Nitrogen fixation, 220
Nitrogen metabolism, summary, *248*
Nor-epinephrine
  action of, 289
  biosynthesis of, 239–**240**
  function in nerve transmission, 293
Nucleic acids
  composition, 79–80
  size, 87
  structure, 82–*84*

(*see also* Ribonucleic acids, Deoxyribonucleic acids, Messenger RNA, Protein synthesis)
Nucleosides, 81
Nucleotides
  biosynthesis of, 234–237
  definition, 81
  of metabolic importance, 87–91
  terminology, 82, 83
  in Vitamin B_{12}, **91**
Nucleolus, 120
Nucleus, of a cell, 120

Oleic acid, **64**, 209
One-carbon metabolism (*see* Single-carbon metabolism)
Ornithine, **247**
Ornithine Cycle, 245–*247*
Oxalacetic acid, **183**
  function in Tricarboxylic Acid Cycle, 182–*183*–184
  synthesis from phosphoenolpyruvate, 187
Oxalic acid, **9**
Oxalosuccinic acid, **183**, 184
β-Oxidation of fatty acids, *202*–203
  (*see also* Fatty acids, oxidation of)
Oxidative decarboxylation
  of α-ketoglutaric acid, *183*, 184
  of pyruvic acid, 179–182
Oxidative phosphorylation, 143
Oxyhemoglobin, 295–296
Oxytocin, **25**, 286–**287**

Palmitic acid, 8, 64
Pancreas, hormones of, 284
Pancreozymin, 288
Pantothenic acid, **91**, 97
Papaverine, **242**
Paper chromatography, 128–*129*–130
Parathyroid hormone, 287
Pectins, 61
Penicillin, 252
Pentoses, **45**, 188–195
Pepsin, 226
Pepsinogen, 227
Peptidases, *226*–228
Peptide bonds, **15**, 24
Peptides, 24–26
Permeases, 225
Peroxidases, 244
Phenylalanine, 20, 224
  biosynthesis of, *238*
  conversion to tyrosine, 238–239
  metabolism of, 237–239
Phenylketonuria, 239
pH optima, for enzymes, *110*–111

Phosphatidic acids
  biosynthesis, 210
  structure, **68**
Phosphatidyl cholines, **68, 68,** 210–*211*
Phosphatidyl ethanolamines, 68, 211
Phosphatidyl inositols, 68
Phosphatidyl serines, 68, 211
Phosphocreatine (*see* Creatine phosphate)
Phosphodiesterases, 200
Phosphoenolpyruvic acid, *172,* **175**–176
  in aromatic biosynthesis, *238*
  formation from oxalacetic acid, 187
Phosphofructokinase, 172
Phosphoglucomutase, 168, 172
Phosphogluconate pathway, 187–*188*–192
  as a source of TPNH, 189
6-Phosphogluconic acid, **188**
6-Phosphogluconolactone, **188**
Phosphoglyceric kinase, *172*
Phosphoglyceromutase, *172*
Phospholipase *A*, 201
Phospholipids
  as emulsifiers, 198
  glycerol phospholipids, 67, **68, 69**
  sphingosine phospholipids, 70
Phosphomonoesterases, 199
Phosphopantetheine, **206**
Phosphorylase, 169–171
  hormone control of activity, *284*–285
Phosphorylcholine, **211**
Photosynthesis, 148–153, 192–195
  as a source of TPNH, 150–152
  CO_2 fixation, 193
  light reactions, 148–*151*–153
  path of carbon in, 192–195
Photosynthetic phosphorylation, 152
Phytoglycolipids, 70
Phytokinins, 291
Pigments, plant, 76–78
Pituitary gland, hormones of, 285–287
Plant growth hormones, 289–292
Plant pigments, 76–78
Plasmalogens, **69**
Platelets, 300
Polysaccharides
  digestion of, 159–161
  formation of, 167–171
  hydrolysis of, 159–161
  structures and occurrence, 59–62
  (*see also* Individual polysaccharides)
Polysomes, 260
Porphyrins, 76, **77,** 146–**147**
Proenzymes (*see* Zymogens)
Progesterone, **215, 282**
Prolamines, 36
Proline, 19, 223

Protamines, 35
Proteins
  classification of, 34–36
  denaturation, 34
  hydrolysis of, 225–228
  purification of, 36–40
  structures of, 14–15, 26, 28–33
Protein structure
  alpha helix conformation, 31
  extended chain conformation, 30
  folded conformations, 32, 33
  types of bonding involved, 30
Protein synthesis
  formation of messenger-RNA, 255–257
  function of messenger-RNA, 258–260
  function of soluble-RNA, 257–*259*–260
  role of DNA, 255–*256*
  summary, *256*
Proteolytic enzymes, 225–228
Prothrombin, 300–302
Purines
  biosynthesis of, 234, 235, *237*
  structures of, **80**
Pyranose rings, in sugars, 48
Pyridoxal phosphate, 97, **221**–222
Pyridoxamine phosphate, **221**–222
Pyrimidines
  biosynthesis of, 234, 235–*236*
  structures of, **80**
Pyruvic acids, *172,* **176,** 178
  decarboxylation of, 177, 179–182
Pyruvic decarboxylase, 177
Pyruvic kinase, *172*
Pyruvic oxidase, 180

Radiation
  effects on nucleic acids, 273
  and malignant growth, 273–275
Radioactive tracers, 127–128
Radioautograph, 130
Recombination of viruses, 121–*122*
Reducing sugars, 55
Repression of enzyme synthesis, 268–*269*–
    270
Ribitol, **53**
Riboflavin, 90, 97
Ribonucleic acids, 79
  control of biosynthesis, 255–257
  messenger-RNA
    formation of, 255–257
    functions of, 258–260
  soluble-RNA or transfer-RNA, 257–*259*–
    260
  structure, 82–86
Ribose, **45**
Ribose 5-phosphate, 189

Ribosomes
  as location of protein synthesis, *256*, 258–260
  as location of ribosomal-RNA, 80
  as subcellular particles, *120*
Ribulose, **47**
Ribulose 1,5-diphosphate, 189, **193**–194
  as CO_2 acceptor in photosynthesis, 193
Ribulose 5-phosphate, **188**–189, 194
RNA (*see* Ribonucleic acid)

Schiff's bases, in transamination, 222
Secretin, 288
Sedoheptulose 7-phosphate, **190**–192
Serine, **17**
  from glyceric acid 3-phosphate, 230
  role in single-carbon metabolism, 230–231
Shikimic acid, **238**
Sialic acids, 54
Sickle-cell anemia, 250
Silk fibroin, structure, *31*
Single-carbon intermediate compounds
  origin of, 230–233
  role in purine and pyrimidine biosynthesis, 234–237
Single-carbon metabolism, 229–234
"Sodium pump," and nerve transmission, 292
Somatotropin, 286
Sphingomyelins, **70**
Sphingosine, 69, **70**
Squalene, **213**
  biosynthesis, 212–*213*
  conversion to cholesterol, 213–214
Starch, 59–**60**, 159–161, 167–171
Stearic acid, 8, 64
Steroid hormones, 280–283
Steroid and sterols
  cholesterol biosynthesis, 212–216
  typical structures of, **71**–**73**
  metabolism of, 214–216
  (*see also* Bile acids, Steroid hormones)
Stilbestrol, **281**
Substrate, definition, 99
Succinic acid, **9**
  in Tricarboxylic Acid Cycle, 183, 184
Succinic dehydrogenase, 183, 184
Succinyl-Coenzyme A, 184
Sucrase, 161–*162*
Sucrose, **59**
  digestion of, 161–*162*
Sugar derivatives, 52–54
Sugars (*see* Monosaccharides)

Testosterone, **215**, **281**
Tetrahydrofolic acid, 230–*231*–236

Thiamine pyrophosphate, 97
  as cofactor for α-ketoglutaric dehydrogenase, *183*, 184
  as cofactor for pyruvic decarboxylase, 177
  as cofactor for transketolases, 191
  mechanism of function in decarboxylation reactions, 180–181
Thioalcohols, 4
Threonine, **17**, 223
Thrombin, 300–302
Thromboplastin (thrombokinase), 300–301
Thymidylic acid, 235, 236
Thymine, **80**
Thyroglobulin, 288–*289*
Thyroid hormones, 288–289
Thyrotropin, 286
  and thyroxine production, 288–289
Thyroxine, **241**
  biosynthesis, 240–241
  release and hormone action of, 288–*289*
TPN (*see* Triphosphopyridine nucleotide)
Tracers, radioactive, 127–128
Transaldolases, 190–192, 194
Transaminases, 221–224
Transamination, 221–224
Transcarbamylases, 266–267
Transformation, bacterial, *252*
Transketolases, 190–192, 194
Transmethylation, 231–234
Tricarboxylic Acid Cycle, 182–*183*–187
Triglycerides
  biosynthesis, 210–211
  hydrolysis of, 198–*200*
  structures of, **66**
Triose-phosphate isomerase, 172, 174
Triosephosphates, *172*, **173**
Triphosphopyridine nucleotide
  in fatty acid biosynthesis, 204–208
  in isocitric dehydrogenase reaction, 184
  in mevalonic acid biosynthesis, *212*
  reduction of, in photosynthesis, 150–152
  structure of, 89
Tropins, 286
Trypsin, 226
Trypsinogen, 228
Trytophan, **19**, 224
Tyrosine
  conversion to alkaloids, 241
  conversion to epinephrine, *240*
  conversion to thyroxine, 240–241
  formation from phenylalanine, 238–239
  structure, **20**

Ultracentrifuge, 40
Unsaturated fatty acids, **64**, 209

Uracil, **80**
Urea, formation of, **246**-*247*
Urea cycle (*see* Ornithine Cycle)
Uric acid, **245**
Uridine, **81**
Uridine-diphosphate-glucose, 168-**169**-*170*
Uridine triphosphate, 168-**169**
Uronic acids, **53**, 61-62

Valine, **17**, 224
Vasopressin, 25, 286-**287**
Viruses, 87, 121-122, 251, 273-274
Virus recombination, 121-*122*
Vitamin A$_1$, **74**
Vitamin B$_{12}$, 91, 97, 232
Vitamin C (*see* Ascorbic acid)
Vitamin D, **75**
Vitamin E, **75**

Vitamin K, **75**
    and blood coagulation, 301-302
Vitamins
    fat-soluble, 74-75
    relation to coenzymes, 95-98
    (*see also* individual vitamins by names)

Warfarin, 302
Waxes, 71

Xanthophylls, 76
Xylose, **45**
Xylulose, 47
Xylulose 5-phosphate, **190**

Zymogens, 114
Zymogen activation, 227-228